Also by Anthony Robbins

Unlimited Power
Awaken the Giant Within
Notes From a Friend
Giant Steps

UNLIMITED POWER

A BLACK CHOICE

Anthony Robbins
and
Joseph McClendon III

SIMON & SCHUSTER

Simon & Schuster
Rockefeller Center
1230 Avenue of the Americas
New York, NY 10020

Designed by Irving Perkins Associates

Manufactured in the United States of America

1 3 5 7 9 10 8 6 4 2

Library of Congress Cataloging-in-Publication Data

Robbins, Anthony.
Unlimited power : a Black choice / Anthony Robbins and
Joseph McClendon III.
p. cm.
An adaptation of: Robbins, Anthony. Unlimited Power. 1986.
Includes index.
1. Success—Psychological aspects. 2. Afro-Americans—Psychology.
I. McClendon, Joseph. II. Title.
BF637.S8R558 1997
158.1'089'96073—dc21 96-39232
CIP

ISBN 0-684-82436-1

To all the Black men and women who are making this nation and our world a better place by their compassion, love, courage, and persistence . . .

May you always live with passion!

—Anthony Robbins

Dedicated to the greatest gift that lives within each and every one of our souls. This, the gift of love that comes with the very first beat of our hearts and exists in every breath we take, is the golden thread that binds us all together.

Most of all from me to Mrs. Every Jo McClendon and Mr. Joseph McClendon, Jr.

In memory of Alan Wade Stubbings.

—Joseph McClendon III

Acknowledgments

When it came time to express my deepest appreciation to those who contributed their precious support, input, questions, suggestions, and hard work on this project, my heart grew with anticipation. It dawned on me that, due to the nature of this book, virtually every person I have had the privilege to call friend has in some way or another contributed to my growth and, therefore, to the growth of this book. To those on the forthcoming list, please allow me to give a deep, heartfelt *thank you* for creating an environment in which I have been able to learn and grow. To those I haven't mentioned, please know that I value your friendship and presence as one of the greatest gifts in my life.

Thank you, first, to the greatest family in the world—Mom, Dad, Ava, Anita, Lisa, Nick, and Rudee—for kicking my butt through life and believing in me. Many thanks also to Deena Banks, Karen Risch, Vicki St. George, and the crew at Just Write for helping me do only that—just write! To Laura Kalb, Veronique Boss, Marina McPherson, Pam Hendrickson, Deb Hinz, Lisa Bell, and everyone on the RRI staff for bending over backward in dealing with my constant phone calls. To Dominick Anfuso, Ana DeBevoise, Bob Asahina, and Cassie Jones for your patience with and belief in this book. To Sam Georges for your great sense of humor, your friendship, and your profound wisdom; you are truly the master of questions. To Bill Stafford for believing in me from jump street. To Violet Farley for your wonderful insight. To Terry Schmidt for your wonderful ability to drive. To my great friend John Lewis Parker and your family for your companionship and wisdom. To Danny Harris for your vision. To Jeff Joseph for your friendship and quick wit. To Rick, John, and James for allowing me to kick out some of the funkiest jams this man has ever slammed. To Ms. Sonia Satra for your inspiration and your faith in me. To Kerrie Pohn, Alvin, and Lumpy for tolerating my late hours and constant rambling. To Greg Gibson for your mind-boggling language solutions. To Lloyd Duplechan, Alan Slater, Jim

Sergeant, Houston Houston, Chris Houston, Brian Beeler: you guys are the best. To Lori Trehan for all those hours of debate and chiseling away at the core. To Debra Russell for your love and friendship over the years. To Albert Saab: you the man. And last, but certainly not least, to my dearest friends, Tony and Becky Robbins, for your loving support and eternal friendship.

—JOSEPH MCCLENDON III

Contents

Introduction

BY ANTHONY ROBBINS

For nearly two decades, I have devoted myself to pursuing the answers behind what creates an extraordinary quality of life. I've always been fascinated (almost obsessed) with the desire to understand the force that makes us do what we do, think what we think, love what we love, and hate what we hate. How is it that some individuals, when faced with extreme social injustice, unfairness and abuse, rise above these conditions and become souls of inspiration—performing at levels that far exceed anyone's expectations and producing extraordinary levels of success, joy, and happiness—not just for themselves but for all of those they have the privilege to touch? What causes certain people to pull empowering meanings from the inevitability of life's storms and be able to positively influence their family, friends, and communities?

When I first studied United States history, I was embarrassed to learn that ours was a country that created a Declaration of Independence to ensure freedom for all, yet had withheld this liberty from a large sector of its citizens. Through omission and blatant exclusion, African Americans were regarded as less significant and denied the same rights as others who didn't share their heritage and skin color.

Yet how inspiring it is now to see so many great Black men and women, many of whom I have had the honor and privilege to meet and consult, who have pierced the color barrier and are today shaping our culture and the experiences that allow us to think and feel at a deeper level of awareness and passion. Our world has been shaped by people like Quincy Jones, a man from the ghetto whose family had to literally eat rats to survive and who has for fifty years been the heart, soul, and dean of American music. Oprah Winfrey is the icon of daily television; she connects every single day with the American people to such an extent that she has become one of the most listened to, observed, and influential women in the nation. I believe Nelson Mandela is one of the most extraordinary souls alive today. Here is a man who was imprisoned and physically, psychologically, and emotionally tortured for twenty-seven years, yet somehow through it all maintained a level of dignity and courage that defied every abuse thrown at him. Here is a man who was unwilling to trade his freedom for a promise of silence to injustice, a brilliant man of unwavering principle whose vision is surpassed only by his compassion. Can you imagine the rage you would feel if you were unfairly imprisoned for more than a quarter of a century? One has to ask how any human being could experience this and not be filled with hate and an obsession to retaliate. Yet, as we know today, this man has proven what we are all capable of—he has put the rage and the wounds of the past behind him to serve the greater good and create a future for all the races of his nation. He has been willing to do whatever it takes to make this happen—even to the degree of appointing Frederick de Klerk—the very man who led the nation and ideology who instigated his condemnation—to be his partner in governing.

These exceptional people and so many others throughout history—from Jesse Owens to Martin Luther King, Jr.—are not just extraordinary human beings, but role models and mentors for all of us regardless of heritage. I can only imagine the pride you must have as an African American knowing that, in spirit, the blood of these and the multitude of other Black men and women of valor and distinction pulses through your veins. I know you will understand my eagerness to share these stories as a collection—as a testament to the strength and wisdom of the people who lived them.

In the two years preceding the completion of this book, I also witnessed less noble incidents unfold—among them, the Rodney King beating, the social unrest as a result of the policemen's trial, and the racial tension sparked by the O.J. Simpson trial. Yet in the midst of all this, the human spirit prevailed and the magnitude of our heroes was brought forth to me once again as I witnessed the power and dignity of the Million Man March in October of 1995.

The sight of so many African Americans conducting an unprecedented, peaceful yet strong demonstration of unity made me more determined than ever to increase the number of African Americans who could access and utilize the technologies in this book. In these people I recognized a passionate commitment—one of incredible courage and conviction—to create a destiny of fulfillment for themselves and their children, despite the pain and frustration of the past. This burning conviction hit close to home.

You see, my own obsession for striving to make the world a better place comes from the fact that I once believed life was fierce and formidable; my obsession with freedom comes from the fact that I once didn't possess any; my obsession with learning, growing, and sharing the finest tools for change comes from the fact that I have personally felt the pain of what seemed to me to be unbearable injustice and inhumanity.

We all need a certain amount of pain or dissatisfaction to compel us into change. One day I realized that the behavior I was demonstrating was pitifully far from the person I truly was inside; I was living a life of hostility, despair, and self-loathing. It was out of that pain that I finally began to convert my rage into power—the power to move me forward, the power to focus on solutions. I developed an unwavering commitment to create freedom for myself and everyone I could touch. I found role models in each of the areas of my life I needed to improve, I learned the specific actions they had taken to achieve the results I wanted, and I followed through on those actions. I made the shift that to this day allows me to be both deeply fulfilled and intensely driven—gratified without being complacent. My history continues to compel and inspire me.

In 1984 at the age of twenty-four, I wrote my first book, *Unlimited Power.* It was the beginning of a journey that has now given me the privilege of sharing these tools with more than one and a half million people from nearly every walk of life. I have managed to cross every socioeconomic level; I have traveled the world and worked with some of the most challenged and most successful people—from the President of the United States to local community leaders, from NBA stars and top-rated actors to bottom-line thinkers in corporate business—entrepreneurial geniuses and top financial traders who have earned as much as half a billion dollars in one day—and from those homeless and struggling to survive to whole cities hoping to reengineer for greater prosperity.

I work both personally and via the efforts of the Anthony Robbins Foundation with inner-city youths, those facing the ravages of drug addiction, and even prisoners, teaching them to empower themselves, to be so strong, to be so powerful that nothing on this earth—no inequity, injustice, challenge, or circumstance—can prevent them from creating and becoming whatever and whoever they want in life.

However, having said all of this, I don't pretend to know what it's like to be Black. I've never experienced the sting of racism, or the dull, numbing twist of discrimination. There is no way I can even begin to understand what it must be like to know that my ancestors were murdered, molested, raped, and separated for the sake of controlling and exploiting what God gave us all as the gift of life. No, I don't know what it is like to be Black—but through the eyes and heart of one of my dearest friends in life I have had the privilege of taking a glimpse at what I can only describe as a crystal clear ocean of possibilities yearning to be bathed in by its beautiful Black people. Through the experience of this man I have vicariously witnessed the elements of what it might take to put together some of the pieces of a magnificent puzzle. He welcomed me into his world and shared with me his heart and passion for making a difference.

It's true, I do not know what it is like to have someone judge me by the color of my skin, but I do understand what it is like to overcome tremendous obstacles. Both in my own experience and in those whose strength and will I admire—among them, my dearest friend, and gifted co-author, Joseph McClendon III—I continue to be inspired by what human beings are capable of doing and becoming when they change two things: their beliefs about what is possible and their strategy for attaining that which they value most in life.

Let me take a moment to tell you about this extraordinary friend of mine, Joseph McClendon III. I first met Joseph in 1986 when he attended one of my seminars in Los Angeles, California. Strange as this may sound, the moment I met him I knew that we would be friends for a lifetime. It's often said that we respect and love in others what we value in ourselves. Joseph has a passion for living, a depth of caring, and a sense of playfulness and joy that touches every soul he meets. His commitment to be and give his best is unmatched. I've watched him integrate and communicate the tools and techniques I teach with a style and flair all his own. He has an unparalleled wit and uncanny sense of humor, and his exceptional skills have led him to become an outstanding Peak Performance Specialist and the Head Trainer of Robbins Research International, Inc.

One of my sincere wishes for you is that you have or find such a friend for your life. Perhaps through these pages Joseph can become for you what he has become for me—a best friend and valued adviser. Together we share in the process of committing our lives to service, making a difference for all people on the largest scale possible. One day as we were discussing how we could reach this very goal, Joseph suggested that we consider adapting *Unlimited Power* specifically for the Black audience. And thus with a decision, the book you are holding came into being. I sincerely hope that this book not only provides you with tools that will empower your life, but touches you in a deep and meaningful way. I don't know you personally, but I do know that if you are holding this book, you must be a special soul who is unwilling to settle for whatever the current circumstances offer. You are a person who wants to make history rather than live in the limitations of the past.

I also hope that reading what Joseph and I will be sharing—my principles and strategies illuminated by his experience—will enhance your appreciation of your history, a history of powerful African Americans who are making a difference in the quality of life for all people. If any of the thoughts, ideas, or strategies in this book touch you in a meaningful way, I will feel deeply honored. I hope you will write to Joseph and me and share with us the story of your success. So let the journey begin!

PART ONE

THE MODELING OF HUMAN EXCELLENCE

CHAPTER ONE

The Human Choice

There is absolute magic in this being called Black—splendor and purpose in every single cell. For within us are the genetics of the warrior, who steps boldly into the future, and the connection of family that binds us together with love. There is unlimited power and innate intelligence in the very soul that drives us.

—JOSEPH MCCLENDON III

THE CONFLICT IS classic: The difference between what we feel in our souls and what we deal with in the real world is all too often like night and day. Inside each and every one of us is a seed of greatness, a deep yearning to grow and contribute, to make a difference. All of us want to believe we deserve the good life—that we can actually achieve it.

So what prevents us from having our dreams? What keeps us from achieving what we long for in the core of our being? There is no question that racial and cultural differences all too often show up as challenges that could impede our forward motion. But if any of us truly believes those differences determine our destiny, then our future is dim indeed. To allow ourselves to fall into the cultural hypnosis of thinking that the outside world ultimately controls our lives—instead of realizing that each day is replete with opportunities to become powerful beyond belief—is to surrender the magic given to us at conception and guaranteed with our very first breath of life.

Deep inside, we all know the real truth: It is in fact our differences—our points of uniqueness—that make every human being worthy of greatness, and adversity strengthens our very souls. Muscles only grow with demand. Anything that doesn't kill us makes us stronger if we learn from it, and challenges are God's way of preparing us for what we ask for.

When I look into the eyes and hearts of others who share my beautiful heritage, I feel alive and proud. When I see how much we've grown, contributed, and loved as a culture over the years, I have a sense of connection that is unshakable. I feel extremely privileged and humble to be able to share my thoughts with you, and I deeply thank you for the opportunity to walk this new path together on this enchanted journey we call life.

As I look at my life today, I can't help but feel incredibly grateful. But it wasn't always that way. Like most people, I experienced a time so full of self-doubt and confusion about who I was and what I was capable of that it all but paralyzed me. While I was raised in a family that taught equality and fairness, often the outside world showed me quite a different picture.

We've all had times in our lives when being different was a liability for the moment—and those moments can seem like an eternity. All too often these "defining" moments can powerfully shape our beliefs about people, opportunities, and the world as a whole, thereby shaping our lives for better or worse. Without warning, something happens. Things change, and we can be thrust into horrific situations. Life turns on a dime, and depending on how we interpret those turns, they can either limit us or accelerate us on our journey to fulfillment.

THE OPPORTUNITY TO TRANSFORM

My own life has been full of incidents where being Black was the catalyst for sometimes vicious treatment. Let me tell you about one such event . . . a long, long time ago.

On a cold, windy November night, out in the middle of nowhere, life as I knew it was about to change. Darkness hung in the air like a thick, black, velvet blanket. And even the thin slice of the moon that shone that evening seemed frozen in place by the emptiness of the desert sky.

It was about 11:30 on a Friday night, and I was riding my motorcycle from Los Angeles to San Jose to visit my father and sister. I was passing through the small town of Oildale near Bakersfield, on the way to Interstate 5. (In those days, to say that Oildale was a "redneck" town was like saying that the Grand Canyon was just a little hole in the ground, or that Adolf Hitler had just a few minor personality glitches he needed to work out!) I had a full tank of gas and only about three more hours to go before I reached my destination. I always traveled late at night to avoid traffic, and I loved the feeling of freedom that being the only one on the road gave me. It was sometimes scary but always exciting. I was blasting down the roadway on my Harley-Davidson at about sixty-five miles per hour, and under normal circumstances I would have been able to pass right by Oildale.

Unfortunately, on this particular evening I had neglected to tighten the rear chain on my bike. With a loud bang it came flying off the sprocket, leaving the bike powerless and out of control. I coasted to a stop, walked back to collect the pieces of chain, then pushed the bike to the nearest freeway off-ramp about a hundred yards away. I pulled into a closed gas station nearby to make the necessary repairs.

I had been there about half an hour when an old Chevy pickup truck appeared with three men in the cab. They pulled into the station and screeched to a stop between me and the pumps. At first I thought they had stopped to help me, but as they stumbled out of the truck I knew I was in trouble. It was obvious they had been drinking, and they seemed so excited over what they had found that they fell all over each other, laughing about who would get to deliver the opening line.

As I stood there, afraid for my life and trying to figure out what to do, I couldn't help thinking that most of us have probably feared this type of situation more than once in our lives. All the stories of vicious mistreatment of Blacks flashed through my mind like some horrible civil rights newsreel from the 1960s on fast-forward. Now it seemed I was about to relive one of those events. For a split second I thought everything was going to be okay, because the large one (the one with the stained overalls and all the teeth missing) stepped to the front and grinned. But my hopes were instantly crushed when he drawled, "Well, niggra, looks lak you picked the wrong place to git broke down at."

After that, everything seemed to happen in slow motion. They all charged me at once, kicking over my bike and trying to pull me out into the open where they could beat me down. "It's time for you to die now, nigger!" one of them shouted as they encircled me. Instinctively I wedged myself between the gas pumps for protection, and I was able to defend myself for a short while, but not before taking some pretty intense hits. Wherever I turned there was another one of them taking a swing at me. In total fear, I realized I did have a weapon: The wrench I had been using to work on the bike was still in my hand. I lashed out with it in hopes of driving them away. It helped for a time, but there were too many of them. I remember being kicked and punched in the head and ribs, actually hearing the impact and knowing the blows were serious. The dull thud of someone's foot in my side or fist in my teeth seemed to be coming out of nowhere, too fast for me to block or dodge. I remember being more angry than scared, feeling like I was going to pass out but fighting to stay conscious. I knew if I lost consciousness, they would rip me to pieces. I don't really know what made them stop, but I do remember running after one of them, yelling at the top of my lungs, ultimately hurling the wrench at him.

Finally, they all piled into the truck and peeled out of there. The rage and hate I felt in those moments was overwhelming. My mind was screaming, *You bastards! How dare you do this to me! How dare you!* I looked down at my shirt and saw my own blood all over it. I felt my insides on fire, and the bitter taste of blood in my mouth brought a lump to my throat. My face felt like it was torn to shreds, my nose and mouth were bleeding, and I was having difficulty breathing. So scared that I couldn't think what to do, I did know there was something seriously wrong. I figured if I didn't get medical help quickly, I would die.

I made my way over to the pay phone at the far end of the station to call for help, but the receiver had been torn off. I couldn't walk any further, and I was afraid the good ol' boys would return to finish me off, so I spent the rest of the night in the back of the gas station praying they wouldn't find me.

The seconds passed like hours as I sat there freezing in a pile of old tires at the back of the station. Finally, at about 6:30 A.M.

when the attendant came to open the station, I crept out from behind the tire pile. The attendant took one look at me and phoned for help. The police arrived and took me to the hospital to deal with my injuries.

About an hour and a half later, I was driven to the sheriff's station in the back of a squad car so I could fill out a police report. The people at the station were cold and unfeeling. With the way they were treating me, you would have thought I was being blamed for what had happened. One of them even asked what the hell I was doing in that part of town anyway, as if I had no business being there. Still shaken and aching from the beating, I was told, "Sit on the bench in front of the desk and wait until we can get to you." As officers came and went, many of them shook their heads in disgust as they walked by. Some even snickered and smirked as if I'd gotten my just deserts. I wanted to cry, but I was so angry and scared that I just sat there and steamed in disbelief. While I felt I couldn't possibly get out of there soon enough, I had to spend several hours at the station—while they ran a warrant check on *me* and impounded my bike!

By being in the wrong place at the wrong time, it was as if I had stumbled back into the dark ages of my not-too-distant ancestors. (To this day, I have serious doubts whether they really ever looked for the men who assaulted me.) I felt violated and, despite an upbringing that stressed fairness and racial harmony, I felt the seeds of prejudice germinating in my own gut. It sickened me to see what I was becoming. For the first time in my life, I found myself reacting to color and culture instead of character. From that point on, anyone who even slightly resembled a redneck was cause for immediate suspicion. Even though intellectually I knew better, another person's race could instantly create rage inside me.

Despite the fact that most of my business and personal interactions included White people, I found myself trusting only the ones I knew, and befriending only those who really went the extra mile to prove their camaraderie. I was leading a double life, and the denial and contradiction were tearing me up inside. I hated who I was becoming with all my heart. I was guilty of the very process that caused those men to attack me viciously without cause, knowing nothing about who I was as a person. The scars on the outside would heal, but I didn't know how to deal with what was eating me alive inside.

THE BATTLE WITHIN

For years after that event, I was living a lie. Outside, I was happy and ambitious by most people's standards, but inside, I was completely steeped in the memory of what had happened. I was angry, bitter, extremely sarcastic—I'm sure you'd agree, rightfully so. But I was wrong to generalize my hatred, and somewhere deep inside I knew it.

The incident was over, but the effect lingered and governed my very being. Not only did I feel rage against White rednecks but perhaps worst of all, I actually began to buy into the idiot idea that the color of my skin made my soul less significant. It made me sad and angry to think how many Black men and women felt like me because they or someone they loved had endured abuse as bad or worse than my own. I didn't want that event to shape the rest of my life. I didn't want to live the rest of my days filled with self-doubt and vengeance. I didn't want to be like those rednecks! Yet I couldn't stop thinking not only about the injustice I had encountered, but the pain my entire race had experienced throughout history—the oppression, the slavery, the mistreatment, the stereotyping of an entire culture. The words "it's not fair" constantly rang in my head like an embarrassing, subliminal reminder of a hideous legacy binding us to hopelessness. I felt like I was losing the battle within myself.

TIME HEALS ALL . . . OR DOES IT?

As time passed, I thought it was over. My hatred softened to bitterness. But at the same time, the ghost of that experience continued to haunt me. It became the filter for all my inner actions, not only with whites but with my own people as well. My low self-worth and my self-doubt translated into suspicion and judgment of anyone like me. If I were so insignificant that I could be mistreated so cruelly with no consequence, then anyone who looked like me must be just as worthless—right?

> *We are responsible for the world in which we find ourselves, if only because we are the only sentient force which can change it.*
>
> —JAMES BALDWIN

Those were the most counterproductive months of my life. But you know what? I didn't feel that way at the time. I had no idea how I was allowing the events of my past to affect me. I'd always been driven, yet something began holding me back. The invisible force of fear and insecurity showed up in little ways I never would have connected to my past. Procrastination, hesitation, failure to follow through, low motivation, and flat-out fear became cancers in my life, draining me of ambition and accomplishment. Even when I was doing well, something always seemed to prevent me from living my dreams. I'm sure there has been a time in your life when you wondered, like I did, what was stopping you from reaching your full potential. I had no idea how my behaviors and feelings of self-worth were skewed by my perceptions of who "we" are and what "we" are capable of in this society. I'd seem to get so far, only to sabotage my own progress.

Always, there was a horrible little voice deep inside me constantly suggesting, *They're right! You don't fit in; you're not smart enough. You're Black, and in this world being Black is a liability, not an asset. What's more, you're not only Black but you're also dark, and that's two strikes against you. No matter how hard you try you'll never be good enough.*

I'd known for a long time most of the world is conditioned to think of Black as less preferable than White, and Blacks have been suffering from lower self-esteem for centuries. I remembered seeing a study on TV where Black children were given an assortment of dolls and asked which ones were the prettiest and the best. All of the children picked White dolls. When they were asked which were bad and ugly, they all picked Black dolls. These were babies, beautiful Black babies, and they had already begun to prefer something other than themselves. They had learned that Black was wrong, bad, and ugly.

I had also seen a show when I was a kid about what life would be like in the future. There were huge, clean cities with monorails, moving sidewalks, and smiling, happy citizens all enjoying the modern conveniences of the day. Everyone had futuristic bubble-domed cars, and they all lived in modern homes with every gadget you could imagine to make their lives fun, effortless, and happy. But there were no Black people. Not one! I remembered turning off the TV in tears at the age of nine and vowing never to watch it again.

I certainly realize this was not necessarily everyone's view of the world, and that the intention of the producers of the show was not to promote prejudice. But to a nine-year-old child, it was scary as hell. I remember thinking, *White people didn't plan on me being around in the future, and wherever we would be, we wouldn't be eligible for the good life to which the White race was entitled.* I remember thinking in those days, *The only Black faces I see on television seem to be subservient, clownish, or in trouble.* I asked my father why I never saw Blacks in the cowboy movies. "Where were we in those days, Dad?" My father had a wonderful sense of humor, and in an effort to soften the blow, he said, "They hadn't invented us yet, son." In reality, until the last two and a half decades, Blacks were effectively omitted from history and denied the same rights others took for granted.

The truth is that my race holds no monopoly on being discriminated against. Around the world, prejudice and discrimination have existed throughout human history on a variety of levels. Every day, persecution rears its ugly head, and unfortunately will probably continue to do so. People are discriminated against because they differ in their religious beliefs or cultural background. In some parts of the world being born female condemns you to a life of subservience and abuse. In some countries you would be hunted and imprisoned for holding different political beliefs. Different groups of people have been randomly selected not only for discrimination but sometimes elimination. Gender, religion, politics, sexual preference—the list of "reasons" for prejudice goes on and on.

The most important lesson we can learn from the sufferings of our ancestors is that their lives changed only when certain individuals rose above their circumstances and used discrimination and persecution as the ultimate challenge to be and become more. This is exactly what Nelson Mandela has done—and as a result, he has changed the face of the future for South Africa, if not the entire world. Throughout history, discrimination has either caused people to give up and fail or to become intensely hungry to create change, to produce a greater quality of life not only for themselves but their children as well. They rally against whatever challenges exist and become so focused on their strengths, assets, and power that their positive impact is ultimately felt by everyone.

But understanding that discrimination is a universal force we either allow to destroy us or strengthen us was not something I believed in those days. While I have a different perspective today (having had the privilege of traveling around the world and opening my eyes to its history), in my days of suffering I not only focused on my own pain but also the immeasurable pain my beautiful race had endured for hundreds of years. The consequences of social conditioning and personal experiences constantly had me at odds with myself, my family, and the people around me. My double life caused a constant division in my soul and a gnawing feeling of being torn apart from within. It wasn't until 1985 that I realized the full extent of the damage. All those years of frustration, hurt, anger, and embarrassment, coupled with a lifetime of what it means to be Black in America, had taken their toll, and it all came to a head one night.

I had always seen myself as a strong man. I had worked so hard, I had given my all, but the rewards just weren't there. Even though by most people's standards I had achieved a lot, I felt empty inside. It seemed like nothing could please me. I became such an angry perfectionist that nothing or no one was good enough, least of all myself. I started alienating everyone around me. My girlfriend was miserable, my co-workers avoided me, and I did a sickening dance of denial for anyone who questioned my behavior. I felt like I was living a lie in a world where I just couldn't win and couldn't understand why. By day I'd hold it together, but every night my guts would start twisting with a million threads of chronic stress and depression. My head would start swirling with panic, and I would become overwhelmed by a numbing confusion. Worn out physically, emotionally, and financially, *I lost it!*

One night I reached a point where I had no idea where I was or what I was doing. I looked up and realized I was in the bathroom, clutching the sink with both hands. Sick to my stomach, I was trying to throw up but nothing would come. Overcome with emotion and fear, I saw my own eyes in the mirror welling with tears. "WHAT THE HELL IS THE MATTER WITH ME?" I screamed. It was as if all my fears, all my inadequacies, all my insecurities were screeching in my head like a thousand little demons hell-bent on driving me insane. I felt stinging anger and hatred toward myself and my inability to get a handle on the situation. I looked at all the things I was trying to do, and it all seemed so hopeless. Society teaches us we must work hard to get the things we want—well, I had done just that and then some, but it seemed the harder I worked the worse it got. Nothing made me happy. My girlfriend was miserable, and I knew it was just a matter of time before she would leave me, too. Everything I did suffered because I was spread so thin. I felt like a complete failure and less than a man.

What was missing? How could I have let this happen to me? What was wrong with me? Why couldn't I break through and finally succeed? Why did I always get so far, so close to success, and either do something stupid to sabotage myself, or watch helplessly as something horrible happened to rob me of my dream? Why . . . why . . . why? Each debilitating question my brain asked, each castrating image that flashed across the screen of my imagination dragged me closer to the ground. I spent the rest of the night on the bathroom floor, hoping I would die and afraid that I really would. I knew I had to go on but my very soul kept shouting, *WHY? WHAT FOR?*

The next morning I found myself at work, standing there like a shell of a man waiting for the next stiff breeze to blow me apart and scatter my paper-thin soul to the four winds. I felt totally defeated, and there was nothing I could do to change it.

Then I heard a voice that broke into my nightmare. It was a coworker who had been a good friend over the years. He took one look at me and knew that something was wrong. He said, "Hey, man, you look awful. What's up?"

"Nothing," I said, hoping he'd mind his own business and leave me alone.

But he didn't. Instinctively he stayed and said, "Look, I don't have to know what's wrong, but I know something that can help you with whatever that 'nothing' really is. I know this sounds crazy, but I was just coming by to tell you about this seminar in L.A. tonight that you need to attend. I know you don't know anything about it, but you just gotta trust me. The guy that's speaking will blow your mind and help you change your life. Just get there." He wrote down the directions for me and made me promise I'd really show up. At this point I'd have done anything to get him out of my face, so I halfheartedly agreed. But my gut was screaming, *No way!* After he left I stuffed the directions in my pocket and forgot about it. The last thing I wanted to do was to go where there were a lot of people.

The rest of the day scraped along at an agonizing pace. Everything I did seemed to go wrong and require more energy and effort than I had to give. I felt defeated and weak, and nothing I did could shake me out of the thick funk that encased my soul. When it was time to go home after work, I was afraid to go. What would I do when I got there—lose it again? Then I remembered the seminar my friend Bill had told me about. I thought, *It can't hurt. I'll just go and stick my head in and see what it's all about. I'll just stay for a few minutes.* I can't remember what made me do it, but at 5:30 P.M. I found myself headed down the freeway toward a hotel near the Los Angeles airport.

Pity Party

I was standing at the back of a crowded seminar room, wondering what the hell I was doing there. Anger, fear, and confusion coursed through my nervous system like battery acid. And then, as if my pain were not enough, it hit me. I was the only Black person there! The only Black face in a room full of happy, dancing "positive" White people. Some looked professional and successful; others, if they weren't already rednecks, looked like they could very easily grow into them. Looking at these people started to bring up all the resentment, frustration, and sarcastic bitterness inside of me. I felt sickeningly judgmental and painfully angry. The very emotions that were destroying my life were staring me right in the face, dancing all around me, daring me to leave. These people were so caught up in their own joy that all I could see was they didn't give a damn about me. No one even seemed to notice me standing there—and if they did, I was sure they were all judging me and avoiding me like the plague.

Then, right when I was feeling the most alone, the most angry, the most alienated, just when I thought I was going to bolt for the door, someone touched me on the shoulder. I spun around ready to lash out at whoever it was, expecting to find some goofy, dancing, Pollyanna, White seminar junkie goading me to loosen up and have a good time. But instead, standing in front of me was a man with his hand outstretched in greeting. His voice cut through the music and my own emotional hell. "Are you okay?" he asked. He had singled me out of the crowd and approached me without fear or judgment. He was a White man, but he stood in front of me as just a man. He didn't seem to care what anybody else would think; he had just made his way through the crowd and extended a welcoming hand. It sounds funny, but my anger, suspicion, and judgment became suspended in curiosity for the moment, and I opened up to this inquisitive stranger. By his suit and demeanor it was clear that he worked for the organization hosting the event, but there was something about the guy that made him different. He told me his name (which I forgot as soon as he said it) and asked me if I had a seat. He seemed to sincerely want to know the answer. Out of a sea of people, he had taken the time to help me.

He asked me again, "Are you okay?" I could tell he wasn't going to leave without a response. I guess I was a little bit in shock at that moment.

"I'm fine, man—thanks," I told him. His warm caring seemed to set me at ease. I remember thinking, *Whoever this speaker is, he sure trains his staff well. This guy is good.* I felt safe and taken care of. We talked for a few minutes, and then he asked me if I was afraid of the firewalk.

"Firewalk?" I asked. "What firewalk? Nobody told me about a firewalk. What the hell is that?"

He grinned from ear to ear and chuckled a little bit. "No one told you it's part of the seminar?"

"Hell no," I said. "What in God's name are you talking about?"

"Well, that's not what the seminar is all about," he said. "It's about how to overcome your fears and discover what's most important in your life. It's about centering yourself in your real purpose. It's about remembering who you really are." He looked at me and with a slight grin on his face he said half-jokingly, "And by the looks of it, you could use some of that right now."

I remember thinking, *How did he know that about me?* But I felt such a connection with this person—as if we had known each other for years and he knew what I was feeling.

Then he said, "It's obvious you've got some pain, but I just want you to know that you don't have to keep it. I want you to know I'll be a friend for you if you want to talk. And don't worry about the firewalk. It's just a simple exercise to demonstrate what you are capable of. You'll be fine."

A firewalk, I thought. Not only had my friend at work not told me what the seminar was all about, but it seems he had left out one little important detail. At the end of the program, all the participants were going to walk across a bed of burning hot coals. Barefoot!

I'm sure the look on my face said, "I'M OUTTA HERE!" but something made me stay.

"*NOW* I'm scared," I told him. "Aren't you?"

His face broke into another huge smile and he laughed out loud. "Nah! I do this all the time. You'll be just fine. Besides, remember what I said: That's not what the seminar is all about anyway. It's about how to get the best out of yourself. It's about how to turn the very fear that stops you into the courage that drives you. It's about how to get leverage on yourself so you really follow through. It's about how to collapse the negative experiences and emotional challenges from your past and use them instead as building blocks to create the future you deserve.

"At the end of the evening, if you choose to, you'll have the opportunity to do the firewalk. You'll see there is nothing to be afraid of. It has nothing to do with religion or 'mind over matter' or any of that stuff. It'll just be a celebration of the changes that you've made."

He explained that the firewalk is just a metaphor for turning our fears into power. There are lots of things you can do in your life that you didn't think were possible. He said, "You need two things in life to succeed. You need the skills and the emotional states of mind—confidence, conviction, passion. And those things are already inside of you, but maybe they're not being employed as much as your fear or worry. You'll learn that the only two things that usually stop us are fear and not having the skills.

"At the end of this evening you will have the emotional states—the courage and confidence—and the skills you need to change your life for good. Tonight's really about having some new choices and learning some tools to make it happen for you. We all can have extraordinary lives. Anyone can wake up every day with passion—but few people do." He said this with such certainty, congruence, and warmth that it made me feel maybe I really could be free from the emotional hell that was costing me so much in my life.

There was something about this man that made me trust him and believe he really did care. For some strange reason, I felt a strong connection with this stranger whom I hadn't even known ten minutes earlier. I didn't want the conversation to end. I thought, *To hell with the speaker! This guy has his stuff together. He really wants to help me—and I believe he can.*

After a few minutes, the music got louder and people started taking their seats. My new friend said he had to go and take care of a few things. He shook my hand and told me to have a great time, then he turned to walk away. He took about four steps, turned around and said, "Hey! I'd like to follow up with you and see how you're doing after the seminar. Do me a favor and let's hook up later and exchange numbers." I thought, *Wow, what service!* I felt I had really made a new friend and connected with a special soul. But after he walked away, I felt a little of the enthusiasm drain out of me. I still felt hopeful but I also thought, *No way in hell am I going to walk on those coals.*

The music stopped and everybody started clapping and cheering. A beautiful woman stepped onto the stage to address the crowd. She told us that just a few years ago she, too, was standing right where we were tonight, scared and doubtful and ready to leave. But she stayed, faced her fears, and transformed her life forever. After she finished her story she announced, "Ladies and gentlemen, my husband . . . Tony Robbins!"

It was the guy who had been talking to me! He wasn't a staff member at all—he was the star of the show. I should have known this unique man who was standing onstage with an incredible presence and approachable demeanor, who had taken the time to connect with me personally even before the program started, was special indeed. And the friendship we had kindled in that moment was more than just polite concern. He wasn't just being nice, he was genuinely reaching out to my soul. And as he looked at me from the front of the room, he knew I got it. Our meeting was predestined, and both of our lives were about to change.

From that point on, I was totally fascinated. I watched as I and the rest of the room transformed. From those with skepticism to those with high hopes, all of us gradually realized our real strength and power—not by positive thinking or persuasion from Tony, but instead by discovering how we function as human beings and engaging the driving force that is in each and every one of us. In minutes we turned decades of sour beliefs and destructive conditioning into confidence and internal pride. Tony's understanding of how the human brain works and his entertaining ability to communicate it made it easy for us all to see the true God-given greatness in our souls. We laughed; some of us cried. We connected, danced, and learned more about ourselves in those few hours than most of us had learned in our entire lives.

Tony helped us think in terms of possibility, and then to turn that possibility into certainty and courage to take on whatever was laid in front of us. It all made such simple sense. I felt as if he were talking directly to me, as if I could relate to everything he was saying. He wasn't some saint or some guru granting us these powers. Instead, he was just a man—a very special man—with a huge heart and an incredible ability to teach us how to do it for ourselves, how to access our own power and specialness not by affirmation, not by enthusiasm, but by having a solid plan and strategies for success. It wasn't him telling everybody what *his* plan was for *us;* it was each of us discovering and creating our own plan for our future. He honored the uniqueness of each and every human being in the room. I think most of all that's why it was so easy for me to relate to him. He wasn't about changing people to fit his vision, but about helping them discover their own.

Tony was truly amazing. He was funny, he was sincere, and he was right on the money with his insights about our lives. Though I barely knew him at this point, I felt proud of and for him. He didn't pump us up or hype us. Instead, he educated and inspired us to expect and demand more from ourselves. This remarkable young man, wise beyond his years, masterfully wove his wealth of information and knowledge into the fabric of our souls. And perhaps the best part was he didn't expect, assume, or require that we agree or even accept his thoughts. Rather, he laid it out in front of us all to inspect it using our own beliefs.

All of this he backed up with a solid technology. I watched him take people who had been struggling with emotional challenges like fears and phobias for years and wipe them out in a matter of moments. He showed us how to change our hesitations and doubts instantly into total congruency and faith. In those moments I saw, heard, and felt the passion for living I had been struggling to find all those years. I felt an insatiable yearning to learn, a deep hunger for more of what would ultimately be my calling as well.

There were three very distinct things that happened to me that night. One, I made an incredible friend for life. Two, I saw the solution for my own challenges and the transformation of my own beliefs about myself and my world. And three, I thought of all the people with similar experiences—inhibitions and fears like mine—who could benefit from this knowledge. I thought, *God, I want my brothers and sisters to know their power as well. I want everyone to know about this, to know about themselves.*

By the end of the evening, I had experienced so many changes I couldn't wait to get back to my life. Tony and I connected again and exchanged numbers. And of course I walked on the coals. The firewalk was just like he said: a metaphor for what is possible, a simple demonstration of our true capability. But most important, the seminar gave all of us the skills and tools to master our own lives.

In the days and weeks following the seminar I immediately, almost effortlessly, started using the tools I had learned—the same tools you will learn in this book—to dramatically change the quality of my life for the better. I had always wanted to play music for a living, but I'd been afraid of failing or losing the security of my job. After the seminar I quit my limiting job of fifteen years, pursued my dream of playing professionally, and in 1991 landed a recording contract with CBS Records. All of my judgment, fears of failure, and inadequacy dropped off like unwanted ballast, and opportunities and possibilities the likes of which I had previously not even dared to dream of appeared. I finally began to live a life rich with love, joy, pride, happiness, possibility, and healthy relationships with others.

And you know what? I wanted even more. All my life I've loved people and have wanted to give back and contribute. That's one of the things Tony and I share a passion for. Physically, financially, emotionally, and spiritually, my life spiraled to new levels, and with it grew my desire to share my passion with my own race. I hungered for more knowledge about these incredible tools for changing lives. In the past, I had read all the "positive thinking" books, listened to all the tapes, and heard so many motivational speakers it was a joke, but nothing delivered like this technology. This wasn't motivation or pump-up fanfare—it was solid tangible skill sets that produced measurable results. In college, my major was psychology. I thought I knew it all, but in reality, I didn't have a clue. I had never experienced anything like this. I wanted so much more, and now I knew it was here for the taking. So I decided I was going to master this technology.

I began to immerse myself in the strategies Tony was teaching. Since then, I've sat in rooms full of CEOs of major companies, children, businessmen and women, psychiatrists and psychologists, people of every culture from all around the world, souls from forty-two different nations. I've discovered we all have at least two things in common:

First, we all have a willingness to make ourselves and the world we live in a better place. Some have that willingness because they've already succeeded and want to give back. Some have it because they've tried everything and nothing else worked. But we all have that hunger, that insatiable yearning to do and give more than we are currently giving. Tony created an environment in which all the discriminatory rules of society were suspended so people could see the power and essence of who we are as humans, then use what we discover for the betterment of all.

Second, we've all made the choice to be, do, and have what we want based upon our willingness to access those states of mind that produce the best results. Race, religion, gender, culture didn't matter—the choice was ours alone. It's not a Black thing or a White thing, it's a human thing. **It's the *human choice* that mat-**

ters the most—and we all have that choice at any moment in time. As long as we keep ourselves in a place of caring, loving, and giving . . . not focusing on ourselves as much as focusing on how to make a difference . . . in a place where we have compassion instead of judgment, curiosity instead of sarcasm, humor instead of hate, and centeredness instead of frustration . . . those choices are always at our disposal—and the tools are here to access those choices.

As my friendship with Tony continues to grow after ten years, I think what brings us together the most is our absolute caring and our passion for sharing what works with as many people as possible. To this day we feel like brothers on the path of making a difference. The words you are reading now come from both of our hearts, to share with you the same tools that have already helped millions create the lives they desire.

Over the past ten years, I have become certified in Tony's technology, eventually becoming Head Trainer for Robbins Research International, Inc. In addition, I started my own peak performance company, Succeleration, offering workshops and seminars to assist groups and individuals get the very best out of themselves. I began teaching postgraduate extension courses at the University of California at Los Angeles. I became proficient in handling fears and phobias in a very short period of time—sometimes a few minutes, sometimes an hour or so.

Perhaps one of the greatest gifts I have received from this technology is that no matter what is put in front of me, I don't have to accept it as being permanent or defeating. Yes, there will be color obstacles. Yes, people will judge me and try to oppress me and my race. But ultimately we can and will climb over those obstacles, or go around them, or even storm right through them to get to the other side. That first night at the seminar, one of the beliefs I adopted was: *There's always a way if you're committed.* Too many people have succeeded for us to deny that each of us already has everything it takes to succeed. It's this sense of certainty that will take us further and faster and make us healthier and happier. If things don't work out, we need never regress to the old beliefs that have held us down for far too long.

Break Away

By now, you may be asking, "What does all this have to do with me? How will this help me get from where I am now to where I want to go? And what does this have to do with *Unlimited Power: A Black Choice?*" Well, while I said earlier that Tony's environment was multicultural, I still have a hunger to reach more of my own people. Tony and I have traveled around the world in the last few years, and we have noticed consistently that only a very small fraction of this valuable, life-changing information has found its way into the Black community. I felt most of our race was missing some essential tools that would change the quality of our lives for the better: how to transform our lives mentally, physically, and emotionally; how to become truly free; how to sever the ties of weakness binding us to the stories of the past but still preserve the pride and strength we need; how to reprogram the negative emotions we allow to affect us daily even though we realize they don't serve us; how to create a plan for the future that not only improves our own lives but those of our children as well. This we can all use. I see so many of us struggling to find our way and missing the boat by doing the same things over and over again. Life is much simpler than we've been led to believe, and these tools are the keys to open some of the doors that previously seemed closed to us.

Too few of us are taking advantage of what is at our fingertips. As a group, we may very well be in our infancy in the areas of success conditioning and personal development. In researching and asking why more of us don't seek this knowledge, I found a wide variety of reasons. Some people said they wanted to hear it from one of our own kind, or that they can't relate to a White man, or that this is something Blacks just don't do. But beliefs like those keep us from having, being, and doing what we want in our lives. We need to take full advantage of *any* resources, whether they be white, black, red, brown, yellow, whatever.

Regardless of those beliefs, we now have no excuses. This, my dear friend, is your opportunity to take advantage of what works and use it to benefit your future. These are the same tools and techniques that have and will continue to make the great greater, the strong stronger, the happy happier, and the successful more successful. These techniques do not discriminate. They play no favorites and show no regard for race, creed, or cultural background. They are natural law, and it is your birthright to use them to the fullest.

Many years ago, Anthony Robbins produced a masterwork for creating change. Since 1985, *Unlimited Power* has been a bestseller, translated into seventeen languages and published around the world. This book has brought to millions of people the strategies and systems that produce lasting change and success. It's an owner's manual for the human brain. These skills and tools are now laid in front of you for your inspection and use in shaping your own life.

Unlimited Power: A Black Choice came out of a discussion Tony and I had about the need for more choices and role models of success within the Black community. There is definitely a need for more information about technologies of positive change within communities other than those that have traditionally received them. Tony and I have worked together to create this book so you will have this message directed to you through the eyes of someone who perhaps has lived part of what you may have lived—someone who has experienced the reality of being Black in today's world.

In writing this book, our wish is that you will find the technologies, strategies, skills, and philosophies taught within these pages to be as empowering for you as they have been for me. The power to magically transform our lives into our greatest dreams lies waiting within us all. It's time to unleash it, so get ready! And by the way, if you're willing to really commit and focus—not just read this book but act upon what you read—then this will be worth so much more than you ever imagined.

This book is the sum total of Tony's and my collaboration, synergistically working together in order to convey this information in a form you and I can personally relate to and prosper from. It uses rich metaphors, examples, and stories that tap into our beautiful Black history, both recent and ancient. It provides more role models, more possibilities, more real-life accomplishments to illustrate these strategies at work.

We genuinely applaud you and your quest to move "we the people" to higher levels of greatness. It is because of you and others like you that we have come so far. We praise your continued success and encourage the open-mindedness of all who are willing to grow. We humbly offer ourselves, our services, and our beliefs as high-octane jet fuel to the human vehicle so that we may all go *farther, faster, now!* So let's get to it. Let's make it happen. And by the way, keep this in mind: There has never been a better time in history for us to be alive. We live in an age where anything is possible—if we are willing to go for it.

Black Power Today

Utopia is what the imagination of man has to say about the possibilities of the human spirit.

—Howard Thurman

Today the pace at which people are able to turn their dreams into realities is truly amazing. We live in an age when, regardless of our skin color or gender, we are capable of achieving some pretty incredible things in very short periods of time—success that would have been unimaginable in earlier times. Looking at the world today, I wonder who could have foretold the rising political stars of such Black leaders as Bobby Rush, Carol Moseley-Braun, Marian Wright Edelman, Thurgood Marshall, Maxine Waters, David Dinkins, or Nelson Mandela. Who could have imagined the immense popularity of entertainment figures like Quincy Jones, Bill Cosby, Oprah Winfrey, Denzel Washington, Whitney Houston, Spike Lee, or the artist formerly known as Prince? Who would have dreamed of the scientific prowess of Muriel Petioni or the astonishing adventures of astronaut Mae Jemison? Who could have expected the literary masterpieces of Toni Morrison, Alice Walker, Walter Mosley, or Cornel West? These are just a few of the many outstanding Black men and women who surround us today.

Look at Robert L. Johnson, president and founder of the Black Entertainment Network (BET). He took a medium that barely existed in the 1980s, cable TV, and created an empire. He too started with just a dream. He created a weekly two-hour show, and now his network broadcasts twenty-four hours a day—the first and *only* Black cable network, servicing more than 2,500 different markets and forty million homes. BET was the first Black-owned company to be traded on the New York Stock Exchange.

What does Robert L. Johnson share with all these other masters, aside from prodigious success? The answer, of course, is . . .

CHAPTER TWO

The Commodity of Kings

There is no such force as the force of a man determined to rise. The human soul cannot be permanently chained.

—W.E.B. Du Bois

Power is a very emotional word, especially as it pertains to the African American culture. People's responses to it are varied, and for some, power has a negative connotation. In the late 1960s, for example, the term *Black power* took on several meanings. For most African Americans, it was a statement of strength and pride, while for much of the rest of the world it elicited confusion and fear. Today, as always, some people lust after power while others feel threatened by it, as if it were something evil or suspect.

How much power do you want? How much power do you think is right for you to obtain or develop? What does power really mean to you?

Neither Tony nor I think of power in terms of controlling or imposing our will upon others. We're certainly not suggesting that you should, either. That kind of power is almost always short-lived. But you must realize that power is a constant in this world. Either you shape your perceptions or someone else shapes them for you. In this world, you do what you plan for yourself . . . or you follow someone else's plan for you. And as history has shown, those other plans don't necessarily have your best interest in mind.

In our opinion, real power is the ability to create the results you desire while simultaneously adding value to the lives of others. Ultimate power is the ability to shape and control your own life. It's the ability to define human needs and fulfill them—both your needs and the needs of people you care about. It's the ability to direct your own thought processes, your own behavior, so you take hold of the steering mechanism of your life and determine your own destiny.

Throughout history, the power to control our lives has taken many different and contradictory forms. In the earliest times, power simply belonged to the one with the greatest physical size, strength, and agility. Those who were the strongest and the fastest had power to direct their own lives as well as the lives of those around them. As time went on and civilization grew, power was a matter of birthright or heritage, and a hierarchy of royalty developed. Surrounding himself with the symbols of his realm, the king ruled with unmistakable authority, and others could derive power only by their association with him. Then came the early days of the Industrial Age when capital was power. The "Golden" Rule applied: "He who has the gold makes the rules." Even though as African Americans we were denied many opportunities during these times, we were still affected by the balance of power in the existing system. To this day most of us consider the control of capital the truest measure of power. All the historic factors continue to play a role: It's still better to have capital than not to have it, and it's better to have physical strength than not to have it. However, one of the largest sources of power today is derived from *specialized knowledge.*

By now, we all know we are living in the Information Age. We are primarily a communication-based culture. Industry still plays a huge role in society, but information is where true power lies. We live in a time when new ideas, movements, and concepts change the world almost daily, whether they are as profound as quantum physics or as simple as the best way to market hair-care products. If there's anything that characterizes the modern world, it's the massive, almost unimaginable flow of information—and therefore, of change. From books and movies to e-mail and the Internet, this new information comes at us in a blizzard of data to be seen and felt and heard. And the anonymity of the newest forms of communication makes race and other bases of prejudice virtually insignificant. You can conduct business with people who might never know the color of your skin, your gender, your age—or even your real name.

In today's society, whoever has the best information and the means to communicate it has what kings used to have—unlimited power.

> *Money is what fueled the industrial society. But in the informational society, the fuel, the power, is knowledge. One has now come to see a new class structure divided by those who have information and those who must function out of ignorance. This new class has its power not from money, not from land, but from knowledge.*
>
> —JOHN KENNETH GALBRAITH

Perhaps the most exciting thing about power being information-based is that today the key to power is available to everyone. In the Middle Ages, if you weren't the king or part of the royal family, it was difficult to obtain power. In the Industrial Age, if you didn't start with a lot of capital, your odds for amassing it were slim. Today, however, any kid with a library card or access to the Internet might create a corporation that could change the world. Those with access to certain forms of specialized knowledge and information can transform not only themselves but also, in many ways, our entire society. What's great about this is that, for the most part, all of us have easy access to specialized knowledge. Therefore, we all have access to potential power.

With that in mind, we're left with an obvious question: Why do some people produce magnificent results and others barely eke out a living? Why do so many of us in this society seem to be behind the times, playing catch-up with our potential, while others set new standards of personal and professional success? In the United States the kind of specialized knowledge needed to transform the quality of our lives is available to everyone. It's in every bookstore, every video store, every library. You can get it from speeches and seminars and courses. And we all seem to want to succeed. The best-seller list is full of prescriptions for personal excellence: *Think Big, Live Your Dreams, Why Should White Guys Have All The Fun?, In Search of Excellence, Think and Grow Rich, Black Pearls, The One Minute Manager, Member of the Club* . . . the list seems to go on forever. If all the information is so easily accessible, why don't we all use it to generate the results we want? Why aren't we all empowered, happy, wealthy, healthy, and successful?

The truth of the matter is that information alone is not enough. Think about it: If all we needed were some ideas and a positive mental attitude, each of us would be living in the lap of luxury. *Action* is the catalyst for every great success. *Action* is what produces results. Knowledge alone is only potential power, and until it comes into the hands of someone who knows how to take effective *action,* it will remain dormant. In fact, the literal definition of the word *power* is "the ability to act."

Too many of us get caught in the mental trap of seeing successful people and thinking they got where they are because they have some special gift. The color of their skin, we think, predisposes them to success (and conversely, the color of our skin can guarantee our failure through no fault of our own). But if there is one thing the last twenty years have shown us, it is that anyone can do anything, regardless of race, creed, color, or gender. This is not to say that some people don't have advantages or that others are never the object of prejudice. But in almost every profession or vocation, there is a representative of one or more minority groups. It could be argued that these "representative" few have been thrust into their roles by affirmative action, and even when people's abilities are equal, opportunities are not. Unfortunately, some measure of inequality is a fact of life. Some people are judged because they are female, disabled, foreign-born, single, fair-haired, overweight, soft-spoken, young—or any other arbitrary characteristic, including the opposite of any of those just listed. All too often people use their differences as an excuse to justify giving up. "Because I'm a woman and women don't get a fair shake in the business world, why bother trying?" Or, "I'm too old to even get started." The good news is that, upon closer observation, we will usually find that the greatest gift extraordinarily successful people have is not some outward characteristic, but *the ability to get themselves to take action.* It's a "gift" that any of us can develop within ourselves. After all, other people had the same knowledge BET cable TV magnate Robert L. Johnson did. Anyone else could have figured out that an all-Black cable network had tremendous social and economic potential. But Johnson alone had the vision, took the necessary action, and made it a reality.

Even though Johnson was told no Black man could make it, he

wasn't willing to accept that belief. He proved a fundamental law of the universe: Every truly great success means overcoming obstacles. You can choose to believe that any man or woman with total resolve will never be stopped by any obstacle, whether racism, physical disability, acts of God, or anything else. In fact, obstacles can actually *serve* you in becoming a bigger success and, ultimately, a greater person because of them.

COMMUNICATION IS POWER

Human beings shape their lives through two types of communication. First, we conduct what we call *internal communication.* These communications are made up of the things we say to ourselves and what we picture in our minds. It's from these resources that many of our internal feelings are generated. Whenever we think a thought or even say something to ourselves, we are experiencing internal communication. Reading this book silently is conducting internal communication.

The second way we communicate is through *external communication:* the words we speak aloud; the way we use our faces; our voice tonality, facial expressions, and body postures; as well as any physical actions we take to express ourselves to the world. It's important to realize that every communication we make, whether conscious or unconscious, internal or external, is an action, a cause set in motion. And all communications have some kind of effect, on ourselves and others as well. In turn, all behaviors and feelings find their original roots in some form of communication.

To master our lives, we must master the way we communicate to ourselves. If we want to change our lives, we must change our actions, and our actions are fathered by decisions. We must have some form of internal communication to get ourselves to take action. In addition, if we are going to influence the actions of others, we must become more conscious of the effect of all the elements of external communication. Dr. Martin Luther King, Jr., was able to influence himself first by mastering his internal communication, maintaining his passion against staggeringly unjust and vicious odds. But his emotions and dreams would have died in his heart had he not mastered external communication as well. To this very day, his words, voice, and face are etched into our memories as bold reminders that his dream still lives. Because he mastered both internal and external communication, he was able to influence a nation of hungry souls to make the lasting changes we all enjoy today. And his voice continues not only to expect more but give more as well.

Because communication is action, it is power. Those who have mastered its effective use can change their own experience of the world and the world's experience of them. When you master your communication, you begin to master your life. Throughout history, people who have made the biggest impact on our thoughts and feelings and on the world as a whole are those individuals who have learned to use communication power.

Take a minute and think about that last statement. Isn't it true that the people who have had the biggest effect on you are those who have mastered the skill of communication? Think of some of the people who have changed our world—Martin Luther King, Jr., John F. Kennedy, Mahatma Gandhi, Malcolm X, Thomas Jefferson, Franklin Delano Roosevelt, Albert Einstein, even entertainers like Bill Cosby, Oprah Winfrey, and Michael Jackson. In a much grimmer vein, think of Adolf Hitler. As horrible as he was, he affected the course of the world. These people were all master communicators. They were able to take their vision—whether it was to transport people into space, or to create a hate-filled Third Reich—and communicate it to others with such conviction and certainty they influenced the way the masses thought and acted. Through their communication power, they changed the world.

Isn't this also what sets a Quincy Jones, a Tom Bradley, a Spike Lee, an Eddie Murphy, or a Colin Powell apart? Are they not masters of the tools of human communication, whether it's to entertain or to influence? Just as these people are able to move the masses with communication, we can use the same tools to move ourselves.

The quality of your external communication will determine the quality of your success in the outer world. It will determine how you interact with others—personally, emotionally, socially, and financially. But what's more important by far is that the level of success you experience *internally*—the happiness, joy, ecstasy, love, or anything else you desire—is the direct result of the way you communicate to yourself. Your internal communication, not the events surrounding your life, will determine whether you are happy, sad, joyful, grateful; whether you will feel the passion and love that you and every human being deserves in this life.

Whether or not you truly experience the emotions you desire is a direct result of the way you communicate to yourself. If a woman continually tells herself there is a glass ceiling that limits how far she can go in this world and therefore she can't ever achieve her goals, then she will never find the courage and strength to make it happen—unlike Mrs. Shirley Chisholm, America's first Black congresswoman. If we as African Americans continually tell ourselves that our color predisposes us to unfair treatment, then whether it's true or not, we will lose the drive and spirit necessary to find the very solutions that will take us into the glorious future that beckons us. We will see only anger and frustration and resentment in the world, and in turn we will not act upon the multitudes of opportunities laid at our feet every day.

Please make sure you understand this simple fact of life: **How we feel is not the result of what is happening in our lives—it is our *interpretation* of what is happening.** History has shown us over and over again that the quality of successful people's lives is determined not by what happens to them, but rather by what they *do* about what happens in their lives. It's our interpretation of what is happening, our internal communication, that affects our lives the most. We must master it. We must focus on what we can do. And there is always something we can do; if not something in the outside world, then something within ourselves that will turn life's challenges into opportunities. We can look at unfairness in life and say, "WE SHALL OVERCOME THIS AND WIN!"

Consider Bill Dower of the U.S. Marine Corps. He joined the Marine Corps in the 1940s with aspirations of rising through the ranks and proving his patriotism. But at that time, most Marine drill instructors made no secret of how they felt about Blacks in the military. To say that Black recruits received unfair treatment is a gross understatement. Dower and two other Black Marines plotted to take the life of a particular drill instructor who had made their lives unbearable by constantly humiliating them, mistreating them, and wearing them down. On the night they were supposed to commit the murder, one of Dower's friends did something that changed all of their lives forever. He challenged them all to look at the situation in an entirely different way. He said, "If we kill this man it will ruin our lives forever, and they will have won. All they've been saying about us will have been true—that we can't take it, we're weak, we haven't got what it takes to make it. This is the ultimate opportunity to prove them wrong."

Instead of buying into the persecution, the recruits created a new meaning out of it. From that point on, whatever was thrown at them they not only took on and conquered, but they even asked for more. They excelled at everything; they attacked their tasks with the spirit of champions. They developed a saying, "Whip it on." If they were told to do a hundred more push-ups than the other men—"Whip it on." Run ten more miles—"Whip it on." "Whatever you throw at us makes us stronger, so whip it on!" And stronger they all became. Decades later, Bill Dower not only became a drill sergeant himself, but was appointed Master Drill Sergeant and trainer of all drill sergeants in the U.S. Marine Corps. He is one of the proudest, strongest Americans we know. Bill Dower and his comrades communicated to themselves that what looked like an impossible situation was really an opportunity to be more than anyone thought they were capable of being.

Remember, you are the one who decides how to feel and act based upon the ways you choose to perceive your life. As simplistic and unnatural as it may sound, **nothing has any meaning except the meaning we give it.** Most of us have allowed the process of interpretation to become automatic. But it's important to realize that if we don't consciously take charge of our interpretations, outside forces will determine our worldview. On the other hand, it's exciting to know we can reclaim that power instantly and change how we experience life on this planet.

This book is about learning how we function as human beings and using that information to take the massive, focused, congruent actions that lead to astounding results. It's about producing what you want in your life *right now!* Think about it. Isn't that what you're really interested in anyway? Isn't that why you picked up this book? Perhaps you want to change how you feel about yourself and your world. Perhaps you'd like to be a better communicator, develop a more loving relationship with someone, learn more rapidly, become healthier, or earn more money. All of these things and more you can create for yourself through the effective use of the information in this book.

Before you can produce new results, however, you must first recognize the results you're already producing. These results may or may not be the ones you desire, but no matter what we do or don't do, we are always producing results. Most of us think our "mental states of mind" are out of our control because they are a result of what's occurring in the outside world. The truth is that we can and do control our states of mind.

If you're depressed, for example, you created and produced the "show" you call depression. If you're ecstatic, you created that, too. Remember, emotions do not just happen to you. We don't "catch" depression. Just like every other result in our lives, we create that emotion through specific mental and physical actions. In order to be depressed, you have to view your life in specific ways. You have to say certain things to yourself in just the right, ugly tone of voice. You have to adopt a specific posture and breathe a certain way to produce the emotion you know as depression. It also helps tremendously if you collapse your shoulders and look down a lot. Talking in mournful-sounding tones and thinking of the worst possible situations also helps produce that emotion. If you throw your biochemistry into turmoil through poor diet or excessive alcohol or drug use, you assist your body in creating low blood sugar and thus virtually guarantee depression.

Here's the point: It takes effort to produce depression. It's deliberate, hard work, and it requires taking specific types of actions. Unfortunately, just like anything else we do often enough, some of us have gotten really good at producing this emotion. And this is just one example. The same holds true for any other emotion, good or bad. Some people have created this state so often, though, that it's easy for them to produce. In fact, often they've linked this pattern of internal communication to all kinds of external events. Some people get so much secondary gain—attention from others, sympathy, love, and so on—that they adopt this style of communication as their natural state of living. Others have lived with it so long it actually feels comfortable. They become identified with the state.

So, What's the Solution?

The great news is that we can change our mental and physical actions to wipe out the emotions that don't serve us and strengthen the ones that do. We can condition ourselves to become ecstatic, or excited, or compassionate by adopting the point of view that creates that emotion. To produce a state of ecstasy, for example, you can picture in your mind the kinds of things that create this feeling. You can change the tone and content of your internal dialogue with yourself. You can adopt the specific postures and breathing patterns that create that state in your body, and *tadah!*—you will experience ecstasy. If you wish to be compassionate, you must simply change your physical and mental actions to match those the state of compassion requires. You'll soon find that you can create any emotion you like, when you like it.

It might be helpful to think of the process of producing emotional states by imagining your internal communication as being like making a movie. To produce the precise results they want on the screen, filmmakers manipulate what you see and hear. If they want you to be scared, they might turn up the sound and splash some special effects on the screen at just the right moment. If they want you to be inspired, they'll arrange the music, lighting, and everything else on the screen to produce that effect. They can produce a tragedy or a comedy out of the same event, depending on what they decide to put on the screen. You can do the same things with the movie screen in your own mind. You can manipulate your mental activity, which is the foundation of all physical action. You can turn up the lights and sounds of the positive messages in your brain, and dim the lights and sounds of the negative ones. You can run your brain as skillfully as John Singleton runs his movie set.

Every small, positive change we can make in ourselves repays us in confidence in the future.

—Alice Walker

Some of what follows may seem hard to swallow—at first, you may find it hard to believe there's a way to instantly summon up your most powerful resources at will. But if you had suggested to Negro slaves 225 years ago that their descendants would be winning elections for government office, heading corporations, and living in the lap of luxury in this country, they would have told you to stop all that dreaming. They would have cautioned you, "Don' let de massa hear you talkin' like dat." If you had suggested one hundred years ago that men would go to the moon, you would have been considered insane. (Where do you think the word *lunatic* came from?) If you had said it would be possible to travel from New York to Los Angeles in five hours, you would have seemed like a crazy dreamer. In reality, all it took was the mastery of specific technologies and laws of aerodynamics to make those things possible. (In fact, right now one aerospace company is working on an aircraft they say will soon take people from New York to California in twelve minutes, by exiting and reentering the earth's atmosphere.) Though perhaps not as swiftly, the changes we've made in the Black community have been created step by step as well. With the application of specific technologies and laws of *human behavior,* we will reach our goals of personal equality and cultural unity that much faster.

I feel so fortunate to be alive in this day and age. I am so thankful for the things our ancestors did to make our lives better today. Although there is much more work to be done to balance this planet, I never stop appreciating the men and women who have sacrificed so much for us all.

Recent history has given us several role models and examples of successful Black men and women: the invincible Jesse Owens, who proved to the world that there was no such thing as ethnic "inferiority" or "superiority" . . . the inimitable General Colin Powell, who was not only instrumental in the U.S. armed forces command during the Gulf War, but a powerful political adviser throughout his distinguished military career . . . the indomitable

Carol Moseley-Braun, first Black U.S. senator . . . the innovative Berry Gordy, who founded the breakthrough Motown Records in 1959 . . . the indestructible Wilma Rudolph, who overcame polio and paralysis to become a three-time Olympic gold medal champion . . . and the countless others whose names have not yet made it into the public eye. Upon close inspection of all these inspiring individuals, we start to see a pattern in them all; a consistent path we call . . .

CHAPTER THREE

The Ultimate Success Formula

The thing is to never deal yourself out. . . . Opt for the best possible hand. Play with verve and sometimes with abandon, but at all times with calculation.

—L. DOUGLAS WILDER

HE HAD ONE thing on his mind: not just to win but to be the very best in the sport. Moving like a hungry panther in the wild, he stalked his prey with cunning and finesse and deadly accuracy. Then, with a blinding forehand smash he sent the tennis ball viciously slicing across the net back to his opponent, stamped, "Special delivery from Arthur Ashe—no return address!" And when the match was over, there he stood, the victor, with that boyish smile of confidence and pride he wore so well.

Even at the young age of twelve, a slightly cocky Arthur Robert Ashe, Jr., knew he wanted to be the best professional tennis player in the world—a goal difficult for anyone to accomplish, let alone a young Black man in the 1960s. He battled vicious racism every step of the way. There actually were laws prohibiting Blacks from playing professional tennis. Arthur Ashe's experiences would have made most of us turn and run, or fight back in frustrated anger. Over and over, he put his future, his reputation, and all too often his life on the line to break through the color barrier and make his dream a reality. As a result, to this day he is known as the greatest Black tennis player of all time. He not only had to continually change his approach on the playing court, he also had to keep changing his approach *off* the court to maintain the dignity and mental stamina needed to reach his goal.

We all know that Arthur Ashe went on to dominate the sport of tennis. But what many of us don't know is that until the time of his death in February 1993 he led a tireless crusade for racial equality and AIDS research simultaneously. His drive and determination still stand as an empowering reminder of what the human spirit can accomplish when it is directed passionately.

What made this man so successful? It's the same thing that men and women from every walk of life knowingly or unknowingly have always used to succeed. We call it the Ultimate Success Formula. It's the fundamental, simple system that causes anyone to succeed in anything they do. It is the path that will guide you through the inevitable obstacles that all human beings experience whenever they set a worthwhile goal.

THE FIRST STEP

There are four steps to the Ultimate Success Formula, and the first is so simple most people tend to pass it by. You must:

1. Know your outcome. What does this mean? It means you must develop absolute clarity about the exact result you want to produce. We use the word *outcome* as opposed to goal because these two words have very different effects on your nervous system. As you'll be learning in the pages to follow, language affects the way we think and feel. It even affects our biochemistry. Many of us have set and then failed to achieve goals. But as we said in the last chapter, we always achieve some "outcome"—whether or not it's the one we desire.

We must not only decide what our outcome is, we must resolve to do whatever is necessary with integrity to make it a reality. So few people take the time to define with precision what they want, and it's hard to hit a target when you don't know what it is. Besides, if you have only a generalized view of what you want, such as, "I'd like to earn more money," one dollar may complete your goal. The secret is to train your brain to continually focus on anything that can help you achieve your heart's deepest desires.

Think of your brain as a highly sophisticated missile-guidance system, one that will hit any target you define for it with precision. But you must know exactly what it is you want. A missile can't hit a fuzzy target or one that you haven't taken the time to define.

If you speak to those who knew him, Arthur Ashe had this step handled from his earliest years. He knew exactly what he wanted. He never focused on obstacles; he focused on the outcome he wanted to produce. Color was not his focus, pain was not his focus—hitting the tennis ball was his focus. Winning tennis matches was his ultimate focus. His brilliance seemed to be due in part to the simple fact that he refused to focus on things he couldn't control. He focused only upon his serve, his volley, his attitude about the game—things he *could* control. The "fact" that there wasn't another Black player of his quality in all of professional tennis didn't rule his mind. Instead, like all great leaders and achievers, he was focused on step one, "What's my outcome?" In fact, he *used* the fact that no other Black man had ever reached such heights in professional tennis as an inspiration rather than evidence it would be impossible.

The Second Step

2. Take massive action—"the cure-all." While it's true very few people ever take the time to define precisely what they want, an even smaller percentage, once they know what they want, actually take action—much less massive action! The one thing that's made the biggest difference in my ability to achieve the most important outcomes of my life is massive action. There is no replacement for it. Massive action truly is the cure-all. You can create changes and results most people never dream of *if* you'll stop sitting around talking about it, planning it, thinking about it, and instead, actually DO IT—whatever "it" is that can move you forward. All journeys start with the first step. Massive, committed, focused, passionate action sends a clear-cut message to the world that you are here to play to win. And the world has no choice but to sit up and take notice—and start the delivery process to hand you your desires.

Did Arthur Ashe just dream and talk about what he wanted? Not a chance. He spent a lifetime out on the court by himself, smacking that ball over and over again until his reactions and moves were no longer rehearsed but woven into the fabric of his very being. He didn't have to think about where to go or what to do on the court. His tennis racket became a natural extension of his mind and body. Ashe paid the price that excellence demands. When he was tired and sore, when he couldn't go any further, he'd "whip it on" and step up to the challenge.

One of our core beliefs is that **what you practice in private you will be rewarded for in public.** But if we don't take that action—if we don't practice in private, if we don't "whip it on"—there are no rewards in public. And we'll have no one to blame but ourselves. Massive action is the ticket, and no one succeeds without it.

THE THIRD STEP

3. You must know what you are getting. Out of the tiny number of people who know their outcomes and take massive action, an even smaller percentage actually master the third step. Far too many people who consider themselves achievers think the secret to success is to know what you want, put your head down, take massive action, and you'll get there eventually. They believe if you just push hard enough, if you just storm forward, you'll make it. We've all heard the term *tunnel vision.* The problem with tunnel vision is that if you don't look up and see where you're going, that tunnel could run you into a drainpipe! These kinds of people believe that because they came up with a plan and worked hard on it, then it has to work no matter what.

In reality, most plans human beings put together do not work the first time. That's part of the learning process. Trial and error is part of growing, strengthening, building, accomplishing, and developing character. If it were all that easy, everyone would have already figured it out. But we must not get caught up in the trap of continuing to do what isn't working. You must sensitize yourself to anything that could give you feedback as to whether or not you are on track. You don't want to start running east looking for a sunset—it's not going to happen no matter how hard you try, how fast you go, or how much massive action you take. You've got to notice what results you are getting *as you take action.* This requires you to pay attention and check in to see what is working and what isn't. It also requires not judging too quickly. Sometimes you need to do something long enough to see whether or not it works. That's the delicate balance we call "learning by experience." Too many people keep on doing what doesn't work simply because they don't take the time to look at the results they are getting in the moment. Remember the definition of insanity: doing the same thing over and over again, expecting a different result.

Arthur Ashe would study his form, serve, forehand, and backhand to see what he was doing right as well as what he could improve. He had coaches to watch and point out both the good and the bad. He learned from his mistakes and his successes. Like anyone who succeeds, he never took it for granted that he knew it all. He constantly evaluated whether what he was doing was working or not. If it wasn't, he immediately moved to step four.

The Fourth Step

4. Change your approach—the ultimate power. Flexibility is power. When we realize we aren't getting closer to our outcomes with our current plans and actions, we must change our approach. We can't give up. We must try something else. Just because you don't get the result you want one way doesn't mean it won't work another way. One of my favorite sayings is, "The amount of people who fail is directly proportionate to the amount of people who give up." History is full of outstanding people who kept changing their approach after they seemed to have failed at doing something one particular way. Where would we all be if our ancestors gave up and quit trying to find new ways to gain equality? Sometimes it's just a little shift in the way you're doing something that gets the result you want. But you must be willing to try something new, to be flexible in your approach to listening and doing things a different way.

Too often all over the world, I've seen people buying into the false belief they have tried everything, or saying they've tried a million approaches, when the fact of the matter is they've tried scarcely a handful of ways—and most of those were probably a variation on the same approach. Sometimes we have to try something radically different to get what we want. Sometimes we have to go against the grain. One of the only things I've seen Tony get upset about is when someone insists he or she has tried everything to get a result. If you were to tell Tony that, he'd very quickly let you know that you are lying to yourself. **If you really would have tried everything, you would have found a way.**

Did Arthur Ashe follow this final step of the formula as well? Of course he did. He'd work day in and day out on a particular serve or stroke, giving it all he had. And when he would reach a plateau or experience difficulty, he would take note of what was going on in his game and change his approach. He'd study other players, get new coaches, do anything that would sustain his forward movement. He continually changed his approach not only on the playing court, but also off the court to maintain the strength of character that propelled him to the number one position in his sport and made him a legend. He learned how to communicate to the world of tennis that he meant business.

If you keep changing your approach, if you are flexible enough to keep trying something new, you will come up with new choices and arrive at your outcome. If you keep evaluating whether or not it's working, sooner or later you'll find what *does* work, and that's where ultimate success comes in.

One final note: Too often, the more successful that people become, the less flexible they tend to be. Out of our desire to preserve our success, we often lose the very power that made us successful in the first place. Avoid this trap by understanding that true success comes from being certain there are many ways to get your outcome.

In review, the four steps of the Ultimate Success Formula are simply:

1. Know your outcome.
2. Take massive action.
3. Have sensory acuity—notice what you are getting.
4. Change your approach until you get the result you want.

The key question is, If the essence of this formula is trial-and-error learning, is there a way to speed things up? You bet there is.

It's called *modeling.* The essence of all that Tony teaches comes from his desire to produce results, make changes, and help other people. But if we took the time to learn through trial and error, we'd be very old before we got very wise. Through the process of modeling we can compress decades into days. We can model someone who has spent twenty or thirty years to figure something out, and in a matter of minutes, hours, weeks, or months, produce the same result. Here's the secret: **Once you know your outcome, find someone who has already produced the results you want.** Who already has lost weight and kept it off? Who already has financial independence? Who already has a deeply fulfilling love life? This book is made up of these role models. Just like the Ultimate Success Formula, there is a strategy for modeling. In the very next chapter you will learn how to duplicate other people's success in a fraction of the time they accomplished it originally.

Is Arthur Ashe the only one who has followed the Ultimate Success Formula? Of course not. Everyone who has ever created outstanding results has followed it to a tee. Consider a more recent example, Robert Townsend. Here's a man who has become one of the world's most successful Black filmmakers and TV personalities by the age of thirty-five. Today he stars in HBO specials and TV series, all the while writing, directing, and starring in his own films. He helped blaze the trail that has made it possible for others to make their dreams a reality in the film industry.

Townsend was one of the first of only a handful of Black filmmakers to compete successfully in a White-dominated film industry. And by the way, did he do this during a time when Black filmmakers were the rage in Hollywood? Not hardly. As a matter of fact, it was quite the opposite. But, again, what did he do? He followed the Ultimate Success Formula. Instead of focusing on the obstacles he focused on his outcomes. A brief conversation with him or anyone who knows him would probably prove that Townsend was obsessed with his outcome. He defined it clearly: He wanted to produce a film that would move people. A film that would crack the thick protective shell of a White-dominated industry. A film that would break the stereotyping of Blacks in films as shuffling, lazy, jiving clowns, servants, or criminals, by parodying them in the very medium which supported them earlier in the century. A film that would utilize the wealth of talent in the Black acting community and create a place for others in the future. And most important, a film that would show a Black filmmaker could produce an economically profitable product, which ultimately is Hollywood's (or for that matter any business's) way of measuring success. Profitability—money—talks.

How did he do it? How did he reach that point at such a young age? Was he lucky? Was he blessed with lots of capital? Were his friends and family connected to the inside world of show business? Did the movie industry welcome him with open arms? Absolutely not. As a matter of fact, they told him his product wasn't bankable and would never sell. Did someone come to him with excess capital and offer to finance his venture? No way. He started at the very bottom and made his own way to the top.

It's a remarkable story. Townsend set out to raise capital for his dream. First he tried to get the money from traditional sources. Everywhere he turned his faith was tested as doors were slammed in his face. When that didn't work, he tried businesspeople and friends in the community. That didn't work, either. He was hit with countless nos and reasons why what he wanted to do couldn't be done. "You have no money, no background, no resources, all the things necessary to pull it off. It just can't be done." Armed with a burning desire to succeed and a passion for his craft, Robert treated every no as a challenge to keep putting one foot in front of the other. Every rejection galvanized his commitment to his outcome. He lived the opposite pattern of those who fail.

You see, most people don't achieve what they want in life because they are so focused on what they *don't* want. They spend 10 percent of their time thinking about their goal, and 90 percent of the time thinking about how they don't want to be rejected, how they don't want to have to work too hard, how much effort their goal will require. But Townsend wasn't like most people. He poured his guts into his dream. Did he say, "It's because I'm Black that it's so hard to get financing"? Perhaps. But truthfully, it's hard for anyone to make a film. It's a business that millions want to be part of, yet only dozens succeed at the ultimate level. Regardless of the source of the challenge, Townsend knew what he wanted and just kept changing his approach until he finally came up with an alternative.

He knew his outcome, he took massive action, and when he realized his actions weren't working, he moved to the fourth step: He got amazingly flexible. Having tried "everything," after being turned down by virtually everyone in town and nearing the end of his rope, young Townsend did what most sane humans would never have considered. He put his faith on the line and challenged himself to come up with a solution. By consistent focus and demand from himself, he came up with a brainstorm that only one in a million people would even consider, let alone have the guts to do: He funded his film with credit cards. In a day when not everybody would send you four or five credit applications in the mail, Townsend got as many cards as he could and maxed them to the limit. He used the money to finance his first film. Everyone told him this was the worst thing he could possibly do, but in his gut he knew he had to. And from that small initial sum of money, against all odds, Townsend directed, produced, and starred in his first film. Through his focused determination and drive, his efforts yielded one of the first successful modern Black comedies. Over the years his creation, *Hollywood Shuffle,* has become a cult classic, and it launched a brilliant career in the entertainment business for Robert Townsend. He used the same grit and faith to produce his second film, *The Five Heartbeats,* after being turned down by almost everybody in the business. It, too, is one of the great Black films of our time. The Ultimate Success Formula is what put Townsend on the map as a filmmaker and catapulted several Black actors into the limelight in the bargain. His legacy paved the way for many Black filmmakers today.

Those who understand these four simple steps can transform the quality of their lives. And the beauty of the Ultimate Success Formula is that it's not a White thing, it's not a Black thing, it's purely a human thing. Spike Lee, John Singleton, Mario Van Peebles, and virtually all the greats have all knowingly or unknowingly done the same thing to produce the outstanding results they have given us. And they all might very well owe a debt of gratitude to a brave young man with a fistful of credit cards. What he did took guts, what he did took faith—but he followed a tried-and-true formula. And it's the same formula you can use right now to begin to make your dreams a reality. Perhaps one of the greatest gifts those who have succeeded have left us is that they've created role models to help us achieve what we truly desire quicker and more effectively. That's why we have a greater opportunity than ever before.

THE SEVEN CHARACTER TRAITS OF ULTIMATE SUCCESS

In one way or another, everything in this book is directed toward providing you with the most effective tools for empowering you to take successful action. People can do virtually anything—as long as they muster the resources to believe they can, and as long as they take effective action.

All this leads to a simple, inescapable fact: **Success is not an accident.** The difference between people who produce positive results and those who do not is not some random roll of the dice. There are consistent, logical patterns of action, specific pathways to excellence, that are within the reach of us all. We can all unleash the power within us. We simply must learn how to use our minds and bodies in the most effective and advantageous ways.

Have you ever stopped to think, *What do Michael Jordan and Michael Jackson have in common that makes them so successful? What do Tina Turner and Ted Turner share that sets them apart from the masses? What did Sammy Davis, Jr., and Martin Luther King, Jr., or B.B. King and Freddie King share?* The one thing they've *all* shared is consistently taking effective action toward the accomplishment of their dreams. But what is it that makes people like this continue day after day to put everything they've got into everything they do? There are, of course, many factors. However, there are seven fundamental character traits that the most successful people of our time have all cultivated within themselves. *Seven characteristics that give them the fire to do whatever it takes to succeed. Seven basic triggering mechanisms that can ensure your success as well.*

TRAIT ONE: PASSION!

People who consistently produce results have discovered a reason, an all-consuming, energizing, almost obsessive purpose that drives them to do, grow, and be more. It gives them the fuel that powers their "success train" and causes them to tap their true potential. It was passion that caused Arthur Ashe to drive to the net continually and force his opponents to make mistakes that cost them games and titles. It was passion that caused Alex Haley to devote his life to write *Roots,* which is perhaps one of the greatest pieces of African American literature of our time. It's passion that sets the career of Tina Turner apart from so many others, and that enabled her to pick up and keep going despite abuse and insurmountable odds. It's passion that makes a Shaquille O'Neal or Hakeem Olajuwon play every game as if their very lives hinged upon the outcome. It's passion that drives computer scientists through years of dedicated effort to create the kinds of breakthroughs that have put men and women into outer space and brought them back. It was passion that led George Washington Carver to work relentlessly to discover hundreds of uses for the peanut, and to develop countless other innovations in a time when most Blacks were struggling to learn to read. It's passion that causes people to stay up late and get up early. It's passion that people want in their relationships. Passion gives life power, and juice, and meaning. There is no greatness without a passion to be great, whether it's the aspiration of an athlete, an artist, a scientist, a parent, or an entrepreneur. You'll discover how to unleash this inner force through the power of goals in Chapter 13.

Trait Two: Belief!

Every religious book on the planet talks about the power and effect of faith and belief on humankind. People who succeed on a major scale differ greatly in their beliefs from those who fail. Our beliefs about what we are and what we can be precisely determine *who* we will be. If we believe in magic, we'll live a magical life. If we believe our life is defined by narrow limits, we've suddenly made those limits real. What we believe to be true, what we believe is possible, becomes what's true, becomes what's possible. This book will provide you with a specific, scientific way to quickly change your beliefs so that they support you in the attainment of your most desired goals. Many people are passionate, but because of their limiting beliefs about who they are and what they can do, they never take the actions that could make their dreams a reality. People who succeed know what they want and believe they can get it. We'll learn about what beliefs are and how to use them in Chapters 6 and 7.

Passion and belief help to provide the fuel, the propulsion toward excellence. But propulsion is not enough, for all it can do is send a rocket flying blindly toward the heavens. Besides that power, we need a path, an intelligent sense of logical progression. To succeed in hitting our target, we need . . .

TRAIT THREE: STRATEGY!

A strategy is a way of organizing resources. Think about Muhammad Ali, the greatest boxer of all time. He had certain strategies he used consistently—his boldness, his humor, his style of fighting were all part of his strategy for success. He even told us what one of those strategies was in advance: "Float like a butterfly, sting like a bee." This truly was a precise description of one of the many strategies he used to dominate the sport in his day. He figured out what he wanted to learn, whom he needed to know, and what he needed to do. He had passion and belief, but he also had the strategy that made those things work to their greatest potential.

Every great entertainer, politician, parent, or employer knows it's not enough to have the resources to succeed. One must *use* those resources in the most effective way. A strategy is a specific type of plan, a way of organizing your resources in such a way as to produce a predetermined outcome. You can open a door by breaking it down, or you can find the key that opens it intact. You'll learn about the strategies that produce excellence in Chapters 9 and 10.

TRAIT FOUR: CLARITY OF VALUES!

When we think of the things that made America great, we think of things like patriotism and pride, a sense of tolerance, and a love of freedom. These things are values, the fundamental ethical, moral, and practical judgments we make about what's important, what really matters. Values are specific belief systems we have about what is right and wrong for our lives. They're the judgments we make about what makes life worth living. Many people do not have a clear idea of what is important to them. Often individuals do things that afterward they regret simply because they were not clear about what they believed was right for them and others. When we look at great successes, they are almost always people with a clear fundamental sense about what really matters. Think of Martin Luther King, Jr., John F. Kennedy, Oprah Winfrey, Michael Jordan, Whitney Houston, Michael Johnson. They're all known for having different visions, but the common link is a fundamental moral grounding. People like these have a clear sense of who they are and why they do what they do. An understanding of values is one of the most rewarding and challenging keys to achieving excellence.

As you've probably already noticed, all of these traits feed on and interact with one another. Is passion affected by belief? Of course it is. The more we believe we can accomplish something, the more we're usually willing to invest in its achievement. Is belief by itself enough to achieve excellence? It's a good start, but if you believe you're going to see a sunrise and your strategy for achieving that goal is to face west, you may have some difficulty. Are our strategies for success affected by our values? You bet. If your strategy for success requires you to do things that do not fit your beliefs about what is right or wrong for your life, then even the best strategy will not work. This is often seen in individuals who begin to succeed only to end up sabotaging their own success. The problem is that there's an internal conflict between the individual's values and his or her strategy for achievement. In the same way, all four of the things we've already considered are inseparable from . . .

Trait Five: Energy!

Energy can be the thundering, joyous commitment of Tina Turner or the artist formerly known as Prince. It can be the entrepreneurial dynamism of Wally Amos or Bill Gates. It can be the unstoppable vitality of Bill Cosby or Aretha Franklin. It is almost impossible to amble languidly toward excellence. People of excellence take opportunities and shape them. They live as if obsessed with the wondrous opportunities of each day and the recognition that the one thing no one has enough of is time. There are many people in this world who have a passion they believe in. They know the strategy that would ensure it, and their values are aligned, but they just don't have the physical vitality to take action on what they know. Great success is inseparable from the physical, intellectual, and spiritual energy that allows us to make the most of what we have. In Chapters 11 and 12, you'll learn and apply the tools that can immediately increase physical vibrancy.

TRAIT SIX: BONDING POWER!

Nearly all successful people have in common an extraordinary ability to bond with others, the ability to develop rapport with people from a variety of backgrounds and beliefs. Sure, there's the occasional mad genius who invents something that changes the world. But if the genius spends all his time in a lonely warren, he will succeed on one level but fail on many others. The great successes—the Kennedys, the Kings, the Gandhis—all had the ability to form bonds that united them to millions of others. Yet the greatest success of this kind is experienced not on the stage of the world; it is felt in the deepest recesses of your own heart. Deep down, everyone needs to form lasting, loving bonds with others. Without that, any success, any excellence, is hollow indeed. You'll learn more about those bonds in Chapter 15.

The final key trait is something we talked about earlier in the first chapter . . .

TRAIT SEVEN: MASTERY OF COMMUNICATION!

This is the essence of what this book is about. The way we communicate with others and the way we communicate with ourselves ultimately determine the quality of our lives. People who succeed in life are those who have learned how to take any challenge life gives them and communicate that experience to themselves in a way that causes them to successfully change things. People who fail take the adversities of life and accept them as limitations. The people who shape our lives and our cultures are also masters of communication to others. What they have in common is an ability to communicate a vision or a quest or a joy or a mission. Mastery of communication is what makes a great parent, a great artist, a great politician, a great teacher. Almost every chapter in this book, in one way or another, has to do with communication, bridging gaps, building new paths, and sharing new visions.

Here's the Deal

In the first portion of this book you will see how to become the captain of your own destiny. You will learn how to take charge and run your own brain and body more effectively than ever before. You will be working with factors that affect the way you communicate with yourself. In the second portion, we'll study how to discover what you really want out of life and how you can communicate more effectively with others as well as how to anticipate the kinds of behaviors that different kinds of people will consistently create. The third portion takes on a larger, more global perspective of how we behave, what motivates us, and what we can contribute on a broader, extrapersonal level. It's about taking the skills you've learned and becoming a leader.

When this book was written, the original goal was to re-create and provide a textbook for human development—a book that would be packed with the best and the latest in human change technology. It's designed to arm you with the skills and strategies that will enable you to change anything you want to change, and to do it faster than you've ever dreamed of before. This should create an opportunity for you in a very concrete way to immediately increase the quality of your life experience. We're hoping this is a work you will come back to again and again, always finding something useful for your life. However, we became concerned that many people would not even get to the parts of the book we think are most important, simply because *several studies have shown that fewer than 10 percent of the people who buy a book read past the first chapter.* As hard as that is for me to believe, I also learned that less than 3 percent of the nation is financially independent, less than 10 percent have written goals, only 35 percent of American women—and even fewer men—feel they are in good physical shape, and in many states one out of every two marriages ends up in divorce. The frightening thing for me to find out is that most of these statistics are far worse for the Black community. Only a small percentage of people really live the life of their dreams. Why? It takes effort. It takes consistent action. To most of us, effort equals pain, and of course we all move away from pain.

> ***I've always believed that if you put in the work, the results will come. I don't do things half-heartedly. Because if I do, then I can expect half-hearted results.***
>
> —MICHAEL JORDAN

Bunker Hunt, the Texas oil billionaire, was asked if he had any one piece of advice he could give people on how to succeed. He said that success is simple. First, you decide what you want specifically, and second, you decide you're willing to pay the price to make it happen—and then pay that price. If you don't take that second step, you'll never have what you want in the long term. I like to call the people who know what they want and are willing to pay the price to get it "the few who do" versus "the many who talk." I challenge you to play with this material, read it all, put it into immediate practice, share what you learn, and enjoy it.

If there's one thing that Black history teaches us it's the indisputable fact that the progress of our ancestors was created by those individuals who consistently demonstrated an almost relentless air of perseverance. The struggles and sacrifices that have been made along the way stand not only as inspiring testaments but a shining reminder of the strength and tenacity that is inside all of us. The number of people who fail is directly proportionate to the number of people who give up. In this chapter, we've stressed the importance of taking effective action. But there are many ways to take action. Most of them depend on a large degree of trial and error. Most people who have been great successes have adjusted and readjusted countless times before they got where they wanted to go. Trial and error is fine, except for one thing: It uses a vast quantity of the one resource none of us will ever have enough of—time.

Here's a question for you: What if there were a way to take action that accelerated the learning process? What if I could show you how to benefit from the same lessons that people of excellence have already learned? What if you could learn in minutes what someone else took years to perfect? Would that be of great value to you? The way to do this is through modeling, a way to reproduce precisely the excellence of others. To find out what they do that sets them apart from those who only dream of success, you must discover . . .

CHAPTER FOUR

The Difference That Makes the Difference

God makes three requests of his children: Do the best you can, where you are, with what you have, now.

—African American folklore

He was only twelve years old when it happened. He and his mom were cleaning the excess paint off the floor with solvent after painting the bathroom in the small, three-bedroom house where he and his brothers and sisters lived nineteen years ago. The deadly combination of the fumes from the solvent, the oil-based paint, and the lack of circulation in the room would change this young Black man's life forever. As he entered the room to resume cleaning, the old electric heater clicked on and ignited the volatile mixture, creating an explosive ball of fire that ripped through the whole house. "I thought I was in hell," he recalls. "All I remember was running the wrong way toward the mirror. All I could see was my horrified eyes as I was trapped inside the swarm of fire that filled the room." The next thing he knew, he was running out of the house and into the street, engulfed in flames. Down the street, a neighbor caught him and put out the fire that now covered his body.

Upon realizing what had happened, the young man got up and ran back into the house to save his mother and siblings. Fortunately, they had left the house, but not without his mother suffering burns over a great deal of her body as well. They were both taken to the hospital and in the days that followed underwent the horrific process of having the skin scrubbed off their bodies. The young man sustained third-degree burns over 85 percent of his body. He begged the doctors not to tell his mother how badly he had been burned, but somehow the grim news got to her and she demanded to see her son. She pulled the tubes and bandages from her body and ran down to see him. The sight of her young son so badly burned and in so much pain was too much for the young mother. Her body went into shock, and she died soon after. The young man was left to deal with his severe injuries and to take care of his young sisters and brothers alone.

At some point in every man's and woman's life there comes a time of supreme challenge—a time when every resource that we have is tested to its fullest. A time when life is inexplicably unfair. A time when our faith, our values, our patience, our compassion, our ability to persist, are all pushed to our limits and beyond. For some people, those times are used as opportunities to become better people, while others allow these experiences of life to destroy them.

For more than a decade now, I have been fascinated by what makes human beings behave the way they do. This is one of the most profound similarities Tony and I share. We wonder, What sets certain men and women apart from each other? What creates a leader, a role model? How is it that there are so many people in this world who live such joyous lives in spite of almost every adversity, while others who would seem to have it all live lives of despair, anger, depression, and hopelessness?

Let me tell you another man's story. Look at the differences between the two men's lives. This second man's life would appear to be much brighter. As one of the world's most famous entertainers, his popularity earned him a huge fortune and endeared him to millions. Over the years he has been called one of the greatest musicians of all time. His innovative style was way ahead of its time, and, to this day, musicians still imitate his sound and his techniques. It seemed that from out of nowhere, this man came onto the scene and forever changed the face of a style of music that only a handful of Blacks dared or even cared to venture into. His passion for playing the guitar became his calling card around the world. He had dozens of admiring friends, a beautiful wife, wonderful homes and recording studios. He seemed to have everything a person could ask for.

Here's the question: Which one of these two men would you rather be? The most obvious answer is the second one. As a matter of fact, I can't imagine anyone choosing the first over the second.

Well, let me tell you a little bit more about each of the two men. The first man is strong, healthy, motivated, and one of the most inspirational souls I know. His name is Herdale Johnson. He is the father of four healthy, happy children and enjoys inspiring others to get the best out of themselves. As an entrepreneur, he has started three businesses and is constantly striving to improve the quality of his life. He donates some of his time to foster homes, entertaining and motivating children. He recently started taking flying lessons and soon hopes to be soaring on his own, which has been one of his dreams for several years. When he learned of his mother's death those many years ago, he vowed to God that if he lived he would make sure his sisters and brothers were taken care of. He kept the promise that he made. All of his sisters and brothers now have lives and careers of their own and were never separated during their childhood.

Herdale is a living example of human spirit and strength. Through all of his challenges, past and present, he always rises to the occasion and deals with whatever life hands him: "If I got through the 'house of terror,' then God will get me through anything that comes at me in this life."

On the other hand, the second man is someone the world knew well. His name is Jimi Hendrix. He was and still is one of the most celebrated guitarist-singer-songwriters of all time. To this day his music is played around the world and his style continues to show up in modern music. It has been said that to have watched him play live was like watching a man possessed with the holy spirit. Hendrix was able to enrich countless lives, over and over again, but he failed to fully enrich the one that should have mattered the most—his own. When he died at the age of twenty-seven of what the coroner ruled "acute toxicity from cocaine and heroin," few who knew him were surprised. In the 1960s, he made it public that he frequently used drugs. This man who seemed to have everything couldn't keep the drugs out of his body long enough to realize what he really had. It has been said that his last days of life were spent depressed, confused, and out of control. Outwardly it would seem that he had everything—talent, fame, riches—but on the inside, he was defeated, empty, and played out.

History is full of examples of people who have taken what most of us would consider handicaps and overcome them to produce major results. What about the guy who developed a severe stuttering problem as a teenager and went on to become one of the world's most recognizable voices? Often referred to as "the voice of God," and most famous for being the voice of Darth Vader in the *Star Wars* trilogy, James Earl Jones didn't let his challenge keep him from his dreams. Did you know that the actor Danny Glover was dyslexic? Or that Michael Jordan couldn't even make his high school junior varsity team? Or that Les Brown, one of the nation's foremost Black motivational speakers, was told at the age of twelve that he was mentally retarded and would never be able to learn like the other kids?

On the other end of the spectrum, think about people like Billie Holiday or Miles Davis, people who seemed to hold the brass ring and ended up losing it all, ruining their precious lives in the end. One might think, *Well, these people were successful.* But here's the catch: *They're dead!* Dead before their time. Death equals failure. And perhaps the worst part about it is that they set examples for others by their actions.

So what is it really that makes the difference between the haves and the have-nots? What's the difference between the cans and the cannots? What's the difference between the do's and the do nots? Why is it that some people overcome horrible, unimaginable adversity and make their lives a triumph, while others, in spite of every advantage, turn their lives into a disaster? Why do some people take any experience and make it work for them, while others take any experience and make it work against them? What's the difference between a Herdale Johnson and a Jimi Hendrix? What really is the difference that makes the difference between success and failure?

> ***There is a way to provide against the onslaught of poverty. It is the recognition of the power of the mind.***
>
> —**A.G. Gaston**

By far, the biggest difference between success and failure is in the way that we communicate to ourselves and the actions that we take. What we do when it seems that we've tried everything and things still keep turning out wrong is all a result of how we communicate to ourselves about what it all means and what we should do with it. People who succeed do not have fewer problems than people who fail. (As a matter of fact, the only people without problems are those in cemeteries.) **It is not what *happens* to us that separates failures from successes. It is how we *perceive* it and what we *do* about what happens that makes the difference.** Rarely do people succeed the first time out. It's only after repeated tries and learning from their mistakes that they finally reach the top. Virtually every success story comes with a history of trying and trying again until success was achieved.

When Herdale received the information from the doctor that four-fifths of his body was covered with third-degree burns, he had a choice about how to interpret that information. The meaning of this event could have been a reason to die, to grieve, or anything else he wanted to communicate. He chose to consistently communicate to himself that this experience had occurred for a purpose and that this would someday provide him with even greater advantages in his goal to make a difference in the world. As a result of this communication with himself, he formed beliefs and values that continued to direct his life from a sense of advantage rather than tragedy.

Or what about Bonnie St. John Dean, who at the age of five had to have her right leg amputated above the knee? Rather than letting it stop her, she went on to become an Olympic medalist in skiing. And it didn't stop there. She also became a White House official, Harvard and Oxford graduate, Rhodes scholar, author, and the vice president of the national Amputee Fund. How did she get herself to do all of that? Simple. She mastered her communication with herself. When her body sent her signals that in the past she had interpreted as pain, as limitation, as exhaustion, she simply relabeled their meaning and continued to communicate to her nervous system in a way that kept her moving forward.

How do people produce outstanding results? I've been curious about that answer for as far back as I can remember. **Fortunately, success leaves clues.** People who produce outstanding results do specific things to create those results. It's not enough just to know that successful people communicate differently to themselves. It's been important to me to know specifically how they did it. What I've learned is that *if we precisely duplicate the actions of others, we can reproduce the same quality of result.* In short, if there were someone who demonstrated great courage and strength even in the most dire of circumstances, I could find out his strategy—how he looked at things, how he used his body in those situations—and I could become more courageous, too. In my life, I had produced the result of being extremely angry, broke, and in debt. It wasn't until I finally realized that all I needed to do was model people who were healthy, happy, and financially secure—find out what they did, how they did it, what they thought, what their beliefs were—and that I could produce the same results they did. This is how I was able to go from a life of despair to a life I love.

In my search for excellence, I studied every avenue of human potential and human behavior I could find. Tony introduced me to a science known as Neuro-Linguistic Programming, or NLP for short. If you analyze it, the name comes from *neuro* for "brain" and *linguistic* for "language." *Programming* is the installation of a plan or procedure. NLP is the study of how language, both verbal and nonverbal, affects our nervous system. According to NLP, our ability to do anything is based upon our ability to direct our own nervous system, specifically our five senses.

In the past, NLP has primarily been taught to therapists and a small number of fortunate business executives. When Tony first exposed me to it, I immediately realized it was something quite different from anything I had ever experienced before. For example, I watched him help a woman who had been in therapy for over three years for phobic responses, and in less than forty-five minutes, no more phobia! (Cases like these directly contradicted my college psychology classes in which it was said phobia "cures" would take several years and patients never really lose the fear; they just learn to live with it better.) NLP provides a systematic framework that teaches us how to direct not only our own states and behaviors, but also the states and behaviors of others. In short, it is the science of how to run your brain in an optimal way to produce the results you desire. I was hooked. I had to know it all!

In the months that followed, I gobbled up the fundamentals of NLP, hungry to learn and to put this knowledge into action. I took classes and attended seminars and soon became certified in the science. Using Tony as a model, I became proficient in helping people overcome fears and phobias and other emotional challenges in a remarkably short amount of time, sometimes working with as many as five and six people with different challenges a day. Best of all, I learned how we function as human beings. If someone else is able to wake up in the morning, quickly and easily and full of energy, that is a result they produced. I now could duplicate that behavior, and, what's more, I could show others how to do the same for their lives.

You see, results spring from *actions*—specific mental or physical actions that trigger certain neurophysiological processes, such as waking up from sleep quickly and easily or getting oneself to immediately take action on the things that matter the most. One of the fundamental understandings of NLP is that we all share the same type of nervous system. Remember: *It makes no difference what the color of our skin is, how tall we are, or where we are from—we're all made the exact same way.* So if anyone in the world can do anything, you can, too, if you run your nervous system in exactly the same way. The process of discovering exactly and specifically what people do to produce a certain result is called *modeling*. The key word is *specifically.* The closer we get to doing everything down to the last detail the same way, the closer we get to producing the same result.

Obviously, some tasks are more complex than others and may take more time to model. But virtually anything any human being does can be modeled, as long as you have the desire and commitment to stick through the changes. And in most cases, you don't have to go through the same hardships as the person you are modeling. You can step in, model the actions that took years to perfect, and produce similar results in a matter of moments, months—or at least in a lot less time.

Most of the credit for bringing NLP to the forefront must be given to two men, John Grinder and Richard Bandler. They looked for people who were most effective at creating the one thing they felt most human beings wanted—change—and studied successful businesspeople, therapists, and others in order to distill the lessons and patterns those people had discovered through years of trial and error. For example, they studied Milton Erickson, perhaps the world's greatest hypnotherapist, and Virginia Satir, one of the best relationship therapists. Grinder and Bandler discovered certain universal patterns that enabled these people to get extraordinary results in short periods of time. Then they taught these patterns to their students, who were able to apply them to produce the same quality of results, even though they did not have the noted therapists' years of experience.

What these men did for human development is legendary. But even with these powerful tools at hand, many people just learned them and didn't use them. They didn't have the personal power to turn them into action, evidence of the fact that *knowledge is not enough.* Action is what produces results. **Action is power.** Most of us know what to do, but we don't do what we know. The more I learned about the modeling process, the more I started to realize this was the key to human change and excellence.

Words are nothing but words; power lies in deeds. Be a man of action.

—Mamado Kouyate

It can be argued that the modeling process is much more difficult for Blacks in this world, because the system was set up without our best interest in mind. But the fact of the matter is that our history is full of role models of success, and everyday changes are being made to improve the quality of our lives. Injustice and prejudice are the cancers of our society, and we must fight them tooth and nail every step of the way. But we must never, never stop looking at the progress we have made and the many role models we have. The strength of so many of these individuals to persevere is a character trait to model in itself. Think of all the abolitionists a century ago who manned the Underground Railroad. They risked their lives every night and day to bring thousands to freedom. They knew slavery wasn't fair, so they kept on, modeling their mentors in turn—people like Harriet Tubman, who showed them how to persevere.

Blacks who have made the biggest differences in this world have all been expert modelers. Since the early days, Blacks were not allowed to read or write; the only way they had to produce results was to watch what they saw others do and secretly do them on their own. They may not have known it, but the procedures they used to get quick, effective results were modeling procedures. They mastered the art of learning everything they could by following other people's experience rather than their own. They learned how to save the one thing that most of us simply don't have enough of: time.

> *I don't think there's anything in the world I can't do. In my creative source, whatever that is, I don't see why I can't sculpt. Why shouldn't I? Human beings sculpt. I'm a human being.*
>
> —MAYA ANGELOU

When asked about achieving their goals, most successful people will say there's nothing mysterious or magical about it. It's not in the genetic makeup. It's a discipline that can be learned. Dennis Kimbro, Les Brown, Maya Angelou, Colin Powell . . . the list goes on and on. They all believe each of us has what it takes and we can access it by adopting role models and modeling their behaviors. Dr. Martin Luther King, perhaps the greatest voice for Black Americans, learned his skills by modeling others who had the ability to move people with their words and voices.

This book, too, is filled with a whole series of models for directing your mind, your body, and your communication with others in a way that will produce outstanding results for everyone involved. However, my goal for you is not only that you learn these patterns of success, but that you also go beyond them by creating your own models.

What I want you to learn is a process, a framework, a discipline that will allow you to duplicate excellence wherever you find it. I want to teach you some of the most effective patterns of NLP and other strategies for tapping into the human potential. However, I want you to become more than just an

"NLPer." I want you to become a person who sees, feels, and knows what you want, models the best, and takes action to make it yours. NLP is not the end-all and be-all of success. Things are always changing and getting better, so I want you to become someone in constant pursuit of outstanding performance technologies—someone who's not stuck, not confined to any one series of systems or patterns, but who instead relentlessly seeks out new and effective ways to produce the results you desire. To model excellence, you should become a detective, an investigator, someone who asks lots of questions and tracks down all the clues to what produces excellence.

Tony and I have taught thousands of entrepreneurs, engineers, athletes, stockbrokers, entertainers—you name it—to excel in their chosen professions, not because we know everything about what they do, but rather because we understand the value of modeling. We found out what the masters in those professions did when they produced their greatest results and showed how they could trigger those performances in themselves on cue.

Modeling has made a tremendous difference in my own life, as well. I've learned the skills of turning people's lives around through NLP and other therapeutic interventions by observing Tony and modeling what he thinks and does. I learned snow boarding, scuba diving, negotiating, guitar playing, meditation, business, skydiving, all in very short amounts of time, by finding a way to precisely model what the masters do.

Building from the successes of others is one of the fundamental principles of accelerated learning. In the world of technology, every advance in engineering or computer design follows naturally from earlier discoveries and breakthroughs. In the business world, if you don't learn from the successes and failures of others, you are doomed to fail or, at the very least, progress slowly. But the world of human behavior is one of the few areas that continue to operate from outdated theories and information. Many of us are still using a nineteenth-century model of how the brain works and how we behave. We put a label called "depression" on something, and guess what? We're depressed and we tend to stay that way.

The truth is that those terms can be self-fulfilling prophecies. Think about it. What misleading labels have been put on the

Black race by others? And even worse yet, *what destructive labels have we put on ourselves that tend to keep us feeling somehow less worthy of success and happiness?* This book teaches a technology that's readily available, a technology that can be used to create the quality of life you desire.

The modeling process is so simple it will seem too good to be true. But the fact of the matter is that you already do it and have been doing it unconsciously all your life. You learned how to ride a bike or tie your shoes by modeling whoever showed you how. The process you are about to learn will go right to the core of the matter and show you how to do it quicker, with precision and more efficiency.

In the modeling process, there are three basic steps that must be followed to reproduce any human outcome. These are the three forms of mental and physical actions that correspond most directly to the quality of results we produce. Imagine them as three numbers to a combination lock on the gates to prosperity and fulfillment. You will learn how to effectively employ these elements in your life in the following chapters, but for now, here are the steps to modeling.

1. Beliefs

How many times have you heard this saying? "Whether you believe you can do something or you believe you can't, you're right." This goes far deeper than you might at first imagine. The beliefs we hold about ourselves and the world in which we live can and do literally change the biochemical makeup of the blood that courses through our veins. For example, when people believe they can do something, they may get excited about the possibility, and the brain sends a message to the adrenal glands, releasing a chemical that causes us to be more alert and to move faster and more deliberately. What people believe, what they think is possible or impossible, to a great extent determines what they can or cannot do. If you're constantly sending your nervous system signals that limit your abilities, you're stopped before you get started. But if you're constantly telling yourself you can accomplish something, then you certainly increase your chances of accessing whatever it takes from yourself to get the desired result. This powerful tool cannot be underestimated. Every religion, every philosophy, every form of human-development teaching has its roots in the importance of a person's belief. So if you can model someone's belief system, you've taken the first step toward acting as that person does, thus producing a similar type of result. We'll look at belief systems further in Chapter 6.

2. Mental Syntax

Syntax is just another word for the order in which things are done. In this case, it means the order in which a person organizes thoughts. We all tend to think in a certain pattern when we do things we are familiar with. Syntax is like a code. There are seven digits in a phone number, but you have to dial them in the right order to reach the person you want. The same is true in reaching the part of your brain and nervous system that could most effectively help you get the outcome you desire. The same is true in communication. Many times people don't communicate well to each other because different people use different codes, different mental syntaxes. Unlock the codes, and you've gone through the second door toward modeling people's best qualities. We'll look at syntax in Chapter 9.

3. Physiology

Throughout the rest of this book, the word *physiology* refers to the way we move our bodies. The way you use your physiology—the way you breathe and hold your body, your posture, your facial expressions, the nature and quality of your movements—actually determines what state of mind you are in. The state you're in will then determine the range and quality of the behaviors you're able to produce. We'll look further at physiology in Chapter 11.

Remember, we're modeling all the time. Here's a simple modeling example from the business world. We live in a culture that's consistent enough so that what works in one place will very often work in another. If someone has set up a successful business selling chocolate chip cookies at a mall in Detroit, chances are the same thing will work at a mall in Dallas. If someone in Los Angeles sets up a successful business delivering pizza in under a half hour, chances are the same thing will work in Florida or New York. All many people do to succeed in business is find something that works in one city and do the same thing somewhere else before the lag time is up. All you have to do is take a proven system and duplicate it—and maybe even better, improve upon it. People who do this are virtually guaranteed success, as long as they follow the modeling process accurately.

Eddie Murphy once said that the way he got so good is that he would sit in front of the TV for hours and imitate all his favorite actors and characters. He would study their movements, speech patterns, and ideas until he could duplicate what they did.

Through this same modeling process, I began to get immediate results both for myself and for others. I continued to seek out other patterns of thought and action that produced outstanding results in short periods of time. Even though we all model to learn, the trouble is that most of us model on a completely unconscious, unfocused level. We assume that the thing we notice the most in one person is the thing to copy. We pick up random bits and pieces from this person or that and then totally miss something much more important from someone else. We model something good here and something bad there. We attempt to model someone we respect but find we don't really know how to do what he or she does.

Listen and learn from people who have already been where you want to go. Benefit from their mistakes instead of repeating them.

—BENJAMIN CARSON

Think of this as a guidebook for conscious modeling with greater precision, a chance for you to become aware of something you've always been doing. But I want to make something clear. Our goal, our outcome for you, is not just that you master the patterns we're describing here. What you need to do is develop your own patterns, your own strategies.

There are phenomenal resources and strategies all around you.

My challenge to you is to start thinking like a modeler, continuously being aware of the patterns and types of actions that produce outstanding results. If someone is able to do something outstanding, the immediate question that should pop into your mind is, *How does that person create that result?* I'd hope you would continue to look for excellence, for the magic in everything you see, and to learn how it's produced—so that you can create the same kinds of results whenever you desire.

Try this. Take a few minutes right now and think about all the things you are good at: driving a car or riding a bicycle, whipping up a tasty dinner, maybe playing a musical instrument. Whatever it is you do well, you'll probably realize that at some point in the development of these talents, you followed the modeling process.

Next we'll explore what determines our responses to the varying circumstances of life. Let us continue by studying . . .

CHAPTER FIVE

The Power of State

To be a champion, you must believe you are the best. If you're not, pretend you are.

—MUHAMMAD ALI

THERE IS A power that can help us overcome the most overwhelming odds. A power that can give us the choice and the freedom in any moment to achieve and be all that we can. It's a power that is at your fingertips at all times. And you are about to learn how to use it NOW . . .

They hated him. He stood in stark contrast to everything they believed to be true about human beings. He stood defiantly between reality and their false sense of superiority. The jeers were deafening as they screamed insults in German. He was surrounded yet completely alone in a merciless, brutal country. In the distance stood Adolf Hitler himself, confidently awaiting the defeat of Jesse Owens by the allegedly superior Aryans. Hitler had declared that Blacks were an inferior race, and Owens' very presence at the Olympics was considered by his "hosts" to be an insult. I'm sure you can imagine how terrified he must have felt, knowing the vast majority of the people there were hoping he would fail miserably. How dare he even attempt to compete against Germany's finest athletes—the super race supposedly destined for world domination! But compete he did, and as we all know, the world was changed by what happened that day.

Somehow in the midst of that seething hate, this brilliant young American centered himself, focused on his goal, and shot down the track and into the pages of history. He had traveled there to represent his country, the United States of America, and the ideals of freedom and individual dignity for which it stood. He must put everything he believed in, everything he had worked for, and everything he *was* on the line. The world was watching.

Single-handedly, Jesse Owens did what no other man had ever done: He shattered the Olympic record and, along with it, Hitler's illusion of racial superiority. How was it that in the face of fear and ridicule this man was able to reach inside and pull out the victor within? In spite of all the negativity surrounding him, he put himself in the "zone"—what Tony and I call the *power of state.*

Let me ask you a question: Have you ever had one of those days when you could do no wrong? You know, one of those days when you had the Midas touch? You knew you were lookin' good, you felt good . . . and you were "all that, and a bag of chips!" Perhaps it was in a sport where you seemed to have all the right moves or maybe in a business meeting where you had all the right answers. You were clever and sharp and witty. Maybe it was a time when you impressed yourself by suddenly doing something you never did before and coming out on top. You can probably also remember days when just the opposite happened, when you just couldn't seem to get it together, nothing went your way, and everything you touched seemed to fall apart.

What's the difference? After all, you're the same person. You have the same personal references and resources available. Why is it that some days you can consistently produce outstanding results and other days you'd swear you were jinxed? Why do even the best athletes have days when they do everything right, only to follow them with days when they can't buy a basket or a base hit?

> *Emotion is what makes me what I am today. It makes me play bigger than I am.*
>
> —CHARLES BARKLEY

The difference in the results you get is the state of mind you are in. There are empowering states of mind that tap into our real power: courage, certainty, joy, ecstasy, pride, and love. And there are disempowering, paralyzing states like fear, doubt, anxiety, sadness, frustration, hatred, and confusion.

Have you ever been in a restaurant and had a waitress snarl,

"Whaddya want?" Do you think she always talks to her customers like that? It's possible she's had such a difficult life that she does. But it's more likely she's had a bad day handling too many tables, maybe even been stiffed by a few customers. She's not a bad person; she's just in an unresourceful state. If you can change her state, you can change her behavior.

The state of mind we are in at any given moment determines the behavior we display. Understanding this simple fact is the key to mastering our potential and achieving excellence. We always do the best we can given the resources available, but sometimes we find ourselves in unresourceful states, like the waitress who's been stiffed one too many times. I know there have been times in my life when I did or said something I regretted later. Perhaps you have, too. It's important to remember these times when someone treats you poorly, so you can feel compassion for the person instead of anger.

Here's what's great about all this: **We can take control of our own states of mind and subsequently alter our behaviors and the results we get.** What if you could snap your fingers and go into a powerful, confident, empowered state of mind anytime you wanted? A state of mind charged with energy and excitement, alive with possibility? Well, you *can.*

By the time you finish this book, you're going to know how to put yourself into your most resourceful, empowering states and get yourself out of your disempowering states whenever you choose. **Remember, the key to power is taking action.** Our goal is to share with you how to use the states that lead to decisive, congruent, committed action. In this chapter we're going to explore what states are and how to make them work for us.

EFFECTIVELY "TRAIN YOUR BRAIN"

For the most part, we all go in and out of different states of mind without consciously being aware of it. Something happens—we see or hear something—and we automatically respond by going into a state. It may be a resourceful and useful state or an unresourceful and limiting state, but there's not much that most of us do to control it. The difference between those who fail to achieve their dreams in life and those who succeed is the difference between those who never consciously choose the states they're in and those who consistently put themselves in a state that supports them in reaching their goals.

Let's try something. Make a list of ten to fifteen things you want in life. Do you want love? Well, love is a state—a feeling or emotion we signal to ourselves and feel within ourselves based on certain stimuli from the environment. Do you want respect? When we feel respected we are in a very specific state of mind. Even the material things you may have written down come with a particular state of mind. If you want a car or a house, for example, you want them because they will make you *feel* a certain way. They will give you access to a specific state of mind. **Almost everything we want comes down to a state of mind—and only *we* produce these states within ourselves.** Maybe you want money. It's not that you crave little pieces of green paper with dead presidents on them. You want what money represents to you: love, confidence, freedom, or whatever states you think it can help provide. So the key to love, the key to joy, the key to the one power that humans have sought for years—the ability to direct their lives—is the ability to know how to direct and manage your states of mind.

The first key to directing your state and producing the results you desire in life is to learn to effectively run your brain. In order to do this, we need to understand a little bit about how it works. We need to know what creates a state in the first place. For centuries, humans have been fascinated by ways to alter their states and thereby their experience of life. They have tried fasting, drugs, rituals, music, sex, food, hypnosis, chanting. These things all have their uses and their limitations. However, you are now going to be opened up to much simpler ways that are equally powerful and in many cases quicker and more precise, without the side effects and consequences.

The world we live in is first and foremost shaped by the mind.

—Charles Johnson

But MOM! How come it seemed like such a smart idea when I did it?

All human behavior is a result of the state of mind we are in. If we produce different communications and behaviors when we're in resourceful states than when we're in unresourceful ones, then the next question is, What creates our states of mind? There are two main components of state. The first is our *internal representations,* and the second is *the condition and use of our bodies.* What and how you picture things, as well as what and how you say things to yourself about the situation at hand, create the state you're in and thus the kinds of behaviors you produce.

For example, how do you treat someone you care about when he or she comes home much later than promised? Your behavior will greatly depend on the state you're in when your loved one returns, and to a large degree this will be determined by what you have been picturing in your mind as the reason for the lateness. If for hours you had been picturing this person in an accident,

How We Create Our States and Behaviors

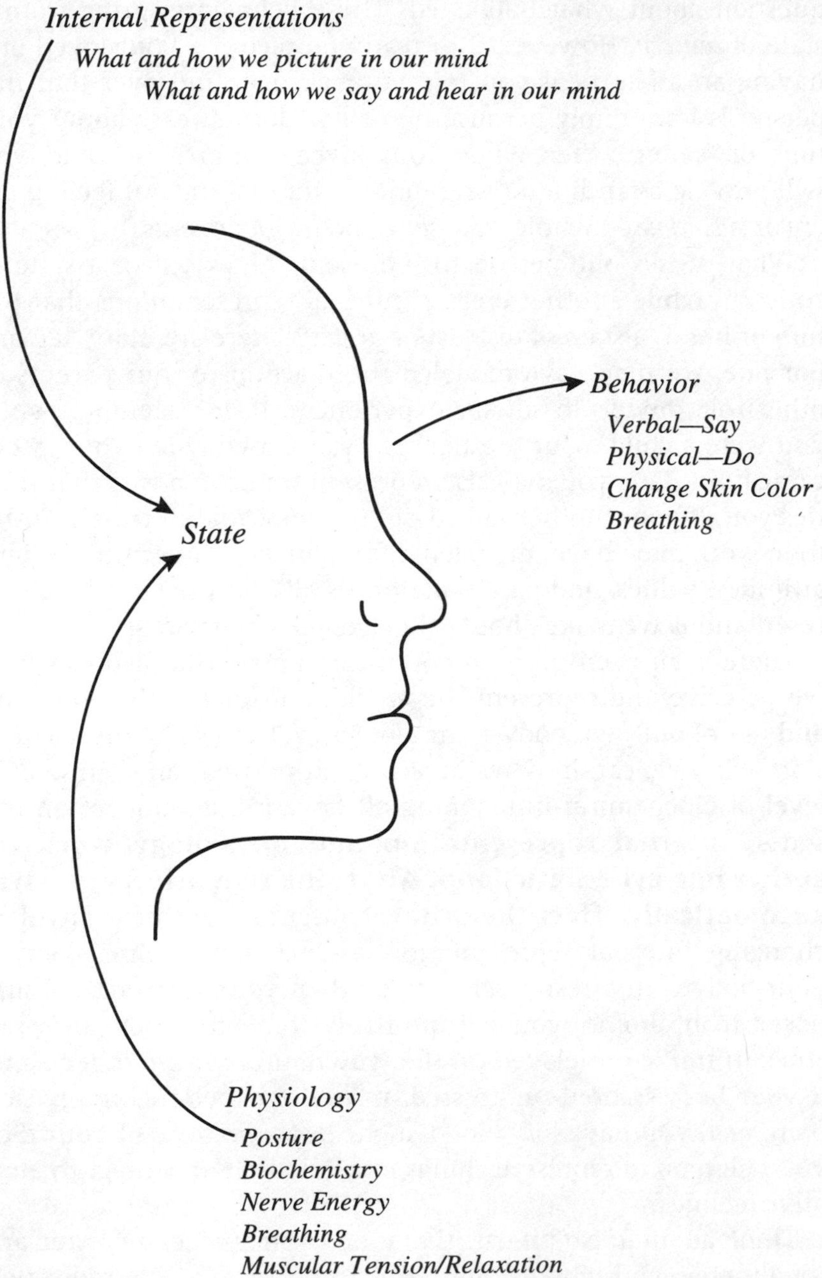

bloody, dead, or hospitalized, as the person walks in the door you may greet him or her with tears, a sigh of relief, a big hug, and a question about what happened. These behaviors spring from a state of *concern*. However, if instead you pictured your loved one having an affair, or if you told yourself over and over that this person is late simply because he or she doesn't care about your time or feelings, then when your loved one arrives home, you will provide a far different reception. Out of a state of feeling *angry* or *suspicious*, a whole new set of behaviors results.

What causes one person to represent things out of a state of concern, while another creates internal representations that put him or her in a state of distrust or anger? There are many factors. For one, we may have modeled the reactions of our parents or other role models in similar experiences. If, for example, when you were a child, your mother always worried when your father came home late, you may also represent things in a way that worries you. If your mother talked of how she couldn't trust your father, you may have modeled that pattern. Thus, our beliefs, attitudes, values, and past experiences all affect the kinds of representations we make about other people's behaviors.

There is an even more important and powerful factor in how we perceive and represent the world, and that is the condition and use of our own body—our *physiology.* Things like muscle tension, what we eat, how we breathe, our posture, and our overall level of biochemical functioning all have a huge impact on our states. **Internal representation and physiology work together in a cybernetic loop. Anything that affects one will automatically affect the other.** Thus, changing states involves changing internal representation and changing physiology. If your body is in a resourceful state when your loved one is supposed to be home, you will probably think that person is just stuck in traffic or delayed on the way home. On the other hand, if your body is tired or stressed, if you're experiencing physical pain, or if you have low blood-sugar levels because of your diet, you will tend to represent things in a way that may magnify negative feelings.

Think about it: Isn't it true that when you are feeling rested and totally alive and vibrant, you tend to perceive the world differently than when you're tired or sick? The condition of your physiology literally changes the way you represent things and thus your experience of the world. These two factors, *internal representations* and *physiology,* are constantly interacting with each other to create the state we are in. And the state we are in determines the type of behaviors we produce. Thus, to control and direct our behaviors, we must control and direct our states, and to control our states, we must control and consciously direct our internal representations and physiology. How would your life be better if you could control your states of mind?

PERCEPTION AND REPRESENTATION: WHAT'S "REAL"?

To direct our experiences in life, we must first understand how we experience. All humans receive and represent information about their environment through five senses: vision or sight, audition or hearing, kinesthesis or touch and feel, gustation or taste, and olfaction or smell.

We make most of the decisions that affect our behavior primarily using only the first three of these senses: the visual, auditory, and kinesthetic systems. The brain takes signals from these senses and filters them into an internal representation. Thus, your experience of the event isn't precisely what happened but rather a personalized internal "re-presentation." The conscious mind of an individual can't use all the signals being sent to it. You would probably go stark raving mad if you consciously had to make sense of thousands of stimuli ranging from the pulse of blood through your left finger to the vibration of your inner ear. **So the brain filters and stores the information it needs, or expects to need later, and allows the conscious mind of the individual to ignore the rest.**

This filtering process explains the huge range in human perception. Two people can see the same traffic accident but give utterly different accounts of it. One may have paid more attention to what was seen, another to what was heard. They saw it from different angles. In the first place, they both have different physiologies they use in the perception process. One may have twenty-twenty vision while another may have poor physical resources in general. Perhaps one had personally been in an accident before and had a vivid representation already stored. Whatever the case, the two will have very different representations of the same event. And they'll go on to store those perceptions and internal representations as new filters through which they will experience other events in the future. All too often what really happened and how a person describes it are two different things.

Since we don't know how things "really" are, but only how we represent them to ourselves, why not represent them in a way that empowers ourselves and others, rather than creating limitations? The key to doing this successfully is *memory management*—the forming of representations that consistently create the most empowering states for an individual. In any experience, you have many things you can focus on. Even the most successful person can think of what isn't working and go into a state of depression or frustration or anger—or focus on all the things that work in her life. No matter how terrible a situation is, you can represent it in a way that empowers you.

> *I had to practically hypnotize myself into thinking I was going to be a success.*
>
> —JOHN SINGLETON

It's a fact that people who are successful are able to tap into resourceful states of mind on a consistent basis. Isn't that the difference between people who succeed and people who don't? Think back to Herdale Johnson. Despite being terribly burned, he found a way to consistently put himself in a resourceful state. We can represent things in a way that puts us in a positive state, or we can do the opposite.

Ever wonder how Nelson Mandela survived all those years in prison without letting the injustice of it drive him crazy? And what about the people he loved? By his own account, Mandela treated every day as a God-given opportunity to shape himself mentally, physically, and spiritually. He constantly visualized himself walking out of bondage stronger and leading his people to the freedom they so desperately deserved. Few of us can even imagine what he must have endured. Yet every day, he trained his brain to be what he knew it had to be to become that leader. It was a challenge he would win—and the world won in the process.

Do you think he was ever scared? Of course he was. Do you think he ever wanted to give up? Of course he did. But the difference is that he changed all of that to something that empowered him to succeed. Nelson Mandela learned to use his internal representations to support his actions.

Like Mandela, we can all learn to change our states. And when we do, we harness the power to guide our behaviors in a way that ensures we take the action that produces *new* results in spite of our fears or other limiting factors.

Ultimately, it doesn't really matter what has happened to you; it's how you represent it. Think about the word *represent.* It's never too late to re-present it (present it again) to ourselves. Have you ever had something happen that at the time seemed to be all bad yet later you were glad that it happened or you learned from it? The artist formerly known as Prince was booed off the stage at a Rolling Stones concert. I'm sure it was devastating to him at the time, but the end result was that he became more determined. He used the experience as a major publicity piece for his popularity, and he now represents his "disaster" as a learning experience.

We must represent things to ourselves in a resourceful manner. Failure to do this will usually mean failure even to attempt that which you desire, or at best a feeble, halfhearted attempt that will produce like results. If I say to you (as Tony did to me), "Let's walk on fire," the stimuli I produce for you, in words and in body language, go to your brain, where you form a representation. If you picture people taking part in some terrible satanic rite or burning at the stake, you won't be in a very good state. If you form a representation of yourself burning, your state will be even worse.

If, on the other hand, you picture people clapping and dancing and celebrating together, if you see a scene of total joy and excitement punctuated by the rhythmic pounding of authentic African drummers—the "real" scene at one of Tony's firewalks—you will be in a very different state. If you see a representation of yourself and your friends walking healthfully and joyously, and if you say, "Yes, I absolutely can do this," and move your body with total confidence, then these neurological signals will put you in a state where you will most likely take action and walk.

The same is true for everything in life. If we represent to ourselves that things aren't going to work, they won't. If we form a representation that things will work, then we create the internal resources we need to produce the state that will support us in producing positive results. What distinguishes a Jesse Owens or a Nelson Mandela from other people is that these two legends represented the world as a place where they could produce any result they truly desired most.

Choose Your Representations So That They Support You

If internal representations and physiology work together to create a state that produces behaviors, what determines the specific kind of behavior we produce when we're in that state? One person in a state of love will hug you, while another will just tell you she loves you. The answer is *our references from our past.* When we go into a state, our brain accesses possible behavioral choices based on what we've experienced in the past. The number of choices is determined by our models of the world. Some people, when they get angry, have one major model of how to respond, so they may lash out as they learned to do by watching their parents. Or maybe they just tried something, and it seemed to get them what they wanted, so that became a stored memory of how to respond in the future.

We all have a lifetime of references to draw from. We all have worldviews, models that shape our perceptions of our environment. From people we know and from books and movies and television, we form an image of the world and what's possible in it. In Bonnie St. John Dean's case, it was the memory of a strong mother making no excuses and doing whatever it took to get her outcomes that gave her the strength to keep pushing until she got what she wanted. She had a model of success and inspiration that helped her represent her situation as something that in no way prevented her from being utterly successful. She unconsciously modeled her mother.

What we need to do is to model successful people and find out the specific beliefs that cause them to represent the world in a way that allows them to take effective action. We need to find out exactly how they represent to themselves their experience of the world. What do they do visually in their minds? What do they say? What do they feel? Once again, if we produce the exact same messages in our bodies, we can produce similar results. That's what modeling is all about. Yes, it's that simple. **Success no longer has to be a game of chance.**

One of the constants in life is that results are always being produced. If you don't consciously decide what results you want to produce and represent things accordingly, then some external trigger—a conversation, a TV show, whatever—may put you in states that create behaviors that do not support you. Life is like a river. It's moving, and you can be at the mercy of the river if you don't take deliberate action to steer yourself in a direction you have predetermined. If you don't plant the mental and physiological seeds of the results you want, weeds will grow automatically. If you don't consciously direct your own mind and states, your environment may produce undesirable, haphazard states. The results can be disastrous. So it's critical—on a daily basis—to stand guard at the door of your mind, to know how you are consistently representing things to yourself. You must daily weed your garden.

If you continually focus on all "bad" things in life, all the things you don't want or all the possible problems, you put yourself in a state that supports those types of behaviors and results. For example, are you a jealous person? No, you are not. You may in the past have produced jealous states and the types of behaviors that spring from them. **However, you are not your behavior.** By making these kinds of generalizations about yourself, you create a belief that will govern and direct your actions in the future. Remember, your behavior is the result of your state, and your state is the result of your internal representations and your physiology, *both of which you can change in a matter of moments.* If in the past you have been jealous, it simply means you have represented things in a way that created this state. You now can represent things in a new way and produce new states and accompanying behaviors.

Remember, we always have a choice of how to represent things to ourselves. If you represent to yourself that your lover is cheating on you, like Lawrence Fishburne's title character in Shakespeare's *Othello* does, pretty soon you will find yourself in a state of rage and anger. He begins to agonize over his wife's infidelity even *before* he has any evidence it is true—he experiences it in his body as if it were, so that by the time he sees Desdemona again, he is abusive and angry. Othello attacks her verbally, and everything she says, though innocent, he construes as proof of his suspicions. The tragedy is that he is unable to see the truth—to represent the situation accurately—until after he has killed his loyal wife.

In working with people who have stage fright, when I ask them how they are representing public speaking to themselves, they inevitably say they picture standing in front of a roomful of people as they stumble over their words, perspire nervously, and panic. Even as they describe this scene, they almost always start to stammer and sweat. When I get them to change the pictures in their heads to someone who is relaxed, calm, and in control, and get them to breathe and hold their bodies in a more relaxed state, they no longer experience the panic. Once they can begin to actually *enjoy* the representations they make of public speaking, they no longer dread the real thing.

You can change *your* pictures of negativity to images of success. This new picturing process will put you in a state where you will behave differently. There may be times when you will get a little nervous, but why waste time and emotion thinking about it now?

If you have confidence, you'll always find a way to win.

—CARL LEWIS

If we take control of our own communication with ourselves and produce visual, auditory, and kinesthetic signals of what we do want, outstanding positive results can be consistently produced, even in situations where the odds for success seem limited or nonexistent. The most powerful and effective managers, coaches, parents, and motivators are those who can represent the circumstances of life to themselves and to others in a way that signals success to the nervous system in spite of seemingly hopeless external stimuli. They keep themselves and others in a state of total resourcefulness so that they can continue to take action until they succeed. Didn't Martin Luther King, Jr., take what was a seemingly hopeless situation and represent it as a foundation for hope, peace, and equality? Remember his famous "I Have a Dream" speech? That very speech was a bright example of how he represented the world to himself. He saw a world where children of all races and religions played together without hatred or prejudice. This representation electrified his soul and caused him to use his body in such a way that he produced the behavior known as *leadership*.

Remember, human behavior is the result of the state we're in. If you've ever produced a successful result, you can reproduce it by taking the same mental and physical actions you did then. I'm emphasizing this over and over so it is embedded within you: **The kind of behavior people produce is the result of the state they are in. How they specifically respond out of that state is based on their models of the world**—that is, their stored neurological strategies.

Most people take very little conscious action to direct their states. They wake up depressed or they wake up energized. Good breaks lift them up; bad ones bring them down. One difference between people in any field is how effectively they marshal their resources. It's most clear in athletics. No one succeeds all the time, but there are certain athletes who have the ability to put themselves in a resourceful state almost on cue, almost always rising to the occasion. Why did Reggie Jackson hit all those October home runs? How did Shaquille O'Neal or Earvin "Magic" Johnson develop the uncanny ability to hit all those shots at the buzzer? They were able to summon their best when they needed it, when the pressure was the greatest.

State change is what most people are after. We want to be happy, joyous, ecstatic, centered. As Black Americans, we want to feel proud, confident, and strong. We don't want to be frustrated, angry, upset, or bored. So what do most people do? Some turn on a TV set that gives them new representations they can internalize, so now they see something and laugh. They're no longer in their frustrated state. They go out and eat, or they smoke a cigarette, or they take a drug. On a more positive note, they might exercise.

The only problem with most of these approaches is that the results are not lasting. And as you're aware, television doesn't always have our best interest in mind. When the TV show is over or we return from a workout, we still have the same internal representations about our lives. We remember them and feel bad again after the excess food or drug has been consumed. And in many cases, there's a price to pay for the temporary state change. By contrast, this book will show you how to directly change your internal representations and physiology, without the use of external devices which many times create additional problems in the long run.

Why do people use drugs? Not because they like sticking needles in their arms, but because they like the experience and don't know any other way to get into that state. Tony and I have seen kids who were hard-core drug users kick the habit after a firewalk because they were given a more elegant model of how to achieve the same high. One kid who said he'd been on heroin for years finished the firewalk and told the group, "It's over. I never felt anything from a needle that even comes close to what I felt on the other side of those coals." That didn't mean he had to walk on fire every day. He just had to regularly access this new state. By doing something he thought was impossible, he had developed a new model of what he could do to make himself feel good.

The successes in this world are those who have mastered the skill of accessing the most resourceful states. Black, White, or otherwise, that's what separates them from the pack. The key thing to remember from this chapter is that your state has awesome power, and you can control it. You don't have to be at the mercy of whatever the world seems to hand you.

There is a factor that determines in advance how we will represent our experience of life—a factor that filters the way we represent the world to ourselves. A factor that determines the kinds of states we will consistently create in certain situations. It has been called the greatest power. Let us now investigate the magic power of . . .

CHAPTER SIX

The Birth of Excellence: Belief

In every crisis, there is a message. Crises are nature's way of forcing change—breaking down old structures, shaking loose those negative habits so that something new and better can take their place.

—SUSAN TAYLOR

AT 2:30 A.M. on a Monday morning the phone rang and woke me from a short but deep sleep. The voice on the phone was my older sister, so hysterical that all I could make out from her broken speech was that our mother was in the hospital, and I had to come quickly. Within ten minutes, I was in the car heading down the highway toward the small town where they lived—about three hours away. By the time I arrived at the hospital, the sun was starting to peek over the horizon. I ran to the front desk, and the receptionist directed me to the emergency waiting room at the end of the operating wing.

As I entered the intensive-care waiting room, my sister stood up and ran to me. Visibly shaken, she was clutching her infant daughter, trying to speak, when the door on the other side of the room opened. In walked a man dressed in surgery scrubs. It was immediately obvious that he and my sister knew each other, so their silence was horrifying. As he looked into her eyes without saying a thing, my sister and I knew that whatever the news was, it wasn't good. I'll never forget his words when he finally did speak.

"Your mother has cancer," he told us. "We took one-third of a grapefruit-sized tumor out of her intestine. It's malignant, and she has about three months to live." The impact of those words was like a white-hot, razor-sharp saber, piercing right through the center of my pounding heart. I felt my knees go numb and my face turn to a ball of fire. My heart dropped, and my sister let out a mournful sound I hope never to hear again. She started to fall, and I reached out and grabbed her by the shirtsleeve to keep her up.

My first thought was, *What can we do to change this?* My world stood still. The doctor went on to advise that we should leave as soon as my mother was able for the Alaska trip she had been wanting to take. Within a couple of months, he predicted, she would be bedridden. I looked away and thought to myself, *NO WAY. We are going to beat this!*

By the time I looked back to where the doctor was standing he was heading out the door. "Stop!" I shouted. "Please don't tell that to my mother." Realizing this was not the first time the doctor had to deliver this message to family members, I saw the compassion in his eyes as he said, "I'm sorry, son, there's nothing that can be done. I have to tell her. It's part of my job."

"Doctor," I said, "I understand that it's your job to tell her what you found and to give her your opinion, but it's *not* your job to tell her she's going to die. You have no right to give her that death sentence. You can tell her she's sick, you can tell her she has cancer and how bad it is, but please, *please* don't tell her she is going to die."

I had recently read a wonderful book by Dr. Deepak Chopra in which he wrote that nine times out of ten when patients are told by a physician they are going to die by the end of a certain time period, they follow the prediction exactly, dying three months or six months later *to the day.* He even cites cases in which people were mistakenly diagnosed with a terminal disease and either developed the disease or died of its complications.

I told the doctor, "I appreciate your diagnosis, but I won't accept your verdict." Then he and I went back and forth arguing until we reached a stalemate. I told him that no matter what, there was no way in hell I was ever going to let him tell that to my mother—not those particular words. I knew what the consequences were and was not willing to accept them. Just to be sure, I was in her room when she regained consciousness and made certain I was there every time he came to visit her. Anytime the doctor started working toward telling my mom she was history, I changed the subject and rushed him out of the room, or made jokes, or did whatever it took to prevent her from hearing her death sentence. He did tell her that she had cancer and that it was very serious, but I never let him tell her she was going to die.

Instead, my mother and I set out on a journey of healing her body with her thoughts. We visualized, we wrote, we laughed, all the time keeping a keen eye on beating her illness. She truly believed she was going to be around for years to come, and do you know what? I remember once hearing her say she believed she would be around to watch her grandkids grow and go to school. I'm elated to say that at this time, now seven years later, my mother is still with us. Because she was never told she was going to die in three months, she was never given the belief that her situation was hopeless.

It has been said that our beliefs are the core of our very being, who we deem ourselves to be, what we think we can and can't do. They are convictions and opinions about ourselves and the world in which we live and are the filters we use to determine the quality of our existence here on this planet. We usually think of beliefs in terms of creeds or doctrines, and that's what many beliefs are. But in the most basic sense, a belief is any guiding principle, faith, or passion that can provide meaning and direction in life. Beliefs are like commanders of the brain. When we congruently believe something is true, it is like delivering a command to our brain as to how to represent what is occurring. My mother believed fervently she was going to get better—and she did. That's what gave her the strength and tenacity to go through the sometimes agonizing process of healing herself. Because she believed in the transcendent power of her Maker and her abilities, she was empowered in a way that almost defies understanding. Her beliefs transformed her daily from a critically sick woman to a vital, happy soul. In the most profound sense, they kept her alive.

It is the mind that makes the body.

—SOJOURNER TRUTH

Belief delivers a direct command to your nervous system. When you believe something is true, it becomes your reality and you behave accordingly. Handled effectively, beliefs can be the most powerful forces for creating good in your life. On the other hand, beliefs that limit your actions and thoughts can be as devastating as resourceful beliefs can be empowering. Religions throughout history have empowered millions of people and given them strength to do things they thought they could not. Beliefs help us tap the richest resources deep within us, creating and directing these resources in the support of our desired outcomes. If you think about it, the beliefs that our forefathers had about the promised land and their right to be free is what gave them the strength to carry on. We have all benefited from their actions. Beliefs help you see what you want and energize you to get it.

In fact, there is no more powerful directing force in human behavior than belief. In essence, human history is the history of human belief. The people who have changed history—whether Christ, Mohammed, Gandhi, Edison, Einstein, or Mandela—have been the people who have changed our beliefs.

The more we learn about human behavior, the more we learn about the extraordinary power that beliefs have over our lives. In many ways, that power defies the logical models most of us have. But it's clear that even at the level of physiology, beliefs (congruent internal representations) control reality. A remarkable study was once done of a woman who had multiple personalities. In one persona, her blood-sugar levels were completely normal. But in a different, diabetic persona, her whole physiology changed to become that of a diabetic. Her belief had become her reality.

In a similar vein, there have been numerous studies in which a person in a hypnotic trance is touched with a piece of ice represented to him as a piece of hot metal. Invariably, a blister will develop at the point of contact. What counted was not reality but belief—the direct unquestioned communication to the nervous system. The brain simply does what it's told.

Most of us are aware of the placebo effect: People who are told a drug will have a certain effect will many times experience that effect even when given a pill with no active properties. Norman Cousins, who learned firsthand the power of belief in eliminating his own illness, concludes, "Drugs are not always necessary. Belief in recovery always is."

One remarkable placebo study concerned a group of patients with bleeding ulcers. They were divided into two groups. People in the first group were told they were being given a new drug that would absolutely produce relief. Those in the second were told they were being given an experimental drug, but that very little was known about its effects. Seventy percent of those in the first group experienced significant relief from their ulcers. Only 25 percent of the second group had a similar result. In both groups, patients received a drug with no medicinal properties at all. The only difference was the belief system they adopted. Even more remarkable are the numerous studies of people who, given drugs known to have harmful effects, have experienced no ill effects at all when told they would experience a positive outcome.

Studies conducted by Dr. Andrew Weil have shown that the experiences of drug users correspond almost exactly to their expectations. He found he could lead a person given a dose of an amphetamine to feel sedated or a person given a barbiturate to feel stimulated. "The 'magic' of drugs resides within the mind of the user, not in the drugs," Weil concluded.

In all these instances, the one constant that most powerfully affected the results was belief, the consistent, congruent messages delivered to the brain and nervous system. If you believe in success, you'll be empowered to achieve it. If you believe in failure, those messages will tend to lead you to experience that as well. **Ultimately, whether you say you can do something or you say you can't, you're right.** Both kinds of beliefs have great power. The question is, What kinds of beliefs are best to have, and how do we develop them?

If you have no confidence in self, you are twice defeated in the race of life. With confidence, you have won even before you have started.

—Marcus Garvey

The birth of excellence begins with our awareness that *our beliefs are a choice.* Most human beings go though life never realizing this simple but powerful fact. You can choose beliefs that limit you, or you can choose beliefs that support you. The trick is to choose the beliefs that are conducive to success and the results you want and to discard the ones that hold you back.

The biggest misconception people often have of belief is that it's a static, intellectual concept, an understanding that's divorced from action and results. Nothing could be farther from the truth. Belief is the doorway to excellence precisely because there's nothing static about it.

It is our belief that determines how much of our potential we'll be able to tap. Beliefs can turn on or shut off the flow of ideas. Imagine the following situation. Someone says to you, "Please get me the salt," and as you walk into the next room, you say, "But I don't know where it is." After looking for a few minutes, you call out, "I can't find the salt." So you look again, and still you can't find the salt. Then that someone walks up, takes the salt right off the shelf in front of you, and says, "Look, dummy, it's right here in front of you. If it was a snake, it would have bitten you." When you said, "I can't," you gave your brain a command to overlook the salt (in psychology, we call this a *scotoma*). Remember, every human experience, everything you've ever said, seen, heard, felt, smelled, or tasted, is stored in your brain. When you congruently say you cannot remember, you're right. When you congruently say you can, you give a command to your nervous system that opens up the pathways to the part of your brain that can potentially deliver the answers you need.

Where do beliefs come from? Why do some people have beliefs that push them toward success while others have beliefs that only help them fail? If we are going to try to model the beliefs that foster excellence, the first thing we need to find out is where those beliefs come from.

1. The Primary Source of Beliefs Is the Environment

This is where the cycles of success breeding success and failure breeding failure are played out in the most relentless fashion. The real horror of ghetto life is not the daily frustrations and deprivations. People can overcome those. The real nightmare is the effect the environment has on beliefs and dreams. If all you see is failure, if all you see is despair, it's very hard for you to form the internal representations that will foster success. Remember, in the last chapter we said modeling is something we all do consistently. If you grow up in wealth and success, you can easily model wealth and success. If you grow up in poverty and despair, that's where your models of possibility come from.

Dr. Benjamin Bloom of the University of Chicago studied one hundred extraordinarily successful young athletes, musicians, and students. He was surprised to find that most of the young people hadn't begun by showing great flashes of brilliance. Instead, most received careful attention, guidance, and support, and then they began to develop. The belief that they could be special came before any overt signs of great talent.

Environment may be the single most potent generator of belief, but it's not the only one. If it were, we'd live in a static world where the children of wealth would know only wealth, and the children of poverty would never rise above their origins. Instead there are other experiences and ways of learning that can also be incubators of belief.

2. Events, Small or Large, Can Help Foster Beliefs

There are certain events in everyone's lives that they will never forget. For example, where were you the day the riots broke out following the acquittal of the men who beat Rodney King? For many people, it was a day that forever altered their worldview. In the same way, most of us have experiences we'll never forget, events that had such an impact on us that they were installed into our brains forever. These are the kinds of experiences that form the beliefs that can change our lives.

3. Beliefs Are Formed and Expanded Through Knowledge

A direct experience is one form of knowledge. Another is gained through reading, seeing movies, viewing the world as it is portrayed by others. Knowledge is one of the great ways to break the shackles of a limiting environment. No matter how grim your world is, if you can read about the accomplishments of others, you can create the beliefs that will allow you to succeed. Dr. Robert Curvin, a Black political scientist, wrote in the *New York Times* how the example of Jackie Robinson, the first Black player in baseball's major leagues, changed his life when he was a youngster: "I was enriched by my attachment to him; the level of my expectations was raised by his example."

Black Americans have received the message from society that we are, at the very least, not preferred. This has been done blatantly and covertly throughout our history. Even if by omission alone, if a race of people has been denied their rights and the benefit of knowing their real history, the obvious result would be self-doubt and low esteem. Yet, even in the horrific discrimination of the 1950s, certain Black Americans refused to allow the environment to dictate who they were. They chose to see themselves in a more positive light. They created and found role models to become their beacons of possibility, even though they understood the realities of the day. Fortunately, though, we are starting to see ourselves in a more positive light. Our presence is rightfully woven within the fabric of modern society. And with it comes new and more empowering beliefs about ourselves. Today we have a world rich with examples of possibility, and part of the purpose of this book is to remind us of this immutable fact.

4. Some of Our Beliefs Today Are Created Through our Past Results

The most powerful way to destroy a limiting belief is to create an experience that violates it. If you can get yourself to do something you previously thought you couldn't do—even once—suddenly that limiting belief will turn and take its place with all the other old disempowering beliefs that used to spoil your life. Think back to when you were a kid and you thought you'd never learn to ride a bike, swim, or drive a car. But the minute you accomplished those things, you proved you were indeed capable, and those limiting beliefs were shattered forever. If you succeed once, it's far easier to form the belief that you'll succeed again. With each small success comes the momentum that strengthens the legs of certainty we call belief.

The first time I had to conduct my class at UCLA was the most difficult. I had to teach a roomful of scientists and engineers, most of them with more Ph.D.'s than I had fingers, and I was told they weren't going to be very receptive to my style or the content of my material. The dean warned me they wouldn't go for any of that "New Age, mind-body, woo-woo stuff." They were stiff and analytical, I was told, so I shouldn't try anything different. But since I had never taught any other way, I decided to stick with what I knew was best despite his advice.

When the day came, I surprised myself and the dean. The class was a great success, and the engineers loved it. Every day they would return with a new sense of curiosity and possibility. I have made so many new friends and assisted them in making some major changes for the better.

Once I found that I could succeed at teaching, I was able to form a belief that allowed me to return again and again. After five semesters, the class was among the top ten in the engineering and management department. There was a time I believed it wasn't possible for me to communicate to people like this and have a positive impact. But having that first success violated the limiting belief and opened the doors to a new belief of what I was capable of. Repeating that successful behavior began to give me the certainty that ultimately allowed me to have the long-term impact I've had on the students. This process of building momentum, of going from uncertainty to certainty, is the same process that successful entertainers, business owners, and people from just about any other walk of life go through. They start out attempting what seems to be unknown and uncertain, graduating into behaviors they feel comfortable and confident in doing. The secret is to learn how to believe before the results occur. When we create the results in advance, believing it can be done becomes a self-fulfilling prophecy.

5. The Fifth Way to Establish Belief Is Through Creating in Your Mind the Experience you Desire in the Future as if It Were Here Now

Just as past experiences can change your internal representations and thus what you believe is possible, so can your imagined experience of how you want things to be in the future. Tony calls this *experiencing results in advance.* And if you think about it, that's exactly what you are doing when you vividly imagine the future. I call it *future vibing.* When the results you have around you are not supporting you in being in a powerful and effective state, you can simply create the world the way you want it to be and "step into" that experience, thereby changing your states, your beliefs, and your actions. Remember the adage: As you think, so you are. Use your imagination to create your desired states of mind. After all, if you're in sales, is it easier to make $10,000 or $100,000? The truth is it's easier to make $100,000. Let me tell you why. If your goal is to make $10,000, what you're really trying to do is make enough to pay the bills. If that's what your goal is, if that's what you represent to yourself about why you're working so hard, do you think you'll be in an excited, empowered, resourceful state as you work? Are you bursting with excitement, thinking, *Boy, oh boy, I've got to get to work so I can make enough to pay my lousy bills?* I don't know about you—that just doesn't get my motor running!

But selling is selling. You have to make the same calls, meet the same people, deliver the same products, no matter what you're hoping to achieve. So it's a lot more exciting, a lot more enticing, to go out with the goal of making $100,000 than $10,000. And that state of excitement is much more likely to activate your taking the kinds of consistent actions that will tap your higher potential than just hoping to go out and make a living.

Obviously, money is not the only way to motivate yourself.

Whatever your goal may be, if you create in your mind a clear image of the result you want and represent it to yourself as if you've already achieved it, then you will put yourself in the kind of states that will support you in creating the results you desire.

All these things are ways to mobilize belief. Most of us form our beliefs haphazardly. We soak up things—good and bad—from the world around us. But one of the key ideas of this book is that you're not just a leaf in the wind. **You can control your beliefs.** You can control the ways you model others. You can consciously direct your life. You can change. If there's a key word in this book, that's it—*change.*

So if you're ready to start making some changes in the quality of your life, then let me ask you a question: What are some of the beliefs you have about who you are and what you're capable of? Please take a moment and jot down five key beliefs that have limited you in the past. Don't pass up this opportunity to take a look at the things that have slowed you down or even stopped you in the past. Instead, get excited that you are about to take a step in the direction of changing the things that limit you and finding the things that empower you.

5 Limiting Beliefs

Examples: "I'm not smart enough," "I'll never get ahead because I'm Black."

1.
2.
3.
4.
5.

Now, make a list of at least five positive beliefs that can now serve to support you in achieving your highest goals.

5 Empowering Beliefs

Examples: "What I don't know, I can learn," "Because I'm Black, I have the strength to accomplish whatever I want."

1.

2.

3.

4.

5.

All negative beliefs at the very least hinder our forward motion. You should know better than anybody how yours have affected your life. What has it cost you in the past to have these beliefs? How have they slowed you down or held you back from your dreams—or perhaps kept you from even dreaming or hoping at all? One of the greatest abilities that we as human beings possess is the ability to consciously make change. It's critical for us to realize that belief systems are no more permanent than the clouds in the sky or the hair on your head. If you're driving a Honda and decide you would be happier with a BMW or Mercedes, it's in your power to change.

Your internal representations and beliefs work in much the same way. If you don't like them, you can change them. We all have a hierarchy, a ladder of beliefs. We have core beliefs, things that are so fundamental we would die for them. These are things like our ideas about patriotism and family and love. But most of our lives are governed by beliefs about possibility or success or happiness we've picked up unconsciously over the years. The key is to make sure those beliefs work for you, that they're effective and empowering.

All my life I've had this almost criminal optimism. I didn't care what happened, the glass was always going to be half full.

—QUINCY JONES

We've talked about the importance of modeling. Modeling excellence begins with modeling belief. Some things take time to model, but if you can read and think and hear, you can model the beliefs of the most successful people on the planet.

Where do your personal beliefs come from? Do they come from the average man on the street? Do they come from TV and radio? Do they come from whoever talks the longest and the loudest? If you want to succeed, it would be wise for you to choose your beliefs carefully, rather than walking around like a piece of flypaper, picking up whichever belief sticks. An important thing to realize is that the potentials we tap, the results we get, are all part of a dynamic process that begins with belief. Think of the process in terms of the following diagram.

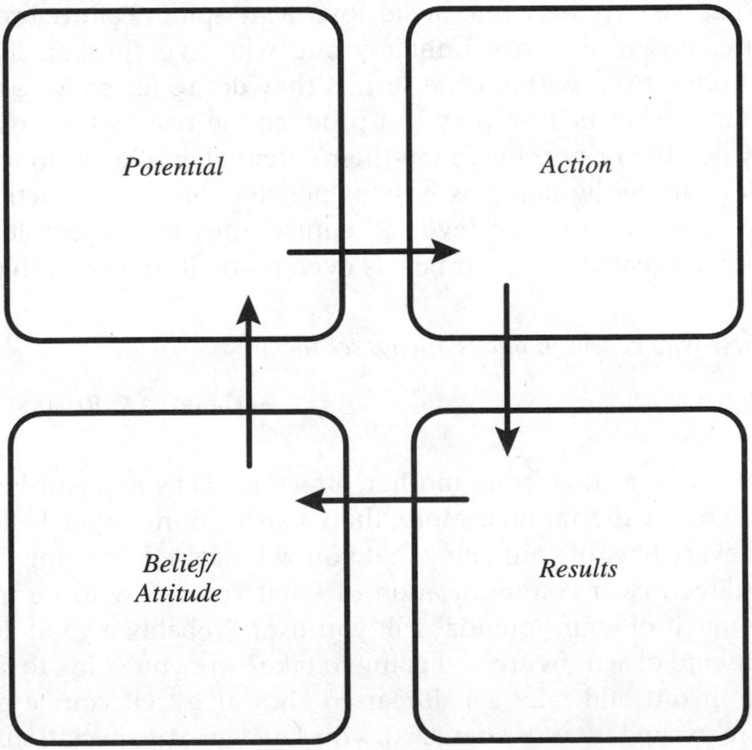

Let's say a person has a belief that he's ineffective at something. Let's say he's told himself he's a bad student. If he has expectations of failure, how much of his potential is he going to tap? Not very much. He's already told himself that he doesn't know how to succeed. He's already signaled his brain to expect failure. Having begun with those sorts of expectations, what sorts of actions will he probably take? Will they be confident, energized, congruent, assertive? Will they reflect his real potential? Not likely. If he's convinced he's going to fail, why make the effort to try hard? He's started with a belief system that stresses what he can't do, a system that subsequently signals his nervous system to respond in a certain way. He's tapped a limited amount of his potential. He's taken halfhearted, tentative actions. What sort of results come out of all this? Chances are they'll be pretty dismal. What will these dismal results do to his beliefs about subsequent endeavors? Chances are they'll reinforce the negative beliefs that started the whole chain.

What we have here is a classic downward spiral. Failure breeds failure. People who are unhappy and who live "broken lives" have often been without the results they desire for so long that they no longer believe they can produce the results they want. They do little or nothing to tap their potential and begin to focus on how to get by doing as little as possible. From such actions, what results do they achieve? Of course, they are miserable results that break down their beliefs even more, if that's possible.

Those who believe in ghosts always see them.

—CHARLES V. ROMAN

Let's look at this from another direction. Let's say you begin with great expectations. More than expectations—you believe with every fiber of your being that you will succeed. Starting with that direct, clear communication of what you know to be true, how much of your potential will you use? Probably a good deal. What kind of actions are you going to take? Are you going to drag yourself out and take a halfhearted shot at it? Of course not! You're excited, you're energized, you have great expectations of success, you're going to go great guns. If you put out that sort of effort, what sort of results will be generated? Chances are they'll be pretty good. And what does that do to your belief in your ability to produce great results in the future? It's the opposite of the vicious cycle. In this case, success feeds on success and generates more success, and each success creates more belief and momentum to succeed on an even greater scale.

Do resourceful people screw up? Sure they do. Do affirmative beliefs guarantee positive results every time? Of course not. If anyone tells you he's got a magic formula to guarantee perpetual, flawless success, you'd best grab your wallet and start walking in the opposite direction. But history has shown time and again that if people maintain the belief systems that empower them they'll keep coming back with enough action and enough resourcefulness to succeed eventually. George Washington Carver failed hundreds of times with his projects, but he continued to believe in his ability to succeed in the long term. He allowed himself to be empowered by success, and he refused to be cowed by his failures. His belief system was geared toward excellence, and he finally achieved it. When he did, he changed the history of this country.

Sometimes it's not necessary to have a tremendous belief or attitude about something in order to succeed. Sometimes people produce outstanding results simply because they don't know something is difficult or impossible. Sometimes just not having a limiting belief is enough. For example, there is a story of a young man who fell asleep during math class. He woke up as the bell rang, looked up at the blackboard, and copied the two problems that were there. He went home and labored on his "homework" all day and all night. He couldn't figure out either one, but he kept trying for the rest of the week. Finally, he got the answer to one and brought it to class. The teacher was absolutely stunned. It turned out the problem he'd solved was supposedly unsolvable. If the student had known that, he probably wouldn't have solved it. But since he didn't tell himself it couldn't be done—in fact, quite the opposite; he thought he absolutely had to solve it—he was able to find a way to do it.

Remember, another way to change your belief is to have an experience that disproves it. That's another reason why we use physical metaphors like board breaking or the firewalk. I don't care if people can bust plywood or walk on hot coals, but I do care that people can do something they thought was impossible. If you can do even one thing you thought was utterly impossible, it causes you to rethink all your beliefs.

NOTE: If you haven't done so yet, put this book down and take a look at the beliefs that empower you and disempower you. Do this exercise before moving on to the next chapter. This is where you will start to effect change in your behaviors. Give yourself the gift of some basic new and empowering beliefs. This does not have to be a scary exercise. Lighten up and have fun! At the end of the next chapter you will be using some or all of the beliefs on this list to make some changes in your belief systems, so take the time to do this now.

The next question is, Is the figure below concave or convex?

It's a silly question. The answer is, It depends on how you're looking at it. Your reality is the reality you create. If you have positive internal representations or beliefs, it's because that's what you've created. If you have negative ones, you've created those, too. There are any number of beliefs that foster excellence. The following chapter contains seven that are particularly important as pertains to success. They are . . .

CHAPTER SEVEN

The Seven Lies of Success

In every adversity, look for the benefit that can come out of it. Even bad experiences offer benefits, but you have to look for them.

—Eric V. Copage

It's been said many times and many ways for the past, oh . . . half a dozen centuries or so, that we are all responsible for the lives we live. We choose the paths we are on. Life hands us some pretty crazy circumstances, but the fact remains, we always have a choice. If we choose bliss, and are willing to do what it takes to have it, that's what we get. If we choose misery, we get that, too. As you learned in the last chapter, belief is the foundation of excellence. The fundamental choices we make about how to perceive events and what to do about them are based upon our beliefs. They're how we turn our brain on or off. So the first step toward excellence is to find the beliefs that guide us toward our desired outcomes.

Remember the Ultimate Success Formula of Chapter 3? Know your outcome, take massive action, know what results you're getting, and have the flexibility to change until you're successful? The same is true of beliefs. You have to find beliefs that support your outcome, beliefs that get you where you want to go. If your current beliefs are not doing that, then it is imperative you become aware of them and try some new ones on for size.

People are sometimes put off when Tony and I talk about the "lies" of success. Who wants to live by lies? But all that is meant by lies is that we don't know how the world really is. We don't know if the line is concave or convex. We don't know if our beliefs are true or false. What we can know, though, is if they work—if they support us, if they make our lives richer, if they make us better people, if they help us and help others.

The word *lies* is used in this chapter as a constant reminder of these facts. In this context, the word *lie* does not mean "to be deceitful or dishonest" but, rather, is a useful way to remind us that no matter how much we believe in a concept, we should be open to other possibilities and continuous learning. We suggest you look at these seven beliefs and decide whether they're useful for you. We have found these beliefs time and again in successful people we have modeled. To model excellence, you have to start with the belief systems of excellence. These seven beliefs have empowered people to do more, take greater action, and produce greater results. We're not saying they're the only useful beliefs of success. They are a start. They've worked for others, and we'd like you to see if they can work for you.

Belief No. 1: Everything happens for a reason and a purpose, and it serves us. Do you remember the story of Herdale Johnson? What was the central belief that helped him overcome adversity? Instead of letting what happened to him be a crutch or an excuse, he decided to use it as a challenge to make him stronger, and to raise his siblings. He decided to use his story as an example of strength for others who might think they have insurmountable problems. And what about Bonnie St. John Dean? She could very easily have lived a bitter life of self-pity and anger. Instead she took what was given her and used it to win.

We can learn so much from people like these. No matter how much negative feedback they get from their environment, they think in terms of possibilities. They think everything happens for a reason, and it serves them. They believe every adversity contains the seed of an equivalent or greater benefit.

I can guarantee you that people who produce outstanding results think this way. I believe as soon as something happens to you, whether good or bad, your job is to start looking immediately for the benefit. Sometimes it's hard, but if you keep looking you will find it, and that's when your life will change for the better. Think about it in your own life. There are an infinite number of ways to react to any situation.

Let's say you fail to land a job you had counted on, one that you were certain you deserved. Some of us would be hurt and frustrated. We might sit home and mope, or go out and get drunk. Some of us would be mad. We might blame the company, figuring they were a bunch of ignorant individuals. Or we might blame ourselves for ruining a sure thing.

All of that might allow us to let off some steam, but it doesn't help us. It doesn't bring us any closer to our desired outcome. It takes a lot of discipline to be able to retrace your steps, learn painful lessons, mend fences, and take a good look at new possibilities. It's too easy for Black men or women to blame the color of our skin as the fundamental reason for a lot of our misfortune. And you know what? A lot of it is true. It's hard to look for the benefit when injustice has been done. But that's the only way to get a positive outcome from what seems like a negative result.

> *Someone was hurt before you; wronged before you; hungry before you; frightened before you; beaten before you; humiliated before you; raped before you; yet someone survives.*
>
> —Maya Angelou

There is an old story of an African farmer who one day went out to his stable to find that his prize bull had escaped in the night and was nowhere to be found. The news of his loss spread throughout the nearby village, and everyone said to him, "That's too bad. That's a terrible thing to have happened!" To this the farmer simply replied, "Maybe so." A few days later while out working in his field, the farmer looked up to see his bull returning home, and to his surprise, he had a new friend with him: a wild steer. When the news got to the village, everyone said, "Wow, you're a lucky man." To this the farmer replied, "Maybe so." A few days later while trying to corral the new steer, the farmer's only son was trapped against the fence by the animal and suffered a broken leg. When the village people heard of this they all said, "What bad luck! Now your son is hurt. He won't be able to help you on the farm, and your crops will be late." To this the farmer said, "Maybe so." Two days later, there was a disturbance outside the farmer's hut. He opened it to find ten warriors standing there. "We are from the king's army, and we know that you have a young son. We are here to take him with us into battle." "Come in," said the farmer, "I'll introduce you to my son." There in the bed was the young son with his leg broken, unable to walk. Seeing that the boy was useless to them, the warriors left and went off to battle without him.

Every time something perceivably bad happened, the wise old farmer had the foresight to realize that there was some good hidden within it. Too many of us make the mistake of dwelling on how bad things appear to be in the moment, instead of realizing that the stage is set for a benefit to come from the situation. Often, when things look their worst, something wonderful is right around the corner waiting to be discovered. Adopting this belief and developing the tendency to look for the benefit serves as a catalyst for recovery. Remember, what we do in the moment makes the critical difference in our outcome.

Take a moment to think again about your beliefs. Do you generally expect things to work out well or to work out poorly? Do you expect your best efforts to be successful, or do you expect them to be thwarted? Do you see the potential in a situation, or do you see the roadblocks? Many people tend to focus on the negative more than the positive. The first step toward changing that is to recognize it. Belief in limits creates limited people. The key is to let go of limitations and operate from a higher set of resources. The leaders in our culture are the people who see the possibilities, who can go into a desert and see a garden. Impossible? What happened in Israel? If you have a strong belief in possibility, it's likely you'll achieve it.

I don't believe in failure. It's not failure if you enjoyed the process.

—OPRAH WINFREY

Belief No. 2: There is no such thing as failure. There are only results. Most people in our culture have been programmed to fear this thing called failure. At least 75 percent of the personal coaching I do with clients has to do with fear of rejection or failure. Yet, all of us can think of times when we wanted one thing and got another. We've all flunked a test, suffered through a frustrating romance that didn't work out, put together a plan only to see everything fall apart. It's safe to say that most successes in this world have come only after numerous failures—except that super-achievers don't call them failures; they call them outcomes or results.

The Wright brothers didn't fly the first time they tried. As a matter of fact, they failed miserably. But fortunately for us all, they had an outcome in mind and understood the law of trial and error: The amount of people who fail is directly proportionate to the amount of people who give up. If we just keep trying and changing our approach, chances are we will win in the end.

People always succeed in getting some sort of results. The super successes of our culture aren't people who never fail, but those who know that if they try something and it doesn't give them what they want, they've had a learning experience. They use what they've learned and simply try something else. They take some new actions and produce some new results.

Think about it. What is the one asset, the one benefit you have today over yesterday? The answer, of course, is experience. People who fear failure make internal representations of what might not work in advance. This is what keeps them from taking the very action that could ensure the accomplishment of their desire. Are you afraid of failure? Well, how do you feel about learning? You can learn from every human experience and succeed in anything you do. In fact, "failure" is a large part of winning. But it is not perceived as such by people who achieve greatness. They don't dwell on failure or attach negative emotions to something that doesn't work. They focus on what they can learn.

As someone once said, if you're not failing on a regular basis, you're not playing big enough. There's a famous story about Thomas Edison. After he'd tried 9,999 times to perfect the lightbulb and hadn't succeeded, someone asked him, "Are you going to have ten thousand failures?" He answered, "I didn't fail. I just discovered another way not to invent the electric lightbulb." He had discovered how another set of actions had produced a different result.

Every man got the right to his own mistakes. Ain't no man that ain't made any.

—Joe Louis

Winners, leaders, masters in their chosen fields—people with personal power—all understand that if you try something and do not get the outcome you want, it's simply feedback. You use that information to make finer distinctions about what you need to do to produce the results you desire. Buckminster Fuller once wrote, "Whatever humans have learned had to be learned as a consequence only of trial and error experience. Humans have learned only through mistakes." Sometimes we learn from our mistakes, sometimes from the mistakes of others. Take a minute to reflect on the five greatest so-called "failures" in your life. What did you learn from those experiences? Chances are they were some of the most valuable lessons you've learned in your life.

Did you know that a jetliner is off course most of the time? It's true. The winds and air currents are continually testing the airplane by blowing it around instead of allowing it to fly a perfectly straight line. The pilot and autopilot are continually making adjustments to put the plane back on course. Think of your life as a great airship headed toward paradise. Your mind is the pilot and autopilot. Whenever you seem to be off course, simply remind yourself that it's part of getting where you want to go, remember your outcome, and then adjust yourself to get back on course. It's a wonderful model for the process of living successfully. But most of us don't think that way. Every error, every mistake, tends to take on emotional baggage. It's a failure. It reflects badly on us.

For example, many people get down on themselves because they're overweight. Their attitude about being overweight doesn't change anything. Instead, they could embrace the fact that they've been successful in producing a result called excess fat and that now they're going to produce a new result called being thin. They would produce this new result by producing new actions.

If you're not sure what actions to take to produce this result, take special note of Chapter 12, or model someone who has produced the result called being thin. Find out what specific action that person produces mentally and physically to remain thin consistently. Produce the same actions, and you will produce the same results. As long as you regard your excess weight as a failure, you'll be immobilized. However, the minute you change it to a result you produced—and therefore one you can change now—then your success is assured.

There are many of us brimming with hope and anticipation for the future, yet there are too many more who have given up. It may take daily positive thinking to convince ourselves that we, individually, are special, gifted, deserving people. We can personally inspire others by exorcising our demon—our cynicism, our destructive habits—and by acknowledging the value inside our hearts and heads, and putting it to use.

—Eric V. Copage

Some time ago, Tony taught me to ask myself a great question: "What would I attempt to do if I knew I could not fail?" Think about it. How would you answer that? If you really believed you could not fail, you might take a whole new set of actions and produce powerful new results. Wouldn't you be better off trying them? Isn't that the only way to grow? So I suggest you start realizing right now that there's no such thing as failure. There are only results. The results that our ancestors produced so many years ago are called a better way of life that we all enjoy and sometimes take for granted today. You always produce a result. If it's not the one you desire, just change your actions and you'll produce new results. Cross out the word *failure,* circle the word *outcome* in this book, and commit yourself to learning from every experience.

Belief No. 3: Whatever happens, take responsibility. I recently read General Colin Powell's autobiography in which he talks about always taking responsibility for your actions and condition. He recalls a time early in his career when he was in a hurry to get somewhere, and when he arrived he found he had lost his sidearm. In the Army this was a serious offense, one to be dealt with severely. He never once started making excuses or trying to blame anyone else; he immediately took responsibility. He went directly to his superior and reported it, and for his courage he was granted leniency. What great leaders and achievers have in common is that they operate from the belief that they create their world. The phrase you'll hear time and again is, "I am responsible. I'll take care of it."

The overwhelming majority of achievers and successful individuals share the viewpoint that no matter what happens, whether good or bad, they created it. If they didn't cause it by their physical actions, maybe they did so by directing their thoughts and influencing their world. Now, I don't know if this is true. No scientist has yet proved that our thoughts create our reality. But it's a useful lie. It's an empowering belief. I personally believe that we create our experiences in life—either by behavior or thought—and we can learn from both.

Most of our society thinks in terms of the negative when we speak of taking responsibility for something. If we've made a mistake, we should own up to it. But there is another very important aspect of taking responsibility: We need to take ownership of the good things we have created also. Many people feel somehow arrogant or self-centered if they talk about the positives in their lives. Our society has conditioned us to believe that people who openly talk about their own accomplishments are braggarts and only out for themselves. While there are limits to how far we might go in acknowledging our accomplishments, we are robbing ourselves of a very important motivational tool if we don't.

By taking responsibility for our accomplishments and acknowledging our successes, we are literally conditioning our nervous system to do more of the same. Remember, as human beings we are motivated either by pain or pleasure. We all move away from pain and toward pleasure. If your nervous system sees that it will get pleasure for accomplishing something, it will do more of it. That's how we learn. That's how we perpetuate forward motion. On the other end of the spectrum, if we don't accept responsibility for our successes and failures, then our nervous system doesn't get conditioned the way we want. Now this doesn't mean you have to shout your accomplishments from the tops of buildings, or call everyone and make them all aware of what you've done. It simply means that you must acknowledge the success to yourself and take pride in what you have created. Pat yourself on the back, or close your eyes and give thanks. Whatever you do, just be aware that you did something for the better and that you appreciate it.

Nobody can hinder you from doing what you want, if that's what you set your mind to do.

You can always find a hook to hang your excuses on, but they're just excuses. You don't have anyone to blame but yourself. Nobody makes you fail.

—UNKNOWN

If you don't believe you're creating your world, whether it's your successes or failures, then you're at the mercy of circumstances. Things just happen to you. You're an object, not a subject. Our history shows that others don't necessarily have our best interests in mind when it comes to decisions made about us. What each and every single one of us must do is to take charge of our own circumstances.

John F. Kennedy had this belief system. Dan Rather once said that Kennedy became a true leader during the Bay of Pigs incident, when he stood before the American people and said that the Bay of Pigs was an atrocity that never should have happened—then took full responsibility for it. When he did that, he was transformed from an able young politician to a real leader. Kennedy did what every great leader must. Those who take responsibility are empowered. Those who avoid it are disempowered.

The same principle of responsibility holds true on a personal level as well. Most of us have had the experience of trying to express a positive emotion to someone else. We try to tell them we love them, or that we understand a problem they're having. But instead of getting that positive message, they pick up a negative one instead. They get upset or hostile. Often our tendency is to get upset right back, to blame them, to hold them responsible for whatever ill will is generated. That's the easy way out, but not always the wisest. The fact is, your communication may have been the trigger. You can still produce the communication result you desire if you remember your outcome—the behavior you want to create. It's up to you to change your behavior, your tone of voice, your facial expressions, and so on. We say that the meaning of a communication is the response you get. By changing your actions, you can change your communication. By retaining responsibility, you retain the power to change the result you produce. Stop, take a deep breath, and try again to relay your true intention.

Belief No. 4: It's not necessary to understand everything to be able to use everything. Let me ask you a question. Can you explain how and why electricity works? Can you tell me with complete accuracy where it comes from, the different voltages and currents? Do you understand amperage and wattage as they pertain to specific demands and loads? For most of us the answer is a resounding NO! As a matter of fact, you'd find that only a minute fraction of the entire world population could answer those questions with any degree of accuracy. Yet every single one of us can go over to the wall and flick the light switch to get the result of electricity. We don't have to understand how it works to benefit from it.

This is a fact of life that most successful people understand. They don't believe they have to know everything about something in order to use it. They know how to use what's essential without feeling a need to get bogged down in every detail. If you study people who are in power, you'll find they have a working knowledge of a lot of things but often they have little mastery of each and every detail of their enterprise.

We talked in the first chapter about how modeling can save us one of our irreplaceable resources: time. By observing successful people to discover what specific actions they create to produce results, we are able to duplicate their actions—and thus their results—in much less time. Time is one of the things no one can create for you. But achievers invariably manage to be time misers. They extract the essence from a situation, use what they need, and don't dwell on the rest. Of course, if they're intrigued by something, if they want to understand how a motor works or how a product is manufactured, they take the extra time to learn. But they're always aware of what they need to produce the result; they always know what's essential and what's not.

You can spend all your time studying the roots, or you can learn to pick the fruit. Successful people aren't necessarily the ones with the most information or the most knowledge. There were probably plenty of scientists and engineers at Stanford and Cal Tech who knew more about computer circuitry than Steve Jobs or Steve Wozniak, but these two were more effective at using what they had. They were the ones who got results.

I remember reading in *Think and Grow Rich* many years ago about Henry Ford of Ford automobile fame. As it turns out, Mr. Ford scarcely had a grade-school education. When he was questioned by a reporter about his lack of book knowledge and how it handicapped him, he took the man into his office. There he showed him a brand-new invention. It had several buttons on it and resembled an early telephone. He told the reporter that he didn't have to know everything, because with this invention he had an army of people who either knew the answer or would go out and find it. Ford was able to spend his time on things that mattered more to him than trying to find answers. It's imperative to recognize that all great leaders and achievers—Black, white, and otherwise—understood that if they didn't know the answer to a particular problem, they would seek help. They knew where to go to get the answers.

Belief No. 5: People are your greatest resource. Back in the early 1970s when Black history started to become a real part of the educational system and I started to learn about people like W.E.B. Du Bois and George Washington Carver, I started to see that we, too, have a rich history full of role models and possibility thinkers. It wasn't until then that I started to have respect for my ancestors and the people around me. Upon closer observation, I realized that all leaders and achievers throughout time were people who loved people. Individuals of excellence—people who produce outstanding results—almost universally have a tremendous sense of respect and appreciation for humanity. They have a sense of team, a sense of common purpose and unity. If there's any insight at the heart of the new generation of business books such as *Success Runs in Our Race, The 7 Habits of Highly Effective People, Innovation and Entrepreneurship, In Search of Excellence,* or *The One Minute Manager,* it's that there's no long-lasting success without rapport among people, and that the way to succeed is to form a team that works together effectively. By now we've all heard about the efficiency of Japanese factories, where workers and management eat in the same cafeteria and both have input into evaluating performance. Their success reflects the wonders that can be achieved when we respect people rather than trying to manipulate them.

You think and achieve as a team, the individual accolades will take care of themselves. . . .
Talent wins games but teamwork and intelligence win champions.

—MICHAEL JORDAN

When Thomas J. Peters and Robert H. Waterman, Jr., authors of *In Search of Excellence,* distilled the factors that made companies great, one of the key things they found was a passionate attention to people. "There was hardly a more pervasive theme in excellent companies than respect for the individual," they wrote. The companies that succeeded were the ones that treated people with respect and dignity, the ones that viewed their employees as partners, not as tools. They note that in one study, eighteen out of twenty Hewlett-Packard executives interviewed said the company's success depended on HP's people-oriented philosophy. HP isn't a retailer dealing with the public, or a service company dependent on goodwill. It's dealing at the most complex frontiers of modern technology. But even there, it's clear that dealing effectively with people is seen as the preeminent challenge.

As you read this book, keep in mind the image of a pilot readjusting the trim on a plane to guide it safely to its glorious destination. It's the same with life. We have to remain alert constantly and recalibrate our actions to make sure we're going where we want to go. To say you treat people with respect and to do it are not the same thing. Those who succeed are the most effective in asking others, "How can we do this better?" "How can we fix this?" "How can we produce greater results?" They know that one person alone, no matter how brilliant, will find it very difficult to match the collaborative talents of an effective team.

In addition, we must respect ourselves as well. It starts with awareness of self-progress and acknowledgment of achievement. Often we look outside ourselves for those reassuring comments and rewards, but the fact of the matter is, it has to come from within if it is to do the most good.

Belief No. 6: Work is play. History has shown that the majority of people who achieve massive success love what they do. Think about it—can you name one who didn't have a passion for his or her work? One of the keys to success is making a successful marriage between what you do and what you love. Alex Haley once said, "When I write, I'm in love. There's nowhere else I'd rather be, nothing else I'd rather be doing."

Maybe we all don't write as well as Mr. Haley, but we can all do our best to find work that invigorates and excites us. It's no secret that people who hate their jobs rarely succeed. And we can bring to whatever we do at work many of the aspects of what we do at play. Mark Twain said, "The secret of success is making your vocation your vacation." That's what successful people seem to do.

We hear a lot about workaholics these days, and there are some people whose work has become something of an unhealthy obsession. They don't seem to get any pleasure out of their work, but they reach the point where they can't do anything else. We might assume that these people work so frantically because they are moving up the corporate ladder or are intent on some other goal they expect to give them pleasure.

On the other hand, researchers are finding surprising things about other workaholics who seem maniacally focused on work because they love it. It challenges them, it excites them, it makes their life richer. These people tend to look at work the way most of us look at play. They see it as a way to stretch themselves, to learn new things, to explore new avenues.

Are some jobs more conducive to this than others? Of course! The key is to work your way toward those jobs. If you can find creative ways to do your current job, it will help you move toward work that's even better.

We talked earlier about the synergistic nature of a coherent belief system, and how positive beliefs support other positive beliefs. As Tony would say, there aren't any dead-end jobs. There are only people who have lost the sense of possibility, people who have decided not to take responsibility, people who have decided to believe in failure. We're not saying you have to become a workaholic or that you should choose to orient your world around your work. But we are suggesting that you will enrich your work and your life if you bring to your job the same curiosity and vitality you bring to your play.

Most people don't have a clue about what they would rather be doing instead of the job they currently have. Let me ask *you* point-blank: If you knew you couldn't fail, what would you be doing for a living? What do you love? How could you incorporate it into something that brought you financial and emotional satisfaction? Most of us never take the time to think it through. Take out a piece of paper or your journal and jot down a few things. Let your imagination go. Have fun!

Belief No. 7: There's no abiding success without commitment. If there's a single belief that seems almost inseparable from success, it's that there's no great success without great commitment. If you look at the top achievers in any field, you'll find they're not necessarily the best and the brightest, the fastest and the strongest. You'll find they're the ones with the most commitment. The great Russian ballerina Anna Pavlova said, "To follow, without halt, one aim: there's the secret of success." It's just another way of stating our Ultimate Success Formula: Know your outcome, take massive action, develop the sensory acuity to know what you're getting, and keep refining it until you get what you want.

We see this in any field, even those where natural ability would seem to have the strongest influence. Take sports. What made Larry Bird one of the best players in basketball? A lot of people are still wondering. He was slow. He couldn't jump. In a world of graceful gazelles, he sometimes looked like he was playing in slow motion. But when you came right down to it, Larry Bird succeeded because he had a massive commitment to success. He practiced harder, he had more mental toughness, he played harder, he wanted it more. He got more out of his skills than almost anyone else. Jackie Robinson made his way into the record books the same way, by consistently using his commitment to excellence as a force driving him to put everything he had into everything he did.

Commitment is an important component of success in any field. Before he hit the big time, Dan Rather was a legend as the hardest-working television newsman in Houston. They still talk about the time he did a spot hanging on to a tree as a hurricane roared toward the Texas coast. I heard someone talking about Michael Jackson the other day, saying that Jackson was an overnight wonder. Overnight wonder? Does Michael Jackson have great talent? Sure he does. And he's been working at it since he was five years old. He's been an entertainer since then, practicing his singing, perfecting his dancing, writing his songs. Sure, he had some natural talent. He was also brought up in an environment that supported his career; he developed belief systems that nurtured him; he had many successful models available to him; he had a family that guided him. Yet the bottom line was that he was willing to pay the price. Tony and I like to use the term WIT—Whatever It Takes. Successful people are willing to do whatever it takes to succeed. (Of course, it should go without saying that you do whatever it takes to succeed without harming another person.) That, as much as anything else, is what separates them from the pack.

Are there other beliefs that foster excellence? Sure there are. When you think of them, so much the better. Throughout this book, you should be aware of additional distinctions or insights that you can add. Remember, success leaves clues. Study those who succeed. Find out the key beliefs that enhance their ability to take effective action consistently and produce outstanding results. These seven beliefs have done wonders for others before you, and we believe they can do wonders for you if you commit yourself to them consistently.

I can almost hear some of you thinking, *Well, that's a big if. What if you have beliefs that don't support you? What if your beliefs are negative, not positive? How do we change beliefs?* You've already taken the first step, awareness. You know what you want. The second step is action—learning to control your internal representations and beliefs, how to run your brain.

So far we've begun to put together the pieces that I believe lead to excellence. We started with the idea that information is the commodity of kings, and master communicators are those who know what they want and who take effective actions, varying their behavior until they achieve their outcomes. In Chapter 4, we learned that the pathway to excellence is through modeling. If you can find people who have created massive success, you can model the specific actions they consistently take that produce results—their beliefs, mental syntax, and physiology—so you can produce similar results in a shorter learning time. In Chapter 5, we talked about the power of state. We've seen how powerful, resourceful, and effective behavior can change your neurophysiological state. In Chapter 6 we learned about the nature of belief, how empowering beliefs unlock the door to excellence. In this chapter, we've explored seven beliefs that are the cornerstones of excellence.

In the next chapter you will learn some powerful techniques that can help you make use of what you've learned and that will affect your life on a much more personal level. It's time for . . .

CHAPTER EIGHT

Mastering Your Mind: How to Run Your Brain

> *It is impossible to raise and educate a race in the mass. All revolutions and improvements must start with individuals.*
>
> —John W. E. Bowen

Now it's time to have some fun with the person you know best: you! This chapter is about active solutions. You're about to learn how to change your states so you can produce whatever you want, when you want it. You see, people don't usually lack resources; they lack control over the resources they have. In this chapter you will learn how to be in control, how to instantly change your states of mind, which will in turn change your actions and ultimately the results you get. Like the ripples caused by the stone tossed into a still pond, the changes you make now will affect your entire life and assist you in not only picking the fruits of your desire but in also squeezing every last drop of nectar out of it.

The systems of change Tony and I teach are very different from the ones used in many schools of therapy. A large number of therapists believe that in order to change, you have to go back to deep-seated negative experiences and experience them again. The idea is that people have negative experiences in life that build up inside them like steam, until finally the pressure gets too great and they burst or overflow. The only way to get in touch with this process, the therapists say, is to reexperience the events and pain all over again, then to try to let it go once and for all.

To be flat honest with you, our experience tells us that's one of the least effective ways to help people overcome their challenges. When you ask people to go back and reexperience some terrible trauma, you're putting them into the most painful, least resourceful state possible. If you put someone in an unresourceful state, the chances of producing new resourceful behaviors and results are greatly diminished. In fact, this approach may even reinforce the painful or unresourceful pattern. By continually accessing neurological states of limitation and pain, it becomes much easier to trigger these states in the future. The more you relive an experience, the more likely you are to use it again. Maybe that's why so many traditional therapies take so long to produce results.

Now, please don't misunderstand. Traditional therapy does produce results. I have several friends who are traditional therapists. My initial education was in traditional therapy. I believe all therapists sincerely care about helping their patients. However, the question is, Could these results be produced with less pain for the patient, and in a shorter period of time? The answer is yes—if we model the actions of the most effective therapists in the world, which is exactly what Bandler and Grinder, the fathers of NLP, did. In fact, by mastering a simple understanding of how your brain works, you can become your own therapist, your own personal consultant. You can go beyond therapy and change any feeling, emotion, or behavior for yourself in a matter of moments.

Producing more effective results begins with creating a new model for the process of change. If you believe your problems store up inside you until they overflow, that's exactly what you'll experience. Instead of all that pain building up like some sort of toxic gas, imagine your neurological activity to be more like a CD player. Human beings have experiences that are recorded, and we store them in the brain like tracks on a CD. Our recordings can be played back at any time if the right stimulus in our environment is present—if the right button is pushed. Depending on which recordings are selected, we will feel and act accordingly.

So we can choose to remember experiences—"songs"—of joy and love or push buttons that create pain. If your therapist continues to push the buttons of disempowerment over and over again, you may be reinforcing the very negative state you wish to change. We may be forgetting that we all have multitudes of great recordings available, too.

Let's consider a different approach. What if you could simply program your CD player so it plays a completely different song? You hit the same button, but instead of playing a sad song, it brings up an ecstatic one instead. Or else you could rerecord the disc—you could take the old memories and change them. The point is, selections that aren't being played won't build up and explode. That's absurd. And just as it's a simple procedure to reprogram a CD player, it's easy to change the ways we produce unresourceful feelings and emotions. Think about it; we don't have to experience all that remembered pain to change our state. All we have to do is change the negative internal representation to a positive one that is automatically triggered and causes us to produce more effective results. We have to rev up the circuits of ecstasy and turn off the juice to the circuits of pain.

Optimum Performance Technologies look at the structure of human experience, not the content. While we are sympathetic to pain from a personal point of view, when we're helping you to create change we couldn't care less about what happened in your past. What we *do* care very much about is how you put together in your mind what happened. How do you personally produce the state of depression or the state of ecstasy? The main difference is the way you structure your internal representations.

A mind is a terrible thing to waste.

—UNITED NEGRO COLLEGE FUND

Remember, all human beings construct internal representations through five senses—sight, sound, touch, taste, and smell. So whatever experiences we have stored in the mind are represented through these senses, primarily through the three major modalities: visual, auditory, or kinesthetic.

Our five senses or representational systems are the ingredients from which we can build any experience or result. If anyone is able to produce a particular result, that result is created by specific actions, both mental and physical. Remember the modeling process? If you duplicate the exact same actions, you can duplicate the results that person produces. In order to produce a result, you must know what ingredients are necessary. However, it's not enough just to know what ingredients are needed. If you want to produce the exact result, you must know exactly how much of each ingredient is needed. Too much or too little of any particular ingredient will not produce the kind and quality of the desired result.

Humans wanting to make a change usually want to change one or both of two things: how they feel (state) or how they behave (the actions they take). For example, a chain smoker often wants to change how he physically and emotionally feels (nervous, anxious, restless) and also his behavioral pattern of reaching for cigarette after cigarette. In the chapter on the power of state, we made it clear that there are two ways to change people's states and thus their behaviors—either to change their physiology, which will change how they feel and the kind of behavior they produce, or to change their internal representations. Now we will learn how to specifically change the way we represent (think) of things so that they empower us to feel and to produce the kind of behavior that supports us in the achievement of our goals. It's much easier than you may think. As a matter of fact, we use the same procedure to install negative states and behavior, so we might as well use it for the better.

Even though we are all unique, there are two things we all can change about our internal representations. 1) We can change *what* we represent. For example, if we imagine the worst possible scenario, we can change to picturing the best possible scenario. Or 2) we can change *how* we represent something. Once we discover the different ways we represent things and how they affect us, we can take charge of our own mind and begin to represent things in a way that empowers rather than limits us. Think of it as discovering the operating manual for your brain.

When we find a result that someone else is producing, we need to know more than just how they picture or speak to themselves. We need sharper tools to really access what's going on in the mind. That's where *submodalities* come in. They are like the precise amounts of each ingredient required to create a result. To be able to understand and thus control a visual experience, we need to know more about it. We need to know if it's bright or dark, in black and white or in color, moving or stationary. In the same way, we'd want to know if an auditory communication is loud or quiet, near or far, resonant or tinny. We'd want to know if a kinesthetic experience is soft or hard, sharp or smooth, flexible or stiff. I've made a list of submodalities below.

Checklist of Possible Submodalities

Visual:

1. Movie or still frame
2. Panorama or framed (if framed, the shape of frame)
3. Color or black and white
4. Brightness
5. Size of picture (life-size, larger, or smaller)
6. Size of central object(s)
7. Self in or out of picture
8. Distance of picture from self
9. Distance of central object from self
10. 3-D quality
11. Intensity of color (or black and white)
12. Degree of contrast
13. Movement (if so, fast or slow tempo)
14. Focus (which parts—in or out)
15. Intermittent or steady focus
16. Angle viewed from
17. Number of pictures (shifts)
18. Location
19. Other

Auditory:

1. Volume
2. Cadence (interruptions, groupings)
3. Rhythm (regular, irregular)
4. Inflection (words marked out, how)
5. Tempo
6. Pauses
7. Tonality
8. Timbre (quality, where resonating from)

9. Uniqueness of sound (gravelly, smooth, and so on)
10. Movement of sound spatially
11. Location
12. Other

Kinesthetic:

1. Temperature
2. Texture
3. Vibration
4. Pressure
5. Movement
6. Duration
7. Steady—Intermittent
8. Intensity
9. Weight
10. Density
11. Location
12. Other

For Pain:

1. Tingling
2. Hot—Cold
3. Muscle tension
4. Sharp—Dull
5. Pressure
6. Duration
7. Intermittent (such as throbbing)
8. Location
9. Other

Another important distinction is whether an image is associated or disassociated. An associated image is one you experience as if you were really there. You see it through your own eyes, hear and feel as if you were actually at that time and place in your own body. A disassociated image is one you experience as if you were watching it from outside yourself. If you see a disassociated image of yourself, it's like watching a movie of yourself doing something.

Take a minute to remember a recent pleasant experience you've had. Perhaps you hugged someone you love or saw a great movie. Experience it as though you were there right now. See what you saw through your own eyes: the events, images, colors, brightness, and so on. Hear what you heard: the voices, sounds, and so on. Feel what you felt: emotions, temperature, and so on. Experience what that's like.

Go on, try it now. Put down the book and try it . . .

Now try this. See and feel yourself stepping away from the situation. Watch yourself having the experience from a distance of forty feet away.

What's the difference in your feelings? In which case were the feelings more intense, the first example or the second? The difference between these is the difference between an associated experience and a disassociated experience. In one you're in it, in the other you're watching it.

By using submodality distinctions like association versus disassociation, you can radically change your experience of life. We can do this in an instant, anywhere, anytime. Remember, we've learned that all human behavior is the result of the state we're in, and that our states are created by our internal representations—the things we picture, say to ourselves, and so on. Just as a filmmaker can change the effect his or her movie has on an audience, you can change the effect any experience in life has upon you. A filmmaker can change the camera angle, the volume and type of music, the speed and amount of movement, the color and quality of the image, and thus create any state he or she wants in the audience. You can direct your brain in the same way to generate any state or behavior that supports your highest goals or needs. Stop for a moment and think of the possibilities!

Use Submodalities to Change How You Feel About Anything

It's very important that you do the following exercises, so you might want to read each one through, then stop and actually do it before reading on. This is your first action step toward taking control of your life. Also, it might be fun to do the exercises with someone else. Take turns giving and receiving the cues.

1. Once again, think of a very pleasant memory. It doesn't matter whether it was recent or long ago. Just close your eyes, relax, and think of it.
2. Now take that image and make it brighter and brighter. As the image brightens, be aware of how your state changes.
3. Next, bring your mental picture closer to you.
4. Now stop, and make it bigger.

What happened when you manipulated the image? It changed the intensity of the experience, didn't it? For the vast majority of people, making an already pleasant memory bigger, brighter, and closer creates an even more powerful and pleasant image. It puts you in a much more intense state of mind.

Many people access their brain primarily in a visual framework. They react to the pictures they see in their heads. Others are primarily auditory, and still others are kinesthetic—these people react most strongly to what they hear or feel. We all have access to all three but most of us rely on one primary submodality. So after you've varied the visual frames, let's try the same thing with the other two representational systems.

Bring back the pleasant memory we've worked with so far. Now increase the volume of the voices or sounds you hear. Give them more rhythm, more bass, a change in timbre. Make them stronger and more affirmative. Now do the same with the kinesthetic submodalities. Make the memory warmer and softer and smoother than it was before. What happens to your feelings about the experience now?

Not all people respond in the same ways. Kinesthetic cues in particular elicit different responses in different people. You probably found that making the image brighter or larger enhanced it. It gave the internal representation more intensity, made it more appealing, and, most important, it put you in a more positive, resourceful state. Whenever I do these exercises in counseling sessions, I can see exactly what's happening in a person's mind just by watching their physiology. The breathing gets deeper, the shoulders straighten, the face relaxes, and the whole body seems more alert. It's quite interesting to observe.

Now, let's try the same thing with a negative image. I want you to think of something that upset you and caused you pain. Take that image and make it brighter. Bring it closer to you. Make it bigger. What's going on in your brain? What happens to your breathing? (Most people find that the negative state has intensified. The bad feelings they felt before are more powerful than ever.) Now put the image back where it was. What happens if you make it smaller and dimmer and farther away? Try it, and note the difference in your feelings. You'll discover that the negative feelings have lost their power.

Now try the same thing with the other modalities. Hear your own internal voice, or whatever's going on in the experience, in a loud, staccato tone. Feel the experience as hard and firm. Chances are the same thing will happen—the negative feeling will be intensified. It's important that you experience and understand this on an emotional as well as intellectual level. Pay close attention to what happens to you personally. Let's find out how you tick. I want you to do these exercises in a focused, intense way, being careful to note which modalities and submodalities have the most power for you. You might want to run through these steps again in your mind, being aware of how the manipulation of the image changes your feelings about it. Take the time to do this and you will find one of the keys to how and why you function the way you do.

Now take the negative image you began with and make it smaller. Be aware of what happens as the image shrinks. Now defocus it—make it fuzzier, dimmer, and harder to see. Now move it away from you—push it back so you can barely see it. Finally, take the image and push it far away—all the way to an imaginary sun. Notice what you hear and see and feel as it disappears from the world.

Do the same thing with the auditory modality. Bring down the volume of the voices you hear. Make them more lethargic. Take away their rhythm and snap. Do the same thing with your kinesthetic perceptions. Make the image feel wispy and insubstantial. What happens to the negative image when you go through this process? If you're like most people, the image loses its power—it becomes less potent, less painful, or even nonexistent. You can take something that has caused great pain in the past and make it impotent, let it dissolve and disappear completely.

By now you can probably see from this brief experience just how powerful this technology can be. And this is just the tip of the iceberg. In just a few minutes, you've taken a positive feeling and made it stronger and more empowering. You've also been able to take a powerful negative image and strip it of its power over you. In the past, you've been at the mercy of the results of your internal representations. Now you should know that things don't have to work that way. How can you use this tool in your life?

You can live your life one of two ways. You can let your brain run you the way it has in the past. You can let it flash the same old pictures, sounds and feelings it has in the past, and you can respond automatically on cue, like Pavlov's dog reacting to the bell. *Or you can choose to consciously run your brain yourself.* You can take bad experiences and images and sap them of their power. You can represent them to yourself in a way that no longer overpowers you, a way that cuts them down to a size you know you can effectively handle.

Every single one of us has experienced insecurity about something. Perhaps it was a job or a task that seemed too big or too difficult. We didn't feel like we'd ever get done, so we didn't even begin. If you imagine that task as being a small picture, you'll feel like you can handle it, and you'll take the appropriate action instead of being overwhelmed. At this point, all this may sound too simple to you, but when you try it, you'll discover that changing your representations can change how you feel about a task, and in turn, change your actions.

Also, here's an added attraction. You can take good experiences and enhance them! You can take the little joys of life and make them bigger, brighten up your vision of the day, and feel yourself become lighter and happier. This is a way to create more juice, more joy, more flavor in your life. Remember in the second chapter we talked about the commodity of kings? The king had the ability to direct his kingdom. Well, your kingdom is your brain. Just as the king can run his kingdom, you can run yours—if you begin to take control of how you represent your experience of life.

There does not have to be powerlessness. The power is within ourselves.

—FAYE WATTLETON

Our language gives us many examples of the power of our representations. What do we mean when we say that a person has a bright future? How do you feel when a person says the future looks dim? What are you saying when you talk about shedding light on a subject? What do we mean when we say someone blew something out of proportion or has a distorted image of something? What do people mean when they say something weighs heavily on their mind or they feel they have a mental block? What do you mean when you say that something sounds about right or rings a bell, or that everything clicked?

We tend to assume those phrases are just metaphors. They're not. They're often very precise descriptions of what's going on inside the mind. Think back to a few minutes ago when you took an unpleasant memory and enlarged it. Remember how it accentuated the negative aspects of the experience and put you in a negative state? Can you find a better way to describe that experience than to say you blew it out of proportion? So we *instinctively* know how powerful our mental images are—we just need to turn that intuition into a tool for taking control of our lives.

Here's a simple exercise that has helped many people. Have you ever had times when your brain just wouldn't shut up? I call it the internal dialogue from hell. Sometimes our brains just keep chattering the same thing over and over again. We debate points with ourselves or try to win old arguments or settle old scores. Try this: The next time it happens to you, just turn down the volume. Make the voice in your head softer, farther away, and weaker. That takes care of the problem most of the time. Or do you have one of those internal dialogues that's always limiting you or doubting you? Try this: Hear it say the same things, only in a sexy voice, with an almost flirtatious tone and tempo—"You can't do that." How does it feel now? You may feel that you're even more motivated to do what the voice is telling you not to. Try it now and experience the difference.

Let's try another exercise. This time, think of something you have been totally motivated to do. Something pleasurable, like going to the movies, or playing a sport, or taking a special trip—anything you looked forward to doing. Now, relax and form as clear a mental picture of that experience as possible. I'm going to ask you some questions about it. Pause and answer each question one by one. Remember, there are no right or wrong answers. You might want to jot down your responses so you can review them later.

While you are looking at the image, is it moving or is it still? Is it in color or black and white? Is it close or far away? Is it to the left, to the right, or in the center? Is it high, low, or in the middle of your field of vision? Is it associated—do you see it through your own eyes?—or is it disassociated—are you watching it as it happens? Does it have a frame around it, or do you see a panorama that goes on forever? Is it bright or dim, dark or light? Is it focused or unfocused? As you do this exercise, be sure to note which submodalities are the strongest for you, which ones have the most power when you focus on them. As you notice these things, also notice your emotions as you discover them.

Now run through your auditory and kinesthetic submodalities in this motivated situation. When you hear what's going on, do you hear your own voice, or do you hear the voices of others in the scene? Are the sounds you hear loud or quiet? Do they have varied inflections, or are they a monotone? Are they rhythmic or staccato? Is the tempo slow or rapid? Do the sounds come and go, or are they steady? What's the main thing you're hearing or saying to yourself? Where is the sound coming from? When you feel it, is it hard or soft? Warm or cool? Rough or smooth? Flexible or rigid? A solid or a liquid? Sharp or dull? Where is the feeling located in your body? Is it sour or sweet?

Please take the time to do this exercise. Some of those questions may seem difficult to answer at first, but I hope you'll stick with it. If you have a tendency to form your internal representations primarily as feelings, you may have thought you don't make pictures. But as you become more aware of your own modalities, you'll learn to improve your perceptions as time goes on. So you might first remember what you were feeling at that time. Once you're in that state and you have a rich, powerful internal representation, it's much easier to ease into a visual frame to work on visual submodalities or into an auditory frame to experience auditory submodalities. This process is called *overlap*.

Now that you've seen and experienced the structure of something you were once strongly motivated to do, I want you to think of something you would *like* to be strongly motivated to do that at present you have no special feeling for, like doing laundry or paying bills. Once again, form a mental image. Now run through the exact same questions, carefully noting how your responses differ from those you had for the thing you were strongly motivated to do. As you do this, be sure to note which submodalities are strongest and have the most power to affect your state.

Now take the thing you were motivated by—let's call it experience No. 1—and the thing you want to be motivated by—experience No. 2—and compare them side by side. There are differences in the submodalities, aren't there? We can predict this, of course, because *different representations produce different types of results in the nervous system*. Now take what you've learned about which submodalities motivate you and then, bit by bit, readjust the submodalities of experience No. 2 so that they match those of experience No. 1. Again, these will be different for different people, but chances are the image of experience No. 1 will be brighter than that of experience No. 2. I want you to concentrate on the differences, and manipulate the second representation so it becomes more and more like the first one. If the picture is dull in the second experience, then focus it and make it sharp and clear. Remember to do the same with the auditory and kinesthetic representations as well. Do this now.

Now, how do you feel about experience No. 2? Are you more motivated? You should be, if you matched the submodalities of experience No. 2 with those of No. 1. (For example, if experience No. 1 was a movie and experience No. 2 was a still frame, you made experience No. 2 into a movie.) Continue the process with all the visual, auditory, and kinesthetic submodalities. When you find the specific triggers (submodalities) that cause you to go into a desirable state, then you can link these triggers to undesirable states and thereby change them in a moment.

Remember, similar internal representations will create similar states or feelings. And similar feelings or states will trigger similar actions. Also, if you find out what specifically makes you feel motivated to do just about anything, you then know exactly what you have to do with any experience to make yourself feel motivated. From that motivated state, you can get yourself to take effective action.

We're always curious about how someone is able to produce any result, mental or physical. For example, people will come to me for counseling and say, "I'm so depressed." We don't ask, "Why are you depressed?" This is asking them to represent to themselves and me why they are feeling bad, and that would just put them into a depressed state. We don't want to know why they're depressed; we want to know *how* they're depressed. We'll ask instead, "How do you do that?" Usually I get a startled look, because the person doesn't realize that you have to do certain things in your mind and physiology to get depressed. So I'll ask, "If I were in your body, how would I get depressed? What would I picture? What would I say to myself? How would I say it? What tonality would I use?" These processes create specific mental and physical actions, and thus specific emotional results. Once we know the process, we can show them how to change the structure of the process to get a better result.

Many of us still harbor feelings of inadequacy and insignificance about our color and our past. These feelings can stifle even the strongest of souls. What if we were to take all those things we were hesitant to do in the past and attach to them the submodalities of pleasure and pride? Remember, few things have any inherent feeling. You've learned what is pleasurable, and you've learned what is uncomfortable. You can simply relabel these experiences in your brain and immediately create a new feeling about them. What if you took all your problems, shrank them down, and put a little distance between them and you? The possibilities are endless. You really are the captain of your own ship in this life.

Something very important to remember is that repetition is the mother of skill. The more you practice anything, the easier it is to use it. The more often you consciously trigger these simple submodality shifts, the better you'll become at quickly producing the result you want. Find what works best for you. You may find that changing the brightness or dimness of an image has a stronger effect on you than changing its location or size. Once you know this, you'll know that brightness should be one of the first things to manipulate when you want to change something.

BANISH BAD PATTERNS FOREVER

Now at this point you may be thinking, *These submodality changes are great, but what's going to keep them from changing back? I know I can change how I feel at the moment, and that's valuable, but it would be great if I had a way to make change more automatic, more consistent.*

Good thing you asked. You're about to learn another process to do just that—the *swish pattern*. It can be used to deal with some of the most persistent problems and bad habits people have. It's quick, it's easy, and it's fun. A swish pattern takes existing internal representations that normally produce unresourceful states, and causes them instead to automatically trigger the new resourceful states you desire. When you find out what internal representations make you feel like overeating, for example, with the swish pattern you can create a new internal representation of something more powerful that would cause you, if you saw or heard it, to push food away. If you link the two representations, whenever you think of overeating the first representation will instantly trigger the second and put you in a state of not desiring food. The best part of the swish pattern is that once you implant it effectively, you don't ever have to think of it again. The process will happen automatically, without any conscious effort. Here's how the swish pattern works. Try it and have fun with it.

Step No. 1: Identify the behavior you want to change. Now make an internal representation of that behavior as you see it through your own eyes. If you want to stop biting your fingernails, imagine a picture of you lifting your hand, bringing your fingers to your lips, and biting your nails.

Step No. 2: Once you have a clear picture of the behavior you want to change, you need to create a different representation, a picture of yourself as you would be if you made the desired change and what that change would mean to you. You might picture yourself taking your fingers away from your mouth, creating a little pressure on the finger you were going to bite, and seeing your nails perfectly manicured and yourself as well dressed, magnificently groomed, more in control, and more confident. The picture you make of yourself in that desired state should be disassociated. The reason for this is that we want to create an ideal internal representation, one that you will continue to be drawn to rather than one you feel you already have.

Step No. 3: "Swish" the two pictures so that the unresourceful experience automatically triggers the resourceful experience. Once you hook up this triggering mechanism, anything that used to trigger biting your nails will now trigger you into a state where you are moving toward that ideal picture of yourself. Thus, you're creating a whole new way for your brain to deal with the old triggers.

Here's how to do the swish: Start by making a big bright picture of the behavior you want to change. Then, in the bottom right-hand corner of that picture, make a small, dark picture of the way you want to be. Now take that small picture, and in less than one second have it grow in size and brightness until it literally bursts through the picture of the behavior you no longer desire. As you do this process, say the word "wooosh" with all the excitement and enthusiasm you can. I realize this may sound a bit juvenile. However, saying "wooosh" in an excited way sends a series of powerful, positive signals to your brain. Once you've set up the pictures in your mind, this whole process should only take about as long as it takes to say "wooosh." When you're done, in front of you should be a big, bright, focused, colorful picture of how you want to be. The old picture of how you were has been smashed to smithereens.

The key to this pattern is speed and repetition. You must see and feel that small dark picture become huge and bright and explode through the big picture, destroying it and replacing it with an even bigger, brighter picture of how you want things to be. Take a moment to experience the great feeling of seeing things the way you want them. Then open your eyes for a split second to break the state, and when you close your eyes again, do the swish once more. Start by seeing the thing you want to change as large, then have your small picture grow in size and brightness and explode through. Whoosh! Pause to experience it. Open your eyes. Close your eyes. See what you want to change. See the original picture and how you want to change it. Whoosh it again. Do this five or six times, as fast as you can. Remember, the key to this is speed; and to have fun doing it. What you are telling your brain is, "Do this, see this, 'Whoosh!' Do this, see this, 'Whoosh!' Do this, see this, 'Whoosh!' Do this . . ." until the old picture automatically triggers the new picture, the new states, and thus the new behavior.

Now make the first picture, and what happens? If, for example, you swished a pattern of biting your fingernails, then when you imagine yourself biting them, you would find it hard to do. It actually would feel unnatural. If not, you would run the pattern again. This time, you would do it more clearly and more rapidly, being certain to experience only for a moment the positive feeling you get from the new picture before opening your eyes and beginning the process again. It may not work if the picture you choose to move toward isn't exciting or desirous enough. It's very important that it be extremely attractive—something that puts you in a motivated or desirous state, something that is more important to you than the old behavior. Sometimes it helps to add new submodalities, like smell or taste. The swish pattern produces results amazingly quickly because the brain tends to move away from unpleasant things and toward pleasant ones. By making the picture of no longer needing to bite your fingernails much more appealing than the picture of biting them, you've given your brain a powerful signal about which kind of behavior to move toward.

You can also do this with fears or frustrations. Take something you're afraid to do. Now picture it working out the way you want it to, and make this picture really exciting. Now swish the two of them seven times. Think of the thing you feared. How does it make you feel now? If the swish pattern has been done effectively, the moment you think of the thing you feared, you should automatically switch to thinking of how you want it to be.

Another variation of the swish pattern is to imagine a slingshot in front of you. Between the two posts is a picture of the present behavior you want to change. Place a small picture of how you want to be in the sling. Then mentally watch this little picture being pulled farther and farther away from you until the sling is stretched as far as possible. Then let it go, and watch as it explodes forward, right through the old picture in front of you, into your brain. It's important that when you do this, you mentally pull the sling all the way back before letting it go. You still "wooosh" as you release it and break through the old limiting picture of yourself. If you've done this correctly, when you let go of the sling the picture should come at you so fast that your head actually snaps back. Stop right now and take a moment to think of some limiting thought or behavior you would like to change, and use this slingshot/swish pattern to change it.

Remember that your mind can defy the laws of the universe in one crucial way. It can go backward. Time can't, nor can events—but your mind can. Let's say you go into your office, and the first thing you notice is that an important report you needed was not written. The incomplete report tends to put you in a less-than-resourceful state. You feel mad. You feel frustrated. You're ready to go out and scream at someone. But screaming won't produce the result you want. It will only make a bad situation worse. The key is to change your state to one that will allow you to get things done. That's what you can do by rearranging your internal representations.

In just the few exercises we've done so far, you've seen that you have the ability to totally control your own state. How would your life be if you remembered all your good experiences as bright, close, and colorful; joyous, rhythmic, and melodic; feeling soft, warm, and nurturing? And what if you stored your bad experiences as fuzzy little still-frame images with almost inaudible voices and insubstantial forms you could not feel because they were far away from you? Most successful people do this unconsciously. They know how to turn up the volume of the things that help them and turn off the sound of the things that don't. What you've learned in this chapter is how to model them.

Not everything can be solved by these processes, but it's a great start. And I'm certainly not suggesting that you ignore problems. Some things need to be addressed. Yet it's important for us to remember to constantly assess the consequences of our communication, and ask ourselves regularly, "If I continue to represent things to myself this way, what will likely be the final result in my life? What direction is my present behavior taking me, and is that where I want to go?" Now is the time to examine what our mental and physical actions are creating. Too many of us can look back and wish we had done things even just a little bit differently. Most of the time those little things are simply the way that we communicated with ourselves.

Something else that might be very important to note is that most of us have a particular pattern of associating and disassociating. There are definite advantages and disadvantages to both sides. Many people spend most of their time disassociated from their representations. They rarely seem to be emotionally moved by anything. Disassociation has one advantage; if you keep out of deep emotions about some things, you can have more resources to handle them. Here in America and around the world, it seems that we must disassociate from all the prejudice and racial injustice that go on around us. However, if this is your consistent pattern of representing most of your experiences in life, you're really missing out on that spark that life has to offer. To me, life is all about experiencing the joy and excitement that abounds all around us. If we are disassociated all the time, we are missing a great deal of life's gifts. It bothers me to see so many of our young Black children caught up in the perception that being cool is the way to go through life. Coolness to me is just another way of disassociating from the emotions of life and not dealing with reality.

On the other hand, if the majority of your internal representations are fully associated, you may find yourself an emotional mess. You may have great difficulty coping with life because you feel every little thing. We all know someone who becomes an emotional wreck over the slightest things. A person who is fully associated with everything in life is extremely vulnerable and will usually take things too personally.

Balance is the name of the game. The trick is to get in the habit of consciously choosing whether or not we are associated or disassociated. Remember, we can, in the moment, associate to, or disassociate from, anything we want.

What we're really doing as we work with submodalities is relabeling the stimulus system that tells the brain how to feel about an experience. Your brain responds to whatever signals (submodalities) you give it. If you provide signals of one type, the brain will feel pain. If you provide different submodalities, you can feel fine in a matter of moments. For example: I once had a young medical student come to me in a panic about his difficulty in taking tests. He was a very bright young Black man with a very sharp wit but he doubted whether he could get through medical school because he didn't test well. He was on the verge of dropping out of college because of his fears. He told me he couldn't even study for tests because his mind would go crazy with thoughts of failure, anxiety attacks, and issues of self-worth. I asked him to describe what happened when he thought about taking a test. Through tears, he told me that he saw himself alone in a dark, cold room with no windows, and no sounds except the crackling of the brittle paper his test was printed on, and his mother's voice telling him he can't succeed. The picture was always to his lower left and was almost a still frame. I wrote all of this down and then had him imagine everything in the opposite. The room was filled with light and sound. It was warm, and his other classmates were taking the test right alongside him. The paper that he was to be tested on was now soft and pliable, and the whole scene was in color and in motion. He laughed out loud when he changed the tone of his mother's voice to that of Minnie Mouse on helium. After switching all this he began to feel more confident—in a matter of ten or fifteen minutes. Then we did a series of intense swish patterns. He left my office confident and eager to take his next test. Today this talented doctor holds an internship in a Washington, D.C., hospital, with a promising career ahead of him.

Often when I tell people about this process, they have great difficulty believing that this can be done so quickly and so easily. But isn't that what we all do in the end anyway? Think about it. Perhaps it was when we took a driver's test or asked someone for a date, or had a job interview, or whatever. Isn't it true that somewhere along the line, when we finally gather our courage and do it, we change submodalities and see, hear, and feel ourselves succeeding—even if it is just for the instant that it takes to make the first move? In fact, once you learn the signals that produce specific results in your brain, you can cause yourself to feel however you'd like to feel about virtually anything.

ONE FINAL CAVEAT . . .

There is a larger set of filters of human experience that can govern or affect your ability to maintain new internal representations—or even to make the changes in the first place. Those filters concern what we value most and what unconscious benefits we may be receiving from our present behavior (we'll discuss unconscious secondary gain in Chapter 18, on the process of reframing). If pain is sending you important signals about something you need to change in your body, then unless you address that need, the pain will most likely come back because it is serving you in an important way.

You've learned a lot in this chapter. Not only can you enhance the quality of your life but you can also assist others to do the same. Now it's time to take a look at another way we humans experience life and how we can utilize it for the better. Let's examine . . .

CHAPTER NINE

The Syntax of Success

Let all things be done decently and in order.

—I CORINTHIANS 14:40

THROUGHOUT THIS BOOK, we've talked about why human beings do what they do; what causes us to take action or pull back. We've learned how to use this information to get ourselves to produce the results we really want for our lives. And perhaps most important, we've learned that regardless of color, gender or background, we all have the same type of nervous system. And it's only through our conditioning—through our habitual thoughts and actions—that we train ourselves to either succeed or fail. We've shown that people who are able to produce outstanding results consistently take a set of specific actions, both mental (what they consistently do in their minds) and physical (what they consistently do in the world). Through the process of modeling we've learned that if we take the same actions in the same way, we can create the same (or very similar) results as virtually anyone else in the world.

Now, let's fine-tune the process. There is another important factor that affects our ability to produce the results we want. It's called the syntax of action. Syntax simply means the order in which things are done. The syntax—the way we order our actions—can and will make a major difference in the kind of results we get.

What's the difference between "The dog bit Calvin" and "Calvin bit the dog?" What's the difference between "Ellen ate the lobster" and "The lobster ate Ellen"? There's a huge difference, especially if you're Ellen or Calvin. The words are exactly the same.

The difference is syntax, the way they're arranged. I know this sounds elementary, but it is critical to understand if we are to effectively model the results of successful people. The meaning of the experience is determined by the order of the signals provided to the brain. The same stimuli are involved, the same words, yet the meaning is different. The order in which things are presented causes them to register in the brain in a specific way. It's like the digits of your phone number. There are perhaps hundreds of thousands of different combinations in which the same seven numbers can be arranged, but only the exact right sequence will produce the result you want. Again, if you press the correct numbers in a different order, you will not get your outcome.

We'll use the word *strategy* to describe all these factors—the kinds of internal representations, the necessary submodalities, and the required syntax—that work together to create a particular result.

Without a doubt, we have a strategy for producing just about anything in life: the feeling of love, attraction, motivation, decision, whatever. If we discover what our strategy for love is, for example, we can trigger that state at will. If we discover what actions we take, in what order, to make a decision, then whenever we're indecisive we can become decisive in a matter of moments. We will know which keys to hit and how to produce the results we want in our internal biocomputer.

Here's an example of how strategies work. If someone makes the greatest chocolate cake in the world, could you bake a cake of the same quality? Of course you can, if you have that person's recipe and are willing to follow it. A recipe is nothing but a strategy, a specific plan of what resources to use and how to use them to produce a specific result. If you believe we all have the same neurology, then you believe we all have the same potential resources available to us. It is our strategy—that is, how we use those resources—that determines the results we produce. This is the law of business as well. One company may have superior resources, but the company with strategies that best use its resources will usually dominate the marketplace.

Remember Wally "Famous" Amos? He created one of the greatest chocolate chip cookie sensations in the world. How did he do it? Thousands of people have had great recipes for chocolate chip cookies, but Wally Amos became a success because he developed a unique strategy. He didn't have money, he didn't have resources; as a matter of fact he was at the end of his rope after his talent agent business hit the skids. Depressed and down on his luck, Wally developed a plan and a strategy for doing one of the things that he loved doing: baking cookies. When he was a young boy, Wally's aunt had given him her recipe for cookies and taught him how to bake. So, refusing to give up, Wally started baking cookies full-time to make ends meet. Then Wally did something that no one else had ever tried before. Instead of selling his cookies, he gave them away. That's right, he gave them away. He went to concerts and shows where there were a lot of people and gave his product away for free. People loved them so much that they came from miles around and even started ordering cookies through the mail. Using his past experience as a promoter, he marketed himself and his cookies as bigger than life. He developed a persona that was totally unique. He placed his own smiling face next to one of his delicious cookies, with a stylized logo on each package and a huge sign above his store. He put together a strategy to distribute his product and set out to conquer the cookie industry. In a few months, the "Famous Amos Chocolate Chip Cookie Co." was born. And what started out as a small store on Sunset Boulevard in Hollywood grew to be one of the most recognized cookie companies in the world, for a time dominating the industry—all because Wally had the insight to develop a strategy for success. He developed an identity, he created a need, he developed a system for marketing and distributing . . . all these things were strategies that were later duplicated by the people who tried to compete with him. But Wally had the edge. Before there were cookies in malls, Wally "Famous" Amos was distributing cookies all over the country. He had a strategy.

So, say we want to bake a cake. What will we need to bake the same quality cake as the expert? First, we'll need the same recipe, and then we need to follow it exactly. When we follow the same recipe to the letter we will produce the same results, even though we may never have baked another thing in our lives. The expert baker may have worked through years of trial and error before finally developing the ultimate recipe. You don't have to go to the same school of hard knocks. You get to save time and effort by following his recipe, by modeling his efforts.

There are strategies for anything else in life: financial success, creating and maintaining vibrant health, feeling happy and loved throughout your life. We all know there are people out there who already have financial success or great relationships. If we want the same things in our lives, we need to discover the strategy they use in each instance, and apply it to produce similar results and save tremendous amounts of time and effort. That's the power of modeling.

As you already may have guessed, there is a strategy for following any recipe to produce a desired result. First, the recipe tells us the ingredients we will need to get the results we want. In the "baking" of human experience, those ingredients are our five senses. All human results are built or created from some specific use of the visual, auditory, kinesthetic, gustatory, and olfactory representational systems—sort of like the flour, water, eggs, and sugar in our recipe for baking a cake. What else does this recipe tell us? The correct amounts of those ingredients. In reproducing human experience, we need to know not only the ingredients, but also how much of each ingredient we need. We can think of submodalities as being the amounts, because they tell us specifically how much we need. For example, how much visual input—how bright, how dark, how close is the experience? What's the tempo, the texture? (You remember this stuff from Chapter 8!)

So, is that all you need to know in order to produce the same quality of cake as the expert? Of course not—not unless you also know the syntax or order in which things are to be done. When do you add the sugar and the eggs? When do you beat and when do you stir? What would happen if you put in first what the original baker put in last, and then put the whole thing in the oven before you stirred it? Would you produce a cake of the same quality? I doubt it. If, however, you use the same ingredients, in the same amounts, in the same sequence, then you will of course produce similar results.

We all have a strategy for everything we do, good and bad. We all have a strategy and syntax for motivation, for buying, for love, for being happy, for being attracted to someone. We're not always conscious of it, but certain sequences of specific stimuli will always achieve a specific outcome. Strategies are like the combination to the vault of your brain's resources. Even if you know the numbers, if you don't use them in the right sequence, you won't be able to open the lock. However, if you get the right numbers and the right sequence, the lock will open every time. So you need to find the combination that opens your vault and those that open other people's vaults as well.

How? It's much easier than it may seem. Think of your five senses as the building blocks of your syntax. We all deal with sensory input on two levels—internal and external. A syntax is simply the way we put together the blocks of what we experience externally and what we represent to ourselves internally.

Here's an example. We can have two kinds of visual experiences. The first is what you see in the outside world. As you read this book and look at the black letters on the white background, you're having a visual external experience. The second is visual internal. In the previous chapter, remember how we played with visual modalities and submodalities in our mind? We really weren't there to see the beach or the clouds or the happy or frustrating times that were represented in our mind. Instead, we experienced them in a visual manner.

The same is true of the other modalities. You can hear a song playing on the radio. That's auditory external. Or you can hear a voice in your mind. That's auditory internal. If the tone of the voice is what is important, that is auditory tonal. If the words (meaning) conveyed by the voice are what is important, that's auditory digital. Perhaps you can feel the texture of the armrest of the chair you're sitting in. That's kinesthetic external. Or you can have a deep feeling inside that something makes you feel good or bad. That's kinesthetic internal.

In order to create a recipe, we must have a system to describe what to do and when. So we have a simple notation system to describe strategies. We represent sensory processes in a shorthand notation, using V for visual, A for auditory, K for kinesthetic, i for internal, e for external, t for tonal, and d for digital. When you see something in the outside world (visual external), it can be represented as Ve. When you have a feeling inside, it's Ki. Consider the strategy of someone who gets motivated by seeing something (Ve), then saying something to herself (Aid) that creates the driving feeling (Ki) inside. This strategy would be represented in the following way: Ve-Aid-Ki. You could "talk" all day to this person about why she should do something, and it's highly unlikely you'd succeed. However, if you "showed" her a result and mentioned what she would say to herself when she saw it, you could put that person into state almost on cue. In the next chapter, we'll show you how to elicit the strategies people use in specific situations. For now, I want to show you how those strategies work and why they're so important.

Even though we all have specific strategies for getting certain results, very few of us consciously know how to use those strategies so that we can predict our results. So we are left to the mercy of our emotions and outside circumstances. We go in and out of various states, depending on what stimuli hit us. All you need to do is figure out your strategy, and you can produce a desired state on cue. You also need to be able to recognize other people's strategies so you can know exactly what they react to.

For example, is there a way in which you consistently organize your internal and external experiences to make a purchase? Most definitely. You may not know it, but the same syntax of experiences that attract you to a particular car may also attract you to a particular house. There are certain stimuli that, when presented in the right sequence, will immediately put you in a state that's receptive to buying. We all have sequences we consistently follow to produce specific states and activities. Presenting information in another person's syntax is a powerful form of rapport. In fact, if it's done effectively, your communication becomes almost irresistible because it automatically triggers certain responses.

What other strategies are there? Are there persuasion strategies? Are there ways to organize material so that it becomes almost irresistible? Absolutely. Motivation? Seduction? Learning? Athletics? Selling? Absolutely. How about depression? Or ecstasy? Are there specific ways to represent your experience of the world in certain sequences that create these emotions? You bet. There are strategies for efficient management. There are strategies for creativity. When certain things trigger you, you go into that state. You just need to know what your strategy is in order to access a state on cue. And you need to be able to figure out the strategies others use so you can know how to give people what they want.

What we need to find is the specific sequence, the specific syntax, that will produce a certain outcome, a certain state. If you can do that, and you're willing to produce the action needed, you can create your world as you desire it. Other than the physical necessities of life like food and water, almost everything else you might want is a state. All you have to know is the syntax, the right strategy, for getting yourself there.

GETTING RIGHT ON TARGET WITH THE RIGHT SYNTAX

Early in his career, Tony had a very successful modeling experience with the U.S. Army. He met with a general and promised that he could take any training program the Army had developed and cut the time in half, while simultaneously increasing the competency of all the people involved. Pretty big claim, right? The general was intrigued but not convinced. So Tony was given a contract to improve training programs and simultaneously teach a group of officers how to use modeling to improve many other training programs. But here was the catch: He would be paid nothing unless he produced the results he had promised. Even if he cut the time by 25 percent, he would receive no compensation.

Tony's first project was a four-day program to teach enlisted men how to fire a .45-caliber pistol effectively and accurately. In the past, an average of only 70 percent of the soldiers who took the program qualified afterward, and the general had been told this was the best that could be expected. At this point, Tony began to wonder what he had gotten himself into. He had never shot a gun before in his life! In addition, he heard a rumor that a couple of people in the training group were going to do anything they could to sabotage his work because they were angry about the amount of money he was to be paid. What was he to do?

First, Tony took the giant image of failure he'd been creating in his mind and literally shrank it down to size. He changed his belief systems from, "The best in the Army can't do what they're asking, so obviously I can't make this happen" to, "The pistol coaches in the Army are the best in the world at what they do.

But they don't have a clear understanding of the precise elements of how a person's syntax of internal mental actions can immediately affect performance. And if I take what I know and model these coaches and the Army's best shooters, we'll create a new program that will be even more effective, one that will clearly achieve my objective." Having put himself in a state of total resourcefulness, he told the general he would need access to his best shooters in order to find out specifically what they did—in their minds and physical actions—that produced the result of effective and accurate shooting. Once he discovered "the difference that made the difference," he could teach it to soldiers in less time and produce the desired results.

Along with his modeling team, Tony discovered the key beliefs of some of the best shooters in the world and contrasted them with the beliefs of the soldiers who had not shot effectively. Next, he discovered the common mental syntax and strategies of the best shooters and replicated them so he could teach them to a first-time shooter. Then he modeled the key components of their physiology.

Having discovered the optimum strategy for producing the result called effective shooting, he designed a one-and-a-half-day course for first-time shooters. The results? When tested in less than two days, 100 percent of the soldiers qualified, and the number who qualified at the highest level—expert—was three times higher than after the standard four-day course. By teaching these novices how to produce the same signals to their brains as the experts did, he had helped to make them experts in less than half the time. He then took the men he had modeled, the top shooters in the country, and taught them how to enhance their strategies. The result an hour later: One man scored higher than he had in six months, another shot more bull's-eyes than he had in any competition in recent memory, and the coach gave both of these men a run for their money. One colonel called it the first breakthrough in pistol shooting since World War I.

Through the years, Tony and I have worked on many modeling projects together. In business and teaching it is an invaluable tool for rapid progress and results. Through the years, I've modeled Tony and taken those skills into the business and teaching environment. But I have also used them for myself. For example, for years I have loved the sound of the great blues guitar players. My favorite player is the legendary B.B. King. I had played bass for several years, but guitar was a whole different bag. I knew how much time and practice it had taken to get good on bass, and I thought it would take even longer to play the blues licks that I heard in my head, so I just didn't ever try. It's a great example of how my belief about something kept me from doing it. I made big, bright pictures in my head of hours and hours of painstaking practice, wrong notes, frustration and, even worse, neglecting to do the things that took priority in my life. I thought it would take three or four years before I would be able to play those blues licks I loved.

Then one night I was watching BET and there was a music video with the King himself performing with the group U2. The cameras were capturing the band and B.B. backstage as they readied themselves for the performance. They talked about how they would play the song live and who would do what. B.B. said, "I don't know no chords. I don't believe I have to play all that stuff. Y'all are going to have to play those." Then he took a deep breath, threw his head to the side, and played one of those signature B.B. King blues licks on "Lucile," his Gibson guitar. He said, "I just believe in playin' what I do best." He ripped off another lick and said, "I don't know all that fancy stuff. I just play this." As I watched and listened, I realized that what I was witnessing was the exact syntax and strategy of how B.B. King plays on his beloved instrument, Lucile. He was telling me his beliefs, showing me his physiology, and demonstrating his syntax!

It suddenly occurred to me that I could apply the modeling system to playing blues guitar. I ran out to the video store and rented two tapes of B.B. King live, came home and proceeded to study them. I watched how he held his guitar, where he put his fingers, how he breathed and held his body. Anybody who has ever seen B.B. King play will recognize his stance, and that interesting way he tilts his head back and to the side as he breaks off a sizzling riff. He has a slight smile on his face as if to say, "This is heaven, right here." I then went out and bought a book of his songs, which showed me what notes he played the most. As it turned out, there is a certain sequence of notes, a scale, that he favors. So I went out and bought a guitar (and of course, named it) and then set out to model the King. I held my guitar like him, I used my body like him, I put my fingers in the same places as him. I adopted the belief that all you have to do is know the scale, listen to what's in your head, and trust. I took those old beliefs about taking two years to get good, and I shrunk them down and blew them out. I could afford to practice only about two hours a day, but it was an intense two hours. Now, I'm not going to try and tell you I'm as good as B.B. King. But I will say that after about three and a half months I can hold my own with guitar players who have been playing for years. One of my favorite things to do now is sit in with other musicians and play the blues. I've learned a new way to model the best.

The point here is for you to realize that even when you have little or no background information and even when circumstances seem impossible, if you have an excellent model of how to produce a result, you can discover specifically what the model does and duplicate it—and thus produce similar results in a much shorter period of time than you may have thought possible.

A simpler strategy is one used by many athletes to model the best in their fields. If you wanted to model an expert basketball player, you might first watch carefully to see what his technique is (Ve). As you watch, you might move your body in the same motions (Ke), until they feel like a part of you (Ki). (If you've ever watched basketball, you may have done this involuntarily. When the player you are watching needs to turn or pivot, you turn and pivot for him as if you were the one playing.) Next, you would want to make an internal picture of an expert playing the game (Vi). You've gone from visual external to kinesthetic external to kinesthetic internal. Then you would make a new visual internal image, this time a disassociated image of yourself playing the game or a specific play (Vi). It would be like watching a movie of yourself modeling the other person as precisely as possible. Next you would step inside that picture and, in an associated way, experience how it would feel to perform the same action precisely the way the expert athlete did (Ki). You would repeat that as often as it would take for you to feel completely comfortable doing it. Thus you would have provided yourself with the specific neurological strategy that could help you move and perform at optimum levels. Finally, you would try it in the real world (Ke).

You could map the syntax of this strategy as Ve-Ke-Ki-Vi-Vi-Ki-Ke. This is one of hundreds of ways you could model someone. Remember, there are many ways to produce results. There are no right or wrong ways—there are only effective or ineffective ways to produce your desires.

Obviously, you can produce more precise results by having more accurate and precise information about all the things a person does to produce a result. Ideally, in modeling someone, you would also model his or her internal experience, belief systems, and syntax. However, just by watching a person you can model a great deal of their physiology. And physiology is the other factor (we'll talk about it in Chapter 11) that creates the state we are in and thus the kinds of results we produce.

One of the best ways to find out someone's beliefs and syntax is simply to ask, "What do you believe about your work, your skills, your life, your talent, that you think gives you the competitive edge? What is it that you know or realize about this subject that very few people appreciate, and therefore makes you more successful? How do you go about making this result happen? What's the first thing that you do to produce this result?" You'd be surprised how much information people are willing to give you if you just ask. If you listen carefully, people will give you their entire syntax and beliefs in one conversation. Or do as I did with B.B. King. Find books, tapes, or videos on who or what you want to model. All the information you need is available; you just have to seek it out.

> *Before we even attempt to teach children, we want them to know each of them is unique and very special. We want them to like themselves, to want to achieve and care about themselves.*
>
> —MARVA COLLINS

There is a very important area where understanding and applying strategies makes a major difference. The field of teaching and learning has always been plagued with the question "Why 'can't' some kids learn?" We're convinced there are two main reasons. First, we often don't know the most effective strategy for teaching someone a specific lesson or task. Second, teachers seldom have an accurate idea of how different kids learn. Most learning institutions still teach all students one way. Remember, we're all different and we all have different strategies. If you don't know someone's learning strategy, you're going to have a great deal of trouble trying to teach them.

For example, some people have great difficulty in spelling. Is it because they're less intelligent than good spellers? Of course not. Successful spelling may have more to do with the syntax of your thoughts—that is, how you organize, store, and retrieve information in a given context. Whether you are able to produce consistent results is simply a matter of whether your present mental syntax supports the task you're asking your brain to accomplish. Anything you've ever seen, heard, or felt is stored in your brain. Countless research projects have shown that people in a hypnotic trance can remember (that is, access) things they were unable to recall consciously. Have you ever forgotten something really important and then later remembered it? Chances are, your inability to remember it in the moment was due to your not performing the proper syntax for retrieval. Perhaps later when you were relaxed your brain was accessing more easily. In fact, one method of remembering something is to relax and think of something else.

If you are not spelling effectively, the problem is probably in the way you are representing words to yourself. What's the best strategy for spelling? It's certainly not kinesthetic. It's difficult to feel a word. It's not really auditory, because there are too many words you can't sound out effectively. So what does spelling entail? It entails the ability to store visual external characters in a specific syntax. The way to learn to spell is to make visual pictures that can be easily accessed at any time.

Take the word *Albuquerque*. The best way to learn to spell it isn't to say the letters over and over again—it's to store the word as a picture in your mind. In the next chapter, we're going to learn some of the ways people access different parts of their brain. For example, Bandler and Grinder, the founders of NLP, discovered that where we move our eyes determines which part of our nervous system we have clearest access to. We'll go into these "accessing cues" in detail in the next chapter. For now, just note that most people remember visual images best by looking up and to the left. The best way to learn to spell Albuquerque is to place the word up and to your left, and form a clear visual image of it. Try it now.

At this point we need to add another concept: chunking. On average, most humans can consciously process only five to nine chunks of information at once (like phone numbers, grocery lists, and combinations). People who learn rapidly can master even the most complex tasks because they chunk information into small steps and then reassemble them into the original whole. In other words, they group sets of things together and use each set as one chunk. So, the way to learn to spell Albuquerque is to break it down into three smaller chunks like this: *Albu/quer/que.* I want you to write the three parts on a piece of paper, hold them above and to the left of your eyes, see *Albu,* then close your eyes and see it in your mind. Open your eyes. See *Albu.* Don't say it, just see it; then close your eyes and see it in your mind. Continue to do this four or five or six times until you can close your eyes and clearly see *Albu.* Next, take the second chunk, *quer.* Flash on the letters faster and follow the same process with this chunk, and then with the *que* chunk, until the entire image Albuquerque is stored in your mind. If you have a clear picture, you'll probably have a feeling (kinesthetic) it's spelled right. Then you'll be able to see the word so clearly you can spell it not only forward but backward. Try it. Spell Albuquerque. Then spell it backward. Once you have that, you've got that word spelled forever. I guarantee it. You can do that with any word and become a superb speller, even if you've had trouble spelling your own name in the past. The trick is to take the time to do it. Chunking works with names also. If you take the time to store someone's name and face in this manner, you will remember it more easily.

Another huge aspect of learning is discovering people's ideal learning strategies. We all learn differently and at different paces. As we said earlier, everyone has a particular neurology, a particular mental terrain they use most often. However, our current teaching systems tend to assume that everyone learns the same way and at the same pace. My belief is that this way of teaching is very unfair because of the inherent assumption that those who don't learn that particular way are somehow slower or less intelligent than the others.

Here's an example: Not long ago, a young man came to my office for help. He told me that he was at the end of his rope and he didn't know what to do with his life. You see, Kevin was twenty years old and had been diagnosed as suffering from attention deficit disorder (ADD). Clutched in his hand was a magazine containing an article about him, written by his doctor. She told how, after several years of suffering from ADD and other learning disorders, Kevin was able to lead a "normal" life because she had prescribed the drug Ritalin for him. She wrote that while he would always have trouble with attention, the drug had made him much better. Only one problem: Kevin was miserable. He said that he originally was put on the drug because he couldn't concentrate and couldn't learn like the other students. He kept saying, "I just can't get a *feel* for what they want me to learn." With tears in his eyes he said, "Whenever I try to think of my future I get confused. I don't think I can learn. I'm so afraid I can't learn and I'll never feel happy." Whenever he would talk about learning or thinking or concentrating he would tense up like the hide stretched across an African ceremonial drum, all the while clutching the magazine so tightly that I thought he was going to cut off the circulation to his arm.

I could tell right away that Kevin tended to process a great deal of his experience (information) kinesthetically, because he kept saying he couldn't get a feel for things. I also observed that his frustration increased as he tensed up. Once I realized how he processed information, I was in a position to help him. This young man had the greatest grasp of the things he felt. However, much of the standard teaching process is visual or auditory. His problem wasn't that he had trouble learning. It was that his teachers had trouble teaching him in a way in which he could effectively perceive, store, and retrieve information.

The first thing I had him do was to relax and take some deep breaths. The change in his physiology made an immediate difference in his outlook and his ability to concentrate. Next, I had him tear up the article. "This is not you, Kevin," I told him. "These are just words on a piece of paper, and it's quite possible that whoever wrote this just might not understand how you need to learn." That got his attention—he had been expecting the usual battery of questions. Instead, I started talking with him about all the great ways he used his nervous system. I said, "I bet you're good in sports." He said, "Yeah, I'm pretty good." It turned out that he loved to ride mountain bikes. We talked about biking for a while, and he immediately got excited and attentive, in a state of feeling effective. He was in a more receptive state and he was concentrating like a champ. I explained to him that he had a tendency to store information kinesthetically and that had great advantages in life. His learning style wasn't wrong or even ineffective—it was just different.

I showed Kevin how to relax and put himself in a good state. Then we started to talk about what he wanted to do with his future. He decided he wanted to pursue mountain biking because he really loved the sport. There was a great deal that he needed to study and learn to do it right. However, his kinesthetic style made learning difficult for him. So I showed him how to do it visually, and worked with his submodalities to give him the same feeling about learning that he had about biking. Within thirty minutes he was concentrating and learning and planning his future. In the next few months Kevin weaned himself off Ritalin and has never gone back to it. He started his own carpet business, and within a year and a half, he was featured as a top rider in a very prominent cycling magazine. Today he's a healthy, happy young man with a very bright future ahead of him.

What about "learning disabled" kids? Many times, these young people are not so much learning disabled as they are strategy disabled. They need to learn how to use their resources. Tony taught certain strategies to a schoolteacher who worked with learning disabled kids, ages eleven to fourteen, who had never scored higher on a spelling test than 70 percent, with most scores falling in the 25 to 50 percent range. She quickly realized that 90 percent of her "disabled" students had auditory or kinesthetic spelling strategies. Within a week after she began using the new spelling strategies, nineteen of twenty-six kids scored 100 percent, two scored 90 percent, two 80 percent, and the other three 70 percent. She says that there has been a major shift in the behavior problems—"As if by magic, they've disappeared." She will now be presenting this information to the school board for introduction to all the schools in her district.

We're convinced one of the greatest challenges in education today is that teachers are unaware of the learning strategies of their students. They simply are unaware of the "combinations" of the students' mental vaults. It's not that they don't care; most teachers are extremely committed. Inner-city children, whether they be White or Black, may learn differently than their middle-class counterparts. It's quite possible that a person's cultural or socioeconomic background can affect their preferred learning strategy. But what's most important to realize is that all children have the right and capability to learn anything they want. As parents, teachers, and concerned citizens, we have to learn how to meet those needs and expand the ways in which all of us learn, and thereby increase the quality of life for society as a whole. Up until now, our whole education process has been geared to what kids *should* learn rather than teaching children how they *can* learn anything. Optimum Performance Technologies shares with us a specific set of strategies different people can use in different ways in order to produce the results they desire—whether that is to spell more effectively, or to feel more inspired on a consistent basis.

Think of all the ways you can adapt these tools to the various areas of your personal and professional life. After all, the same problems that we find in the educational field show up in almost every other area. We use the wrong sequence and get the wrong result. Remember, effort is not enough. We have to use the right system to get results. Type in the right numbers and the computer will give you the file that you want. Use the proper recipe and you can consistently bake the cake you desire. Remember, we have a strategy for everything. If you're a salesperson, would it help to know the buying strategy of your customers? You bet it would. If they are strongly kinesthetic, do you want to begin by showing them the beautiful colors of the cars you're selling? Of course not. You'd want to zap them with a strong feeling. You'd want them to sit at the steering wheel, feel the upholstery, hook into the feelings they'd get moving along the open road. If they were visual, you'd start with the colors, lines, and other visual submodalities that work for their strategy.

As peak performance coaches, the first thing we do is ascertain exactly what triggers an individual or a group of individuals to produce their finest performance or results. And what we've discovered is that each individual is unique. If you're a sports coach, would it help to know what motivates different players, what sort of stimuli work best to get them in their most resourceful states? Would you want to be able to break down specific tasks into their most efficient syntax? You bet you would. Just as there's a way to form a DNA molecule or a way to build a bridge, there's an optimum syntax for every task. Remember that in everything we do, we have a consistent strategy or pattern, and most of the time we are unconscious about what the strategy is. But once we are aware of it we can use this strategy, this recipe if you will, to consistently produce any result that we want for the rest of our lives. And I ask you, what kind of improvement could you make if you elicited a particular strategy (for yourself or someone else) and then made it more effective?

You may be saying to yourself at this point, "Well, that's great for you, but I don't have the type of background to look at someone and figure out their strategies. I can't speak with people for a few minutes and know what stimulates them to buy, or to be in love, or to do anything else. I can't read minds." The reason you don't know is that you don't know what to look for—or how to ask for it. I truly believe that if you ask for almost anything in the world in the right way, with enough conviction and enough commitment, you'll get it. Remember, the number of people who fail is directly proportional to the number of people who give up. Some things take great conviction and energy to pursue: You can get them, although you really have to work at them. But strategies are easy. As a matter of fact, you'll be surprised how fast and easily you can elicit them. You can do it in a matter of minutes. In the next chapter we're going to learn . . .

CHAPTER TEN

How to Elicit Someone's Strategy

We must not, in trying to think about how we can make a big difference, ignore the small daily differences we can make which, over time, add up to big differences that we cannot foresee.

—MARIAN WRIGHT EDELMAN

EVER SEE ANY master locksmiths at work? It looks like magic. They play with a lock, hear things you aren't hearing, see things you aren't seeing, feel things you aren't feeling—and somehow manage to figure out the entire combination to a safe.

Master communicators work the same way. You can figure out anyone's mental syntax: You can open the combination to the vault of his or her mind or your own. You have to look for things you weren't seeing before, listen for things you weren't hearing before, feel things you weren't feeling before, and ask the questions you didn't know to ask before. If you do that elegantly and attentively, you can elicit anyone's strategies in any situation. You can learn how to give people precisely what they want, and you can teach them how to do the same thing for themselves.

The key to eliciting strategies is knowing that people will tell you everything you need to know about their strategies. They'll tell you in words. They'll tell you in the way they use their body. They'll even tell you in the way they use their eyes. You can learn to read a person as skillfully as you can learn to read a map or a book. **Remember, a strategy is simply a specific order of representations—visual, auditory, kinesthetic, olfactory,**

gustatory—that produces a specific result. All you need to do is get people to experience their strategy and take careful note of what they do as they do it. I live by the saying "As we think, so we are." If you get someone to think about an experience and associate to it, that person will to some degree experience and demonstrate the strategy he or she uses to accomplish the task.

To effectively elicit someone's strategies, we must first know what to look for, which clues tell which part of a person's nervous system is being used. We need to find out the main representational system. Some people are primarily visual: they tend to see the world in pictures and achieve their greatest sense of power by tapping into the visual part of their brain. Because they're trying to keep up with the pictures in their brain, visual people tend to speak quickly and move quickly. They don't care exactly how they get it out; they're just trying to put words to the pictures. These people tend to speak in visual metaphors. They talk about how things *look* to them, what patterns they *see* emerging, whether the future is *bright* or *dark*. They may ask, "Do you *see* what I mean?" or "How does that *look* to you?"

On the other hand, people who are primarily auditory tend to be more selective about the words they use. They tend to have more tonally rich voices, and their speech is slower, more rhythmic, more measured. Since words mean a lot to them, they are careful about what they say. They tend to say things like, "That *sounds* right to me," or "I can *hear* what you're saying," or "Everything *clicks*." Remember, these qualities are generally unconscious to them.

Then there are those people who are more kinesthetic. They tend to be even slower in their speech and actions than the people who are primarily visual or auditory. They experience the better part of their world through their feelings. Their voices tend to be deeper, and their words often slide out slowly and smoothly. (Think about Barry White; he is a perfect example.) Kinesthetic people use metaphors from the physical world. They're always *grasping* for something *concrete*. Things are *heavy* and *intense*, and they need to *get in touch* with things. They say things like, "I'm *reaching* for an answer, but I haven't got a *hold* on it yet," or "That really *feels* good to me."

Although all of us can use any of these three modes, we each tend to favor one the most. **When you're learning about other people's strategies, you also need to know their main representational system so you can present your message in a way that gets through.** When you are dealing with a kinesthetically oriented person, for example, you don't want to talk a million miles a minute and describe elaborate pictures of things. You'll drive the person nuts. You've got to speak so that your message matches the way his or her mind works. So you'd want to talk more slowly and speak of the feelings that relate to the subject at hand.

You're probably starting to realize by now that just by watching and listening to people you can get an immediate impression of which systems they are using in that moment and which one they favor. Neuro-Linguistic Programming (NLP) utilizes even more specific indicators of what's going on in someone's mind.

"THE EYES ARE THE MIRROR TO THE SOUL"

There's much truth to that romantic saying. In fact, science has revealed that there is a definite correlation between what the eyes are doing and what a person is thinking or feeling, or how the person is processing information. That's right: Simply by observing a person you can tell which representational system he or she is using.

Take a second to answer this question: What color was the first car you rode in? Really try to remember it. To answer that question, 90 percent of people will look up and to the left. That's where right-handed people and even some left-handed people access visual-remembered images. Here's another question: How would Mickey Mouse look in an afro? Take a moment to picture this. This time your eyes probably went up and to the right. That's where most people's eyes go to access created or imagined images.

Just by looking at people's eyes, it's possible to know what sensory system they're accessing. Why? It's this simple: A person's eyes must be in a particular position to think certain things. The sequence of positions tells you the "how" of what someone is doing. Memorize the following charts so you can understand and recognize eye-accessing cues.

Representative Eye Accessing Cues

As people represent information internally, they move their eyes, even though that movement may be slight. With a normally organized, right-handed person the following holds true, and the resultant sequences are systematic. (NOTE: There are some people who are organized in a right-to-left reverse manner.)

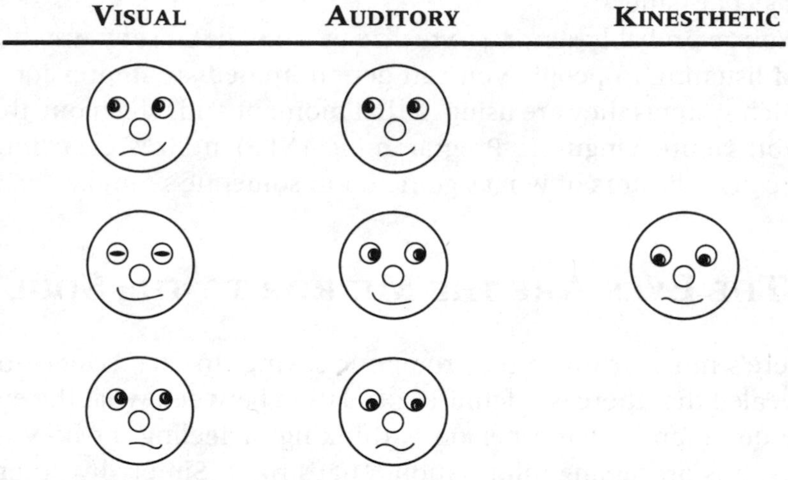

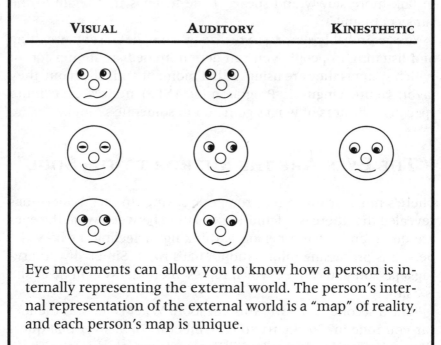

Eye movements can allow you to know how a person is internally representing the external world. The person's internal representation of the external world is a "map" of reality, and each person's map is unique.

Carry on a conversation with someone and observe his or her eye movements. Ask questions requiring the person to remember images or sounds or feelings. Which way do the eyes go for each of the questions? Verify to yourself that the chart works.

Here are some questions you might ask to elicit some responses to read.

To Get	You Might Ask
Visual Remembered Pictures	"How many windows are there in your house?" "What is the first thing you see when you wake up in the morning?" "What did your boyfriend or girlfriend look like when you were sixteen?" "Which is the darkest room in your house?" "Which of your friends has the shortest hair?" "What was the color of your first bicycle?" "What was the smallest animal you saw on your last trip to the zoo?" "What was the color of your first teacher's hair?" "Think of all the different colors in your bedroom."
Visual Constructed	"How would you look if you had three eyes?" "Imagine a police officer with a lion's head and a rabbit's tail, with the wings of an eagle." "Imagine the skyline of your city going up in wisps of smoke." "Can you see yourself with golden hair?"
Auditory Remembered	"What was the first thing you said today?" "What was the first thing someone said to you today?" "Name one of your favorite songs from when you were younger." "What sounds of nature do you like best?" "What's the seventh word in the Pledge of Allegiance?" "What's the ninth word in the song 'Mary Had a Little Lamb'?"

	"Sing 'The Rose' to yourself."
	"Listen in your mind to a small waterfall on a quiet summer day."
	"Listen in your mind to your favorite song."
	"Which door in your house slams the loudest?"
	"Which is softest, the slam of your car door or the slam of your trunk lid?"
	"Who of your acquaintances has the pleasantest voice?"
Auditory Constructed	"If you could ask any question of Thomas Jefferson, Abraham Lincoln, and John F. Kennedy, what question would you ask?"
	"What would you say if someone asked you how we could eliminate the possibility of nuclear war?"
	"Imagine the sound of a car horn becoming that of a flute."
Auditory Internal Dialogue	"Silently repeat this question to your self: 'What's most important to me in my life now?' "
Kinesthetic Words	"Imagine the feeling of ice melting in your hand."
	"How did you feel this morning just after you got out of bed?"
	"Imagine the feeling of a block of wood changing to silk."
	"How cold was the ocean last time you tested it?"
	"Which carpet in your house is the softest?"
	"Imagine settling down to a nice hot bath."
	"Think of what it would feel like to slide your hand over a rough piece of bark onto a soft, cool piece of moss."

As a rule and a way to remember the basics, think of the eyes having to look up for pictures, to the side for sounds, and down for feelings. Also, in all of the eye positions, generally to the right are constructed thoughts and to the left are stored memories. If, for example, a person's eyes go up to the left, she just pictured something from her memory. If they go toward the left ear, she listened to something from memory. When her eyes go down to the right, she is accessing the kinesthetic part of her representational system.

With all of this information in mind, by physically and intentionally placing your eyes in a particular position, you can then access information you need. If you're trying to remember something you saw a few days ago, looking down to the right will not help you see that image. However, if you look up to the left, you'll discover that you'll be able to remember the information more rapidly. Once you know where to look for information stored in your brain, you'll be able to get to it quickly and easily. (For about 5 to 10 percent of people, the direction of these accessing cues will be reversed. See if you can find a left-handed friend or an ambidextrous person with reversed accessing cues.)

Just like our eye patterns, there are other aspects of people's physiologies that give us clues about their modes. When people are breathing high in the chest, they're usually thinking visually. When breathing is even, from the diaphragm or the whole chest, they're probably in an auditory mode. Deep breathing low in the stomach indicates kinesthetic accessing. Observe three people breathing, and note the rate and location of their breathing. These are clues as to what is going on in a person's mind at any given moment.

Even people's voices can tell us things about them. Visual people speak in quick bursts and usually have high-pitched, nasal, or strained tonalities. Low, deep tonality and slow speech are usually kinesthetic. An even rhythm and clear, resonant tonality indicate auditory accessing. You can even read skin tone. Depending on the tone of a person's skin you can even tell what's going on by the changes in color. Obviously, darker people are not as easily read as lighter ones, but there are more than enough clues to get an accurate reading on anyone. When you think visually, your face tends to grow paler. A flushed face indicates kinesthetic accessing. When the head is up, it's in a visual mode. If it's balanced or slightly cocked (as in listening), it's in auditory. If it's down or the neck muscles are relaxed, it's in kinesthetic.

You're probably starting to get it now that even with the most minimal communication, you can get clear, unmistakable cues about how a person's mind works and what sorts of messages the person uses and responds to. **The simplest way to elicit strategies is simply to ask the right questions.** Remember, there are strategies for everything—for buying and for selling, for being motivated and for being in love, for attracting people and for being creative. The best way to learn about these is not to observe, but to do. So do these exercises with someone else if at all possible. By the way, I hope that every time we ask you to do an exercise, you participate fully. That's the best way to get the results you want!

Eye Accessing Cues and Questions to Ask

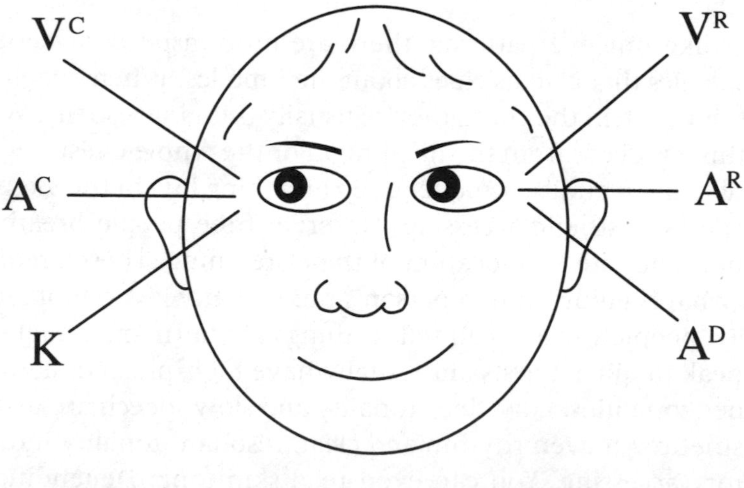

V^R *Visual remembered:* Seeing images of things seen before, in the way they were seen before. Sample questions that usually elicit this kind of processing include, "What color are your mother's eyes?" and "What does your coat look like?"

V^C *Visual constructed:* Seeing images of things never seen before, or seeing things differently than they were seen before. Questions that usually elicit this kind of processing include, "What would an orange hippopotamus with purple spots look like?" and "What would you look like from the other side of the room?"

A^R *Auditory remembered:* Remembering sounds heard before. Questions that usually elicit this kind of processing include, "What's the last thing I said?" and "What does your alarm clock sound like?"

A^C *Auditory constructed:* Hearing words never heard in quite that way before. Putting sounds or phrases together in a new way. Questions that tend to elicit this kind of processing include, "If you were to create a new song right now, what would it sound like?" and "Imagine a siren sound made by an electric guitar."

A^D *Auditory digital:* Talking to oneself. Statements that tend to elicit this kind of processing include, "Say something to yourself that you often say to yourself" and "Recite the Pledge of Allegiance."

K Kinesthetic: Feeling emotions, tactile sensations (sense of touch), or proprioceptive feelings (feelings of muscle movement). Questions that elicit this kind of processing include, "What does it feel like to be happy?" "What is the feeling of touching a pine cone?" and "What does it feel like to run?"

Remember, the key to effectively eliciting strategies is putting the person in a fully associated state of mind. Then there is no choice but to tell you exactly what the strategies are—if not verbally, then nonverbally, by eye movements, body change, and so forth. State is the hotline to strategy. It's the switch that opens the circuits to a person's unconscious. It's the combination that unlocks the vault. Trying to elicit a strategy when a person isn't in a fully associated state is like trying to paint a picture with no paint. Besides, you don't want an intellectual discussion; you want people to reexperience the state and thus the syntax that produced it.

Again, think of strategies as recipes. If you meet a pastry chef who bakes the greatest cake in the world, you may be disappointed to learn that she doesn't know exactly how she makes it. She does it unconsciously. She couldn't answer you if you asked the amounts of the ingredients. She might say, "I don't know—a pinch of this and a dash of that." So instead of asking her to tell you, have her show you. Put her in the kitchen and have her bake the cake. You would note every step she took, and before she threw in that dash of this or that, you would immediately grab it and measure it. By following the chef through the entire process, noting the ingredients, the amounts, and the syntax, you would then have a recipe you could duplicate in the future.

When we elicit someone's strategy we do it the same way. You must put the person back in the kitchen—back to the time when he was experiencing a particular state—and then find out what was the very first thing that caused him to go into that state. Was it something he saw or heard? Or was it the touch of something or someone? After he tells you what happened, watch him and ask, "What was the very next thing that caused you to be in that state? Was it . . . ?" and so on, until he's in the state you're pursuing.

Every strategy elicitation follows this pattern. You have to get the person in the appropriate state by having him remember a specific time when he was motivated, or felt loved, or felt creative, or whatever strategy you want to elicit. Then get him to reconstruct his strategy by asking clear, succinct questions about the syntax of what he saw, heard, and felt. Finally, after you have the syntax, get the submodalities of the strategy. Find out what specifically about the picture, sounds, and sensations caused the person to be in that state. Was it the size of the picture? The tone of the voice? And so on.

How to Elicit a Motivation Strategy

Try this technique for eliciting a motivation strategy with someone else. First, put the person in a receptive state. Ask, "Can you remember a time when you were totally motivated to do something?" You're looking for a congruent answer: one in which the person's voice and body language give you the same message in a clear, firm, believable way. Remember, she won't be aware of much of her sequence. If it's been a part of her behavior for a while, she does it very quickly. In order to get each of her steps, you have to ask her to slow down and then pay careful attention to what she says and what her eyes and body tell you.

Again, the person must be in state and fully associated to get the best results. Think about this. If you ask a person, "Can you remember when you felt very motivated?" and the person shrugs and says, "Yeah," it means she's not yet in the state you want. Sometimes someone will say yes and shake her head no. Same thing. She isn't really associated to the experience; she's not in state. So you have to make sure she's tapped into the specific experience that put her in the right state. Ask, "Can you remember a specific time when you were totally motivated to do something? Can you go back to that time and step back into that experience?" That should do it almost every time. If the person gets frustrated, have her relax for a minute and then go right back to it.

When you get her in a totally involved state, ask, "As you remember that time, what was the very first thing that caused you to be totally motivated? Was it something you saw, something you heard, or was it the touch of something or someone?" If she answers that she once heard a powerful speech and immediately felt motivated to do something, her motivational strategy begins with auditory external (A^e). You wouldn't motivate her by showing her something or by having her do something physical. She responds best to words and sounds. Remember, your outcome is to simulate duplication of the stimulus to produce the same state and result.

Now you know how to get her attention. But that's not the whole strategy. People respond to things both externally and internally. So you will need to find the internal part of her strategy as well. Next you ask, "After you heard that speech, what was the very next thing that caused you to be totally motivated to do something? Did you picture something in your mind? Did you say something to yourself? Or did you have a certain feeling or emotion?"

If she answers that she got a picture in her mind, the second part of her strategy is visual internal (V^i). After she hears something that motivates her, she immediately forms a mental picture that gets her more motivated. Chances are it's a picture that helps her focus on what she wants to do.

Now, you still don't have her whole strategy, so you need to keep asking, "After you heard something, then saw a picture in your mind, what was the very next thing that caused you to be totally motivated? Did you say something to yourself? Did you feel something inside, or did something else happen?" If at that point she gets a feeling that makes her totally motivated, she's completed her strategy. She has produced a series of representations, in this case Ae-Vi-Ki, which create the state of motivation. She has heard something, seen a picture in her mind, and then felt motivated. Most people need an external stimulus and either two or three internal ones before they're finished, although some people have strategies involving a sequence of ten or fifteen different representations before they reach the desired state.

Now that you know the syntax of this person's strategy, you need to find out the submodalities. So you ask, "From what you heard, what about it motivated you? Was it the tone of the person's voice, the actual words themselves, the speed or rhythm of the voice? What did you picture in your mind? Was it a big picture, bright . . . ?" Once you have asked all this, you can test the responses by telling her in the same tone about something you want to motivate her to do, then tell her what she'll picture in her mind and the feelings it will create. If you do all this accurately, you will see the person go into a motivated state right before your very eyes. If you doubt the importance of syntax, try changing the order subtly. Then tell her how it will feel and what she'll say to herself, and you'll see her giving you an uninterested stare. You've got the right ingredients in the wrong order.

Strategy Elicitation

Can you remember a time when you were totally _____ed? Can you remember a specific time?

Go back to that time and experience it . . . *[get the person in state]* As you remember that time . . . *[keep the person in state]*

A) What was the very first thing that caused you to be _____ed? Was it something you saw? Was it something you heard? Was it the touch of something or someone? What was the very first thing that caused you to be totally _____ed? After you *[saw, heard, or were touched]*, what was the very next thing that caused you to be totally _____ed?

B) Did you . . . *make a picture* in your mind? *say something* to yourself? *have a certain feeling* or *emotion?* What was the very next thing that caused you to be _____ed? After you *[saw something, said something to yourself, and so on]*, what was the very next thing that caused you to be totally _____ed?

C) Did you . . . *make a picture* in your mind? *say something* to yourself? *have a certain feeling* or *emotion?* Or did something else happen? What was the very next thing that caused you to be _____ed?

Ask if the person was very _____ed at this point. If so, the elicitation is complete. If not, continue eliciting syntax until he or she answers yes to the above question.

The next step is simply to elicit the specific submodalities of each representation in this person's strategy. So if the first step of the strategy was visual, you would ask:

1. What about what you *saw?* (Visual external)
2. What was it specifically about what you saw that motivated you? Was it the size of it? Brightness of it? The way it moved?

> *Continue this process until you have all the submodalities for the strategy. Then simply talk about something you want to motivate that person to do by using the same syntax and the same key submodality words, then judge by the results you produce in that person's state.*

How long does it take to elicit someone's strategy? It depends on the complexity of the activity you want to know about. Sometimes it takes only a minute or two to learn the precise syntax that will motivate the person to do just about anything you want.

Let's say you're a basketball coach and you want to motivate someone whose strategy begins with auditory external to become a great forward. Although he has some talent and some interest, he's not really motivated to make a commitment. So how would you start? Would you take him out and have him watch your best players at work? Would you show him the court? Would you talk very fast to get his juices going, to show him how excited you are? No, of course not. Every bit of that behavior would work on a person with a visual strategy, and it would turn this person colder than a plate of bad salmon in the fridge.

Instead, you need to sell him by connecting with the auditory stimuli that get him going. You wouldn't be talking fast like a visual person would, and you wouldn't go into a slow, drooping kinesthetic rap. You would talk in a well-modulated, steady, clear, resonant voice. You would speak in the exact same submodalities of pitch and tempo that you learned trigger the beginning of his motivation strategy. You might say something like this: "I'm sure you've heard a lot about how successful our basketball program has been. It's really the talk of the school right now. We've been drawing great crowds this year. It's amazing the noise they make. I've had kids say the crowd noise has done wonders for them. It's kept them going at levels they never expected they could reach. And the roar when they make a basket is amazing. I've never heard anything like it in all my years of coaching." Now you're speaking his language. You're using the same representational system he does. You could spend hours showing him the big new arena, and he'd be drifting off to some distant daydream. Let him really hear the roar of the crowd as he sinks the basket or assists or rebounds, and you've got him hooked.

That's only the first part of the syntax, the hook that gets him going. That by itself won't get him fully motivated. You need to put together the internal sequence as well. Depending on what descriptions he gives you, you might go from the auditory cues to something like this: "When you hear the roar of the hometown crowd, you'll be able to picture yourself playing the best game of your life. Feeling absolutely motivated to play the best game of your life."

USING MOTIVATION STRATEGIES IN THE WORKPLACE

If you have a business, motivating your employees is most likely a major concern. If it's not, you probably won't have the business for very long. But the more you know about motivational strategies, the more you realize how difficult it is to motivate well. After all, if each of your employees has a different strategy, it's hard to come up with a representation that will fill all their needs at once. If you simply run your own strategy (which is what most managers do), you're going to motivate only the people who are like you. You could give the most cogent and well-thought-out motivational lecture in the world, and unless it addressed the specific strategies of different people, it wouldn't do any good.

So what can you do about it? Understanding strategy should give you two clear ideas. **First, every motivational technique aimed at a group should have something for everyone—something visual, something auditory, and something kinesthetic.** That way you will reach everyone at some level. You should show them things, you should let them hear things, and you should give them feelings. And you should be able to vary your voice and intonations so you hook all three types. Those are the traits of a great communicator and motivator.

Second, there's no substitute for working with people on an individual basis. You can provide the broad cues to a group that will give everyone something to work with. To tap into the full strategies different people use, it would be ideal to elicit individual strategies. Individual coaching is the preferred method to make sure you reach everyone.

What we've looked at so far is the basic formula for eliciting anyone's strategy. To be able to use it effectively, you need to get more details about each step of the strategy. You need to add the submodalities to the basic pattern.

For example, if a person's buying strategy begins with something visual, what is it that catches her eye? Bright colors? Great size? Does she go bonkers at the sight of certain patterns or wild, splashy designs? If she's auditory, is she attracted to sexy voices or to powerful ones? Does she like loud clatter and rumbles or a finely tuned, efficient hum? Knowing someone's main modality is a great start. To be precise, to really punch the right buttons, you need to know more. All of this may sound complicated and tedious, but you will be amazed how simple it really is and get even more excited about the results you will get. It's definitely worth the time.

Those who are willing to go the extra mile to learn and elicit strategies are the ones who excel in their fields. And understanding strategy is absolutely essential to success in sales. There are some salespeople who understand it instinctively. When they meet a potential client, they immediately develop rapport and elicit his or her decision-making strategies. They might begin, "I noticed you're using our competitor's copy machine. I'm curious. What was the first thing that caused you to want to buy that machine? Was it something you saw or read about it . . . or did someone tell you about it? Or was it the way you felt about the salesperson or about the product itself?"

Everybody has their own buying strategies. So to be effective, a salesperson must take clients back to a time when they bought something they loved. This will access that buying state. The object is to find out what caused them to decide to buy it. What were the key ingredients and submodalities? A salesperson who learns how to elicit strategies will be learning customers' exact needs, then be empowered to truly satisfy those needs and create a long-standing customer. When you elicit someone's strategy, you can learn in moments what might otherwise take days or weeks to learn.

Know Your Own Strategies

Now that you understand strategy elicitation, let's take a look at some of its other applications. Consider some disempowering strategies. How about overeating? It's estimated that 75 percent of the U.S. population is overweight. Overeating and other eating disorders are a very serious challenge. How do people get to be so overweight? Easy. They've developed a bingeing or overeating strategy. And it's running their lives. I have coached several people to handle weight challenges by helping them discover their strategies.

One lady told me that even when she's not hungry, she quickly finds herself with the overwhelming urge to eat, and it all happens in a matter of a few moments. I took her back to one of those times and asked her what caused her to feel like eating. She said that usually it was something she saw, namely an ad on TV, or if there was a box of food in plain sight. She said that as soon as she saw it, she would make a picture in her mind of a ham sandwich and a bag of chips, then she'd say to herself, "Damn, that looks good! What should I eat?" That would create feelings of hunger in her stomach and she would immediately take action and get something to eat. She may not have been hungry at all before, or even have just eaten an hour ago, but the trigger would appear and she would respond by overeating. And those triggers were everywhere! Also, whenever she was driving, she'd see billboards and fast-food signs that would trigger the same strategy and direct her to the nearest drive-up window.

Once I tapped into her strategy and made her aware that she did the same thing every time, we changed her behavior by changing her strategy. Using swish patterns, pattern interrupts, and collapsing anchors (you'll learn about these methods in the next few chapters), I set it up so that seeing food triggered images of herself, bloated and sick, with cellulite pockets all over her body. In response, she would now say to herself, "I look like Jabba the Hutt! I'd rather take a deep breath and smile than pig out." Then she would imagine herself working out and getting fitter and saying to herself, "This feels great and I'm getting fitter and fitter." Then she would reward herself with a pat on her own back and say to herself, "You're the best, and I'm proud of you." The old stimuli now trigger her new strategy that supports her health and fitness.

You, too, can discover strategies with which your unconscious mind is creating results you do not desire. And you can change those strategies—now!

WHAT'S LOVE GOT TO DO WITH IT?

What about love? Can you make someone feel totally loved by triggering a love strategy? The answer is yes. Once you discover someone's strategies, you can make him or her feel totally loved by triggering the exact stimuli that caused this feeling to occur within that person. You can also figure out what your own love strategy is. Love strategies are different from many other strategies in one key way. Instead of a three- or four-step procedure, there's usually only one step. There's one touch, one thing to say, or one way of looking at a person that makes him or her feel totally loved. This doesn't mean we all need only one thing to feel loved, but there generally is one sense that dominates the others.

You can elicit someone's love strategy the same way you elicit any other strategy. Put the person in state first. Remember, state is the outcome; state is the juice that gets the circuits going. So ask, "Can you remember a time when you felt totally loved?" To make sure he or she is in the right state, follow up with, "Can you remember a specific time when you felt totally loved? Go back to that time. Remember how it felt? Reexperience those feelings in your body now. Experience it now as you did then."

Next ask, "As you remember that time and feel those deep feelings of love, is it *absolutely necessary* that a person show you love by giving you things, taking you places, or looking at you in a certain way? Is it absolutely necessary that this person show love in this way for you to feel totally loved?" Note the answer and its congruency. Next, put the person back into state and say, "Remember that time when you felt totally loved. In order for you to feel these deep feelings of love, is it absolutely necessary for the person to express his/her love in a certain way for you to feel totally loved?" Judge the verbal and nonverbal responses for congruency.

Finally, ask, "Remember how it feels to be totally loved. In order for you to feel those deep feelings of love, is it necessary that someone touch you in a certain way for you to feel totally loved?"

Once you've discovered the key ingredient that creates these deep feelings of love for a person, you need to discover the specific submodalities. For example, ask, "How specifically would someone need to touch you to make you feel totally loved?" Have the person demonstrate, then test it. Touch him or her that way, and if you've done it accurately, you'll see an instantaneous shift in state. You have now tapped into that person's love strategy.

We all have a certain look, a certain way of having our skin stroked, a certain tone of voice, that reduces us to Jell-O. Most of us don't know what it is, but in state, we're able to come up with one thing that makes us feel absolutely, totally loved.

A minority of people will at first come up with two love strategies instead of just one. They'll think of a touch, and they'll also think of something they love to be told. So you have to keep them in the right state and ask them questions to get them to make a distinction. If they could have the touch but not the sound, would they feel totally loved? If they had the sound but not the touch, would they feel totally loved? If they're in the right state, they'll be able to make a clear distinction without fail. Remember, we need all three—visual, auditory, and kinesthetic—but there's one that opens the vault.

Eliciting Love Strategies

Can you remember a time when you felt totally loved? Can you remember a specific time? As you go back to that time and experience it . . . *[get the person in state]*

Visual

In order for you to feel these deep feelings of love, is it *absolutely necessary* for your partner to show you he/she loves you by . . . taking you places? giving you things? looking at you in a certain way?

Is it *absolutely necessary* that your partner show you he/she loves you in this way for you to feel totally loved? *[judge by physiology]*

Auditory

In order for you to feel these deep feelings of love, is it *absolutely necessary* for your partner to . . . tell you he/she loves you in a certain way? *[judge by physiology]*

Kinesthetic

In order for you to feel these deep feelings of love, is it *absolutely necessary* for your partner to . . . touch you in a certain way ? *[judge by physiology]*

[Now elicit the submodality] How, specifically? Show me (tell me, demonstrate for me).

[Thoroughly test the strategy. Judge by congruent physiology.]

Think of how valuable it will be to know the love strategy of your partner or your child. This can be one of the most powerful understandings you develop in supporting your relationship. If you don't know their love strategies, it can be pretty sad. I'm sure we've all been in the situation at least once in our lives when we loved someone and expressed our love, but we weren't believed; or someone expressed love to us, but we didn't believe it. The communication didn't work because the strategies didn't match.

There is an interesting dynamic that develops in relationships. In the very beginning of a relationship, in the courting stage, we are very motivated. So how do we let people know we love them? Do we just tell them we love them? Do we just show them or just touch them? Of course not! During courting, we do it all. We show each other, we tell each other, we touch each other all the time. As time goes on, most of us just aren't as mobilized anymore. We feel comfortable in the relationship. We know the person loves us, and we love that person. So how do we then communicate our feelings of love? Probably just as we would like to receive them. If so, what happens to the quality of the feelings of love in the relationship? Let's take a look.

If a husband has an auditory love strategy, how is he most likely to express his love to his wife? By telling her, of course. But what if she has a visual love strategy so that she feels deeply loved only after she receives certain visual stimuli? What will happen as time goes by? Neither member of this relationship is going to feel totally loved. When they were courting, they did it all—showed, told, and touched—and triggered each other's love strategies. Now the husband comes in and says, "I love you, honey," and she replies, "No, you don't!" He asks, "What are you *talking* about? How can you *say* that?" She may say, "Talk is cheap. You never *give* me flowers anymore. You never *take* me places with you. You never *look* at me in that special way." "What do you mean, look at you?" he may ask. "I'm *telling* you I love you." She is no longer experiencing her deepest feelings of being loved because the specific stimuli that trigger that feeling are no longer being consistently applied by her husband.

Or how about one of the greatest mismatches of all time—a kinesthetic man and a visually oriented woman? He comes home and wants to hug her. "Don't touch me," she says. "You're always grabbing at me. All you ever want to do is hug. Why can't we go someplace? Look at me before you touch me." Do any of these scenarios sound familiar? Can you see now how a relationship you had in the past ended because in the beginning you did it all, but as time went by you began to communicate love in only one way, and your partner needed it in another, or vice versa?

Remember, most of us think our map of the world is the way it is. We think, *I know what makes me feel loved. That must be what works for everyone else.* We forget that the map is not the territory. It's only how we see the territory.

So how does it feel to possess such a powerful tool? Now that you know how to elicit a love strategy, sit down with your partner and find out what makes him or her feel totally loved. And having elicited your own love strategy, teach your partner how to trigger your feelings of being totally loved. The changes this understanding can make in the quality of your relationship are worth your investment in this book many times over.

You can model any strategy, as long as you put someone in state and find out specifically what he or she does, in what order and sequence. The key isn't to merely learn a few strategies and use them. The most important thing is to constantly stay attuned to what people do well, and then to find out *how* they do it—what their strategies are. That's what modeling is all about.

People have spent a lifetime trying to find a way to feel totally loved. They've spent fortunes trying to get to "know themselves" with analysis, and they've read dozens of books on how to succeed. Eliciting strategies is a technology to accomplish these and many other goals elegantly, efficiently, and effectively—now!

So far you've learned how to access resourceful states and behaviors using modeling and strategy elicitation. As you've already seen, one way to get in a resourceful state is through syntax and internal representation. Another way is through physiology. Earlier, you discovered how mind and body are linked in a cybernetic loop. In these last few chapters you've explored the mental states of mind. Now let's take a look at something equally powerful . . .

CHAPTER ELEVEN

Physiology: The Avenue of Excellence

If you do what you've always done, you'll get what you've always gotten.

—MOMS MABLEY

FOR THE PAST few years, I have had the honor of being a member of the faculty at UCLA in the Engineering and Management Department. One of my classes, "Reengineering Yourself for the Next Century," has consistently been a breakthrough course for most of the engineers and managers who attend. What's interesting is that the biggest breakthrough for most of the students is not necessarily in the information they learn, but in the *way* they learn it.

You see, in my experience, engineers are some of the sharpest and most knowledgeable men and women I know, but where they excel in knowledge and information, they usually lack in flexibility. The turning point comes when I get them to loosen up and move their bodies. At any given moment you could walk into my class and find thirty-five to forty adults dancing around to music, clapping their hands, hooting and hollering, laughing out loud, flapping their arms, and in general acting like a bunch of crazy kids without a care on a warm spring day.

You might wonder, *What's going on here?*

What is going on is that they're accessing that part of themselves where most of their power lies. What is going on is the other half of the cybernetic loop: physiology. That "craziness" is about acting as if you felt more resourceful, more powerful, happier than ever before. Acting as if you were totally energized. Acting as if you absolutely knew you were going to succeed. You see, one way to get yourself into a state that supports your achieving any outcome is to act "as if" you are already there. Acting "as if" is most effective when you put your physiology in the state you'd be in if you were already effective.

> *People think of me as close to royalty. . . . I carry myself the way I do because I am royalty within myself.*
>
> —IMAN

For the purposes of this book, the word *physiology* means anything pertaining to your body: movement, posture, facial expressions, etc. Physiology is the most powerful tool we have for instantly changing states, for instantly producing dynamic results. There's an old saying: "If you would be powerful, pretend to be powerful." Truer words were never spoken. We expect people to get powerful results from our seminars, results that will change their lives. But for that to happen they must be in the most powerful physiology possible. Remember, all powerful action is preceded by powerful physiology.

If you adopt a powerful, dynamic, excited physiology, you automatically adopt the same kind of state of mind. The biggest leverage we have in any situation is physiology—because it works so fast, and it works without fail. Physiology and internal representations are totally linked. If you change one, you instantly change the other. If you change your physiology—that is, your posture, your breathing patterns, your muscle tension, the tonality of your voice—you instantly change your internal representations and your state. Remember, any physical movement has an effect on your state of mind.

On those days when we are physically beat, our outlook on the world is generally pretty pessimistic. When we feel tired or our muscles are weak or we have pain somewhere, we perceive the world quite differently from when we feel rested, alive, and vital. Physiological manipulation is a powerful tool for controlling your own brain. So it's extremely important that we realize how strongly it affects us, that it's not some extraneous variable but an absolutely crucial part of a cybernetic loop that's always in action. This area of human motivation is grossly overlooked: You can think and talk all day, but without physical movement, nothing is going to get done.

When your physiology runs down, the positive energy of your state runs down. When your physiology brightens and intensifies, your state does the same thing. So physiology is the lever to emotional change. In fact, you can't have an emotion without a corresponding change in physiology. Think of it this way: **There is no emotion without motion.** And you can't have a change in physiology without a corresponding change in state.

There are two ways to change state: by changing *internal representations* or by changing *physiology.* If you want to change your state in an instant, the first place to go is your physiology. A sudden, radical shift in your breathing, your posture, your facial expression, and, for that matter, anything physical will result in a shift in your state.

Have you ever been driving late at night and started to get drowsy? What's the first thing you do? You shake your head vigorously from side to side, adjust your position in the seat, and maybe even stop the car to stretch, run in place, or at least walk around the car. If you start to grow tired, there are certain things you can do with your physiology to continue to communicate a tired state to yourself: a slump in shoulder position, relaxation of many major muscle groups, and the like. You can become tired simply by changing your internal representations so that they give your nervous system a message that you are tired. If you change your physiology to the way it is when you feel strong, it will change your internal representations and how you feel at that moment. If you keep telling yourself that you're tired, you're forming the internal representation that keeps you tired. If you say you have the resources to be alert and on top of things, if you consciously adopt that physiology, your body will make it so. **Change your physiology and you change your state.** All of our lives we've heard teachers say, "Sit up and pay attention." Now you know why. It's hard to learn or pay attention in a lousy physiology.

In the chapter on belief, you read a little about the effects that beliefs have on health. Everything that scientists are finding today emphasizes one thing: Sickness and health, vitality and depression, are often decisions. They're things we can decide to do with our physiology. They're usually not conscious decisions, but they're decisions nonetheless.

God gives nothing to those who keep their arms closed.

—MAMADO KOUYATE

Do you think people sit and actually say, "I'd rather be depressed than happy"? No way. But what do depressed people do? We think of depression as a mental state, but it has a very clear, identifiable physiology. Most of us could describe the physiology of a depressed person with pinpoint accuracy. Depressed people often walk around with their eyes down. (They're accessing in a kinesthetic mode and/or talking to themselves about all the things that make them feel depressed.) They drop their shoulders. They take weak, shallow breaths. They do all the things that put their body in a depressed physiology. Are they deciding to be depressed? They sure are. Depression is a result, and it requires very specific body "language" to create it. Remember, at all times, we all have a choice.

PEANUTS® **By Charles M. Schulz**

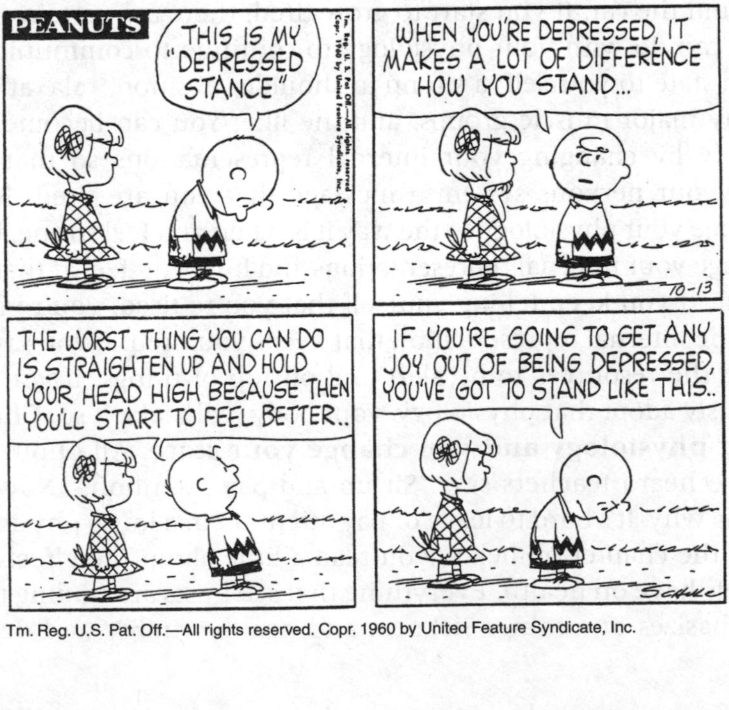

The great thing about all of this is that we can just as easily create a state of mind that empowers us and makes us feel great. We can create ecstasy by changing our physiology in specific ways. After all, what are emotions? They're a complex association, a complex configuration of physiological states. Without changing any of his internal representations, I can change the state of any depressed person in seconds simply by making him move, breathe, and gesture in a new way. You don't have to look and see what pictures a depressed person is making in his mind. Just change his physiology, and wham! you change his state.

It's a fact that if you put yourself in a resourceful physiology, you can't be depressed. Try this. Stand up right now. Stand tall and breathe deeply, pulling air into your diaphragm. Throw your shoulders back and look upward as you put a sheepish, silly grin on your face. Move your body. See if you can feel depressed in that posture. You'll find that it's almost impossible. Instead, your brain is getting a message from your physiology to be alert and vital and resourceful. Often when I do this exercise in my seminars, people start to laugh because they can't get depressed. Wouldn't that be a great tool to use the next time you feel a little down?

This may sound simplistic, but when people come to me and complain they can't do something, I say, "What would happen if you acted like you could?" They usually respond with something like, "Well, I don't know how." I say, "So . . . act like you did know how. Stand the way you would be standing if you did know how to do it. Breathe the way you'd be breathing if you did know how to do it right now. Make your face look as if you could do it right now." As soon as they stand that way, breathe that way, and put their physiology in that state, they instantly feel they can do it. It works without fail because of the amazing leverage of being able to adapt and change physiology. Over and over again, simply by changing physiology, you can make people do things they could never do before—because the second they change their physiology, they change their state.

You try it. Think of something you imagine you can't do but would like to be able to do. Now how would you stand if you knew you could do it? How would you talk? How would you breathe? Right now, put yourself as congruently as possible in the physiology you would be in if you knew you could do it. Make your whole body give you the same message. If you have trouble doing it, think of someone who can do it and adopt what you imagine that person's physiology to be. Make your stance, breathing, and face reflect the physiology you'd have if you knew you could do it. What you'll notice is that now there is a distinct difference in your state of mind from the one you were in. If you are congruently maintaining the right physiology, you will feel "as if" you can handle what you didn't think you could before. Or at least you can find a way.

Break Through with a More Resourceful Physiology

That's what happens when we teach karate-style board breaking. We use this exercise as a metaphor for breaking through one's fears. By using the modeling process, we are able to get people to break through solid wood boards in a matter of minutes—a task that normally would take several years to master. Some people walk up all fired up and ready to go. With very little coaching, they are able to do it healthfully and confidently with ease. Then there are others who will step in front of me in total fear and apprehension. They may have changed their internal representation of what was going to happen, so they imagine the worst possible scenario. Or the sight of the wood may take them out of state as they approach it. These people are usually shaking and about to bolt out of the room like frightened rabbits. Some are even crying and frozen with fear. I know they wouldn't have made it this far if they really didn't want to break through, so I help them break through their fear right there in that moment and take action against seemingly impossible odds. In reality, I need only to do one thing—change their state. Remember, all human behavior is the result of the state we are in for the moment. When we feel strong and resourceful we will attempt to do things we wouldn't do if we felt weak and scared. So wood breaking doesn't teach people intellectually; it gives them the experience of changing their states right then and there to support their goals, regardless of how they felt previously. It proves to them that even at the worst possible time, when everything inside of us is telling us we can't, we can get ourselves to take action and get the results we want.

So what do I do with shaking, crying, frozen, panicked people standing in front of me like scared gazelles on the Serengeti plains, ready to bolt? Actually there are several things I could do, such as have them picture themselves on the other side after they've done it successfully. Tell them to imagine celebrating because they did it. This changes their focus and with it their internal representations. In a matter of two to four seconds, these persons are in a resourceful state—you can see them change their breathing and facial expression. But most of the time I just go directly to the source—bypass all other communication—and change their physiology directly. For example, I can take a crying person and have her look up. By doing this, she begins to access the visual aspects of her neurology instead of her kinesthetic. Almost immediately, she stops crying. I tell her to stand tall, breathe deep, look up, and say, "YES!" This immediately changes the one thing that will govern her performance immediately: her physiology. This radical shift in physiology changes everything in an instant. When I see her in that strong, powerful, resourceful physiology, I then tell her to go, and the same person who was paralyzed with fear a split second earlier now bursts through purposefully and celebrates on the other side.

Obviously, you don't have to break wood to use this technique in your life. Try this for yourself: If you are upset or crying and want to stop, look up. Put your shoulders back and get into a visual state. Your feelings will change almost instantaneously. You can do this for your kids, too. When they get hurt, have them look upward, and the crying and pain will be stopped, or at least decrease tremendously, in a moment.

Over the years I have had hundreds of men and women come to me with a fear of approaching the opposite sex or a fear of confronting their superiors on the job. The same technique can be practiced whenever we feel we can't do something. After doing work on changing the internal representations, I simply have them stand the way they would if they were confident and strong, and they feel like they can do whatever they want in an instant. The ideal is to change both physiology and voice tone. Having done this, we can immediately feel resourceful and be able to follow through with the actions necessary to produce the results we desire.

It's important to remember that at all times we have the ability to change the biochemical and electrical processes of our bodies by changing our physiologies and internal representations. Studies show that when people get depressed, their immune systems follow suit and become less efficient—their white-blood-cell count drops. Have you ever seen a Kirlian photograph of a person? It's the representation of the body's bioelectrical energy, and it changes remarkably as a person changes state or mood. Because of the linking of mind and body, in intense states our whole electrical field can change and we can do things that wouldn't otherwise seem possible. Everything I've experienced and read tells me that our bodies have far fewer limits—both positive and negative—than we have been led to believe.

Remember the saying "As we think, so we are." Well, there have been reams and reams of material written on research done in the field of the mind-body connection. You've no doubt heard stories (like the ones in Chapter 6) of how people were told they were receiving a particular drug that would increase their heart rate and speed them up, when, in fact, they were given just the opposite: They were given a depressant and even in some cases a sedative. Yet these people responded as though they were on amphetamines, and their vital signs increased. Some patients were given sugar tablets and told these were the cure to their disease, and miraculously they recovered. Dr. Deepak Chopra, in his book *Quantum Healing,* tells several stories of people who cured themselves of terminal cancer by changing their internal representations. On the flip side is one particular case that sticks out in my mind, concerning a man who was scheduled for a simple prostate operation the next day. His charts got mixed up with another man's who was suffering from advanced malignant cancer. The man with the prostate operation was visited that evening by a death counselor who thought he was seeing the terminal patient. He told the man there was no hope and that he had only a short while to live. Later on that evening, the man died of heart failure. It can only be speculated, but he probably started making internal representations of someone who is dying, and his body responded to those signals by checking out. Exactly the same process goes on around us every day. Dr. George L. Engel of the University of Rochester Medical Center has developed a lengthy file of newspaper items from all over the world concerning sudden deaths under unexpected circumstances. In each case, it was not that something awful happened in the outside world. Rather, the culprit was the victim's own negative internal representations. In each case, something made the victim feel powerless, helpless, and alone.

The sad part about the whole thing to me is that there seems to have been more research and emphasis on the harmful side of the mind-body relationship than on the helpful side. We always hear about the horrible effects of stress or about people losing the will to live after the death of a loved one. We all seem to know that negative states and emotions can literally kill us. But we hear less about the ways positive states can heal us.

One of the most famous stories on the positive side of the ledger belongs to Norman Cousins. In his ground-breaking work, *Anatomy of an Illness,* he described how he made a miraculous recovery from a long, debilitating illness by laughing his way to health. Laughter was one tool Cousins used in a conscious effort to mobilize his will to live and to prosper. A major part of his regimen was spending a good deal of his day immersed in films, television programs, and books that made him laugh. This obviously changed the consistent internal representations he was making, and the laughter radically changed his physiology—and thus the messages to his nervous system of how to respond. He found that immediate, positive physical changes ensued. He slept better, his pain was lessened, his entire physical presence improved.

Eventually he recovered completely, even though one of his doctors initially said he had a one-in-five-hundred chance of making a full recovery. Cousins concluded, "I have learned never to underestimate the capacity of the human mind and body to regenerate—even when prospects seem most wretched. The life force may be the least understood force on earth."

Some fascinating research that is beginning to surface may shed some light on Cousins' experience and others like it. The studies focus on how our facial expressions affect the way we feel and conclude it's not so much that we smile when we feel good or laugh when we're in good spirits. Rather, smiling and laughing set off biological processes that, in fact, make us feel good. They increase the flow of blood to the brain and change the level of oxygen, the level of stimulation of the neurotransmitters. The same thing happens with other expressions. Put your facial expression in the physiology of fear or anger or disgust or surprise, and that's what you'll feel. All of these things are real, and this suggests we should not only take a closer look, but utilize what we find to our advantage. The chemicals in our very blood change with the expressions on our face, as well as every movement we make.

Act like you want to be and you'll soon be like you act.

—ANONYMOUS

There are about eighty muscles in the face, and they act as tourniquets, either to keep the blood supply steady while the body is experiencing wild swings or to alter the brain's blood supply and thus, to some degree, the brain's functioning. In a remarkable paper written in 1907, a French physician named Israel Waynbaum theorized that facial expressions actually change feelings. Other researchers today are finding the same thing. As Dr. Paul Ekman, Professor of Psychiatry at the University of California in San Francisco, told the *Los Angeles Times* (June 5, 1985), "We know that if you have an emotion, it shows on your face. Now we've seen it goes the other way, too. You become what you put on your face. . . . If you laugh at suffering, you don't feel suffering inside. If your face shows sorrow, you do feel it inside." In fact, Ekman says, the same principle is used regularly to beat lie detectors. People who put themselves in a physiology of belief, even when they're lying through their teeth, will register "truth."

The more we learn about the mind-body connection, the more we potentially free ourselves from the limitations of past beliefs about our abilities. Some people teach that all you really have to do is take good care of your body. If your body is working at peak levels, your brain will work more effectively as well. The better you use your body, the better your brain is going to work. That's the essence of the work of Moshe Feldenkrais. He used movement to teach people how to think and how to live. Feldenkrais found that simply by working on a kinesthetic level, you can change your self-image, your state, and the overall functioning of your brain. In fact, he states that the quality of your life is the quality of your movement. His works are an invaluable source for creating human transformation through changing physiology in a very specific way.

One very important aspect of physiology is *congruency*. If I'm giving you what I think is a positive message, but my voice is weak and shaky and my body language is disjointed and unfocused, I'm incongruent—and you'll pick up on it. Incongruity keeps me from being all I can be, from doing all I can do, and from creating my strongest state.

Have you ever really wanted to do something but another part of you stops you from doing it? Congruence is power. When our physiology matches our thoughts we can get ourselves to take massive action. People who consistently succeed are those who can commit all of their resources, mental and physical, to work together toward achieving a task. Take a minute now and think of the three most congruent people you know. Isn't it true that these individuals have a physiology that matches their intentions?

Developing congruency is a major key to personal power. When our body and words match, we're giving clear signals to our brain that this is what we want to produce. And our mind responds accordingly. Being aware of your current level of congruency will help you develop it. If you say to yourself, "Well, yeah, I guess this is what I ought to be doing," and your physiology is weak and indecisive, it will send a weak, indecisive message to your brain. Think about it. How congruent was Martin Luther King, Jr., when he spoke? The man had astonishing physical presence. Do you think he would have believed what he was saying if he were in a weak, indecisive physiology? Do you think you would have? Of course not. His words definitely matched his physiology, didn't they?

If you say, "Consider it done; I will absolutely accomplish it," and your physiology powerfully matches your words, you absolutely will do it. Congruent states are what we all want to move toward, and the biggest step you can take is to be sure you're in a firm, decisive, congruent physiology. If your words and your body don't match up, you're not going to be totally effective. Can you think of any time when you weren't congruent, and it cost you something as a result? Perhaps you wanted to ask for a raise or a date and you were turned down, or worse yet, you didn't even ask. Conversely, think about those times when you had conviction about what you were going to do, and you did what you set out to do with purpose and determination. What was the difference? How were your facial expressions, your breathing, your posture?

Probably the best way to develop better congruency is to model the physiologies of others who are congruent. You can elicit their strategies or simply act as if you are doing what they do in the moment. If you want to be effective, you want to use your brain in the same way. If you mirror someone's physiology exactly, you will tap the same part of your brain.

What is your congruency level? Could you be congruent more often? Take a few minutes now and think of five people who have powerful physiologies that you would like to mirror. You don't have to know them personally. How do their physiologies differ from yours? What is their posture? Their breathing? How do they move? Take some time and study them; it will be well worth your while. What are some of their key facial expressions and gestures? Take a moment and sit exactly the way one of these people sits. Make similar facial expressions and gestures. Notice how you feel.

> ***When we recognize where our power truly comes from, then we become blessed.***
>
> —BEN VEREEN

Here is a great exercise Tony conducts in a seminar. He has people mirror other people's physiologies, and they find they'll access a similar state and get a similar feeling. Try it now, and you'll have lots of fun doing this. First, find someone else to do this process with. Have that person recall a specific intense memory and, without telling you about it, go back into that state and hold it. Now I want you to mirror that person exactly. To mirror someone means to do exactly as they are doing. Mirror the way he or she is sitting, duplicating exactly how the legs are positioned. Mirror the hand and arm positions. Mirror the amount of tension you see in the face and body. Mirror the position of the head and any movements you see in the eyes or neck. Mirror the mouth, the skin tension, the rate of breathing. Try to put yourself in the exact same physiology your partner is in. By duplicating that person's physiology, you will be providing your brain with the same signal as his or her brain. You'll be able to feel similar or the same feelings. Often you'll see your version of the same pictures your partner's seeing and think your version of the same thoughts your partner's thinking.

Once you've done this, and while you are still in state, note a couple of words you would use to describe the state you're in—that is, what you feel while you are mirroring the person exactly. Now, ask the other person, "While you remain in state, tell me two or three words that describe what you are feeling." About 80 to 90 percent of the time, you will have used the same word to describe the state you were in. There are many people in every seminar who actually start seeing what the other person is seeing. They've described exactly where the person was or identified the people he or she was picturing mentally. Some of the accuracies defy rational explanation. It's almost like a psychic experience—except there's no psychic training. All we do is deliver to our brains the exact same messages as the person we're mirroring. I can't guarantee you'll succeed the first time out, but if you ever come close, you'll find yourself in the same state of anger or pain or sadness or elation or joy or ecstasy that the other person is in.

Some recent research gives scientific support to this. According to an article in *Omni* magazine, two researchers have found that words have a characteristic electrical pattern in the brain. Neurophysiologist Donald York of the University of Missouri Medical Center and Chicago speech pathologist Tom Jenson found that the same patterns hold true from person to person. In one experiment, they were even able to find the same brain wave pattern in people who spoke different languages. They've already taught computers to recognize those brain wave patterns so they can interpret the words in a person's mind even before they're spoken! The computers can literally read minds, much the way we can when we precisely mirror physiology.

LEADERS SHOW YOU HOW THEY LEAD

Some time ago after reading the original *Unlimited Power*, I decided to model some individuals I thought were most powerful and congruent. I rented videos of Martin Luther King, Jr., Muhammad Ali, Malcolm X, John F. Kennedy—and of course, working with Tony, I had constant access to him as a model. Some unique aspects of physiology—special looks or tonalities or physical gestures—can be found in people of great power. If you can model the specific physiology, you'll tap into the same resourceful parts of the brain and start to process information the way they do. You'll literally feel the way they felt. I found that as I modeled them I felt powerful and was able to tap into my own power more easily. As they say, "Try it; you'll like it."

It's important to note that some strategies require a level of physiological development or programming you do not yet have. You may have modeled the world's greatest baker, but if you try to bake his recipe in an oven that only gets up to 225 degrees, while his goes to 625, you are not going to produce the same result. However, by using his recipe, you can maximize the result you get even with your own oven. And if you model the way he got his oven to increase its output over the years, you can create the same result—if you're willing to pay the appropriate price.

One of my most powerful beliefs is that we always have choices in any situation, and as long as we are decisive, the more choices the better. Being attentive to physiology creates choices. Why do people take drugs, drink alcohol, smoke cigarettes, overeat? Aren't these all indirect attempts to change state by changing physiology? This chapter has provided you with the direct approach to quickly change your states. By breathing or moving your body or facial muscles in a new pattern, you immediately change your state. It will produce the same results as food, alcohol, or drugs without harmful side effects to either your body or your psyche. Remember, in any cybernetic loop, the individual who has the most choice is in control. In any device, the most critical aspect is flexibility. All other things being equal, the system with the most flexibility has more choices and more ability to direct other aspects of the system. It's the same with people. The people with the most choices are the ones most in charge. Modeling is about creating possibility. And there's no faster, more dynamic way than through physiology.

So take a look around in your life. Who is powerful and who is not? Choose those who are successful, happy, healthy, powerful, playful, and positive to model. I guarantee these people are the ones with the physiology to match their attributes. Copy their gestures, their posture, their breathing. Experience what they are feeling and experiencing. Give yourself the gift. These new choices will elevate your life. Now, let's take a look at another aspect of physiology—the foods we eat, the way we breathe, and the nutrients we supply to ourselves. Together they are the basis of . . .

CHAPTER 12

The Fuel of Excellence

We live inside this unbelievable cosmos, inside our unbelievable bodies—everything so perfect, everything so in tune. I got to think God had a hand in it.

—RAY CHARLES

SEVERAL YEARS AGO at one of his two-week-long Certification programs, Tony started talking about nutrition, the effects of our food intake, and how we use our bodies. Here it was, 12:30 at night, and he had been onstage working since 8:30 that morning. Yet he was still bouncing around and full of life, and this was the fifth day in a row that he'd kept up this pace. The rest of us, on the other hand, were about ready to drop like bags of wet sand from exhaustion. Not only was Tony full of energy, he was giving it out to the crowd and keeping the rest of us enthused, excited, and empowered all night. I thought that if he could produce these types of results, maybe I ought to listen very closely to what he had to say about this matter.

No one can deny that some people just seem to have more energy than others. I used to believe it was just a matter of genetics, but I'm happy to have found out that it's not necessarily true. People are constantly asking me, "How do you keep going? You sleep on the average of six to six and a half hours per night. You exercise, you play hard, and you always seem to be so up. How do you do it?" The answer is very simple, and it's no big secret . . . ENERGY.

There are three fundamentals that determine the quality of our lives: the thoughts we think, the way we move our bodies, and the things we put into our bodies. So far we've discussed the first two. Our internal representations are the thoughts we think, and our physiology is the way our bodies move. However, without the third component—energy—the other two would cease to exist, or, at the very least, function poorly. Everything we talk about in this book, from claiming your personal power to taking control of your own life, also depends on a healthy level of biochemical functioning. It assumes you're cleansing and nurturing your body, not clogging and poisoning it. The fact of the matter is, you can change your internal representations all day long, but if your biochemistry is messed up, it's going to make the brain create distorted representations. In this chapter, we'll look at the basics of physiology—what you eat, what you drink, and how you breathe. You'll be surprised and pleased to know it is much simpler than you may have been led to believe.

The level of energy and enthusiasm that characterizes me now is in stark contrast to what life used to be like for me. I know firsthand the importance of energy and the magic that an abundance of it can unleash. Ten years ago I used to require no fewer than ten hours of sleep. My blood pressure was through the roof, and the slightest bit of exercise sent me to the couch for an afternoon nap. When flu season came around I was one of the first to sign up for the Disemboweling, Stuffy Head, Wish You Were Dead, and Afraid You Were Going to Die Asian or Hong Kong or whatever so-called bug hit the States that year. I looked older, acted older, and felt older than I do today.

It's no secret that high blood pressure claims the lives of countless African American men per year. And although some of the contributing factors to these high mortality rates must surely be the day-to-day pressures of being Black in America, it's not too presumptuous to attribute it to our diet and living habits as well.

If health research over the past decade has proved one thing, it's that the quality of our physiology affects our perceptions and behaviors. We see more evidence every day that the American diet of junk food, fast food, and additives and chemicals is causing "trapped" wastes in the body, contributing to everything from cancer to crime. One of the most horrifying things I ever read was the diet of a chronic juvenile delinquent, recounted by Alexander Schauss in *Diet, Crime and Delinquency.*

For breakfast, the kid ate five cups of Sugar Smacks cereal with a half teaspoon of added sugar, one glazed doughnut, and two glasses of milk. He snacked on a foot-long rope of licorice and three six-inch beef jerky sticks. Then for lunch he had two hamburgers, French fries, more licorice, a small serving of green beans, and little or no salad. He snacked on some white bread and chocolate milk before dinner. Then he had a peanut butter and jelly sandwich on white bread, a can of tomato soup, and a ten-ounce glass of sweetened Kool-Aid. Later, he had a bowl of ice cream, a Marathon candy bar, and a small glass of water.

How much more sugar could a body take in, after all? A society that raises its young on a diet that even remotely resembles this is asking for trouble. Do you think these "foods" affected his physiology and thus his state and behavior? You bet. On a questionnaire, this fourteen-year-old boy checked the following symptoms: After I fall asleep, I wake up and cannot get back to sleep. I get headaches. I have itching or crawling sensations on my skin. My stomach or intestines are upset. I get bruises or black-and-blue marks easily. I have nightmares or bad dreams. I get faint, dizzy, or have cold sweats or weak spells. I get hungry or feel faint if I do not eat often. I often forget things. I add sugar to most things I eat or drink. I am very restless. I cannot work under pressure. It's hard to decide things. I feel depressed. I constantly worry about things. I get confused. I get depressed or feel the blues over nothing. I blow little things out of proportion and easily lose my temper. I get fearful. I feel very nervous. I am highly emotional. I cry for no apparent reason.

Do you wonder that, coming from this state, this young man created delinquent behaviors? Fortunately, he and many like him are now making radical changes in their behavior, not because they are being punished with long jail sentences, but because a major source of their behavior, their biochemical state, has been changed through diet. Criminal behavior is not just "in the mind." Biochemical variables influence state and thus behavior.

It's not too far-fetched to realize that at least some of the high rate of violence and gang-related crimes might be directly related to the poor dietary habits of our youth. Do you think that the average inner-city youth has a diet that is anywhere near what he needs to support a peaceful, productive lifestyle? This issue infuriates me, and I continually speak on the subject whenever I can.

Now, I do realize we all have different ideas of how and what to eat and drink. But the fact of the matter is, most of us have been *conditioned* by society to believe what we do. I encourage you to take a look at the following information with a very open mind, for the difference it can make in the quality of your life is invaluable.

The Six Principles of Living Health

Although Tony had studied the greats in the medical field, he wasn't looking for credentials. What he wanted was results. So he modeled people who were producing results in their bodies, people who were vibrant and healthy, and he set up a sixty-day program for healthy living. I applied these principles daily, and the results were astounding. More important, I finally found a way to live that was hassle-free and not diet-oriented (notice what the first three letters in the word *diet* spell)—a way that respected how my body worked. Over the years, Tony and I have watched so many others adopt these simple principles and make amazing changes in their lives. We have seen thousands of people shed thousands of pounds of unwanted weight with a fraction of the work they previously thought it would require.

Please be aware that much of what follows will challenge things you've always believed. Some of it will go against the notions you now have of good health. But these six principles have worked spectacularly for us and the people we've worked with, as well as thousands of others who practice a science of health called natural hygiene. We ask only that you please think carefully about whether they could work for you and whether your current health habits are the most effective way to take care of your body. Apply all six principles for ten to thirty days, and judge their validity by the results they produce in your body rather than by what you may have been educated to believe. Understand how your body works, respect it, and take care of it, and it will take care of you.

The first and probably the most important key to living health is the power of breath. If you get nothing else from this chapter but an understanding of the importance of deep breathing, you can dramatically increase the level of your body's health. Think about it: You can go several weeks without food, a couple of days without water, but you can survive only about three or four minutes without air. As simplistic as this may sound, most of us take for granted the importance of not only the quality of air we breathe, but the way we breathe it as well. Yet nothing could be more important. The foundation of health is a healthy bloodstream, the system that transports oxygen and nutrients to all the cells of your body. If you have a healthy circulation system, you'll live a long, healthy life. What controls that system? Breathing. That's the way you fully oxygenate the body and thus stimulate the electrical process of each and every cell.

Let's take a closer look at how the body works. Breathing not only controls the oxygenation of the cells, it also controls the flow of lymph fluid, which contains white blood cells to protect the body. What is the lymph system? Some people think of it as the body's sewage system. Every cell in your body is surrounded by lymph; you have four times as much lymph fluid in your body as you do blood. Oxygen and nutrients are carried in the blood, which is pumped from your heart through your arteries to the thin, porous capillaries. The oxygen and nutrients are then diffused into the lymph surrounding the cells. The cells, having an intelligence or affinity for what they need, take oxygen and nutrients necessary for their health and then excrete toxins, some of which go back into the capillaries. But dead cells, blood proteins, and other toxic material must be removed by the lymph system—and the lymph system is activated by deep breathing.

The body's cells depend on the lymph system as the only way to drain off the large toxic materials and excess fluid that restrict the amount of oxygen. The fluid passes through the lymph nodes, where dead cells and all other poisons except blood proteins are neutralized and destroyed. How important is the lymph system? If it were totally shut down for twenty-four hours, you would be dead as the result of trapped blood proteins and excess fluid around the cells.

The bloodstream has a pump, your heart. But the lymph system doesn't have one. The only way lymph moves is through deep breathing and muscular movement. So if you want to have a healthy bloodstream with effective lymph and immune systems, you need to breathe deeply and produce the movements that will stimulate them. Beware any "health program" that doesn't first and foremost teach you how to fully cleanse your body through effective breathing.

Dr. Jack Shields, a highly regarded lymphologist from Santa Barbara, California, conducted an interesting study of the immune system. He put cameras inside people's bodies to see what stimulated cleansing of the lymph system. He found that a deep diaphragmatic breath is the most effective way to accomplish this. It creates something like a vacuum that sucks lymph through the bloodstream and multiplies the pace at which the body eliminates toxins. In fact, deep breathing and exercise can accelerate this process by as much as fifteen times.

It doesn't take too much common sense to realize that of all the elements necessary for good health, oxygen is the most critical. Dr. Otto Warburg, Nobel Prize winner and director of the Max Planck Institute for Cell Physiology, studied the effect of oxygen on cells. He was able to turn normal, healthy cells into malignant cells simply by lowering the amount of oxygen available to them. His work was followed up here in the United States by Dr. Harry Goldblatt. In the *Journal of Experimental Medicine* (1953), Goldblatt described the experiments he conducted with a species of rats that had never been known to have malignant growths. He took cells out of newborn rats and divided them into three groups. One of the three groups of cells was put in a bell jar and deprived of oxygen for up to thirty minutes at a time. Like Dr. Warburg, Goldblatt discovered that after a few weeks many of these cells died, the movement of others slowed, and still others began to change their structure, taking on the appearance of malignant cells. The other two groups of cells were maintained in bell jars whose oxygen content was consistently maintained at atmospheric concentrations.

After thirty days, Dr. Goldblatt injected all three groups of cells into three separate groups of rats. After two weeks, when the cells had been reabsorbed into the animals, nothing happened with the two normal groups. However, all the rats in the third group—those whose cells had been periodically deprived of oxygen—developed malignant growths. This work was followed up a year later. The malignant growths remained malignant, and the normal cells remained normal.

What does this tell us? The researchers came to believe that lack of oxygen seems to play a major role in causing cells to become malignant or cancerous. It certainly affects the quality of life of the cells. Remember that the quality of your health is really the quality of the life of your cells. Thus, fully oxygenating your system would seem to be a number one priority, and breathing effectively is certainly the place to start.

The problem is that most people don't know how to breathe. One in every three Americans gets cancer. Yet athletes experience only one case of cancer to every seven in average Americans. Why? These studies begin to give us an explanation. Athletes are giving the bloodstream its most important and vital element: oxygen. Another explanation is that athletes are stimulating their bodies' immune systems to work at maximum levels by stimulating the movement of lymph.

This may sound funny, but most of us don't know the right way to breathe. That's right. In my seminars, I ask the audience to take a deep breath. It's amazing: Like bread dough rising in the oven, their shoulders simultaneously move toward the ceiling. But when we raise our shoulders to breathe, we are in fact cutting off as much as a quarter of our lung capacity. Our lungs are larger at the bottom, and when we raise our shoulders we are pushing our diaphragm in the opposite direction it is designed to go—actually closing down the bottom fourth of our lungs to fill the top two-thirds. Have you ever seen a sleeping baby breathe or a puppy taking a nap? Watch their stomachs as they breathe in and out, in and out. The action is in their tummies, not their chest cavities.

Let me share with you the most effective way to breathe in order to cleanse your system. Breathe in this ratio: **Inhale one count, hold four counts, exhale two counts.** So, if you inhaled for four seconds, you would hold for sixteen and exhale for eight. Why exhale for twice as long as you inhale? That's when you eliminate toxins via your lymph system. Why hold four times as long? That's how you fully oxygenate the blood and activate your lymph system. When you breathe, start from deep in your abdomen, like a vacuum cleaner that's getting rid of all the toxins in the blood system.

How hungry do you feel after you exercise? Do you want to sit down and eat a big steak after you've just run four miles? We know, in fact, that people don't. Why not? Because through healthy breathing, your body is already getting what it needs most. So here's the first key to healthy living. **Stop and take ten deep breaths, in the above ratio, at least three times a day.** Starting in the abdomen, take a deep breath through your nose, hold your breath for a count four times that of your inhalation, then exhale slowly through your mouth for a count two times the length of your inhalation. Never strain yourself. See what numbers you can build up to by slowly developing greater lung capacity. Take ten of these deep breaths three times a day, and you'll experience a dramatic improvement in the level of your health. There is no food or vitamin pill in the world that can do for you what excellent breathing patterns can do.

The second key to maximizing your energy is the principle of eating water-rich foods. Seventy percent of the planet is covered with water. Eighty percent of your body is made up of water. What do you think a large percentage of your diet should contain? You need to make certain that 70 percent of your diet is made up of foods that are rich in water. That means fresh fruits or vegetables, or their juices freshly squeezed.

Some people recommend drinking from eight to twelve glasses of water a day to "flush out the system." Do you know how crazy that is? In the first place, most of our water isn't so great. Chances are it contains chlorine, fluoride, minerals, and other toxic substances. Drinking distilled water is usually the best idea. But no matter what kind of water you drink, you can't cleanse your system by drowning it. The amount of water you drink should be dictated by thirst.

Instead of trying to flush your system by flooding it with water, all you have to do is eat foods that are naturally rich in water—water-content foods. There are only three kinds on the planet: fruits, vegetables, and sprouts. These will provide you with an abundance of water, the life-giving, cleansing substance. When people live on a diet that is low in water-content foods, an unhealthy functioning of the body is almost guaranteed. As Alexander Bryce, M.D., states in *The Laws of Life and Health,* "When too little fluid is supplied, the blood maintains a higher specific gravity and the poisonous waste products of tissue or cell change are only cast off very imperfectly. The body is, therefore, poisoned by its own excretions, and it is not too much to say that the chief reason of this is because a sufficient amount of fluid has not been supplied to carry off in solution the waste matter the cells manufacture."

Your diet should be consistently assisting your body with the process of cleansing, rather than burdening it with indigestible foodstuff. The buildup of waste products within the body promotes disease. One way to keep the bloodstream and body as free as possible from wastes and toxic poisons is to limit ingestion of those foods or nonfoods that strain the eliminative organs of the body; the other is to provide enough water to the system to assist in the dilution and elimination of such wastes.

Why is heart disease our biggest killer? Why do we hear about people keeling over and dropping dead on the tennis court at the age of forty? One reason may be that they've spent a lifetime clogging their system. Remember, the quality of your life is dependent upon the quality of the life of your cells. If the bloodstream is filled with waste products, the resulting environment does not promote a strong, vibrant, healthy cell life—nor a biochemistry capable of creating a balanced emotional life for an individual.

Dr. Alexis Carrel, a Nobel Prize winner in 1912 and a member of the Rockefeller Institute, set out to prove this theory by taking the tissue from chickens (which normally live an average of eleven years) and keeping their cells alive indefinitely simply by keeping them free of their own wastes and supplying them with the nutrients they needed. These cells were kept alive for thirty-four years, after which the Rockefeller Institute became convinced they could keep them alive forever and thus decided to end the experiment.

What percentage of your diet is made up of water-rich foods? If you were to make a list of all the things you've ingested in the past week, what percentage would be rich in water? Would it be 70 percent? I doubt it. How about fifty? Twenty-five? Fifteen? When I ask this in my seminars, I usually find that most people eat about 15 to 20 percent water-content foods. And that's definitely higher than the population as a whole. Let me tell you something: *15 percent is suicidal.* If you don't believe me, just check out the statistics for cancer and heart disease. Review what kinds of foods the National Academy of Sciences recommends you avoid and the amount of water content available in those foods.

If you look to nature for the biggest and most powerful animals, you'll discover they're herbivores. Gorillas, elephants, rhinoceroses, and so on all eat only water-rich foods. Herbivores live longer than carnivores. Think of a vulture. Why do you think it looks that way? It doesn't eat water-rich foods! If you eat something that's dried and dead, guess what you're going to look like? I'm only half-kidding on this point. Do you want to slow down the aging process? *Eat more water-rich foods!* How can you make sure that 70 percent of your diet consists of water-content foods? It's actually very simple. **Just be certain from now on to have a salad with each meal.** Make fruit the snack you reach for instead of a candy bar. You'll feel the difference when your body runs more efficiently and allows you to feel as great as you really are!

The third key to living health is the principle of effective food combining. When a medical doctor named Steven Smith celebrated his one hundredth birthday and was asked what allowed him to live so long, he replied, "Take care of your stomach for the first fifty years, and it will take care of you for the next fifty." Truer words were never spoken.

Many great scientists have studied food combining. Dr. Herbert Shelton is the best known. But do you know who was the first scientist to study it extensively? It was Dr. Ivan Pavlov, the man best known for his ground-breaking work with stimulus-response. Some people turn food combining into something very complicated, but it's actually pretty simple: Some foods should not be eaten with others. Different types of foods require different types of digestive juices, and not all digestive juices are compatible.

For example, do you eat meat and potatoes together? How about cheese and bread, or milk and cereal, or fish and rice? What if I were to tell you that those combinations are totally destructive to your internal system and rob you of energy? You'd probably say that I'd made sense to this point, but now I've lost my head.

Let me explain why these combinations are destructive and how you can save yourself large amounts of nerve energy you may currently be wasting. Different foods are digested differently. Starchy foods (rice, bread, potatoes, and so on) require an alkaline digestive medium, which is initially supplied in the mouth by the enzyme ptyalin. Protein foods (meat, dairy, nuts, seeds, and the like) require an acid medium for digestion—hydrochloric acid and pepsin.

Now, it is a law of chemistry that two contrary mediums (acid and alkali) cannot work at the same time. They neutralize each other. If you eat a protein with a starch, digestion is impaired or completely arrested. Undigested food becomes soil for bacteria, which ferment and decompose it, giving rise to digestive disorders and gas.

Incompatible food combinations rob you of energy, and anything that produces a loss of energy is potentially disease-producing. It creates excess acid, which causes the blood to thicken and thus move more slowly through the system, robbing the body of oxygen. Remember how you felt after you dragged yourself from Thanksgiving dinner last year? How conducive is that to good health, to a healthy bloodstream, to an energetic physiology? To producing the results you desire for your life? What is the number one selling prescription drug in the United States? It used to be the tranquilizer Valium. More recently, it was Tagamet, a drug for stomach disorders (now available over the counter). Maybe there's a more sensible way to eat. That's what food combining is all about.

Here's a very simple way to think about it: **Eat only one condensed food at a meal.** What's a condensed food? It's any food that's not rich in water. For example, beef jerky is condensed, whereas watermelon is water-rich. Some people don't want to limit their intake of condensed foods, so let me tell you the least you can do. Make sure you don't eat starchy carbohydrates and protein at the same meal. Don't have those meat and potatoes together. If you feel you can't live without both, have one at lunch and the other at dinner. That's not so hard, is it? You can go to the finest restaurant in the world and say, "I'll have the steak without the baked potato, and I'll have a big salad and some steamed vegetables." That's no problem; the protein will mix with the salad and vegetables because they're water-content foods. You could also order the baked potato (or two) without the steak and have a huge salad and steamed vegetables. Will you leave a meal like this feeling hungry? Absolutely not.

Do you wake up tired in the morning, even after six or seven or eight hours of sleep? While you're sleeping, your body is working overtime to digest the incompatible combinations of food you've put in your stomach. For many people, digestion takes more nerve energy than almost anything else. When foods are improperly combined in the digestive tract, the time it takes to digest them can be as much as eight, ten, twelve, fourteen hours, even more. When foods are properly combined, the body is able to do its job effectively, and digestion lasts an average of three to four hours, so you don't have to waste your energy on digestion. (After eating a properly combined meal, you should wait at least three and a half hours before ingesting any other foods. Also, it is important to note that the drinking of fluids at meals dilutes the digestive juices and slows the digestive process.)

An excellent source for a thorough treatment of the subject of food combining is Dr. Herbert Shelton's *Food Combining Made Easy.* Also, Harvey and Marilyn Diamond have written an excellent book called *Fit for Life,* filled with recipes for properly combined meals.

The fourth key to a long and healthy life is the law of controlled consumption. Do you love to eat? So do I. Want to learn how to eat a lot? Here it is: Eat a little. That way, you'll be around long enough to eat a lot.

Medical study after medical study has shown the same thing: The surest way to increase an animal's life span is to cut down on the amount of food it eats. Dr. Clive McCay conducted one famous study at Cornell University. In his experiment, he took laboratory rats and cut their food intake in half. It doubled their life span. A follow-up study done by Dr. Edward J. Masaro at the University of Texas was even more interesting. Masaro worked with three groups of rats. One group ate as much as it wanted; a second group had its food intake cut by 60 percent; and the third group was able to eat as much as it wanted, but its protein intake was cut in half. Want to know what happened? After 810 days, only 13 percent of the first group remained alive. Of the second group, whose food consumption was cut by 60 percent, 97 percent were still alive. Of the third group where food intake remained high, but protein consumption was cut in half, 50 percent were still alive.

Is there a message in this? Dr. Ray Walford, a famous UCLA researcher, concluded, "Undernutrition is thus far the only method we know of that consistently retards the aging process and extends the maximum life span of warm-blooded animals. These studies are undoubtedly applicable to humans because it works in every species studied thus far." The studies showed that physiological deterioration, including the normal deterioration of the immune system, was markedly delayed by food restriction. So the message is simple and clear: **Eat less, live more.**

Hey, I'm like you. I love to eat. It can be a form of entertainment. But make sure your entertainment isn't killing you. If you want to eat large quantities of food, go ahead. Just make sure they're water-rich foods. You can eat a whole lot more salad than you can steak to remain vibrant and healthy. Try it, you'll like it—and what's more, your body will like you for it.

The fifth key to living healthier is the principle of effective fruit consumption. Fruit is the most perfect food. It takes the least amount of energy to digest and gives your body the most in return. The only food your brain can work on is glucose. Fruit is primarily fructose (which can be easily converted into glucose), and it's most often 90 to 95 percent water. That means it's cleansing and nurturing at the same time.

The only problem with fruit is that most people don't know how to eat it in a way that allows the body to use its nutrients effectively. You must always eat fruit on an empty stomach. Why? The reason is that fruit is not primarily digested in the stomach. It digests in the small intestine. Fruit is designed to go right through the stomach in a few minutes and into the intestines, where it releases its sugars. But if there is meat or potato or starch in the stomach, the fruit gets trapped there and begins to ferment. Did you ever eat some fruit for dessert after a big meal and find yourself burping the uncomfortable aftertaste for the rest of the evening? That's because you didn't eat it properly. You must always eat fruit on an empty stomach. When you eat is also important. It is best not to eat immediately before you go to bed. An excellent habit to develop is to eat no food other than fruit after 9:00 P.M.

The best kind of fruit is fresh fruit or freshly squeezed fruit juice. You don't want to drink juice right out of a can or glass container. Why not? Much of the time the juice has been heated in the sealing process, and its structure has become acidic. Do you want to make the most valuable purchase you can? **Buy a juicer.** What if you don't have the money? Let me ask you: Do you own a car? Sell the car and buy a juicer. The juicer will take you much further. Or just buy the juicer now! You can ingest juice as you would the fruit itself, on an empty stomach. And juice is digested so fast that you can eat a meal fifteen or twenty minutes later.

This is not just opinion. Dr. William Castillo, head of the famed Framington, Massachusetts, heart study, has stated that fruit is the finest food you could possibly eat to protect yourself against heart disease. He said fruit contains bioflavonoids, which keep the blood from thickening and plugging up the arteries. It also strengthens the capillaries, and weak capillaries often lead to internal bleeding and heart attacks.

Tony once talked with a marathon runner who was pretty skeptical by nature, but got him to agree to make proper use of fruits in his diet. Can you guess what happened? He took 9.5 minutes off his marathon time. He cut his recovery time in half, and he qualified for the Boston Marathon for the first time in his life.

Here's one final thing to keep in mind about fruits. What should you start a day with? What should you have for breakfast? Do you think it's a smart idea to jump out of bed and clog your system with some huge amount of food you'll take all day to digest? Of course not.

What you want is something that is easy to digest, that provides fructose the body can use right away, and that helps cleanse the body. When you wake up, and for as long into the day as is comfortably possible, eat nothing but fresh fruit or freshly squeezed fruit juice. Keep this commitment until at least twelve noon each day. The longer you can go with just fruit in your body, the greater the opportunity for your body to cleanse itself. If you start to wean yourself from coffee and the other garbage you used to load your body down with at the start of the day, you'll feel a new rush of vitality and energy you won't believe. Try it for the next ten days and see for yourself. This one change is the thing that gave me the biggest energy boost in the beginning.

The sixth key to a vital, healthy life is understanding the protein myth. Have you ever heard it said that if you tell a big enough lie loud enough and long enough, sooner or later people will believe you? No bigger lie has ever been told than the one that human beings require a high-protein diet to maintain optimum health and well-being.

Chances are you're pretty conscious of your protein intake. Why is that? Some people are looking for an increased level of energy. Some think they need protein to help with endurance. Some eat it for strong bones. But excess protein has the exact opposite effect in every one of those cases.

Let's find a model of how much protein you might really need. When do you think people are most in need of protein? Probably when they're infants. Mother Nature has provided a food, mother's milk, that supplies the infant with everything it needs. Guess how much of mother's milk is protein—50 percent, 25 percent, 10 percent? Too high in every case. Mother's milk is 2.38 percent protein at birth and reduces to 1.2 to 1.6 percent protein in six months. That's all. So where do we get the idea that humans need massive amounts of protein?

No one really has any idea how much protein we need. After ten years of studying human protein ingestion needs, Dr. Mark Hegstead, past professor of nutrition at Harvard Medical School, confirmed the fact that most human beings seem to adapt to whatever protein intake is available to them. In addition, even people like Frances Lappé, who wrote *Diet for a Small Planet* (which for almost a decade promoted the concept of combining vegetables in order to get all the essential amino acids), now says that she was incorrect, that people do *not* have to combine their proteins, that if you eat a fairly balanced vegetarian diet, you will get all the protein you need. The National Academy of Sciences says that the adult American male needs fifty-six grams of protein a day. In a report by the International Union of Nutritional Sciences, we find that each country has adult male daily protein requirements that vary from thirty-nine to one hundred ten grams per day. So who really has any idea? Why would you need all that protein? Presumably to replace what you lose. But you lose only a tiny amount through excretion and respiration a day. So where do they get those numbers?

We could give you a hundred reasons why eating meat for protein is one of the worst things you could do. For example, one of the by-products of protein metabolism is ammonia. Meat contains high levels of uric acid. Uric acid is one of the body's waste or excretory products resulting from the work of living cells. The kidneys extract uric acid from the bloodstream and send it on to the bladder to be passed out with the urea as urine. If uric acid is not promptly and thoroughly removed from the blood, the excess builds up in the tissues of the body and later creates gout or bladder stones, not to mention what it does to your kidneys. People with leukemia are usually found to have very high levels of uric acid in their bloodstream. The average piece of meat has fourteen grains of uric acid. Your body can eliminate only about eight grains of uric acid in a day. In addition, do you know what gives meat its taste? Uric acid from the dead animal you're consuming. If you doubt this, try eating kosher-style meat before it's spiced. As the blood is drained out, so is most of the uric acid. Meat without uric acid has no flavor. Is that what you want to put in your body—the acid normally eliminated in the urine of an animal?

Moreover, meat is teeming with putrefactive bacteria. In case you're wondering what putrefactive bacteria are, they are colon germs. As Dr. Jay Milton Hoffman explains in his book, *The Missing Link in the Medical Curriculum Which Is Food Chemistry in Its Relationship to Body Chemistry*: "When the animal is alive, the osmotic process in the colon keeps putrefactive bacteria from getting into the animal. When the animal is dead the osmotic process is gone and putrefactive bacteria swarm through the walls of the colon and into the flesh. They tenderize the meat." In other words, what ages or softens the flesh are the putrefactive bacteria.

If you absolutely must eat meat, this is what you should do. First, get it from a source that guarantees it's pasture grazed, that is, a source that guarantees it doesn't have growth hormones or DES (diethylstilbestrol). Second, drastically cut your intake. Make your new maximum one serving of meat per day.

We're not saying that simply by not eating meat you will be healthy, nor are we saying that if you do eat meat you cannot be healthy. In fact, many meat eaters are healthier than vegetarians simply because some vegetarians have a tendency to believe if they don't eat meat, they can eat anything else. We're certainly not advocating that.

Are dairy products any better? In some ways, they're even worse. Every female mammal makes milk with the right balance of elements for its species. Many problems can result for humans from drinking the milk of other animals, including cows. For example, powerful growth hormones in cow's milk are designed to raise a calf from ninety pounds at birth to one thousand pounds at physical maturity two years later. By comparison, a human infant is born at six to eight pounds and reaches physical maturity at one hundred to two hundred pounds twenty-one years later. There is great controversy as to the effect this has on our population.

Dr. William Ellis, a noted authority on dairy products and how they affect the human bloodstream, states that if you want allergies, drink milk. If you want a clogged system, drink milk. The reason, he states, is that few adults can properly metabolize the protein in cow's milk. Its principal protein is casein, which is what a cow's metabolism needs for proper health. However, casein is not what humans need. According to Dr. Ellis, both infants and adults have a great deal of difficulty digesting casein. His studies show that, at least in infants, 50 percent or more of the casein is not digested. These partially digested proteins often enter the bloodstream and irritate the tissues, creating susceptibility to allergens. Eventually, the liver has to remove all these partially digested cow proteins, and that in turn places an unnecessarily heavy burden on the entire excretory system, and on the liver in particular. By contrast, lactalbumin, the primary protein in human milk, is easy for humans to digest.

As for drinking milk for calcium, Dr. Ellis states that after doing blood tests on more than twenty-five thousand people, he found that those who drink three, four, or five glasses of milk a day had the lowest level of blood calcium. So if you're concerned about getting enough calcium, simply eat plenty of green vegetables, sesame butters, or nuts—all of which are extremely rich in calcium and easy for the body to use. For example, turnip greens, weight for weight, contain twice as much calcium as milk. Also, it's important to note that if you consume too much calcium, it can accumulate in your kidneys and form kidney stones. Thus, to keep your blood concentrations relatively low, your body rejects about 80 percent of the calcium you eat.

What's the main effect of milk on the body? It becomes a clogging, mucus-forming mass that hardens and sticks to everything inside the small intestine, making the body's job that much more difficult. How about cheese? It's just concentrated milk. Remember, it takes four to five quarts of milk to make one pound of cheese. The fat content alone is enough reason to limit its intake. If you really desire cheese, cut up a small amount in a big salad. That way you have plenty of water-rich food to counteract some of its clogging effects.

For some, giving up cheese sounds awful. I know you love your pizza and brie. Yogurt? It's just as bad. Ice cream? It's not something that will support you in being your best. You don't have to give up that wonderful taste or texture, though. You can put frozen bananas through a juicer to create something that tastes and feels just like ice cream but is totally nurturing to your body. What about cottage cheese? Do you know what a large number of dairies use to thicken their cottage cheese and cause it to stick together? Plaster of paris (calcium sulfate). No kidding. It's allowed within federal standards, although its use is against the law in California. (However, if the cottage cheese is made in a state where it is allowed, it can be shipped to California and sold there.) Can you imagine trying to create a clean, free-flowing bloodstream—then filling it with plaster of paris?

This whole book is designed for you to take in information, decide what you think is useful, and throw away what you find doesn't work. However, why not test all the principles before you judge them? **Try the six principles of the living health system for the next ten to thirty days—or for your lifetime—and judge for yourself if they produce higher levels of energy and a feeling of vibrancy that supports you in all you do.**

Let me give you one small caveat. If you start breathing effectively in a way that stimulates your lymph system, begin to combine your food correctly, and eat 70 percent water-content foods, what's going to happen? Have you ever seen a fire start in a building with only a few exits? Everyone scrambles for the same exits. Well, your body works the same way. It will start cleaning out the garbage that's been piling up in your system for years, and it may use its newfound energy to do it as fast as it can. So you might suddenly start sneezing up excess mucus. Does that mean you've caught a cold? No, you ate a "cold." You created a "cold" by years of awful eating habits. Your body may now have the energy to use your eliminative organs to rid itself of excess waste products formerly stored in the tissues and bloodstream. A small number of people might release enough poisons from their tissues to the bloodstream to produce a slight headache. Should they reach for the Excedrin? No! Where do you want those poisons, out or in? Where do you want that excess mucus, in your handkerchief or in your lungs? It's a small, temporary price to pay for cleaning out years of horrible health habits. Most people, though, will have no negative reaction at all; they'll immediately feel a heightened sense of energy and well-being.

As we pointed out earlier in this book, the first key to success is always to know your outcome. The six keys in this chapter can be yours to create the experience of health you desire. Take a moment and imagine yourself a month from now having actually followed these principles and concepts. See the person you will be after having changed your biochemistry by eating and breathing effectively. What if you started your day by taking ten deep, clean, powerful breaths that invigorated your whole system? What if you began every day feeling alert and joyful and in control of your body? What if you started eating healthy, cleansing, water-content foods and stopped eating the meat and dairy products that were stressing and clogging up your system? What if you began combining foods properly so your energy was available for the things that really mattered? What if you went to bed every night feeling you had experienced the total vibrancy that allowed you to be all you could be? What if you had energy you never dreamed was possible?

If you look at that person and like what you see, then know it's easily within your grasp! It takes only a little discipline—not too much, because once you break your old habits, you'll never go back. For every disciplined effort there is a multiple reward. So if you like what you see, do it. Start today, and it will change your life forever. My wish for you is that you will allow yourself to experience the wonder of the vibrant health that is your birthright.

Now that you know how to put yourself in the finest state for producing results, let's take the next step and discover . . .

PART TWO

THE ULTIMATE SUCCESS FORMULA

CHAPTER THIRTEEN

Limitation Disengage: What Do You Want?

"I can't believe my good fortune, and I am just so grateful, to be a black woman. A Black American woman. I would be so jealous if I were anything else."

—MAYA ANGELOU

CONGRATULATIONS! YOU HAVE COMPLETED the first section of what I call "The Owner's Guide to Being Human." I've shared with you what Tony and I believe are the basic tools of personal power. You now have the techniques and insights that will allow you to discover how people produce results, and how to model their actions so that you can produce similar results. You've learned how to direct your mind and support your body. You now know how to get yourself to achieve whatever you want and help others achieve what they want.

The next obvious question is . . . *What do you want?* And what do the people you love and care about want? As simple as this question is, you'd be surprised how many people never ask it of themselves, let alone answer it. As a matter of fact, most of the time when I ask people what they want, they answer with what they *don't* want. "I don't want to work so hard," "I don't want to be overweight," etc.

If there's one thing that all successful people have in common, it's that they all know what they want. Remember, the first step is always to know your outcome. Have you ever heard the saying, "Knowledge is power"? Well, knowledge is only potential power. Without action and an outcome, knowledge is little more than digital information. What good is having an ATM card if you don't have a machine in which to use it? If you know where to find the ATM, how to use it, and why, you are in control of your situation. If not, all you have is a fancy piece of plastic.

One of the first things we learned is that the quality of your communication is the quality of your life. In this section we will talk about defining your outcome and refining those communication skills that will allow you to use your abilities in the most effective way for the situation at hand. It's important to be able to map out a strategy so you know precisely where you want to go—and know the things that can help get you there quickly.

Since repetition is the mother of skill, let's quickly review what you've learned thus far. The main thing you now know is there are no limits to what you can do. As Black Americans, we have so many potent references of successful people achieving so much—often in the face of some pretty severe opposition and persecution. Your key is the power of modeling. Excellence can be duplicated. If other people can do something, all you need to do is model them with precision and you can do exactly the same thing, whether it's walking on fire, making a million dollars, or developing a loving relationship. How do you model? First you must realize that all results are produced by a specific set of actions. Every effect has a cause. If you reproduce someone's actions exactly—both internal and external—then you, too, can produce the same result. You begin by modeling someone's mental actions, starting with the person's belief system, going on to the mental syntax, and finally mirroring the physiology. Do all three effectively and elegantly, and you can do just about anything.

You've learned that success or failure begins with belief. Whether you believe you can do something or you believe you can't, you're right. Even if you have the skills and resources to do something, once you tell yourself you can't, you shut down the neurological pathways that make it possible. If you tell yourself you can do something, you open up the pathways that can provide you with the resources for achievement.

You've learned the Ultimate Success Formula: Know your outcome, take massive action, develop the sensory acuity to know what you're getting, develop the flexibility to change your behavior until you find out what works, and you will reach your outcome. If you don't get it, have you failed? Of course not. Like a pilot adjusting an aircraft, you just need to change your behavior until you get what you want.

You've learned about the power of being in a resourceful state, and you've learned how to adjust your physiology and internal representations so they serve you, enable you, and embolden you to achieve your desires. You know that if you're committed to success, you'll create it.

An important point worth adding is that there's an incredible dynamism inherent in this process. The more resources you develop, the more power you have; the more strength you feel, the more you can tap into even greater resources and even more powerful states.

You're just about ready to start designing the life of your dreams—but first I want to tell you about a phenomenon I see happening in the Black community that I think you will find helpful. More than ever before, there is a groundswell of Blacks who are moving in the direction of growth through personal development and human awareness. The best example I can think of is the Million Man March that took place October 16, 1995, in Washington, D.C. The theme of the march was "Atonement," and studies have shown that the impact of the march has been very positive as it pertains to Black men taking control of their lives.

Have you ever been thinking about someone, then the phone rings and it's that very person on the line? Or perhaps you're sitting in your car at a traffic light and feel someone staring at you, only to look at the car next to you and find you were right. Most of us have experienced these or similar unexplained so-called coincidences and happenstances. We may not always be able to explain them, but there is definitely more here than meets the eye.

When I was very young, I remember reading in the Bible that we should pray as though we already have what we want. Why? Because that faith and that emotion will act as a radio transmitter to your Creator. Our bodies, our brains, and our states are like tuning forks in harmony with that higher level of existence. So the better attuned and aligned you are, the more you can tap into this rich knowledge and feeling. Just as information filters to us from our unconscious, it may also filter in to us from sources completely outside ourselves—if we're in a state resourceful enough to receive it.

Still, the key to all of this is knowing what we want. The unconscious mind is constantly processing information in such a way to move us in particular directions. Even at the unconscious level, the mind is distorting, deleting, and generalizing. So before the mind can work efficiently, we must get clear about the outcomes we expect to reach. In his well-known book of the same title, Maxwell Maltz calls this "psycho-cybernetics." When the mind has a defined target, it can focus, direct, refocus, and redirect until it reaches its intended goal. If it doesn't have a defined target, its energy is squandered. It's like a person with the world's greatest chainsaw who has no idea why he's standing in the forest.

In this chapter you will learn how to formulate your goals, dreams, and desires as concrete targets, and how to fix firmly in your mind what you want and how to get it. Have you ever tried to put together a jigsaw puzzle without having seen the picture of what it represents? That's what happens when you try to put your life together without knowing your outcomes. When you know your outcomes, you give your brain a clear picture of which kinds of information being received by the nervous system need high priority. You give your brain the clear messages it needs to be effective.

Winning starts with beginning.

—ANONYMOUS

There are people—we all know some of them—who always seem constantly lost and in a state of perpetual confusion. They go one way, then another. They try one thing, then shift to another. They move down one path and then retreat in the opposite direction. They will usually defend their actions as "for real this time," but they seem always to do the same thing over again. Their problem is simple: They don't know what they want. You can't hit a target if you don't know what it is.

You will need to approach this chapter a little differently than the others. We want you to dream, but it's absolutely essential you do so in a totally focused way. If you just read this chapter, it's not going to do you any good. You'll have some great knowledge, but so what? We're going to ask you to sit down with a pencil and paper or a word processor and create your future. Don't even start unless you have allotted some time to do these exercises.

Now, find or create a place where you can relax and be undisturbed. You can expect to spend about an hour to do this, but we think you'll agree that your future is worth the time. It could be the most valuable hour you ever spend. You're going to learn to set goals and determine outcomes. You're going to make a map of the roads you want to travel in your life. You're going to figure out where you want to go and how you expect to get there. You're going to learn how to give those dreams the wings to take your soul higher than ever before.

Here's a major word of caution, though: Do not put any limitations on what's possible. Of course, that doesn't mean throwing your intelligence and common sense out the window. If you're running east looking for a sunset, you won't find it. However, dare to dream big. When Tony was twenty-four years old and he was writing the first edition of this book, he began to write, "If you're four feet eleven inches tall, there's no sense deciding your outcome is to win the NBA slam dunk contest next year. No matter what you try, it won't happen (unless you work well on stilts)." He told me that he did this because he wanted people to understand that they had to be realistic. Before the book was published, Spud Webb of the Atlanta Hawks, five feet seven inches, won the slam dunk contest. So much for the limitations of not being on stilts! However, don't divert your energy from where it can be most effective. When viewed intelligently, there are no limits to the outcomes available to you. Limited goals create limited lives, so stretch yourself as far as you want in setting your goals. You need to decide what you want, because that's the only way you can expect to get it. Follow these five rules in formulating your outcomes. Did you know that one of the co-discoverers of the North Pole was a Black man? That's right. On April 6, 1909, Matthew Alexander Henson, along with Admiral Robert Edwin Peary, made history. Do you think they found the North Pole without knowing what they wanted? Of course not. They had it all mapped out and knew where and what they wanted to a tee. Start your map now.

1. State your outcome in positive terms. Say what you want to happen. Too often people state what they *don't* want to happen as their goals. For example, don't say, "I don't want to be fat anymore." Instead say, "I will become healthy, fit, and trim."

2. Be as specific as possible. How does your outcome look, sound, feel, smell? We call this being *sensory specific.* Become fully associated: "Remember" it as though you've already received it. Engage all of your senses in describing the results you want. The more sensory specific and sensory rich your description, the more you will empower your brain to create your desire. Also, be certain to set a specific completion date and/or time period.

3. Have an evidence procedure. Know how you will look and feel, and what you will see and hear in your external world after you have achieved your outcome. If you're not sure how you will know when you've achieved your goal, you may already have achieved it. You can be winning and feel like you're losing if you don't keep score.

4. Be in control. Your outcome must be initiated and maintained by you. It must not be dependent upon other people having to change themselves for you to be happy. Make sure your outcome reflects things you can affect directly.

5. Verify that your outcome is ecologically sound and desirable. That is, project into the future the consequences of your actual goal. Your outcome must be one that benefits you and other people. Does the outcome benefit others as well as yourself?

Setting Outcomes
Key Components

Positive:	What exactly do you / we want?
Sensory Specific:	What will you / we see? What will you / we hear? What will you / we feel? What will you / we smell? What will you / we taste?
Evidence Procedure:	How will you / we know the outcome has been realized?

If you knew you could not fail, what would you do? If you were absolutely certain of success, what activities would you pursue, what actions would you take?

Remember, clarity is power. We all have some idea of what we want. Some goals are vague—more love, more money, more time to enjoy life. However, to empower our biocomputers to create a result, we need to have goals more specific than a new car, a new house, a better job.

As you create your list, some of what you write down will be things you've thought about for years. Some will be things you've never consciously formulated before. But you need to consciously decide what you want, because knowing what you want determines what you will get. Before something happens in the external world, it must first happen in the internal world. Something rather amazing happens when you get a clear internal representation of what you want. It programs your mind and body to achieve that goal. To go beyond our present limitations, we must first experience this expansion in our minds, then our lives will follow suit.

Think of this chapter as doing the same for your life—you're now going to create it exactly as you want it. Normally in life you could only go so far, but in your mind you're going to take the time to create a reality greater than what you've experienced in the past. Then you're going to externalize that internal reality. If this all seems silly to you, think about this: Which is sillier, creating a new reality, or doing the same thing you have been doing over and over again and not getting the results you want?

12. Principles of Goal Attainment

1. Start by making an inventory of your dreams, the things you want to have, do, be, and share. Create the people, feelings, and places you want to be a part of your life. Sit down right now, grab your paper and pen, and begin writing. Keep your pen moving nonstop for at least ten to fifteen minutes. Don't try to define how you're going to get this outcome now. Just write it down. There are no limits! Abbreviate whenever possible so you can immediately get on to the next goal. Keep your pen moving the entire time. Take as long as you need to put together a broad sampling of outcomes having to do with work; family; relationships; mental, emotional, social, material, and physical states; and anything else. Feel like a king or queen. Remember, everything is within your grasp. Knowing your outcome is the first key to reaching it.

One key to goal setting is play. Let your mind roam free. Whatever limitations you have are limitations you've created. Where do they exist? Only in your mind. So whenever you start to place limitations on yourself, throw them off. Do it visually. Make a picture in your mind of a wrestler flipping an opponent out of the ring, then do the same with whatever limits you. Take those limiting beliefs and toss them out of the ring, and be aware of the feeling of freedom you have when you do it. This is step one. Make your list now!

2. Let's do a second exercise. **Go over the list you made, estimating when you expect to reach those outcomes: six months, one year, two years, five years, ten years, twenty years.** It's helpful to see what sort of a time frame you're placing on yourself. Some people find their list dominated by things they want today. Others find their greatest dreams are far in the future, in some imagined period of total achievement and fulfillment. If all your goals are short-term, you need to start taking a longer view of potential and possibility. If all your goals are long-term, you need to develop some steps that can lead you in the direction you expect to go. A journey of a thousand miles begins with a single step. Be aware of both the first steps and the final ones.

3. Now, pick your four most important goals for this year. Pick the things you're most committed to, most excited about, things that would give you the most satisfaction. Write them down. Then write why you absolutely will achieve each one of them. Be clear, concise, and positive. Tell yourself why you're sure you can reach those outcomes, and why it's important for you to do so.

Jim Rohn, Tony's first personal-development teacher, always taught him that if you have enough reasons, you can do anything. Our purpose for doing something is a much stronger motivator than the object we pursue. Reasons are the difference between being interested versus being committed to accomplishing something. There are many things in life we say we want, but really we're only interested in them for a time. We must be totally committed to whatever it takes to achieve our outcomes. If, for example, you just say you want to be rich, that's a goal, but it doesn't tell your brain much. If you understand *why* you want to be rich, what being wealthy would mean to you, you'll be much more motivated to get there. Why to do something is much more important than how to do it. If you get a big enough why, you can always figure out the how. If you have enough reasons, you can do virtually anything in this world.

4. Now that you have a list of your four key goals, review them against the five rules for formulating outcomes. Are your goals stated in the positive? Are they sensory specific? Do they have an evidence procedure? Describe what you will experience when you achieve them. In even clearer sensory terms, what will you see, hear, feel, and smell? Also note if the goals are maintainable by you. Are they ecological and desirable for you and others? If they violate any of these conditions, change them to fit.

5. Next, make a list of the important resources you already have at your disposal. When you begin a construction project, you need to know which tools you have. To construct an empowering vision of your future, you need to do the same thing. So make a list of what you have going for you: character traits, friends, financial resources, education, time, energy, and so on. Come up with an inventory of all your strengths, skills, resources, and tools.

6. Now focus on times when you used some of those resources most skillfully. Come up with three to five times in your life when you were totally successful—in business, sports, financial matters, relationships—any time you did something particularly well. It can be anything from a killing in the stock market to a wonderful day with your kids. Write these events down. Describe what you did that made you succeed, what qualities or resources you used effectively, and what about that situation made you feel successful.

7. Next, describe the kind of person you would have to be to attain your goal. Will it take a great deal of discipline or education? Would you have to manage your time well? If, for example, you want to be a civic leader who really makes a difference, describe the kind of person who gets elected and really has the ability to affect large numbers of people. We hear a lot about success, but we don't hear as much about the components of success—the attitudes, beliefs, and behaviors that go into producing it. If you don't have a good grasp of these components, you may find it difficult to put together the whole. So write a couple of paragraphs or a page about all the character traits, skills, attitudes, beliefs, and disciplines you would need to possess in order to achieve all you desire. Take some time on this, at least half an hour or more.

8. In a few paragraphs, write down what prevents you from achieving what you desire right now. One way to overcome the limitations you've created is to know exactly what they are. Dissect your personality to see what's holding you back from achieving what you want. Do you fail to plan? Do you plan, but fail to act? Do you try to do too many things at one time, or do you get so fixated on one thing that you don't do anything else? In the past, have you imagined the worst possible scenario and allowed that internal representation to stop you from taking action? We all have ways of limiting ourselves—our own strategies for failing—but by recognizing them, we can change them now and move on.

9. Take each of your four key goals and create your first draft of a step-by-step plan to achieve them. Ask yourself, "What would I have to do first to accomplish this goal?" or "What prevents me from having this now, and what can I do to change this?" Make sure your plans include something you can do today.

Years ago when asked how he was able to achieve so much in his life (not the least of which was founding Tuskegee University in Alabama), Booker T. Washington stated, "I always started with a plan." We must do the same for our lives. We can know what we want, why we want it, who will help us, and a lot of other things, but the critical ingredient that in the end determines whether we succeed in achieving our outcomes is our *actions*. To guide our actions, we must create a step-by-step plan. When you build a house, do you just get a pile of wood, some nails, a hammer, a saw, then go to work? Would you start sawing and hammering and see what came of it? Would that lead to success? Not likely. To build a house you need a blueprint. You need a sequence and a structure so that your actions build upon and reinforce one another. Otherwise you will just have a wild assemblage of boards. It's the same with your life. You need to put together your own blueprint for success.

Let it be said that many of you already have a plan, and for that you should be congratulated. But if that plan is not getting you where you want to go fast enough, then perhaps it's time to fine tune it. At the very least, all it can do is expedite the plan you might already have.

What are the necessary actions you must take consistently to produce the result you want? If you're not sure, think of someone you can model who has already accomplished what you desire. Start with your ultimate outcomes, then work backward, step by step. If one of your major outcomes is to become financially independent, the step before that might be to become president of your own company. The step before that might be becoming a vice president or other important officer. Another step might be to find a smart investment counselor and/or tax lawyer to help you manage your money. It's critical that you continue to work backward until you find something you can do *today* to support the achievement of that goal. Maybe today you could open a savings account or get a book that teaches you some financial strategies of successful people in our culture.

If you want to be a professional dancer, what do you have to do to reach that outcome? What are the major steps, and what are some things you can do today, tomorrow, this week, this month, this year, to produce the results? If you want to be the greatest composer in the world, what are the steps along the way? By working backward, step by step, for outcomes in everything from business to your personal life, you can map out the precise path to follow from your ultimate goal down to what you can do today.

If you're not sure what your plan should be, just ask yourself what prevents you from having what you want now. The answer to that question will be something you can work on changing immediately. The solving of that problem becomes a subgoal or stepping-stone to the achievement of your greater goals.

10. Now, what's the surest way to achieve excellence? Model

someone who has already done what you want to do. **So come up with some models.** By now you probably recognize there are countless role models and examples to pull from—Black, white, and otherwise. Focus on their accomplishments first. They can be people you know personally or famous people who've achieved great success. Write down three to five names, and specify in a few words the qualities and behaviors that made them successful. After you've done this, close your eyes and imagine for a moment that each of these people is going to give you some advice about how best to begin accomplishing your goals. Write down one main idea that each would give you if he or she were speaking to you personally; jot down the first idea that comes to mind. Maybe it's how to avoid a roadblock or break through a limitation; what to pay attention to, or what to look for. Even though you may not know them personally, with this process they can become excellent advisers on your future.

Now you have a clear internal representation of where you want to go. You've been giving signals to your brain, forming a clear, concise pattern of outcomes. Goals are like magnets. They'll attract the things that make them come true. In Chapter 8, you learned how to run your own brain, how to manipulate your submodalities to enhance positive images and decrease the power of negative ones. Let's apply that knowledge to your goals.

Take a glimpse into your personal history, at a time when you were totally successful at something. Close your eyes and form the clearest, brightest possible image of that accomplishment. Take note of whether you put the image to the left or right, up, middle, or down. Again, notice all its submodalities—the size, shape, and quality of its movement as well as the type of sound and internal feelings it creates.

Now think about the outcomes you've written down. Make a picture of how you would be if you achieved everything you've set down today. Put that image on the same side as the previous one, and make it as big, bright, focused, and colorful as you can. Notice how you feel. You'll already feel much more certain of success than you did when you first formulated your outcomes.

If you have trouble doing this, use the swish method we talked about earlier. Move the image of what you want to be to the other side of your mental frame. Make it defocused and black and white. Then quickly move it to the exact same spot as your successful image, having it break through any representations of possible failure you may have perceived. Have the new image take on all the big, bright, colorful, focused qualities of the image of what you've already accomplished. Do these exercises on an ongoing basis until your brain gets an even clearer, more intense picture of what you expect it to accomplish. Your brain responds most to repetition and deep feelings, so if you can continually experience your life as you desire it, with deep and intense feelings, you are almost certain to create what you desire. Remember, the road to success is always under construction.

11. It's great to have all kinds of different goals. However, what's even better is to put them all together in a meaningful way. **So design your ideal day.** What people would be involved? What would you do? How would it begin? Where would you go? Where would you be? Describe everything in detail, from the time you get up to the time you go to sleep. What kind of environment would you be in? How would you feel when you climbed into bed at the end of a perfect day? All our results, actions, and realities start from creations in our minds, so create your day the way you desire it most.

12. Sometimes we forget that dreams begin at home. We forget that the first step toward success is providing ourselves with an atmosphere that nurtures our creativity, that helps us be everything we can be. **So now it's time to design your perfect environment.** Let your mind go. No limitations—whatever you want is what you should put in. Act as if you're royalty. Design an environment that would bring out the best of all you are as a person. Where would you be—in the woods, overlooking the ocean, in an office? What tools would you have—an art pad, paints, music, a computer, a telephone? What support people would you have around you to make sure you achieved and created all you desired in life?

If you don't have a clear representation of what your ideal day would be, what are your chances of creating it? If you don't know what your ideal environment would be, how could you create it? How are you going to hit a target if you don't even know what it is? Remember, your brain needs clear, direct indications of what it wants to achieve. Your mind has the power to give you everything you want. But it can only do that if it's getting clear, bright, intense, focused signals.

I sincerely hope you have not been taking these last few pages lightly. Please don't make the mistake of passing on this opportunity or waiting to do it later "when you have time." *Make the time now.* You can't reach your outcome if you don't know what it is. If you get anything from this chapter, it should be this: Results are inevitable. *If you don't program your mind for the results you desire, someone else will provide that programming for you.* And, as we all know from experience and history, those "someone elses" rarely have your best interest in mind. If you don't have your own plan, someone else is going to make you fit into their plan. If all you do is read this chapter, you've wasted your time. It's imperative you take the time to do each of these exercises. They may not be easy at first, but believe me, they're worth it; and as you begin to do them, they become more and more fun.

In the book *Why Should White Guys Have All the Fun?* there is a copy of the actual handwritten schedule and plan of multimillionaire Reginald F. Lewis. You would do well to look this over for yourself, and judge by his results. One of the reasons most people don't do well in life is that success is usually disguised behind hard work—and goal setting, or outcome development, is hard work. It's easy for people to put it off and get trapped into making a living instead of designing their lives. Exert your personal power now and take the time to discipline yourself to fully complete these exercises. It's been said that there are only two pains in life, the pain of discipline or the pain of regret, and while discipline weighs ounces, regret weighs tons. There's a great deal of excitement to be gained from applying these twelve principles. I can tell you personally that doing these exercises has literally changed the direction of my life and thousands like me. Do this for yourself.

One more thing: It's important to review your outcomes on a regular basis. If you don't, who will? The more you check in, the more chances you have to adjust and fine-tune your approach. Sometimes we may change while our outcomes remain the same, because we've never stopped to see if we still want to create the same things for our lives. Start by systematically updating your outcomes every few months, then perhaps once or twice a year. Remember, your life is a lifelong project. One very useful strategy is to keep a journal, which will provide you with an ongoing record of your goals at any time in your life. Journals are great to review, to study how your life has developed and how much you've grown. If your life is worth living, it's worth recording.

Does all this work? You bet it does! At the end of one of Tony's Certification programs, he told us to describe our ideal day. He gave us about an hour to do it and, after we were finished, he requested that we write another letter thanking ourselves for having accomplished the things it took to make that day a reality. I thought it was a little silly, but I did it anyway. I told myself how proud I was for the tenacity, drive, and hard work it took to have the things on my list. Everything on the list seemed so out of reach at the time, but I did it anyway. We addressed the letters to ourselves and turned them in to Tony. He told us he would mail them back to us in about six months.

Time passed, and I went on with my life. Fast-forward to two years later, when I had moved to L.A. One night I was sitting in my car, reading my mail and listening to the radio, when all of a sudden my eyes fell upon a letter addressed to me. A weird feeling came over me when I realized it was written in my own handwriting—the letter Tony had sent back to us! I had forgotten all about it and, because I had moved, it had taken all that time to reach me. As I read the letter, my eyes filled with tears. *The life that was described in the letter was the life I was living at the time.* I had gotten everything I had programmed into my mind. Everything I imagined had come to pass. Perhaps what struck me most was that all of those things felt so natural to have, and I had no trouble accepting the thanks and praise from myself for having come through.

Why? I did the exercise that is laid out in front of you now. I gave myself a target, and every day I congruently gave my brain the clear, precise, directed message that this was my reality. Having a clear, precise target, my powerful unconscious mind guided my thoughts and actions to produce the results I desired. It worked for me, and it can work for you.

Where there is no vision, the people perish.

—PROVERBS 29:18

Now you should do one final thing. Make a list of the things you already have that were once goals—all the things in your ideal day you already do, the activities and people for whom you are most grateful, the resources already available to you. I call this a gratitude diary. Sometimes people get so fixated on what they want, they fail to appreciate or use what they already have. The first step toward a goal is seeing what you have, giving thanks for it, and applying it to future achievements. We all have ways to make our lives better at any moment. Achieving your wildest dreams should begin immediately with the everyday steps that can put you on the right path. Shakespeare once wrote, "Action is eloquence." Begin today with eloquent action that will lead to even more eloquent outcomes.

By now I'm sure you recognize the importance of committing your goals and outcomes to paper. Please don't make the mistake of relying on your memory to do these exercises. The moment you commit something to paper it becomes a tangible piece of matter that starts to enhance the attraction process.

In this chapter, you've seen the importance of precision in formulating your outcomes. It's the same in all our communications with ourselves and with others. The more precise we are, the more effective we are. Now it's time to learn the methods and tools to accomplish . . .

CHAPTER FOURTEEN

The Power of Precision

A wise person speaks carefully and with truth, for every word that passes between one's teeth is meant for something.

—Moleti Kete Asanti

WE'VE ALL HAD TIMES IN OUR LIVES when the words that someone spoke moved us emotionally. Perhaps it was a parent, a coach, a teacher, a friend. Maybe it was a speech, like Dr. Martin Luther King, Jr.'s, moving call for human rights, "I have a dream." We can all remember moments when someone spoke with so much force, precision, and resonance that the words stayed with us forever. Words literally have the ability to change our biochemical makeup. Comedians, for example, can make us laugh or even cry with the words they use. The chemicals coursing through our systems will respond and change as we react to what we hear.

When John Grinder and Richard Bandler studied successful people, they found many common attributes. One of the most important was precise communication skills. A manager has to manage information to be successful. They found that the most successful managers seemed to have a genius for getting to the heart of information rapidly and communicating to others what they had learned. They tended to use key phrases and words that conveyed their most important ideas with great precision. Successful people understood they did not need to know everything. They distinguished between what they needed to know and what they didn't need to know, and they focused on the former. Bandler and Grinder also observed that many outstanding therapists used some of the same phrases many times to get immediate results with patients in one or two sessions instead of one or two years.

Remember, we've learned that the words we use to describe experiences aren't the experiences: The map is not the territory. Words are just the best verbal representation we can come up with. So it stands to reason that one measure of success is how accurately and precisely our words can convey what we want—how closely our map can approximate the territory. Just as we can remember times when words moved us like magic, we can also remember times when our communication went utterly, hopelessly awry. Have you ever tried to convey your feelings about something to someone and the person took it the wrong way? Maybe you thought you were saying one thing, but the other person got the opposite message. Just as precise language has the ability to move people in useful directions, sloppy language can misdirect them.

In this chapter, you'll learn about tools that will help you communicate with more precision and effectiveness than you may have had before. You'll also learn how to guide others toward the same outcome. We'll pick up some simple verbal tools any of us can use to cut through the verbal fluff and distortion that surrounds us. Words can be walls, but they can also be bridges. It's important to use them to link people rather than divide them. In my opinion, this tool is of utmost importance as it pertains to Black empowerment. The ability to communicate precisely to ourselves and others is key to how we are perceived—and how effective our actions will be as a result.

Are you ready? I'm about to reveal a crucial piece of information that can make an immediate difference in your life. Do you want to know how to get whatever you want? Well, then, get out a fresh piece of paper—come on, do it now. Across the top I want you to write these words in all capital letters, then underline them: <u>HOW TO GET WHATEVER I WANT.</u> Now skip down a few spaces and follow my instructions *to the letter.* You are about to learn one of the most effective, most precise steps to making your dreams a reality. You are about to learn the number one key to success that all great achievers use to get their outcomes. Are you all set? Okay, then . . . Write this down, very slowly and very carefully . . . ASK. That's right, *ask.* End of story!

Am I kidding? Absolutely not. When I say, "Ask," I don't mean whine or beg or complain or plead or grovel. I don't mean expect a handout or a free lunch or an act of charity. I don't mean expect someone else to do your work for you. What I mean is learn to ask intelligently and precisely. Learn to ask in a way that helps you both define and achieve your outcome. Most people don't realize they must ask before they will ever receive. In the last chapter, you began to learn to do this when you formulated the specific outcomes, goals, and activities you wanted to pursue. Now you need some specific verbal tools. Here are five guidelines for asking intelligently and precisely.

1. Ask specifically. Remember everything you did in the last chapter, when you wrote down in detail what you wanted. Details are the key! You must be able to describe what you want, both to yourself and to someone else. How high, how far, how much? When, where, how, with whom? If your business needs a loan, you'll get it—if you know how to ask. Tony used to ask participants in his seminars what they wanted, and people often said they wanted to make money. So he'd hand them a quarter and say, "Now you have money; you've achieved your goals. How does it feel?" You need to define precisely what you need, why you need it, and when you need it.

2. Ask someone who can help you. It's not enough to ask specifically. You must ask specifically of someone who has the resources—the knowledge, capital, sensitivity, or business experience—to help you. Let's say you're having trouble with your spouse. Your relationship is falling apart. You can pour out your heart to a friend, being as specific and honest as is humanly possible. But if you seek help from someone who has as pitiful a relationship as you do, will you succeed? Of course not. Finding the right person to ask brings us back to the importance of learning how to notice what works. Anything you want—a better relationship, a better job, a better program for investing your money—is something someone already has or already does. The trick is to find these peoplc and figure oul what they do right. Many of us gravitate toward "barroom wisdom." We find a sympathetic ear and expect that to translate into results. But it won't unless the sympathy is matched by expertise and knowledge. An unfortunate practice in our Black communities is for us to gravitate toward and seek advice only from those who share our misfortunes. Although this bonds us together in one way, it all but closes off the avenues out of the vicious loop of defeat.

3. Create value for the person you're asking . . . FIRST! Most people want to see, hear, and/or feel a return for what they are giving. Don't just ask and expect someone to give you something. Figure out how you can help this person first. This will assure him or her that giving to you will be a win-win venture. If you have a business idea and need money to pull it off, one way to do it is to find someone who can both help and benefit. Show the person how your idea can make money for you and benefit him or her as well. Creating value doesn't always have to be that tangible. The value you create may only be a feeling or a new awareness or a dream, but often that's enough. If you came up to me and said you needed $10,000, I'd probably say, "So do a lot of other people." If you said you needed the money to make a difference in people's lives, I might begin to listen. If you specifically showed me how you wanted to help others and create value for them and yourself, I might see how helping you could create value for me as well.

4. Ask with focused, congruent belief. The best way to ensure failure is to convey ambivalence. If *you* aren't convinced about what you're asking for, how can anyone else be? So when you ask, do it with absolute conviction. Express that in your words and physiology. Show that you're sure of what you want, sure you'll succeed, and sure you will create value, not just for yourself but for the person you're asking as well.

Sometimes people do all four of these perfectly. They ask specifically, they ask someone who can help them, they create value for the person they're asking, and they ask congruently—and even after that, they don't get what they want. The reason is they didn't do the fifth thing, which is the most important part of asking intelligently.

5. Ask until you get what you want. This doesn't mean always asking the same person. It doesn't mean asking in precisely the same way. Remember, the Ultimate Success Formula says you need to develop the sensory acuity to know what you're getting, and you have to have the personal flexibility to change. So when you ask, you have to change and adjust until you achieve what you want. When you study the lives of successful people, you'll find they kept asking, kept trying, kept changing—because they knew that sooner or later they would find someone who could satisfy their needs.

There's a great story I first read in the book *Think and Grow Rich* several years ago that inspired me to always ask until I got what I wanted. Back in post-slavery days, a young African American girl about ten or twelve years old was sent by her mother to collect wages from her boss. The boss refused to pay the little girl and told her to come back later. But the little girl refused to leave and just continued to ask for the money. Even after the man threatened her with a whipping, she stood her ground and insisted on her mother's wages. Seeing the determination in the little girl's eyes, the man finally gave her what she asked for. Too many of us give up too easily. Remember, the amount of people who fail is directly proportionate to the amount of people who give up.

Which of these five guidelines is the hardest to follow? For many people it's the one about asking specifically. We don't live in a culture that puts a great premium on precise communication. It may be one of our biggest cultural failings. Language reflects a society's needs. An Eskimo has several dozen words for snow. Why? Because to be an effective Eskimo, you have to be able to make fine distinctions between different kinds of snow. There is snow you can fall through, snow you can build an igloo out of, snow you can run your dogs in, snow you can eat, snow that's ready to melt. I'm from California. I practically never see snow, so the one word I have for it is enough for me.

Many phrases and words used by people in our culture have little or no specific meaning. Tony has a term for these generalized, nonsensory-based words: *fluff.* They're not descriptive language; they're more like vague guesswork. Fluff is "Leasha looks depressed" or "Leasha looks tired." Or even worse, "Leasha is depressed" or "Leasha is tired." Specific language is "Leasha is a thirty-two-year-old woman with light brown eyes and short brown hair who is sitting to my right. She's leaning back in her chair, drinking iced tea, with her eyes defocused and her breathing shallow." It's the difference between giving accurate descriptions of externally verifiable experience and making guesses about what no one can see. The speaker has no idea what's going on in Leasha's mind. Don't take your map and assume you know what another person's experience is.

I set goals—realistic goals—and I focus on them. I ask questions, I read, I listen. I did the same thing in baseball with the Chicago White Sox. I'm not afraid to ask anybody anything if I don't know. Why should I be afraid? I'm trying to get somewhere. Help me, give me direction. Nothing wrong with that. Step by step, I can't see any other way of accomplishing anything.

—MICHAEL JORDAN

Have you ever heard this saying? "When you assume something, you make an ASS out of U and ME." Making an assumption is the mark of a lazy communicator. It's riddled with judgment and often prejudice, and is one of the most dangerous things you can do in dealing with others.

A great example is the assumption that Blacks couldn't make the grade to fly in World War II. Assumed not to have the mental or physical skills White pilots had, Blacks were persecuted and restricted to menial duties in the armed forces. This assumption was crushed when a group of Black airmen became the 99th and 332nd Redtailed P51 Mustangs. As fighter escorts to the bombers over Germany, these brave Americans fought brilliantly and never lost a single bomber to enemy aircraft—a record unmatched by their White counterparts. Despite the prejudice, racism, and persecution heaped on them by the very country they were fighting for, their ability to achieve the results they did forced all the other pilots and crew members to respect them as men. In the end, so many owed their lives to the Tuskegee airmen that their views and beliefs about race and people were changed forever. Many became lifelong friends with the valiant men of the 99th and 332nd. What started out as hatred and spite grew into an unbreakable bond of mutual respect, gratitude, and friendship that continues to this day.

LEARN THE PRECISION MODEL

Much of our language is nothing more than wild generalization and assumption. That sort of lazy language can suck the guts out of real communication. If people tell you with precision what

Precision Model

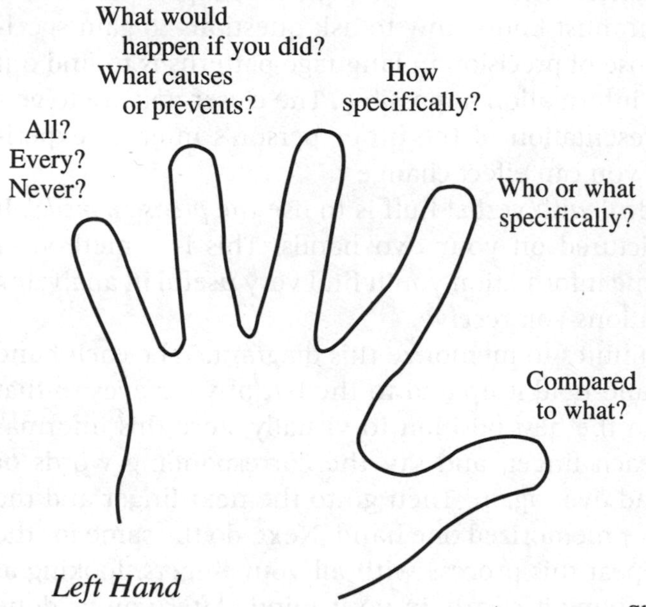
What would
happen if you did?
What causes
or prevents?
How
specifically?
All?
Every?
Never?
Who or what
specifically?
Compared
to what?
Left Hand

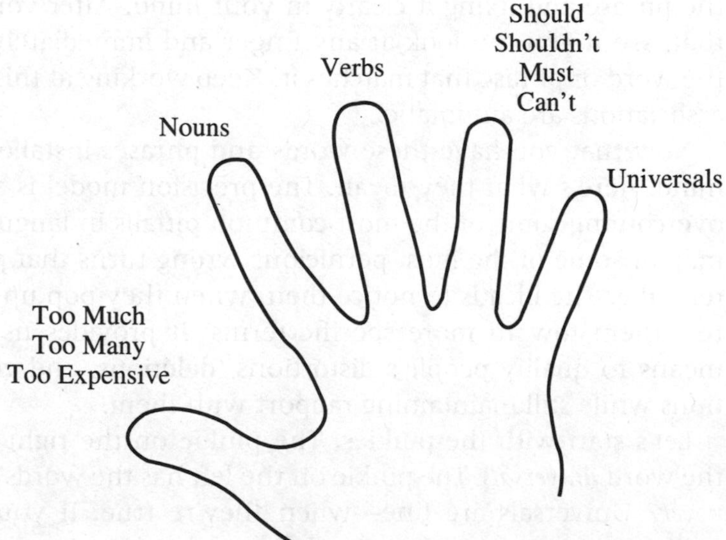
Should
Shouldn't
Must
Can't
Verbs
Nouns
Universals
Too Much
Too Many
Too Expensive
Right Hand

specifically is bothering them, and if you can find out what they want instead, you can deal with it. If they use vague phrases and generalizations, you're lost in their mental fog. The key to effective communication is to break through that fog, to become a fluff-buster. You must know how to ask questions to gain specificity. The purpose of precision in language patterns is to find out as much useful information as possible. The closer you are to getting a full representation of the other person's internal experience, the more you can effect change.

One way to deal with verbal fluff is to use the *precision model.* It may best be pictured on your two hands. This is a method of memorizing some information you'll find very useful in analyzing the communications you receive.

Take a few minutes to memorize this diagram. Take each hand one at a time, and hold it up and to the left of your eyes so that your eyes are in the best position to visually store this information. Look at each finger, and say the corresponding words or phrases over and over again. Then go to the next finger and the next until you've memorized one hand. Next, do the same for the other hand. Repeat this process with all your fingers, looking at the phrase and fixing it clearly in your mind. After you've done that, see if you can look at any finger and immediately think of the word or phrase that matches it. Keep working at this until the associations are automatic.

Now that you have these words and phrases installed in your mind, here's what they mean. The precision model is a guide to overcoming some of the most common pitfalls in language. It's a map of some of the most pernicious wrong turns that people often take. The idea is to notice them when they pop up and redirect them toward more specific terms. It provides us with the means to qualify people's distortions, deletions, and generalizations while still maintaining rapport with them.

Let's start with the pinkies. The pinkie on the right hand has the word *universals.* The pinkie on the left has the words *all? every? never?* Universals are fine—when they're true. If you say that *every* person needs oxygen or *all* the teachers in your son's school have teaching credentials, you're just conveying facts. But more often, universals are a way of soaring into the fluff zone. You see a group of noisy Black kids playing on the street and say, *"All*

Black kids these days are ill-mannered." One of your employees messes up and you say, "I don't know why I pay these people. They *never* work." In both cases—and for much of the time we use universals—we've gone from a limited truth or isolated instance to a general untruth. Maybe those particular kids were acting noisy in that specific situation, but that doesn't mean all Black kids are ill-mannered. Maybe a particular employee seems incompetent in a certain situation, but this doesn't mean all of them are all the time—or even that that particular employee is incompetent all the time.

The next time you hear a generalization like that, simply use the precision model. Repeat the statement, emphasizing the universal qualifier. When you hear, "All Black kids are ill-mannered," ask yourself, "All? Well, I guess not. It's just that these kids playing on the street right now are really loud." Or when you hear, "My employees never work," ask yourself, "Never? Well, I guess that's not true. This one guy sure screwed up in this one instance, but I can't say that's true for the rest of them."

Too often these universals produce stereotypes. Someone may see Black youths involved in gang activities and say, "Blacks are always involved in gangs." Of course this isn't true, but unfortunately many people accept it as fact and view all Black people through that negative filter.

Now bring the next two fingers (the ring fingers) together. On your right hand, examine the restrictive words *should, shouldn't, must, can't.* If people tell you they can't do something, what signal are they sending the brain? A limiting one that makes sure, in fact, that they can't do it. If you ask people why they can't do something or why they have to do something they don't want to do, they usually have no shortage of answers. Break through that cycle by asking the questions that correspond to the left ring finger, such as, *What would happen if you did?* When you ask people what would happen if they were able to do something, it creates a possibility they were previously unaware of and gets them to consider the positive and negative by-products of the activity.

The same process works for you in internal dialogue. When you say to yourself, "I can't do that," what you should do next is ask yourself, "What would happen if I could?" The reply would be a list of positive, enabling actions and feelings. It would create new representations of possibility and thus new states, new actions, and potentially new results. Just asking yourself that question will begin to change your physiology and your thinking to make it more possible. In addition, you could ask, "What prevents me from doing this now?" and thereby become clear about what specifically you need to change.

Now go to your middle fingers, which stand for verbs and *how, specifically?* Remember, your brain needs clear signals to operate efficiently. Fluffy language and fluffy thought dull the brain. If someone says, "I feel depressed," he's just describing a stuck state. He's not telling you anything specific. He's not giving you any information you can work with in a positive way. Break the stuck state by breaking through the fluff. If someone says he's depressed, you need to ask him how specifically he's depressed, what specifically is causing him to feel that way.

When you get him to be more specific, you often must move from one part of the precision model to another. So if you ask the person to be more specific, he may say, "I'm depressed because I always mess up on the job." What's the next question? Is the universal true? It's not likely. So you would ask, "You *always* mess up on your job?" Most likely, the answer will be, "Well, no, not always, I guess." By breaking through the fluff, by getting to specifics, you're on the road to identifying a real problem and dealing with it. What usually happens is that a person has messed up in some small way and made it symbolize some big failing that exists only in his mind.

Now put your index fingers together, the ones that represent nouns and *who specifically?, what specifically?* Whenever you hear nouns—people, places, or things—in any generalized statement, respond with a phrase that includes "who (or what) specifically?" It's precisely what you did with the verbs, going from unspecified fluff to the real world.

Unspecified nouns are some of the worst kinds of fluff. How often have you heard someone say, "They don't understand me," or "They're not going to give me a fair chance"? Well, just who specifically are "they"? This has been done by both Blacks and Whites throughout time. "All Blacks have rhythm. White men can't jump. They hate me cause I'm Black. They hate me because I'm White."

Suppose you've submitted an idea to your employers that you think would really benefit the company, and your proposal has been turned down. If it's a big organization, there's probably one person in particular who's authorized to make decisions. So instead of getting yourself stuck in this vague realm where "they" don't understand, you need to find a way to deal with the real-world person making the real-world decisions. Using an unspecified, nameless "they" can be the worst sort of cop-out. If you don't know who "they" are, you feel helpless and unable to change your situation. But if you focus on specifics, you can regain control. So if someone says, "Your plan just won't work," you need to find out what specific element is bothering that person. A rebuttal like "Yes, it *will* work!" will not maintain rapport or resolve the situation. Often, it's not the whole plan that's the sticking point, but only a small part of it. So if you try to rearrange your whole plan, you're like a plane flying without radar: You might fix everything but the one thing that's the problem. If you specify precisely where the problem is and deal with it, you're on the road to bringing about valuable change. Remember, the closer the map approximates the real territory, the more valuable it is and the more power you have to change the situation.

Now press your thumbs together for the last part of the precision model. The right thumb represents *too much, too many, too expensive.* The other stands for *compared to what?* When you say "too much, too many, too expensive," you're using a form of "deletion," ignoring a possible comparison. Often it's based on an arbitrary thought lodged somewhere inside your brain. You might say more than a week's vacation is too much time away from work. You might think your kid's request for a $299 home computer is too expensive. Step outside your generalizations by making a comparison. Two weeks away from your job may be worth it if you'll come back totally relaxed and able to do your best work. That home computer might be too expensive if you thought it wouldn't do any good. But if you consider it a valuable learning tool, it could be worth many thousands of dollars down the line. The only way to make such judgments rationally is to have valid points of comparison. You'll find that when you start using the precision model, you'll end up using it automatically for all kinds of situations.

For example, I often work with young people and youth-at-risk groups. Often they tell me staying in school is too hard and it's too much work to catch up with their grade level. I usually respond, "Compared to what?"

"Compared to hanging out with my friends," they tell me, "or working the streets." Or compared to struggling later in life to pay bills because of lack of education? Then I find out what specifically "hanging out" is and what they do. Then I might ask how specifically hanging out is like going to school. "Well, it really isn't," they reply.

"That's interesting. What would happen if you felt school was really worth the time and effort?" Their breathing patterns change, and they smile and say, "I don't know . . . I'd feel good, I guess."

"What specifically could we do to help you feel that way about school now?"

"Well, if we would spend more time on science (or music, or history, or whatever), I probably would feel good about it."

"All right. If you were to spend more time on that subject, would you feel that school was worth your time and effort?" They nod in agreement.

What's happened in this conversation? We've found the real-world, specific points we need to deal with. We've gone from a string of generalizations to a string of specifics. Once we get to the specifics, we're able to deal with them in a way that solves our problems. It's that way in almost any sort of communication. The road to agreement is paved with specific information.

In addition, I often use contrast to get someone to look at the consequences of not doing something. If a student says school is too hard, I might ask her, "Compared to what?" When she fails to come up with an answer I might suggest, "Compared to scratching out a living on the streets when you are older?" That will get her to consider the consequences of her present actions—fast!

FLUFF-BUSTING EXERCISES

Here's a fun and interesting experiment. During the next several days, focus on the language other people use. Begin to identify things such as universals and unspecified verbs and nouns. How would you challenge these? Turn on your television and watch an interview program. Identify the fluff that is being used, and ask questions of the TV set that would enable you to get the specific information you need.

Here are some additional language patterns to listen for. Avoid words like *good, bad, better, worse*—words that indicate some form of evaluation or judgment. When you hear phrases such as, "That's a bad idea," or "It's good to eat everything on your plate," you can respond with, "According to whom?" or "How do you know that?" Sometimes people will make statements linking cause and effect, such as, "His comments made me mad," or "Your observations made me think." Now when you hear statements like these you'll know enough to ask, "How specifically does X cause Y?" and in the process become a better communicator.

Another fluffy language pattern to be wary of is verbal mind reading. When someone says, "I just know he loves me," or "You think I don't believe you," you need to ask, "How do you know that?" I also like to ask, "What if that weren't true?" This causes the person to think about the alternative.

The last language pattern to learn is a little more subtle, which is a wonderful reason to give it your attention. What do words like *attention, statement,* and *reason* have in common? They are nouns, yes. But we can't find them in the external world. Have you ever seen an attention, for instance? It doesn't describe a person, place, or physical thing, but rather the process of attending. It's a nominalization, and nominalizations are words that have lost their specificity. When you hear one, you want to turn it back into a process. This gives you the power to redirect and change your experience. If someone says, "I want to change my experience," the way to redirect it is to ask, "What do you want to experience?" If the person says, "I want love," you would respond with, "How do you want to be loved?" or "What is it to be loving?" Is there a difference in specificity in the two forms? There sure is.

Asking the right questions is an invaluable tool for directing communication. One example is the *outcome frame.* If you ask someone what's bothering her or what's wrong, you'll get a long dissertation on just that. If you ask, "What do you want?" or

"How do you want to change things?" you've redirected your conversation from the problem to the solution. In any situation, no matter how dismal, there's a desirable outcome to be achieved. Your goal should be to change direction toward that outcome and away from the problem. Do this by asking the right questions, such as the following *outcome questions*.

"What do I want?"
"What is the objective?"
"What am I here for?"
"What do I want for you?"
"What do I want for myself?"

Remember, try to get responses as sensory specific as possible. If someone says, "I want to be healthy," ask, "What would that feel like?" or, "What does it mean to be healthy?" or, "How will you know when you're healthy?"

Here's another important tool: Choose *how* questions over *why* questions. *Why* questions can get you reasons, explanations, justifications, and excuses. But they usually don't come up with useful information. Don't ask your child why he is having trouble with his algebra. Ask him what he needs to do to perform better. There's no need to ask an employee why she didn't get a contract you were bidding for. Ask her how she can change so you'll be certain to get the next one. Good communicators aren't interested in rationalizations of why something is going wrong. They want to find out how to do it right. The right questions will lead you in that direction.

Let me share with you a final point that goes back to the enabling beliefs we examined in Chapter 7 ("The Seven Lies of Success"). All your communications with others and with yourself should stem from the principle that **everything happens for a purpose and you can use it to serve your outcomes.** That means your communication skills should reflect feedback, not failure. If you're putting together a jigsaw puzzle and a piece doesn't fit, you don't usually take that as failure and stop working on the puzzle. You take it as feedback and try another piece that looks more promising. It's to your advantage to use the same general rule in your communication. For almost any problem in communication, there is a specific question or precise phrase that will transform it. If you follow the general principles we've considered here, you'll be able to find it in every situation. ("Every situation"—start using your precision model now!)

Now we're going to deal with something that is very special to me, as it pertains to humans getting along and working out solutions. Cross-culturally, this next set of tools will definitely make the biggest difference in finding the power in each other. In the next chapter, we'll look at the underpinning of all successful human interaction, the glue that bonds people together. It's called . . .

CHAPTER FIFTEEN

The Magic of Rapport

Nobody can dim the light which shines from within.

—Maya Angelou

Have you ever met someone you clicked with right away? Someone you liked instantly and who seemed to like you just as quickly? Take a second to think about it. Now, go back to that time and try to remember what it was about the person that made you feel so attuned to him or her.

Chances are that you found you both had something in common with each other. Maybe you showed an interest in or had the same opinion about a particular thing or situation. Perhaps you liked the same music or even shared a similar dislike for something. You might not have noticed it, but maybe you had similar patterns of breathing or speech. Maybe you had a similar background or similar beliefs. Whatever you come up with will reflect the same basic element: *rapport.* Simply put, rapport is the ability to find or create something in common with others. Rapport is the ability to enter someone else's world, to make the person feel you understand him or her, to project a strong common bond. It's the ability to go fully from your map of the world to the other person's map. It's the essence of successful communication.

Believe it or not, rapport is the ultimate tool for producing results with other people. It's the master key to influencing with integrity. It provides the ability to sell, persuade, and make a difference. Remember, we learned in Chapter 7 that people are your most important resource. Rapport is the way you tap that resource. No matter what you want in life, if you can develop rapport with the right people, you'll be able to fill their needs, and they will be able to fill yours.

In this book we talk extensively about modeling others. The ability to establish rapport with certain people makes it much easier to model them. In fact, you'll find they are often eager to help you reach your goals and will open up to you even more. Many people make life very complicated and difficult, but it doesn't have to be. All the skills you learn in this book are really ways to achieve greater rapport with people, which in turn makes almost any task easier and more enjoyable.

Want to know the worst cliché ever coined? "Opposites attract." Like many fallacies, it has an element of truth. When people have enough in common, the little differences can add a certain excitement to things. But overall, who is attractive to you? Whom do you want to spend time with?

Think of someone you dislike, someone who rubs you the wrong way and irritates you no end. Chances are this person is so far from being like you that it's a joke. Whom do you like to be around? People who disagree with you on everything, have different interests, like to sleep when you want to play and play when you want to sleep? Of course not. You want to be with people who are like you and yet unique.

When people are like each other, they tend to like each other. Do people form clubs of those who are different from them? No, they get together as fellow war veterans or jazz enthusiasts or baseball card collectors, because having something in common creates rapport. Ever go to a convention? Isn't there an instant bond created among people who've never seen each other before? One of the staples of comedy is a fast-talking, back-slapping extrovert trying to interact with a quiet, self-effacing introvert. How do they get along? Terribly. They're not enough alike to like each other very much.

Whom do most Americans tend to feel better about, the English or the Iranians? Easy answer. And whom do we have the most in common with? Same answer. Think about the Middle East. Why do you think there are problems there? Are the Jews and Arabs alike in their religious beliefs? Do they have the same sort of justice system? Do they have the same language? You could go on and on. All too often it's the same with Blacks and Whites in this country. And Native Americans. And Latinos. And Asian Americans. The problems result from focusing on the ways they're different—the differences in color and culture and custom. Turmoil can result from a massive amount of difference, while harmony tends to result from similarity. It's been true throughout history. It's true on a global scale, and it's true on a personal scale. It's easy to see how and why there are so many race challenges in this world.

The beauty of it is that it doesn't have to be that way. With a little effort, people can create rapport with one another and help bridge those differences. To me, mastering this skill is the single most important step to bridging the color gap. Do Blacks and Whites have a lot of differences? Sure, if you want to view things that way. But they have much more in common, don't they? We're all men and women, brothers and sisters, with similar desires, fears, and aspirations. The way to go from discord to harmony is to focus on similarities. The first step in real communication is learning to connect. Learning how to translate from your map of the world to someone else's. And what allows us to do that? Rapport skills.

How to Build Rapport Instantly

So how do we create rapport? We do it by creating or discovering things in common, a process called *matching* or *mirroring.* There are many ways to create commonality with another person and thus a state of rapport. You can mirror interests, such as having a similar style of dress or favorite activity. Or you can mirror association, such as having similar friends or acquaintances. Or you can mirror beliefs. These are common ways we create friendships and relationships.

All these experiences have one thing in common: They're communicated through words. The most common way to match others is through a verbal exchange of information. However, studies have shown that only 7 percent of what is communicated between people is transmitted through the words themselves. Thirty-eight percent comes through the tone of voice. If you think about the words in the lullaby "Rock-a-bye Baby," you'll see it tells the story of a baby high up in a tree with the wind blowing, then crashing to the ground, cradle and all. Why doesn't the child get scared hearing this? Because the tonality of the mother's voice is soothing the child. I know when I was a kid and my mother raised her voice and said, "JOSEPH!" in a certain tone, that meant much more than my name alone.

Fifty-five percent of communication, the largest part, is a result of physiology or body language. The facial expressions, gestures, and characteristics of movement of the person delivering a communication reveal much more than the words themselves. This explains why a comedian like George Wallace can get up and attack you and say terrible things and make you laugh. Or how Eddie Murphy or Martin Lawrence can swear like drunken sailors and make you laugh. It's not the words, it's the delivery—the tonality and physiology—that makes us laugh.

If we are trying to create rapport merely by the content of our conversation, we're missing out on the most effective ways we could be communicating commonality to the brain of another person. One of the best ways to achieve rapport is through mirroring or creating a common physiology, which is what the great hypnotherapist Dr. Milton Erickson did. He learned to mirror the breathing patterns, posture, tonality, and gestures of his patients, achieving a totally binding rapport in a matter of minutes. People who did not know him suddenly trusted him without question. So if you can develop rapport with just words, think of the incredible rapport you can develop with words and physiology linked together. While the words are working on a person's conscious mind, the physiology is working on the unconscious. Once that happens, there's an irresistible attraction, a tremendous bond. Because it's unconscious, it's even more effective. You're not aware of anything but the bond that's been formed. And here's the clincher: We do this unconsciously anyway when we want someone to like us!

How do you deliberately mirror another person's physiology? What kinds of physical traits can you mirror? Start with voice. Mirror the person's tonality and phrasing, pitch, tempo, pauses, and volume. Mirror favorite words or phrases. How about posture and breathing patterns, eye contact, body language, facial expressions, hand gestures, or other distinctive movements? Any aspect of physiology, from the way a person plants her feet to the way she tilts her head, is something you can mirror. Now, this may sound absurd at first. What if you could mirror everything about another person? Do you know what happens when you do this? People feel as though they've found their soulmate, someone who totally understands, who can read their deepest thoughts, who is just like them. But you don't have to mirror everything about a person to create a state of rapport. If all you do is start with the tone of voice or a similar facial expression, you can learn to build incredible rapport with anyone.

Try this for the next couple of days. Practice mirroring people with whom you spend time. Mirror their gestures and posture, the rate and location of their breathing, the tone, tempo, and volume of their voice. Do they feel closer to you, and do you feel closer to them? Rarely will they notice you doing this, and you can have lots of fun observing what happens.

Remember the mirroring experiment in Chapter 11? When you mirror someone else's physiology, you're able to experience not only the same state, but also the same sorts of internal experiences and even the same thoughts. Now, what if you could do that in everyday life? What if you became such a skillful mirrorer you could know what someone else was thinking? What sort of rapport would you have then, and what could you do with it? It's an amazing possibility to contemplate, but professional communicators do it all the time. Mirroring is a skill like any other; it takes practice to develop. However, you can use it right now and get results.

When you break it down, there are two keys to mirroring: keen observation and personal flexibility. Here's an experiment to do with a friend. Pick one person to be the mirrorer and the other to be the leader. Have the leader run through as many physical changes as possible in a minute or two. Change facial expressions, posture, and breathing. Change big things, like the way you hold your arms, and change small ones, like the tension in your neck. This is a great exercise to do with your children—they'll love it!

When you're through, compare notes. See how well you did at mirroring the other person. Then change positions. You'll probably find you missed at least as many as you hit. Anyone can become an expert mirrorer, but you need to recognize that people use their bodies in hundreds of ways, and the more aware you are of these differences, the more successful you'll be. Even though there are unlimited possibilities, people in a sitting position, for example, usually make a limited number of movements. After some practice, you won't even have to think about doing it—you'll just automatically mirror the postures and physiologies of the people around you.

There are infinite subtleties to effective mirroring, but the foundation is something we touched on in the chapter on eliciting strategy: the three basic representational systems of visual, auditory, and kinesthetic. Remember, everyone uses all three, but most of us have strong preferences for one that we lean on time and time again. Once you've figured out a person's primary representational system, you've radically simplified the job of developing rapport with him or her.

> ***Imagine what a harmonious world it could be if every single person, both young and old, shared a little of what he is good at doing.***
>
> —QUINCY JONES

If behavior and physiology consisted of a random set of factors, you would have to painstakingly identify every cue, then put them all together. But representational systems are like the keys to a secret code. Knowing one fact gives you a clue to a dozen more. As we learned in Chapter 8, there is a whole constellation of verbal and physical behaviors that go along with being primarily visual, a different set for auditory, and still another set for kinesthetic. These behaviors give clues as to how people communicate to themselves and also how they might prefer to be communicated with to create rapport.

Consider someone who operates primarily in an auditory state. If you are trying to persuade him to do something by asking him to picture how it will look, and you talk very, very rapidly, you probably won't get through to him. He needs to *hear* what you have to say, needs to *listen* to your proposal and notice if it *clicks* for him. In fact, he may not even "hear" you, simply because your tone of voice may turn him off from the very start. Another person may be in a primarily visual state, and if you approach her kinesthetically, talking very slowly about how you feel about something, she will probably become irritated at your slow pace and ask you to please get to the point.

Begin to make a list of visual, auditory, and kinesthetic words. For the next several days, listen to the people you are talking with and determine what kind of words they use most. Speak to them using the same kind of words. What happens? Then speak for a while using words that match a different representational system. What happens this time?

Visual, Auditory, and Kinesthetic Words

VISUAL	AUDITORY	KINESTHETIC
see	hear	feel
look	listen	touch
view	sound(s)	grasp
appear	make music	get hold of
show	harmonize	slip through
dawn	tune in/out	catch on
reveal	be all ears	tap into
envision	rings a bell	make contact
illuminate	silence	throw out
twinkle	be heard	turn around
clear	resonate	hard
foggy	deaf	unfeeling
focused	mellifluous	concrete
hazy	dissonance	scrape
sparkling	attune	unbudging
crystal clear	overtones	get a handle
flash	unhearing	solid
imagine	question	suffer

Visual, Auditory, and Kinesthetic Phrases

VISUAL (SEE)	AUDITORY (HEAR)	KINESTHETIC (FEEL)
An eyeful	Afterthought	All washed up
Appears to me	Blabbermouth	Boils down to
Beyond a shadow of a doubt	Call on	Chip off the old block
	Clear as a bell	

Bird's-eye view
Catch a glimpse of
Clear-cut
Dim view
Eye to eye
Flashed on
Get a perspective on
Get a scope on
Hazy idea
Horse of a different color
In light of
In person
In view of
Looks like
Make a scene
Mental image
Mental picture
Mind's eye
Naked eye
Paint a picture
Photographic memory
Plainly see
Pretty as a picture
See to it
Shortsighted
Showing off
Sight for sore eyes
Staring off into space
Take a peek
Tunnel vision
Under your nose
Up front
Well defined

Clearly expressed
Describe in detail
Earful
Express yourself
Give an account of
Give me your ear
Grant an audience
Heard voices
Hidden message
Hold your tongue
Idle talk
Inquire into
Keynote speaker
Loud and clear
Manner of speaking
Pay attention to
Power of speech
Purrs like a kitten
Outspoken
Rap session
Rings a bell
State your purpose
Tattletale
To tell the truth
Tongue-tied
Tuned in/tuned out
Unheard-of
Utterly
Voiced an opinion
Well informed
Within hearing range
Word for word

Come to grips with
Control yourself
Cool/calm/collected
Firm foundations
Floating on thin air
Get a handle on
Get a load of this
Get in touch with
Get the drift of
Get your goat
Hand in hand
Hang in there
Heated argument
Hold it!
Hold on!
Hothead
Keep your shirt on!
Know-how
Lay cards on table
Light-headed
Moment of panic
Not following you
Pain in the neck
Pull some strings
Sharp as a tack
Slipped my mind
Smooth operator
Start from scratch
Stiff upper lip
Stuffed shirt
Too much of a hassle
Topsy-turvy
Underhanded

Sometimes when Tony talks about matching and mirroring in his seminar events, a person becomes concerned or even upset about the approach, saying it's unnatural or even manipulative. But Tony points out that in fact we already mirror people whenever we feel connected to them. You see, anytime you are in rapport with someone, it's natural for you to begin to mirror or match aspects of the person's voice, gestures, facial expressions, and so on. Invariably as Tony explains this, members of the audience are already unconsciously mirroring each other. He also points out that if you travel to different countries and don't at least attempt to speak the language of the land, you are generally not appreciated. Any fool can continue to use his own style and approach without being conscious of the people around him—it takes care, respect, and flexibility to enter other people's worlds. Would you rather be limited to only one tone of voice, one way of speaking, or only one way of using your body? Besides, entering other people's worlds is sure to enhance yours as well. The more we can experience what other people feel like, the more we can connect, the more we'll learn, and the more we will expand ourselves.

In this chapter, we're learning what we do—the recipes for rapport—so we can create that result anytime we wish, even with a stranger. As for mirroring being manipulative, tell me which requires more conscious effort: just to speak at your normal pace and tone, or to find out how someone else communicates so you can enter that person's world? And remember that while you're mirroring another person, you truly experience how he or she feels. If your intent were to manipulate someone else, once you began to mirror, you would in fact begin to feel more like that person—so the question becomes, Are you willing to manipulate yourself?

Here's another point to remember: You're not giving up your identity when you mirror another person, since you are not exclusively a visual, auditory, or kinesthetic person anyway. We should all strive to be flexible. Mirroring simply creates a commonality of physiology that underscores our shared humanity. When I'm mirroring, I can get the benefits of another person's feelings, experiences, and thoughts. That's a powerful lesson to experience about how to share the world with other human beings.

THE SECRET BEHIND CHARISMA

Throughout history, the people who have had the greatest impact on us culturally are those who are strong in all three representational systems. We tend to trust people who appeal to us on all three levels and who project a sense of congruity—all the parts of their personality convey the same thing. Perhaps the greatest example of this was the great Dr. Martin Luther King, Jr. Do you think Dr. King was visually attractive? Most would say yes. Did he have an appealing tone of voice and manner of speaking? You bet he did, especially to the majority of the African American population. Dr. King was a powerful orator and minister who spoke with all the passion of his beliefs—a message that resonated clearly with a huge population of churchgoing Christians. Did he move us emotionally with feelings of patriotism and possibility? History answers that one for us. He moved even those who opposed him. No wonder they call him the Great Communicator!

Think now of a major cultural success like Whitney Houston. Her concerts are packed, her talent is abundant, and she offers everything for the eyes and ears. Visually attractive, she converses with her audiences in a voice deep with feeling, developing tremendous rapport in the process. She appears totally congruent.

Think of a Black man in recent history who stands out in your mind as being powerful, charismatic, able to make a difference. Did you think of Nelson Mandela or of General Colin Powell? Ninety-five percent of the people I poll do. Why? There are many reasons, but let's check a few. Do you feel they are attractive visually? How about from an auditory point of view? Ninety percent of the people I poll agree they are attractive in these ways, too. Can they move you emotionally with their words? Both are supreme masters of communication to affect people. Are they congruent? Absolutely!

Without a doubt, these people are geniuses of the top rank. But you don't need any sort of natural gift to develop rapport skills. **If you can see, hear, and feel, you can create rapport with anyone, just by doing what they do.** Remember, you are looking for things you can mirror unobtrusively. If you mirror a person's nervous twitch or a wandering eye, you might create the impression you are mocking the person.

Also, it should be noted that mirroring and rapport have no color or gender barriers. You don't have to be of the same race or sex for these tools to work. What's great about this is you can duplicate anyone's talents!

Since most of us interact with people on a constant basis, this gives us the opportunity to practice our rapport skills constantly and enter their worlds. As you do this, you will soon find it becomes second nature, and you'll do it automatically without any conscious thought. You'll also find that the process does more than just allow you to achieve rapport and understand the other person. Because of what's known as *pacing* and *leading,* you are able to get that person to follow you. It doesn't matter how different you are or how you met. If you can establish enough rapport with someone, before too long you can change that person's behavior to begin matching yours.

Let me give you an example. Several years ago, a young woman came to me for some help with her emotional challenges. She had been referred to me by her friend, who had neglected to tell her I was Black. It was obvious she was uncomfortable with this. As soon as she saw me, the smile left her face and she became speechless. Having dealt with this several times in the past, I overlooked her reactions, guided her into the office, and asked her to sit down. She sat very rigid and withdrawn in the chair as I started to talk to her and ask some basic questions. Her arms and legs were crossed tightly, and she had a semiworried look on her face. I sat in the chair opposite her in exactly the same posture and began to mirror the rhythm of her breathing. She spoke softly and slowly, so I spoke softly and slowly. She kept saying, "Well, you know," so I kept saying, "Well, you know." She made a rolling gesture with her right hand as she spoke, so I did the same whenever I spoke.

In a very short time, she began to relax and open up more to me, even allowing a smile to come back to her face. Why? Because by matching and mirroring her, I'd established rapport. Before too long, I began to see if I could lead her. First, I gradually sped up the pace of my speech. She in turn sped up her speech. Soon we were laughing and talking freely as though we were best friends, and we were able to get on to the matters at hand. I handled her challenge in about an hour and a half's time. She told me later that she'd been raised by a very prejudiced father and, prior to me, had never had any interactions with a Black person. She admitted she'd been ready to turn around and walk out as soon as she saw that I was a Black man. So you don't need to have ideal circumstances to mirror well—you just need the skill to adapt your behavior to that of someone else.

What I was doing with this woman was pacing and leading. Pacing is just graceful mirroring, moving the way other people move, changing gestures as they change gestures. Once you attain great skill in mirroring someone else, you can change your physiology and behavior almost instinctively as the other person changes. Rapport is not static; it's not something that remains stable once achieved. It's a dynamic, fluid, flexible process. Just as the key to establishing a truly lasting relationship is the ability to change and adjust to what someone else is going through, the key to pacing is the ability to elegantly and accurately change gears when someone else does.

Leading develops naturally from pacing. As you establish rapport with someone, you create a link that can almost be felt. You reach a point where you start to initiate change rather than just mirroring the other person, a point where you have developed so much rapport that when you change, the other person will unconsciously follow you. You've probably experienced being with friends late at night when you're not tired at all, but you're in such deep rapport that when they yawn, you yawn, too. The best salespeople do exactly the same thing. They enter another person's world, achieve rapport, then use that rapport to lead.

An obvious question comes up: What if someone's mad? Do you mirror the anger? Well, that's certainly one choice. Sometimes, by mirroring anger, you can enter someone's world so strongly that when you begin to relax, the person begins to relax also. However, in the next chapter we're going to talk about how to break someone's pattern, whether it's one of anger or frustration, and how to do it quickly. It might be best to break someone's pattern rather than to mirror that anger. Remember, rapport doesn't just mean you're smiling. Rapport means responsiveness. People in gangs create rapport by being angry and violent like each other. This is one of the ways they bond. Occasionally you may need to be just as intense in your communication to a person, since his challenge to you is one of the many ways respect is developed in this part of our culture.

Here's another experiment. Engage someone in conversation. Mirror that person in posture, voice, and breathing. After a while, gradually change your posture or tone of voice. Does the other person follow you after a few minutes? If not, simply go back and pace again. Then try a different lead and make the change less pronounced. If, when you attempt to lead someone, the person does not follow, it simply means you do not have enough rapport yet. Develop more rapport and try again.

> *Whatever reason you had for not being somebody, there's somebody who had that same problem and overcame it.*
>
> —BARBARA REYNOLDS

Remember, the biggest barrier to rapport is thinking other people have the same outlook on life as you do. Excellent communicators rarely make this mistake. They know they have to change their language, tonality, breathing patterns, and gestures until they discover an approach that is successful in achieving their outcome. The real key to establishing rapport is flexibility. You must be willing to experience other people's worlds as they do.

If you fail to communicate with someone, it's tempting to assume he or she is a hopeless fool who refuses to listen to reason. But that virtually guarantees you'll never get through. It's better to change your words and behaviors until they match that person's model of the world.

One primary teaching in Neuro-Linguistic Programming (NLP) is that the meaning of your communication is the response you get. The responsibility in communication rests upon *you.* If you try to persuade someone to do one thing, and he or she does the other, the fault was in your communication. You didn't find a way to get your message through.

This is absolutely crucial in anything you do. Let's look at teaching. The greatest tragedy in education is that most teachers know their subjects, but they don't know their students. They don't know how their students process information; they don't know their students' representational systems; they don't know how their students' minds work.

The best teachers are the ones who establish rapport. There's a story about a classroom in which all the kids—as a prank—arranged to drop their books at exactly 9:00 A.M. to throw the teacher off. Without missing a beat, she put down her chalk, picked up a book, and dropped it, too. "Sorry I'm late," she said. After that, she had the kids eating out of her hand.

The best teachers instinctively know how to pace and lead. They're able to establish rapport so their message gets through. But there's no reason why all teachers can't learn the same thing. By learning to pace their students, by learning to present information in the forms their students can effectively process, they can revolutionize the educational world. We see the problem repeated over and over in inner-city schools throughout the nation. Les Brown was labeled "communicably uneducatable." It wasn't until one teacher came along and recognized how to communicate to him that he was able to rise above his low self-esteem and "failure" mentality.

The founders of NLP give a fascinating example of just how education should work. They tell of a young engineering student whose primary representational system was kinesthetic. At first he had terrible problems learning to read electrical schematics. He found the subject difficult and boring. Basically, he was having trouble making sense of concepts that were being presented visually.

Then one day he began to imagine what it would *feel* like to be an electron floating through the circuit he saw diagrammed in front of him. He imagined his various reactions and changes in behavior as he came in contact with the components in the circuit, symbolized by characters on the schematic. Almost immediately, the diagrams began to make more sense to him. He even began to enjoy them. Each schematic presented him with a new odyssey. It was so enjoyable that he ended up becoming an engineer. He succeeded because he was able to learn through his favored representational system. Think about it: Nearly all the kids who wash out of our educational systems are capable of learning. We just never learned how to teach them. We never established rapport with them and never matched their learning strategies.

I've been emphasizing teaching because, in the end, it's something we all do, whether at home with our kids, at work with our employees or peers, or even just spending time with our friends. What works in a classroom works in a boardroom or living room as well.

There's a final wonderful thing about the magic of rapport: It's the most accessible skill in the world. You don't need textbooks or college courses. You don't need to travel thousands of miles to study at the feet of a master. The only tools you need are your eyes, your ears, and your senses of touch, taste, and smell.

You can begin cultivating rapport right now. We are always communicating and interacting; rapport is simply doing both in the most effective ways possible. Study rapport by mirroring the people in line with you at the grocery store or airline ticket counter. Use it on your job and at home. Next time you go for a job interview, if you match and mirror the interviewer, he or she will like you immediately. Use rapport in your business to create an immediate connection with clients. If you want to become a master communicator, all you need to do is learn how to enter other people's worlds. You already have everything you need to do it now.

There's another way to establish rapport, sets of distinctions that help determine the choices people make. They're called . . .

CHAPTER SIXTEEN

Distinctions of Excellence: Metaprograms

How you perceive experience and how you handle it determine how your life turns out in the long run.

—BILL COSBY

ISN'T IT INTERESTING how people react so differently to things? You could have just heard the funniest, most side-splitting joke, and while you're rolling on the floor laughing with milk shooting out your nose, someone standing right next to you could be thinking, *That's not funny at all!* And still another person would consider it just mildly amusing. You'd think each person was listening in a completely different mental language. This can be even more pronounced when we look at interracial communication. For example, a White man is generally not as offended if he is called "boy" as a Black man would be.

So the question is why people react so differently to identical or nearly identical input. Why does one person see the glass as half-empty and another see it as half-full? Why does one person hear a message and feel energized, excited, and motivated while another hears the exact same message and doesn't respond at all? The plain and simple fact is that if you address someone the right way, you can inspire that person to do anything. But if you address that person the wrong way, all your efforts won't amount to a hill of beans. **The most insightful thought, the most intelligent critique, is totally useless unless it is understood both intellectually and emotionally by the person or persons you are addressing.** If you want to be a master communicator, a master persuader, both in business and in personal life, it is imperative that you know how to find the right keys to open the lock.

> *Every intersection in the road of life is an opportunity to make a decision, and at some point to listen.*
>
> —DUKE ELLINGTON

A very powerful set of distinctions about why people interpret information differently are what we call *metaprograms.* Metaprograms determine how a person processes information and forms perceptions that govern his or her behavior. Metaprograms are the internal programs that determine what we pay attention to. The conscious mind can pay attention to only a limited number of pieces of information at one time, so we delete and generalize information to expedite the process.

Think of your brain as a sort of computer that processes data. It takes in an amazing amount of information and organizes it to make sense to a human being. But a computer can't do anything without specific software. That software provides the structure for the computer to perform certain tasks. Think of metaprograms as the software of the brain. They provide the structure that governs what we will pay attention to, how we make sense of our experiences, and the directions in which they take us. They provide the foundation on which we decide what something means and whether it is boring, interesting, or potentially dangerous. To communicate with a computer, you have to understand its software. To communicate effectively with another human being, you must understand his or her metaprograms.

Every one of us has different patterns of behavior, and we all have patterns by which we organize our experiences to create those behaviors. Through understanding the mental patterns of ourselves and others, we can get our message across more effectively, whether it's trying to get someone to make a purchase or to hear our declaration of undying love. Even though the situations may vary, there is a consistent set of patterns that determines how people understand things and organize their thinking.

Let's take a look at seven patterns of behavior.

Pattern One: Moving Toward vs. Moving Away

The first metaprogram involves the concept of whether we are motivated more by moving toward something or by moving away from something. Remember that all human behavior revolves around the urge to gain pleasure or avoid pain. As simple as it sounds, this bit of information is a fundamental driving force behind all our actions. We pull away from a lighted match to avoid the pain of burning flesh. We sit and watch the moonlight dance across the ripples of a lake because we enjoy the glorious show God has provided for us at that moment.

The same activity will have different levels of motivation for different people. One person may easily be motivated to run up three flights of stairs out of the desire to have an attractive body, while others may be told all day long how their bodies will be transformed if they run up the stairs—and they will never do it. But if someone is claustrophobic, and there are only two ways to the top—one a crowded elevator and the other an open stairway—watch how quickly that person will take the stairs two at a time to avoid the perceived pain. One person may read Alex Haley or Toni Morrison because he enjoys their prose and insight; he's moving toward something that gives him pleasure. Another might read the same writers because he doesn't want people to think of him as uneducated or shallow.

As with the other metaprograms we'll discuss, this process is not one of absolutes. Everyone moves toward some things and away from others. No one responds the same way to each and every stimulus, although everyone has a dominant mode, a strong tendency toward one metaprogram or another. Some people tend to be energetic, curious risk-takers. They feel most comfortable moving toward something that excites them. Others tend to be cautious, wary, and protective; they see the world as a more perilous place and tend to take actions away from harmful or threatening things rather than toward exciting ones. **To find out which way people move, ask them what they want in a relationship, a home, a car, a job, or anything else. Do they tell you what they want—or what they don't want?**

What does this information mean? *Everything.* If you're selling a product, you can promote it two ways: by what it does or by what it doesn't do. You can try to sell cars by stressing that they're fast, sleek, or sexy, or you can emphasize that they don't use much gas, don't cost much to maintain, and are particularly safe in crashes. The strategy you use should depend entirely upon the strategy of the person with whom you're dealing. Use the wrong metaprogram with a person, and you might as well have stayed home. You're trying to move him toward something, and all he wants to do is find a good reason to back away.

Remember, a car can travel along the same path in forward or reverse. It just depends on what direction it's facing. The same is true on a personal basis. Let's say you want your child to spend more time on her schoolwork. You might tell her, "You better study or you won't get into a good college." Or, "Look at Lewis. He didn't study, so he flunked out of school, and he's going to spend the rest of his life pumping gas. Is that the kind of life you want for yourself?" How well will that strategy work? It depends on your child. If she's primarily motivated by moving away, it might work well. But what if she moves toward things? What if she's motivated by moving toward things she finds exciting? If that's how she responds, you're not going to change her behavior by offering the example of something to move away from. You can nag until you're blue in the face, but you're talking in the wrong key, wasting your time and hers. In fact, people who move toward things are often angered by or resentful of those who present things to be moved away from. You would motivate your child better by pointing out, "If you study and get good grades, you can pick and choose any college you want to."

PATTERN TWO: EXTERNAL VS. INTERNAL FRAMES OF REFERENCE

Ask people how they know when they've done a good job. For some, the proof comes from outside. The boss pats them on the back and says their work was great. They get a raise; they win a big award; their accomplishments are noticed and applauded by their peers. When they get that sort of external approval, they know their work is good. That's an *external* frame of reference.

For others, the proof comes from inside. They "just know" when they've done well. If you have an *internal* frame of reference, you can design a building that wins all sorts of architectural awards, but if you don't feel it's special, no amount of outside approval will convince you it is. Conversely, you might do a job that gets a lukewarm reception from your boss or peers, but if you feel it's good work, you'll trust your own instincts rather than theirs. That's an internal frame of reference.

Let's say you're trying to convince someone to attend a seminar. You might say, "You've got to attend this seminar. It's great. I've gone and all my friends have gone, and they've all had a terrific time and raved about it for days. They all said it changed their lives for the better." If this person has an external frame of reference, chances are you'll convince him. If all those people say it's true, he'll often assume it's probably true.

But what if he has an internal frame of reference? You'll have a difficult time convincing him by telling him what others have said. Their feedback doesn't mean anything to him; it doesn't compute. You can convince him only by appealing to things he knows himself. What if you told him, "Remember the series of lectures you went to last year? Remember how you said it was the most insightful experience you'd had in years? Well, I know about something that may be like that; I think if you check it out, you may find you'll have the same kind of experience. What do you think?" Will that work? Sure it will, because you're talking to him in his language.

It's important to note that all these metaprograms are related to *context and stress level*. If you've done something for ten or fifteen years, you probably have a strong internal frame of reference; if you're brand-new, you may not have as strong an internal frame of reference about what is right or wrong in that context. So you tend to develop preferences and patterns over time. But even if you're right-handed, you can still use your left hand in various situations if it is useful to do so. The same is true of metaprograms. You're not just one way; you can vary.

Which frame of reference do most leaders have—internal or external? Truly effective leaders have to have a strong internal frame. They wouldn't be much use as leaders if they spent all their time asking people what they thought of something before taking action. Still, there's an ideal balance to be struck. Remember that few people operate strictly at one extreme. A truly effective leader has to be able to take in information effectively from the outside as well; if not, megalomania results.

PATTERN THREE: SORTING BY SELF VS. SORTING BY OTHERS

We all know selfish, self-centered people, and we all know people who put others' needs before their own. Some people look at human interactions primarily in terms of what's in it for them personally, some in terms of what they can do for themselves and others. Of course, people don't always fall into one extreme or the other. If you sort only by self, you become a self-absorbed egotist. If you sort only by others, you become a martyr.

If you're involved in hiring people, wouldn't you want to know where an applicant fits on this scale? Not long ago a major airline found that 95 percent of its complaints involved 5 percent of its employees. These 5 percent sorted strongly by self; they were most interested in looking out for themselves, not others. Were they poor employees? Yes and no. They were obviously in the wrong positions and obviously doing a poor job, though they might have been smart, hardworking, and congenial. They may have been the right people put in the wrong slots.

What did the airline do? It replaced them with people who sorted by others. The company determined this through group interviews in which prospective employees were asked why they wanted to work for the airline. Most of the individuals thought they were being judged by the answers they gave in front of the group, when in fact they were being judged by their behavior as members of the audience. That is, individuals who paid the most attention and gave the most eye contact, smiles, or support to the person speaking at the front of the room were given the highest rating. Those who paid little or no attention and were in their own world while others were talking were considered to be primarily self-sorting and were not hired. The company's complaint ratio dropped over 80 percent as a result of this move.

That's why metaprograms are so important in the business world. How can you evaluate a person if you don't know what motivates him or her? How can you match the job you have available with the correct person, in terms of required skills, ability to learn, and internal makeup? A lot of very smart people spend their careers totally frustrated because they're doing jobs that don't make the best use of their capabilities. A liability in one context can be a valuable asset in another. In a service business, like an airline, you obviously need people who sort by others. If you're hiring an auditor, though, you might want someone who would sort by self. How many times have you dealt with someone who left you in a confused state because he or she performed well intellectually but poorly emotionally? It's like a doctor who sorts strongly by self. That person may be a brilliant diagnostician, but unless you feel the doctor cares about you, he or she won't be totally effective. In fact, someone like that would probably be better off as a researcher than as a clinician. Putting the right person in the right job remains one of the biggest problems in American business. But it's a problem that could be dealt with effectively if people knew how to evaluate the ways that job applicants processed information.

At this point, it's worth noting that not all metaprograms are created equal. Are people better off moving toward things rather than away? Perhaps. Would the world be a better place if people sorted more by others and less by self? Probably. *But we have to deal with life the way it is, not the way we wish it were.* You may wish your son moved toward things rather than away. If you want to communicate effectively with him, you have to do it in a way that works, not in a way that plays to your idea of how the world should work.

The key is to observe a person as carefully as possible, listen to what is said, what sorts of metaphors are used, what physiology reveals, what sparks attentiveness or triggers boredom. **People reveal their metaprograms all the time. It doesn't take much concentrated study to figure out what people's tendencies are or how they are sorting at the moment.** To determine if people sort by self or others, see how much attention they pay to other people. Do they lean toward people and have facial expressions that reflect concern for what others are saying, or do they lean back and remain bored and unresponsive? Everyone sorts by self some of the time, and it's important to do so sometimes. The key is what you do consistently and whether your sorting procedure enables you to produce the results you desire.

PATTERN FOUR: MATCHING VS. MISMATCHING

I want to try an experiment with you. Look at these figures and tell me how they relate to each other.

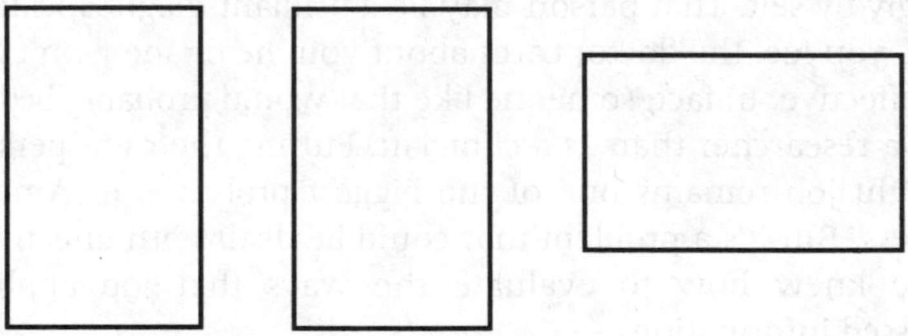

If I asked you to describe the relationship between the three figures, you could answer in many ways. You could say they're all rectangles. You could say they all have four sides. You could say two are vertical and one is horizontal, or that two are standing up and one is lying down, or that no one figure has precisely the same relationship to the other two. You could say one is different and the other two are alike.

I'm sure you can think of more descriptions. What's going on here? They all describe the same picture but take completely different approaches. So it is with matching and mismatching. This metaprogram determines how you sort information to learn, understand, and the like. Some people respond to the world by finding sameness. They look at things and see what they have in common; they're matchers. So when they look at these figures they might say, "Well, they're all rectangles." Another kind of matcher finds sameness with exceptions. This person might look at the figures and say, "They're all rectangles, but one is lying down and the other two are standing up."

Other people are mismatchers—difference people. There are two kinds of mismatchers. One type looks at the world and sees how things are different. This person might look at the figures and say they are all different and have different relationships to one another; they're not alike at all. The other kind of mismatcher sees differences with exceptions, the opposite of a matcher who finds sameness with exceptions—the mismatcher sees the differences first, then adds the things they have in common.

To determine whether someone is a matcher or mismatcher, ask about the relationship between any set of objects or situations and note whether the person focuses first on the similarities or the differences. Can you imagine what happens when a sameness matcher gets together with a difference mismatcher? When one says they're all alike, the other says, "No, they're not, they're all different!" The sameness person's rationale is that they're all rectangles. The difference mismatcher's rationale is that the thickness of the lines may not be exactly the same, or that the angles are not exactly the same in all three of them. So who's right? They both are, of course; it all depends on a person's perception. However, mismatchers often have difficulty creating rapport with people because they are always creating differences. They can more easily develop rapport with other mismatchers.

Why is understanding these distinctions important? Let me give an example from my business. A young mother brought her eight-year-old daughter to me because, as she said, the little girl was causing her problems at home. First I spoke to the mother alone and, after using the precision model, I found the problem was that the girl refused to clean her room to her mother's specifications. The mother would insist, the daughter would refuse, and this would cause a stalemate. Next, I brought the young girl into the room. I asked her why she thought her mother wanted her to see me, but before she could open her mouth, her mother jumped up and said sharply, "She thinks she doesn't have to do what I tell her!" Immediately they started arguing as though I weren't even in the room. I clapped my hands loudly and stood up. Then I told the mother I would like her daughter to answer the question, not her. "As a matter of fact," I continued, "I think I'd like to talk to your daughter alone." Of course, this pleased the daughter because I had stood up to her mom, and it created instant rapport between the two of us. After her mother left the room, I asked the girl some questions. It was obvious that she was a strong mismatcher with a heavy internal frame of reference.

I explained to her that the reason she and her mother didn't get along and she didn't clean her room was that, deep inside, maybe she didn't really think she was capable of cleaning the room. This infuriated her, and she began to tell me all the things she could do if she really wanted. I stuck to my strategy of telling her what I thought about her perceptions of her ability. We argued for a little while longer, then I called her mother back into the room alone. I instructed her to just let the little girl alone and watch her actions without criticism.

The very next morning about 10:30 the mother called me crying. "What did you do to my little girl?" she asked. "I went into her room after she left for school, and it was immaculate. Everything is in its right place, and it's spotless. She must have been up all night cleaning!" You see, the little girl was such a strong mismatcher that whenever her mother told her to do something, she would do the opposite. And because she had such a strong internal frame of reference, she needed to "hear" direction from herself, not someone else. When I told her I thought she thought she couldn't do it, it hit home in both these metaprograms. I knew she would mismatch when I said she thought she couldn't do it and that she would tell herself that she could.

For years psychiatrists called this "reverse psychology." Now you know how to recognize when to use it. Mismatchers are in the minority; the generalizations offered by a survey show that about 35 percent of the people interviewed were mismatchers. (If you're a mismatcher, you'll probably say the surveys are not accurate.) Mismatchers are extremely valuable because they tend to see what the rest of us don't. Usually they aren't the souls of poetic inspiration. Many times, even when they get excited, they'll start mismatching and find a way to get unexcited. But their critical, analytical sensibilities are important to any business.

Matching or mismatching modes are extremely important because they can show up in so many ways, even in nutrition. Extreme matchers can often end up eating food that's bad for them, because they want food that is always the same. They wouldn't want an apple or a plum. There's too much variety in ripeness, texture, and taste. Instead they might eat a lot of junk food because it doesn't change. It might be lousy food, but it warms a matcher's unvarying soul.

Would you use the same persuasion techniques on a matcher and a mismatcher? Would you want them in the same job? Would you treat two kids with different matching strategies in the same way? Of course not. This is not to say that strategies are immutable. People are not Pavlovian dogs. They can modify their strategies to some extent, but only if someone talks to them in their own language about how to do that. It takes tremendous effort and patience to turn a lifelong mismatcher into a matcher, but you can help such a person make the most of this approach and be a little less grumpy in the process. That's one of the secrets of living with people who are different from you. On the other hand, it's useful for matchers to see more differences, for they have a tendency to generalize. It might be useful for a matcher to notice all the differences between this week and last week, or between two different cities (instead of saying Los Angeles is very much like New York). Differences are part of the spice of life.

Can a matcher and a mismatcher live happily together? Sure—just as long as they understand each other. That way, when differences occur, they'll just realize the other person isn't bad or wrong, it's just that he or she perceives things in a different way. You don't have to be totally alike to establish rapport. But you do need to remember the different ways you both perceive things and learn how to respect and appreciate each other.

PATTERN FIVE: CONVINCER STRATEGY

The fifth metaprogram involves what it takes to convince someone of something. The convincer strategy has two parts. To figure out what consistently convinces someone, you must first find out what sensory building blocks the person needs, then discover how often these stimuli must be received before becoming convinced. **To discover someone's convincer metaprogram, ask, "How do you know when someone else is good at a job?** Do you have to 1) see her or watch her do it, 2) hear about how good she is, 3) do it with her, or 4) read about her ability?" The answer may be a combination of these. You may believe someone's good when you see her do a good job and when other people tell you she's good.

The next question is, "How often does someone have to demonstrate she's good before you're convinced?" There are four possible answers: 1) immediately (for example, if she demonstrates she's good at something once, you believe she is), 2) a number of times (two or more), 3) over a period of time (say, a few weeks or a month or a year), or 4) consistently. In the last case, a person has to demonstrate she's good each and every time.

If you're the head of an organization, one of the most valuable states you can achieve with your key employees is trust and rapport. If they know you care about them, they'll work harder and better for you. If they don't trust you, they won't deliver for you. But part of establishing that trust is being attentive to the different needs of different people. Some people will establish a relationship and maintain it. If they know you play fair and care about them, you can establish a bond that will last until you do something to betray it.

This doesn't work for everyone. Some workers need more than that, whether it's a kind word, an approving memo, a show of public support, or an important task to perform. They may be just as loyal and just as talented, but they need more verification from you than others. They need more proof that the bond between you still holds. Likewise, experienced salespeople know customers they had to persuade only once, and they were customers forever. Other customers have to see the product two or three times before they decide to buy, while for others maybe six months can pass before there is a need to sell to them again. Then, of course, there is the salesperson's "favorite"—the customer who has used your product for years, and every time you touch base, he wants to know again why he should use it. This type of person has to be shown every time.

The same process plays out with even greater intensity in personal relationships. With some people, if you can prove your love once, you've proved it forever. With others, you have to prove it every day. The value of understanding these metaprograms is that they provide you with a game plan for convincing someone. You know in advance what it will take to convince that person, so you're no longer upset when you have to convince every time. You *expect* that behavior.

PATTERN SIX: POSSIBILITY VS. NECESSITY

Ask different people why they went to work for their current employer or bought their current car or house. **Some people are motivated primarily by necessity, rather than by what they want.** They do something because they must. They're not pulled to take action by what is possible; they're not looking for infinite varieties of experience. They go through life taking what comes and what is available. When they need a new job or a new house or a new car or even a new spouse, they go out and accept what is available.

Others are motivated to look for possibilities. They're driven less by what they have to do than by what they want to do. They seek options, experiences, choices, paths. While a necessity person is interested in what's known and what's secure, a possibility person is interested in what's not known: What could evolve, what opportunities might develop?

If you were an employer, which kind of person would you most want to hire? Some people would probably answer, "The person who is motivated by possibility." After all, having a rich sense of potential makes for a richer life. Instinctively, most of us (even a lot of people who are motivated by necessity) would advocate the virtues of remaining open to an infinite variety of new directions.

In reality, it's not that cut-and-dried. Many jobs require a great deal of attention to detail, steadfastness, and consistency. People who are motivated by necessity have other virtues, as well. For some jobs, permanence is valued. You want to fill these jobs with people who'll last for a long time. A person motivated by possibilities is always looking for new options, new enterprises, new challenges. If such a person finds another job that seems to offer more potential, it's "Adios, baby!" Not so the somewhat plodding soul who is motivated by necessity, takes a job when circumstances dictate, and sticks with it because working is a necessity of life.

There are many jobs that cry out for a dreamy-eyed, swashbuckling, risk-taking believer in possibility. If your company were diversifying into a whole new field, you'd want to hire someone who'd be attuned to all the possibilities. It's equally important to know what your own personal metaprograms are so if you're ever looking for a job, you can select one that will best support your needs.

The same principle works in motivating your children. Let's say you're trying to emphasize the virtues of education and going to a good college. If your child is motivated by necessity, you have to show him why he needs a good education. You can tell him about all the jobs that absolutely require a degree. You can explain why you need a foundation in math to be a good engineer or in language skills to be a good teacher. If your child is motivated by possibility, you would take a different approach. He's bored by what he has to do, so you'd stress the infinite possibilities open to those with a good education. Show him how learning itself is the greatest avenue for possibility—fill his brain with images of new avenues to be explored, new dimensions to be opened, new things to be discovered. Your objective in each case would be the same, although the paths you take in leading your child would be very different.

Pattern Seven: Working Style

Everyone has their own strategies for work. Some people are not happy unless they're *independent.* They have great difficulty working closely with others and can't work well under a great deal of supervision. They have to run their own show. Others function best as part of a group. We call their strategy a *cooperative* one. They want to share responsibility for any task they take on. Still others have a *proximity* strategy, which is somewhere in between.

They prefer to work with other people while maintaining sole responsibility for a task. They're in charge but not alone.

If you want to get the most out of your employees or children, figure out their work strategies, the ways in which they're most effective. Sometimes you'll find an employee who is brilliant but a pain in the neck, someone who always has to do things her way. Now, she just might not be cut out to be an employee. She may be the kind of person who has to run her own business, and sooner or later she probably will if you do not provide an avenue of expression. If you have a valuable employee like this, you should try to find a way to maximize her talents and give her as much autonomy as possible. If you make her part of a team, she'll drive everyone crazy. But if you give her as much independence as possible, she can prove invaluable. That's what the new concepts of entrepreneurship are all about.

You've heard of the Peter Principle, the idea that all people are promoted to the level of their incompetence. One reason this happens is that employers are often insensitive to their employees' work strategies. Some people work best in a cooperative setting, thriving on a large amount of feedback and human interaction. Would you reward their good work by putting them in charge of some new autonomous venture? Not if you want to make use of their best talents. That doesn't mean you have to keep people at the same level. But it does mean you should give promotions and new responsibilities that utilize their best talents, not their worst ones.

PUTTING IT INTO PRACTICE

Here's an exercise to do today. After reading this chapter, practice eliciting people's metaprograms. Ask them, "What do you want in a relationship (or house or car or career)? How do you know when you have been successful at something? What is the relationship between what you are doing this month and what you did last month? How often does someone have to demonstrate something to you before you are convinced it's true? Tell me about a favorite work experience and why it was important to you."

Does the person pay attention to you while you are asking these questions? Is the person interested in your reaction, or occupied elsewhere? These are only a few of the questions you can ask to successfully elicit the metaprograms we've discussed. If you don't get the information you need, rephrase the question until you do.

Think of almost any communication problem you have with somebody, and you'll probably find that understanding the person's metaprograms will help you adjust communications so that the problem disappears. Think of a frustration in your life—someone you love who doesn't feel loved, someone you work for who manages to rub you the wrong way, or someone you've tried to help who hasn't responded. What you need to do is identify the operating metaprogram, identify what you are doing, and identify what the other person is doing. For example, suppose you need verification only once that you have a loving relationship, and your partner needs it consistently. Or you put together a proposal that shows how things are alike, and your supervisor only wants to hear about the ways they're different. Or you try to warn someone to avoid something, and the person is only interested in hearing about something he or she wants to go after.

When you speak in the wrong key, the message that comes through is the wrong one. It's as much a problem for parents dealing with their children as it is for executives dealing with their employees. Many of us have not developed the acuity to recognize and deal with the basic strategies that others use. When you fail to get your message through to someone, you don't need to change the content. You do have to develop the flexibility to be able to alter its form to fit the metaprograms of the person with whom you're trying to communicate. Often you can communicate most effectively when you use several metaprograms together.

The principles we've dealt with in this chapter are important and powerful. However, note that the number of metaprograms you're aware of is limited only by your sensitivity and imagination. One of the keys to success in anything is the ability to make new distinctions. Metaprograms give you the tools to make crucial distinctions in deciding how to deal with people. You are not limited to the metaprograms discussed here. Become a student of possibility. Constantly gauge and calibrate the people around you. Take note of specific patterns they have for perceiving the world and notice whether others have similar patterns. Through this approach you can develop a whole set of distinctions that can empower you in knowing how to communicate effectively with all types of people.

For example, some people sort primarily by feelings and others sort by logical thoughts. Would you try to persuade them in the same way? Of course not. Some people are turned on by beginnings. They're most excited when they get a new idea off the ground, then tend to lose interest in it and go on to something else. Others are fixated on completion. Anything they do they have to see all the way through to the end, whether it's reading a book or doing a task at work. Some people make decisions based only on specific facts and figures. First they have to know if the parts will work—they'll think about the broader picture later. Others are convinced first by an overall concept or idea. They react to global chunks. First they want to see the big picture—if they like it, then they'll think about the details.

Some people sort by food. That's right, by food. Almost anything they do or consider doing is evaluated in terms of food. Ask them how to get someplace, and they'll say, "Go down the road till you get to Burger King, make a left, and then continue down until you get to McDonald's. Make a right, then make a left at Kentucky Fried Chicken until you get down to that chocolate-brown building." Ask about a movie they went to, and they immediately begin telling you about how bad the concession stand was. Ask about a wedding, and they'll tell you about the cake.

A person who sorts primarily by people will talk mostly about the guests at the wedding or the actors in the film. A person who sorts primarily by activities will talk about what actually happened at the wedding, the plot of the film, and so on.

The other advantage of understanding metaprograms is that it provides a model of balance. We all use metaprograms to varying degrees. For some metaprograms we may lean slightly more to one side than to another; for others we may swing wildly. But there's nothing carved in stone about any of them. Just as you can make the decision to put yourself in an empowering state, you can choose to adopt metaprograms that help rather than hinder you. What a metaprogram does is tell your brain what to delete. So if you're moving toward things, for example, you're deleting the things to move away from. If you're moving away from things, you're deleting those you could be moving toward. To change your metaprograms, all you have to do is become aware of the things you normally delete and begin to focus your attention on them.

Don't make the mistake of confusing yourself with your behaviors or doing it with someone else. You may say, "I know Joe. He does this and this and this." But you don't know Joe. You know him only through his behaviors—and he isn't his behaviors any more than you are yours. If you're someone who tends to move away from everything, maybe that's your pattern of behavior. If you don't like it, you can change. In fact, there's no excuse for you not to change. You have the power now. The only question is whether you have enough reasons to make yourself use what you know.

Making a Change in Metaprograms

There are two ways metaprograms are influenced or changed. One is through Significant Emotional Events—SEEs. If you saw your parents constantly moving away from things and not being able to achieve their full potential as a result, that's a SEE that might have influenced the way you move toward or away from things today. Or if you sorted only by necessity, then missed out on some great job opportunity because the company was looking for someone with a dynamic sense of possibility, that might shock you into changing your approach. Or if you tend to move toward everything, then get taken in by a flashy-looking investment scam, it would probably affect the way you looked at the next proposal that came your way.

The other way you influence metaprograms is by consciously deciding to make a change. Most of us never give a thought to which metaprograms we use. The first step toward change is recognition. Let's say you realize you have a strong tendency to move away from things. How do you feel about it? Sure, there are things you want to move away from. If you put your hand on a hot iron, of course you would want to move it away as soon as you could. But aren't there things you really want to move toward? Isn't a part of being in control making a conscious effort to move toward something? Don't most great leaders and great achievers move toward things rather than away? Begin to stretch a little. Start thinking about things that appeal to you, and actively move toward them.

You could also think of metaprograms on a higher level. Do nations and communities have metaprograms? Well, they have behaviors, don't they? So they have metaprograms, too. We must be careful not to stereotype people, but it is more than possible that whole groups of people, acting as a unit, share similar metaprograms. Their collective behavior many times forms a pattern based upon the metaprograms of their leaders. Their dominant sorting patterns may have been heavily influenced by their history and the treatment of their ancestors. Is it possible that Dr. Martin Luther King, Jr.'s, tendency to move toward things influences us to do the same? I think so. The United States, for the most part, has a culture that seems to move toward things.

Like everything else in this book, metaprograms should be used on two levels. The first is as a tool to guide our communication with others. Just as a person's physiology will tell you countless stories about him, his metaprograms will speak eloquently about what motivates him and what frightens him off. The second is as a tool for personal change. Remember, you are not your behaviors. If you find that any kind of pattern works against you, all you have to do is change it. Metaprograms offer one of the most useful tools for personal calibration and change. And they provide keys to some of the most useful communication tools available. Take some time to calibrate your own metaprograms and those of the people around you. You'll find they are a wonderful tool for assisting you in moving in the direction you most want to go, and to assist others in doing the same.

In the next chapter, we'll look at other invaluable communication tools—tools that will show you . . .

CHAPTER SEVENTEEN

How to Handle Resistance and Solve Problems

I ain't gonna study war no more.

—African American Spiritual

As I look back over the years, I can see that by far the most profound cultural shifts in recent African American history occurred between 1953 and 1969. The hundreds of thousands of beautiful, courageous souls who answered the call of our Black leaders to make a difference sculpted the reality that many of us now take for granted. This same type of painstaking change is now evident in South Africa, beginning with the abolition of apartheid in the 1990s. Although the struggle is not over yet and there is still a long way to go, the concept of basic human rights for all people regardless of color or religious denomination is definitely creeping into the common consciousness of countries all over the world.

In America, the greatest turning point in the fight for equality took place in the 1960s with the adoption of the concepts of nonviolent protest and working within the system. Though dismissed by some as weakness and denial, this approach broke the crooked back of injustice in this country. All in all, most of our success arises from the fact that we have become *flexible* in our approach to claiming our basic human birthright. The cruelties our ancestors faced were unspeakable, but the changes they made in themselves would lay the groundwork for new belief structures on the part of our adversaries of the future.

Whenever you deal with other people, a certain amount of trial and error is inevitable. You can't direct the behavior of others with the same speed, certainty, and effectiveness with which you control your own. But one of the keys to personal success is learning how to speed up the trial-and-error process. You can do this by developing rapport, understanding metaprograms, and learning how to calibrate others so you can deal with them on their own terms. This chapter is about taking the trial and error inherent in human interaction and increasing the pace of discovery by learning to handle resistance and solve problems.

The underlying theme of the first half of this book has been *modeling*. Excellence in modeling is crucial for learning to create rapidly the results you desire. If there's a theme for the second half of this book, it's *flexibility*—a quality all effective communicators share. They know how to gauge others, then keep changing their own behavior—verbal or nonverbal—until they create what they want. The key to effective communication is to begin with a sense of humility and a willingness to change. You can't communicate by force of will; you can't bludgeon someone into understanding your point of view. You can only communicate by constant, resourceful, attentive flexibility.

I've always been fascinated by the music and career of the artist formerly known as Prince. Now there's a man who's definitely flexible! In fact, his whole career is a model of flexibility. His first album was a flop, so he changed his approach. As you know, during his first major concert he was booed off the stage, so he changed his approach. He kept changing until he found what worked—and it didn't take long before he was calling the shots and influencing the world with his music and his style.

Most people don't even know what flexibility really is. The more you use it, the greater your advantage in life. All other things being equal, the person who is most flexible wins. Often, flexibility doesn't come naturally. Many people follow the same patterns of behavior and thought with numbing regularity. Some people are so sure they're right about something, they assume merely using forceful repetition will get them through—a combination of ego and inertia at work. Many times it's easiest to do exactly what we've done before. But the easiest is often the worst thing to do. In this chapter, we're going to look at ways to change directions, break patterns, redirect communication, and profit from confusion. The key to life is to open up as many avenues, try as many doors, use as many different approaches as it takes to solve a problem. If you use only one strategy, you'll be about as effective as a car that runs in one gear. The person with the most choices wins.

Children are the masters of flexibility. It's as if they don't even know the meaning of the word *no*. Recently my seven-year-old niece Rudee Ray tried to convince me to take her to the video store. She used everything in the book—flirting, reasoning, begging, even ordering me to take her. In the end she succeeded because no matter what I said, she kept coming up with other alternatives. I'm sure you've had similar experiences with other young flexibility champions!

Most of us think of settling a dispute as something akin to verbal boxing: You pound the other person with arguments until you get what you want. Much more elegant and effective models can be found in Asian martial arts such as aikido and t'ai chi, where the goal is not to overcome force but to *redirect it*. Rather than meeting force with force, you align yourself with the force directed at you and then guide it in a new direction.

Remember, there is no such thing as resistance; there are only inflexible communicators who push at the wrong time and in the wrong direction. Instead of opposing someone's views, a good communicator is like an aikido master—flexible and resourceful enough to notice resistance, find points of agreement, align with them, and redirect communication in the way he or she wants to go.

> *The best soldier does not attack. The superior fighter succeeds without violence. The greatest conqueror wins without a struggle. The most successful manager leads without dictating. This is called intelligent nonaggressiveness. This is called mastery of men.*
>
> —LAO-TZU

Just as certain words produce specific states of minds, it's important for us to remember that certain words and phrases create resistance and problems. Great leaders and communicators realize this truth and pay close attention to the words they use and the effect the words have. Perhaps the greatest example is the way in which Dr. Martin Luther King, Jr., used words. His speeches were rich with metaphors that painted vivid pictures in the minds of his listeners—powerful statements like, "We must hew from the mountain of hope a stone of justice." Black, White, or other, who could argue with such a statement?

Dr. King was a master of the art of persuasion. He was careful not to create resistance to his proposals through the use of words that triggered negative responses. For example, let's consider just one ever-present, three-letter word: *but.* Used unconsciously and automatically, it can be one of the most destructive words in our language. If someone says, "That's true, but . . ." what is the person saying? That the point being discussed is not true, or that it's irrelevant. The word *but* has negated everything said before it. How do *you* feel if someone says to you that he or she agrees with you, but. . . ? What if the person simply substituted the word *and* instead? What if *you* said, "That's true, and here's something else that's also true," or "That's an interesting idea, and here's another way to think about it"? In both cases, you start with agreement. Instead of creating resistance, you've created an avenue of redirection.

Just as there are phrases and words that automatically trigger feelings or states of resistance, there are other ways of communicating that encourage people to be involved and open. For example, what would happen if you had a tool that could communicate exactly how you feel about an issue without compromising your integrity in any way, yet you never had to disagree with anyone, either? Wouldn't that be fairly powerful? Well, we do have such a tool. It's called the *agreement frame.* It consists of three phrases you can use in any communication to respect the person you're communicating with, maintain rapport, share what you feel is true, yet never resist the person's opinion in any way. And without resistance, there is no conflict.

Here are the three phrases of the agreement frame:

"I appreciate and . . ."
"I respect and . . ."
"I agree and . . ."

In each case, you're doing three things. You're building rapport by entering someone's world and acknowledging the person's communication rather than ignoring or denigrating it with words like *but* or *however.* You're creating a frame of agreement that bonds you together. And you're opening the door to redirect the issue without creating resistance.

For example, suppose someone tells you you're absolutely wrong about something. If you say, "No, I'm not wrong" just as strongly, are you going to stay in rapport? No. Resistance has been created and there is conflict. Instead, respond this way: "I respect the intensity of your feelings about this, and I think if you were to hear my side of it you might feel differently."

Notice you don't have to agree with the content of the person's communication. You can always appreciate, respect, or agree with someone's feeling about something, because if you had the same physiology or the same perceptions, you would feel the same way. You can also appreciate someone else's intent. For example, many times two people on opposite sides of an issue don't appreciate the other's point of view, so they don't even hear each other. But if you use the agreement frame, you will find yourself listening more intently to what the other person is saying—and discovering new ways to appreciate people as a result. Let's assume you're having a discussion with someone on affirmative action. He is for eliminating all racial- or gender-based preference programs because they are discriminatory, while you believe affirmative action merely levels the playing field in an unfair cultural environment. The two of you might see yourselves as rivals, yet you may have the same intent—giving all people the opportunity to fulfill their potential and participate in the American dream. So if the other person says, "Affirmative action means that the best and the brightest may be excluded in favor of less-qualified people who are chosen not for their skills but because their race has been victimized in the past," rather than arguing with him, you could agree with his intent and say, "I really appreciate your desire to make sure that every job, every contract, every place in school is filled with the best people, and I think that affirmative action can actually expand the number of qualified candidates for each position. What about the possibility of . . ."? When you communicate in this way, the other person feels heard and respected, and you encounter no resistance. New possibilities are also introduced. This formula can be used with anyone, because no matter what the other person says you can always find something to appreciate, respect, and agree with. It's impossible to fight with you, because you simply refuse to fight—it's an option that just never comes up.

You can't hold a man down without staying down with him.

—BOOKER T. WASHINGTON

Here's a simple little experiment that provides most people with memorable results. Two people take different sides of a controversial issue and debate it without ever using the word *but,* and without ever belittling or insulting the other's point of view. People find this a liberating experience, somewhat akin to verbal aikido. They're able to appreciate the other person's point of view rather than thinking they have to destroy it. They can argue without getting belligerent or upset; instead, they can make new distinctions and reach points of agreement.

Find someone who'll do this exercise with you. Pick opposite sides of a topic and argue it in precisely the way described above, as a game of finding commonality and leading the discussion in the direction you want it to go. This doesn't mean you should abandon your beliefs; no one wants you to be an intellectual jellyfish. But you'll find you can reach your outcome more effectively by gently aligning and leading rather than pushing violently. And you'll be able to develop a richer, more balanced point of view by being open to other perspectives.

Another worthwhile exercise is to argue for something you *don't* believe. You'll surprise yourself by coming up with new perspectives. Most of us consider discussions to be a win-lose game: We're right, and the other person's wrong. One side has a monopoly on truth, the other resides in utter darkness. I've found time and again I learn more and get where I want to go much more quickly by using the agreement frame. The best salespeople, the best communicators, know it's very hard to persuade others to do something they don't want to do, and very easy to get them to do what they want. By creating an agreement frame, by leading them naturally rather than through conflict, you do the latter, not the former. The key to effective communication is to frame things so that people do what they want to do, not what you want them to do.

Another way to resolve conflicts is to interrupt negative patterns—yours and other people's. We've all found ourselves in stuck states, in which we recycle our own mental dirty dishwasher. Or, to look at it another way, it's like a compact disc with a scratched surface playing the same tired refrain over and over again. The way to get the CD unstuck is to advance to the next track. The way to change a stuck state in yourself or another person is the same: Interrupt the pattern—the tired old refrain—and start anew.

Have you ever been talking on the phone with someone when all of a sudden that little beep signifying call waiting interrupts your conversation? You go to the other line to see who it is, and when you return to the original conversation, you can't remember what you were talking about! This is an example of a pattern interrupt. If someone is in a particular mental, emotional, or behavioral pattern and you interrupt it, it will be hard for that person to continue the original pattern.

Pattern interrupts are usually my first line of attack when dealing with someone on a therapeutic level. Whether I use physical or verbal methods, I am notorious for changing someone's negative state in order to access a better one. I've had people hysterically crying and, by asking a totally unrelated question or having them stand up, I've assisted them to snap out of their unresourceful state of mind, thus opening the door for a new and more empowering pattern. Parents do the same thing with children. Haven't you ever seen a child who was crying because she fell and hurt herself, and as soon as her mother kisses her "booboo" or offers her something sweet, she changes her tune as if nothing ever happened? Sometimes simply asking a question changes the person's focus enough to get him or her on a different train of thought. I recently started using a great question devised by my dear friend Greg Gibson. When someone is stuck in a negative pattern like depression or anger or doubt, I ask, "Has it ever occurred to you not to be that way?" The person usually responds with a "What the heck?" look, and presto change-o! the bad pattern has been broken.

Confusion is one of the best ways to interrupt negative patterns. For example, people might mope around and become depressed because they think they'll evoke sensitive, caring questions from others about what's troubling them. They may be completely unaware they're doing this, but nonetheless they're still doing it. It's their way of getting attention, using their resources in the best way they know how to change their state.

If you knew someone like that, how would you react? Well, you could do the expected. You could sit down and begin a long, sensitive discussion. That might make the person feel a little better in the moment, but it also reinforces the pattern. It tells the person that if she mopes around, she'll get all the attention she wants. What if you did something else? What if you began tickling her, or ignoring her, or barking like a dog in her face? You'll find that this person won't know how to respond to you, and out of her confusion or laughter will emerge a new pattern of thinking or behaving.

Now, clearly there are times when we all need someone to talk to, times when we need a friend. There are genuine instances of grief and pain that require a caring, sensitive ear. But we're talking about patterns and stuck states—repeated behavioral sequences that are self-perpetuating and destructive. The more you reinforce these sequences, the more harm you do. Our aim is to show people that they can change these patterns, that they have the power to change their own behaviors. If you believe you're a ball on a tether waiting for someone to hit you, that's how you'll behave. If you believe you're in control and you can change your patterns to suit your desires, then you'll be able to.

The trouble is, many times our culture tells us otherwise. It says we don't control our behaviors, we don't control our states, we don't control our emotions. Most of us have adopted the belief that we're at the mercy of everything from childhood traumas to raging hormones. The lesson we must learn is that patterns can be interrupted and changed in an instant.

When NLP co-founders Richard Bandler and John Grinder were doing private therapies, they were known as masters of the pattern interrupt. Bandler tells one story about visiting a mental institution and dealing with a man who insisted he was Jesus Christ—not metaphorically, not in spirit, but in the flesh. One day Bandler walked in to meet this man. "Are you Jesus?" he asked. "Yes, my son," the man replied. Bandler said, "I'll be back in a minute." This left the man a little bit confused. Within three or four minutes, Bandler came back with a measuring tape. Asking the man to hold out his arms, Bandler measured the length of his arms and his height from head to toe. Then he left. The man claiming to be Christ became a little concerned. A little while later, Bandler came back with a hammer, some large spiked nails, and a long set of boards. He began to pound them into the form of a cross. The man asked, "What are you doing?" As Bandler put the last nail in the cross, he asked, "Are you Jesus?" Again the man said, "Yes, my son." With a meaningful look Bandler replied, "Then you know why I'm here." Somehow, the man suddenly recalled who he really was. His old pattern no longer seemed like such a good idea. "I'm not Jesus. I'm not Jesus!" the man started yelling. Case closed.

A more positive pattern interrupt is an anti-smoking campaign of a few years ago. It suggested that anytime someone you love reaches for a cigarette, give him or her a kiss instead. In the first place, this interrupts the automatic pattern of reaching for a cigarette. At the same time, it produces a new experience that can cast doubt upon the wisdom of the old one. Pattern interrupts are also valuable in business. One of my clients regularly surprises his staff both with incentive bonuses and unannounced quality inspections. His company's productivity has increased because employees seldom drop into the slump of complacency.

In Chapter 6, I told you about my mother dealing with cancer. Whenever she started to settle into an unresourceful state, I would interrupt her pattern by cracking a joke or asking her a question. She would laugh or try to figure out what I was doing—both of which meant she was no longer in the old state of mind.

We've all been in arguments that take on a life of their own. The original reason behind the dispute may have long since been forgotten but we rage on, getting madder and madder, more and more intent on "winning," on proving our point, because we're stuck in our own disempowering emotions. Arguments like this can completely destroy a relationship. When they're over, you may think, *How in the world did that get so far out of hand?* But while the argument is still going on, you have no perspective whatsoever. Think of situations you have been in lately where you or others were stuck in unresourceful patterns of thinking, feeling, or behaving. What pattern interrupts could you have used?

Take a moment now to create five pattern interrupts you could use in the future, and think of situations where they would be useful. What if you had a pattern interrupt set up in advance, like an early-warning system, to short-circuit arguments before they get out of hand? I've found that humor is one of the best pattern interrupts. It's hard to be angry when you're laughing!

> ***Anger is an emotion that if you carry around for a long period of time, it doesn't allow you to live.***
>
> —JOHN SINGLETON

There are two main ideas in this chapter, and they both go against the grain of what many of us have been taught. **First, you can persuade an opponent more effectively through agreement than through conquest.** We live in a society that revels in competition, that likes to make clear distinctions between winners and losers. Remember the beer commercials a few years back in which two men argued about the same beer? They went back and forth saying, "Less filling . . . Tastes great!" Neither one would bend on his conviction, no matter what. Everything I've learned about communication tells me the competition model is very limited. I've already talked about the magic of rapport and how essential it is to personal power. If you see someone as a competitor, someone to be vanquished, you're starting from the exact opposite framework. The word *compete* is derived from the Latin meaning *to come together*. Build from agreement, not from conflict; learn to align and lead rather than trying to overcome resistance. I know this is easier said than done. However, through consistent awareness we can change our patterns of communication.

Second, our behavioral patterns aren't indelibly carved into our brains. If we do something that limits us repeatedly, we're not suffering from an incurable mental ailment; we're just running an unresourceful pattern. It may be a way we relate to others, or a way we think. **The solution is simply to interrupt the pattern, stop what we're doing, and try something new.** We're not robots wired into almost-forgotten personal traumas. If we do something we don't like, all we have to do is recognize it and change it. What does the Bible say? "We shall all be changed in an instant, in the twinkling of an eye." We *will* be if we *want* to be.

In both cases, the common ground is the idea of flexibility. If you have trouble putting together a puzzle, you won't get anywhere by trying the same solution time and time again. You'll solve it by being flexible enough to change, to adapt, to experiment, to try something new. The more flexible you are, the more options you create, the more doors you can open and the more successful you will be. Remember, we as a people have survived and flourished as a result of being flexible and changing our approach. If we continue to do so, we will get the results we desire. After all, we have changed and adapted throughout history. This is a sign of our strength, for in nature, that which does not adapt shall perish.

In the next chapter, we'll look at another important tool of personal flexibility. We call this . . .

CHAPTER EIGHTEEN

Reframing: The Power of Perspective

Gray skies are just clouds passing over.

—DUKE ELLINGTON

CONSIDER THE SOUND of a car pulling up, the engine shutting off, the car door opening, then slamming shut with a crisp, padded, metal-to-metal sound. *Ka-chunk.* If I were to ask you, "What does that sound mean?" you'd probably shrug your shoulders and say, "It doesn't mean anything to me. Just a car pulling up." When you're in a mall parking lot with cars coming and going and the smell of exhaust permeating the air, that sound probably doesn't have much significance at all. You'd hardly even notice it.

But let's say you're home alone, in bed at 2:30 in the morning. Your peaceful slumber is cracked wide open by the sound of a car pulling up, the engine being shut off, and the car door opening and slamming shut—*ka-chunk*—right outside your bedroom window. Do the sounds have meaning now? You bet they do. That same set of sounds—that signal—will have many different meanings depending on what those sounds have meant to you in similar situations in the past. Your experience may provide you with a context for that signal and thus determine whether it relaxes or frightens you. For example, you may classify the sound as that of your spouse coming home early. But people who have experienced a burglary may think it means an intruder.

Thus the meaning of any experience in life depends on the frame we put around it. If you change the frame—the context—

the meaning changes instantly. One of the most effective tools for personal change is learning how to put the best frames on any experience. This process is called *reframing*.

On a piece of paper, describe the figure below. What do you see?

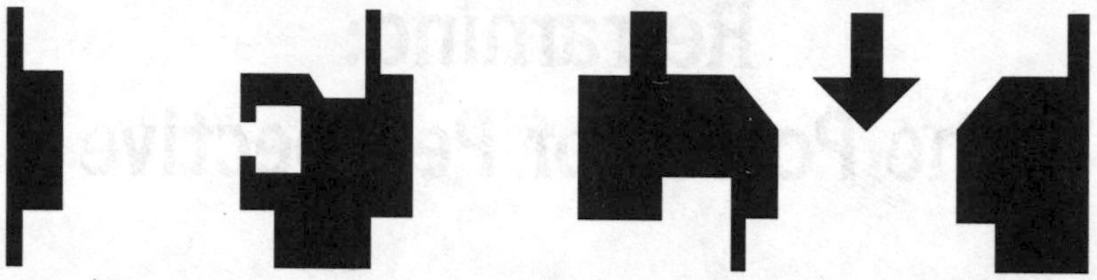

There are many things you could see. You might see what you consider to be a hat on its side, a monster, an arrow pointing down, and so on. Describe to yourself what you see right now. Do you also see the word *fly*? You may have seen it right away because this example has been used for bumper stickers and other promotional items, so your previous frame of reference helped you see it as *fly* immediately. If you didn't see it, why didn't you? Do you even see it now? If you didn't see the word, it's probably because your habitual perceptual frame leads you to expect words on white paper to be written in black ink. As long as you use this frame to interpret this situation, you will not see the word *fly*, since in this case, it's written in white. You must be able to reframe your perception in order to see it. Or perhaps you've seen one of those 3-D paintings that were so popular in 1993. To look at it one way, all you'll see is a mesh of squiggled lines, but when you defocus your eyes you can see the image hidden underneath. The same is true in life. Many times there are opportunities all around to make our lives exactly as we wish them to be. **There are ways to see our biggest problems as our greatest opportunities—if only we can step out of our trained patterns of perception.**

Again, as we've discussed over and over in this book, nothing in the world has any inherent meaning. How we *feel* about something and what we *do* are dependent upon our perception of it. A signal has meaning only in the frame or context in which we perceive it. Misfortune is a point of view. Your headache may feel good to an aspirin salesperson! Many Whites view being Black as an advantage, and vice versa. It's important to remember that perceptions are creative. That is, if we perceive something as a liability, that's the message we deliver to our brain, and the brain produces states that make it the reality. If we change our frame of reference by looking at the same situation from a different point of view, we can change our representation or perception about anything and in a moment change our states and behaviors. This is what reframing is all about.

Remember, we do not see the world as it is. The way things are can be interpreted from many points of view. Our perceptual "maps" define the territory.

Figure A

Figure B

For example, take a look at figure A. What do you see? Of course you see an old, ugly woman. Take a look at figure B. As you can see, this is a drawing of a similar ugly old woman with her chin buried in her fur coat. Look at it carefully and try to figure out what kind of old woman she is. Is she happy or sad? What do you suppose she's thinking about? Yet there's something interesting about this old woman. The artist who drew it claims it's a drawing of her pretty young daughter. If you change your frame of reference, you should be able to see this beautiful young woman. Here's some help. The old woman's nose becomes the chin and jawline of the younger woman's face. The older woman's left eye becomes the younger woman's left ear. The older woman's mouth becomes a necklace around the younger woman's neck. If you still have difficulty, I'll provide you with a drawing that will help you see it. Take a look at Figure C.

Figure C

The obvious question is, Why did you see the ugly old woman in Figure B instead of the beautiful young girl? The answer? You were conditioned in advance to see the old woman.

It is important to note that our past experiences regularly filter our ability to see what is really happening in the world. But there are multiple ways to see or experience any situation. The entrepreneur who buys advance tickets to a concert and sells them at a higher price at the gate can be seen as a despicable person who takes advantage of others—or as someone who adds value to those who could not get tickets or did not want to wait in line. The key to success in life is to consistently represent your experience in ways that support you in producing even greater results for yourself and others.

> *The impulse to dream was slowly beaten out of me by experience. Now it surged up again and I hungered for books, new ways of looking and seeing.*
>
> —RICHARD WRIGHT

Reframing in its simplest form is changing a negative statement into a positive one by changing the frame of reference used to perceive the experience. There are two major types of reframes, or ways to alter our perception about something: context reframing and content reframing. Both alter your internal representations by resolving internal pain or conflict, therefore putting you in a more resourceful state.

Context reframing involves taking an experience that seems to be bad, upsetting, or undesirable and showing how the same behavior or experience is actually a great advantage in another context. Children's literature is filled with examples of context reframing. Rudolph's nose, which caused people to make fun of him, was actually an advantage and made him a hero in the context of a dark and snowy night. The ugly duckling suffered great pain because he was so different, but his difference was his beauty as a full-grown swan.

Great innovations are made by those who know how to reframe activities and problems into potential resources in other contexts. For example, oil was once considered something that destroyed the value of land for crop usage, yet look at its value today. Before George Washington Carver came along the common peanut had but one use, food, but he found thousands of other uses for the peanut and became the first Black scientist to gain major recognition. Several years ago, lumberyards had difficulty disposing of large amounts of waste sawdust from their mills. One guy took that waste and decided to put it to use in another context. He pressed it together with glue and lighter fluid and created something called Presto Logs. After contracting to take away all the "worthless" sawdust from these mills, in two years he developed a multimillion-dollar business, with his major resource costing him nothing! But that's all an entrepreneur is: someone who endows resources with new wealth-producing capacity. In other words, someone who is an expert reframer.

Content reframing involves taking the exact same situation and changing what it means. For example, you might say your son never stops talking. He never shuts up! After a content reframe, you might say that he certainly must be a very intelligent young man to have so much to say. There's the story of a famous army general who was known to have reframed his troops during a heavy enemy attack by saying, "We're not retreating, we're just advancing in another direction." When a person close to us dies, most people in our culture are sad. Why? There are many reasons, such as feelings of loss. Yet when I was in Nigeria recently, I witnessed people celebrating the death of one of their loved ones. Why? They reframe death to mean that the deceased is always with them, that nothing in the universe is ever destroyed, that things just change form. Some consider death as graduation to a higher level of existence, so they are joyous.

Another kind of content reframe is to actually change the way you see, hear, or represent a situation. The next time you're upset about something someone said to you, try this: Envision yourself smiling as this person says the same negative words expressed in the tonality of your favorite singer. Or see the same experience in your mind's eye, only this time with the speaker surrounded by your favorite color. Or you may even change what was said to you in the first place. As you reexperience it, hear an apology this time. Or see the person speaking to you from a perspective that elevates you above him or her. Reframing the same stimulus changes the meaning sent to the brain and thus the states and behaviors associated with it. This book is full of reframes. In fact, "The Seven Lies of Success" is a whole chapter of reframes.

A New Way of Looking at Things

Several years ago a touching and powerful story appeared in *Reader's Digest*, titled, "A Boy of Unusual Vision," about a young boy named Calvin Stanley. It seems Calvin rides a bike, plays baseball, goes to school, and does just about everything else that eleven-year-olds do—except see.

How could this little boy do all these things, while many people in the same situation just give up on life or live in sorrow? One important clue is the fact that Calvin's mother is apparently a master reframer. She has turned every experience Calvin has—experiences that others would have classified as "limitations"—into advantages in Calvin's mind. Since that's what he represents to himself, that's what Calvin experiences. Here are some examples of her communication to him:

Calvin's mother remembers the day her son asked why he was blind. "I explained he was born that way and it was nobody's fault. He asked, 'Why me?' I said, 'I don't know why, Calvin. Maybe there's a special plan for you.' " Then she sat her son down and told him, "You're seeing, Calvin. You're just using your hands instead of your eyes. And remember, there's nothing you can't do."

One day Calvin was very sad because he realized he'd never see his mother's face. But Mrs. Stanley knew what to tell her only child. "I said, 'Calvin, you can see my face. You can see it with your hands and by listening to my voice, and you can tell more about me that way than somebody who can use his eyes.' " The article concluded by noting that Calvin moves in the sighted world with trust and faith and the unshakable confidence of a child whose mother has always been there for him. Calvin wants to become a computer programmer and someday design programs for the blind.

The world is full of Calvins. We need more people who use reframing as effectively as Mrs. Stanley did. I had the good fortune of recently meeting another master reframer when I had the privilege of working in a band with a blind singer by the name of Lee Garrett. He had a wonderful reframe for being blind. He used the word BLIND as an acronym, standing for Building Life In a New Dimension. He said, "God made only a few perfect beings. The rest he gave sight to." What a master of reframing!

Think of a major mistake you've made in the last year. You might feel an instant rush of gloom. But chances are the mistake was part of an experience with more successes than failures. And, as you consider it, you'll begin to realize you probably learned more from that mistake than from anything else you did that month. For example, have you ever gone somewhere expecting to have a bad time and instead met someone special or made an incredible business connection? Unexpectedly making fortunate discoveries is just one of life's great little treasures. Deliberately looking for the benefits in any situation is an important strategy in reframing.

Is there any experience you can't change? Is there any behavior that's an immutable part of your being? Are you your behaviors, or are you in charge of them? **The one thing we've stressed in every part of this book is that you're in control.** You run your brain. You produce the results of your life. Reframing is one of the most powerful ways to take charge of your perceptions, states, and behaviors. Take a moment and reframe these situations:

1. My boss yells at me all the time.
2. I had to pay $4,000 more in income tax this year than last year.

3. We have little or no extra money to buy Christmas presents this year.
4. Every time I begin to succeed in a big way, I sabotage my success.

Here are some possible reframes:

1. It's great that my boss cares enough to tell me how she really feels. She could have just fired me.
2. That's outstanding. I must have made a lot more money this year than last year.
3. Terrific! Then we can become much more ingenious and make something people will never forget instead of buying run of-the-mill gifts. Our presents will be personal.
4. It's wonderful that I'm so aware of what my pattern has been in the past. Now I can figure out what triggered it and change it forever!

Almost any seemingly negative experience can be reframed into a positive. How often have you said, "Someday I'll probably look back and laugh at this"? I say, "Why wait? Why not look back and laugh at it now?" It's all a matter of perspective.

Now take a minute and think of three situations in your life that are challenging you. How many different ways can you see each of the situations? How many frames can you put around them? What do you learn by seeing them differently? How does this free you to act differently?

"Wait a minute," you might be saying. "That's not so easy to do. Sometimes I'm too depressed to do it." HOLD IT! Don't fool yourself. What's depression? It's a state. Remember earlier in the book when we discussed association and disassociation? A prerequisite to being able to reframe yourself is the ability to disassociate from the depressing experience and see it from a new perspective. Then you can change your internal representation and physiology. If you were in an unresourceful state, now you know how to change it.

One way to reframe is by changing the meaning of an experience or behavior. Imagine a situation in which someone does something you don't like, and you think the behavior has a particular meaning. Let's consider a couple in which the husband especially enjoys cooking, and it's important to him that his cooking is appreciated. His wife behaves quietly during the meal. The husband finds this very upsetting. If she's enjoying his meal, she should talk about it. If she's not talking, she must not be satisfied. What could you do to reframe his perception of his wife's behavior?

Remember, what's important to him is appreciation. A meaning reframe involves changing a perception to one that supports what's important to a person and does it in a way he or she had never considered before. We could suggest to the cook that perhaps his mate was enjoying the food so much that she didn't want to waste time talking when she could be eating. Action speaks louder than words, right? Another possibility would be to get him to reframe the meaning of the behavior himself. We could ask, "Has there ever been a time you personally were quiet during a meal you were enjoying very much? What was going on for you?" His wife's behavior is bothersome only within the frame he put on it. In cases like this, it just takes a little flexibility to change the frame.

A second kind of reframe involves working with a behavior you don't like about yourself. Usually you don't like it because you don't like what it says about you as a person or you don't like what it gets for you. The way to reframe it is to imagine another situation or context in which that behavior would be useful in getting you something you do want.

Suppose you are a salesperson. You take great pains to know your product in every detail. But on the sales floor you tend to inundate your customers with so much information they become overwhelmed, sometimes delaying their decision to buy. The question is, Where else would that behavior actually be quite effective? How about technical writing on the product itself, such as in the owner's manual? Knowing a lot of information and being able to have ready access to it could even be useful in studying for a test or helping your kids with their homework. So, you see, it's not the behavior itself that's the problem, but where it's being employed. Can you think of examples in your own life? All human behaviors are useful in some context. Procrastination may seem useless across the board, yet wouldn't it be nice to put off being angry or sad to another day—and then never get around to it?

Make it a habit to reframe images and experiences that bother you. For example, think of a person or experience that's preying on your mind. You come home Friday after a lousy day at work, and all you can think of is the ridiculous project your supervisor gave you at the last minute. Instead of getting away from it, you take the frustration home with you. You're watching television with your kids, and all you're thinking about in this angry state is your "dumb" supervisor and his idiotic project.

Instead of letting your brain make you miserable for the weekend, learn to reframe the experience in a way that makes you feel better. Start by disassociating yourself from it. Take the image of your supervisor and put it in your hand. Put a pair of funny glasses, a big nose, and a mustache on him (or her!). Hear him talking in a funny, screechy cartoon voice. Feel him as being warm and cuddly, and hear him saying he needs your help on this project; could you *please* help? After you've concocted this, maybe you can appreciate that he's under stress and likely forgot to tell you what he needed until the last minute. Maybe you can remember a time when you did the same thing with someone else. Ask yourself if this situation is such a big deal that you should allow it to ruin your weekend.

I'm not saying the problem isn't real. Maybe you need a new job, or maybe you need to communicate better in your current job. But if that's the case, you need to deal with the problem instead of being haunted by some lingering, negative specter in your mind that keeps you reacting and causes you to treat those closest to you in a negative way. Do this effectively a few times, and the next time you see your supervisor you may see him with glasses and a big nose and feel differently as he talks to you. Thus you create new feedback for him and a new way for the two of you to interact, different from the stimulus-response dynamic you had set up with each other before.

EXPAND YOUR INFLUENCE OVER OTHERS—AND YOURSELF

Reframing is crucial not only on a personal level, but in learning how to communicate with others. Think of selling. Think of any form of persuasion. The person who sets the frame, the person who defines the turf, is the one with the most influence. Most of the major successes you can think of, in fields ranging from advertising to politics, are the result of artful reframes—changing people's perceptions so that their new representations about something put them in a state that makes them feel or act differently.

Most reframing is done for us, not by us. Someone else changes the frame for us and we react to it. What is advertising, after all, but a huge industry with the sole purpose of framing and reframing mass perceptions? Do you really think there's anything particularly macho about a specific brand of beer or particularly sexy about a certain cigarette? If you give an aborigine a Virginia Slims cigarette, he wouldn't say, "Hey, this is kinda sexy." But the pitchmen put on the frame, and we respond. If they don't think we're responding well enough, they put on a new frame and see if it works.

One of the greatest advertising reframes was done by Pepsi-Cola. For as long as anyone could remember, Coca-Cola was the preeminent cola drink. Its history, tradition, and standing in the market were unchallenged. There was nothing Pepsi could do to beat Coke on its own turf. If you're up against a classic, you can't say, "We're more of a classic than they are." People just won't believe it. Instead, Pepsi turned the game upside down; it reframed the perceptions people already had. When it started talking about the Pepsi Generation and issued its "Pepsi Challenge," it turned its weakness into strength. Pepsi said, "Sure, the other guys have been king, but let's look at today. Do you want yesterday's product, or do you want today's?" The ads reframed Coke's traditional dominance as a weakness, an indication that it was the product of the past, not the future. And they reframed Pepsi's traditional second-fiddle status as the company's advantage.

What happened? Coke finally decided it had to play on Pepsi's turf. It came up with its "New" Coke, and the rest is marketing history. It's a classic example of reframing, because the whole battle was over nothing but image. It was simply a question of whose frame would stick in people's minds. There's no inherent social content in a carbonated sugar beverage that rots your teeth. There is nothing inherently more contemporary about the taste of

Pepsi versus the taste of Coke. But by changing the frame and defining the terms, Pepsi pulled off one of the great marketing coups in recent history.

Many of us find it easier to reframe when communicating with others than when communicating with ourselves. If we're trying to sell someone our old car, we know we have to frame our presentation in a way that highlights what's good about the car and downplays what's bad. If your potential buyer has a different frame, your job is to change her perception. But few of us spend much time thinking about how to frame our communications with ourselves. Something happens to us. We form an internal representation of the experience and figure that's what we have to live with. Think how crazy that is—it's like turning on the ignition, starting up your car, and then seeing where it decides to go!

Instead, you need to learn to communicate *with yourself* with as much purpose, direction, and persuasiveness as you would in a business presentation. You need to start framing and reframing experiences in a way that makes them work for you. One way is simply on the level of careful, conscious thought.

We all know people who've become gun-shy after an unsuccessful romance. They get jilted or hurt and decide to back off from subsequent relationships. The fact is that the relationship brought them more joy than pain. That's why it was so difficult to give up. But blotting out the good memories and concentrating on the bad puts the worst possible frame on an experience. The idea is to change the frame: See the joy, see the gain, see the growth. Then it's possible to move on from a positive rather than a negative frame and be empowered to create an even greater relationship in the future.

A Quick Way to Eliminate Phobias

In its broadest sense, reframing can be used to eliminate negative feelings about nearly anything. One of the most effective techniques is to picture yourself in a theater. See a troublesome experience as a movie up on the screen. First play it in fast-forward, like a cartoon. Put circus music on it, such as the sound of a calliope. Then play it backward, watching the image become more and more absurd. You'll find the experience soon loses its negative power.

The same technique can work with phobias, but you need to turn up the juice. Here's how we do it. A phobia is often rooted at a deep kinesthetic level, so you need to provide more distance from it in order to do an effective reframe. Phobic responses are so strong that people can react to the mere thought of something. The way to deal with such people is to disassociate them from their representations several times. We call this *double disassociation*.

For example, if you have a phobia about something, try this exercise. Go back to a time when you felt totally empowered and alive. Go back to that state and feel those strong, confident feelings. Now see yourself protected by a radiant, nurturing bubble. Once you have that protection, go to your favorite mental movie theater. Sit down in a comfortable seat with a good view of the screen. Next, feel yourself float out of your body and up into the projection booth, all the time feeling your protective bubble around you. Look down and see yourself sitting in the audience looking up at the empty screen.

After you've done that, look up at the screen and see a still frame, black-and-white image of the phobia or some terrible experience that really used to bother you. You're looking down on yourself in the audience and watching yourself observe what's happening on the screen—you're doubly disassociated from it. In that state, run the black-and-white image backward at an extremely fast pace so you see the thing that's been haunting you appear like a cheap home movie or an old slapstick comedy. Notice your amused reactions to it as you watch yourself in the audience watching this movie on the screen.

Let's take it a step further. Take the part of you that's really resourceful, the part that's up in the booth, and float back down into where your body has been sitting, then get up and walk to the front of the screen. You should be able to do that in a very strong, confident state. Then tell your earlier self, "I've been watching over you and have come up with two or three ways that can help change that experience, two or three reframes of the meaning or the content that will help you handle it differently, now and in the future." These are ways the younger you can now handle situations with the benefit of your present-day, more mature perceptions. All that pain and fear are no longer necessary. You're more resourceful now than when you were younger, and that old experience is just history, nothing more.

After helping your younger self cope with something he or she couldn't handle earlier, stride back to your seat and watch the movie change. Play the same scene in your head, but this time watch as your younger self handles the same situation with utter confidence. When you've done that, walk back to the screen and congratulate your younger self. Give him or her a hug for breaking free of the phobia, trauma, or fear. Then pull that younger self back inside of you, knowing he or she is more resourceful than ever before and an important part of your life. Do this with other phobias or fears you have. Then do the same thing for someone else.

This can be an incredibly powerful experience. I've been able to take people with terrible lifelong phobias and free them of their fears, many times in a matter of minutes. Why does this work? Because to go into a phobic state requires specific internal representations. If you change those representations, you will change the state the person creates when thinking of that experience.

For some people, a number of these exercises involve a level of mental discipline and imaginative power they may not previously have accessed. As a result, several of the strategies may feel awkward at first. However, if you work carefully on them, you'll feel more adept all the time. These are some of the same tools we use to assist people in overcoming lifelong phobias, traumatic memories, and emotional challenges. Remember, life is not as complicated as we've been led to believe. Things we once thought were a part of who we are can be eliminated very easily. The worst thing you can do is nothing at all.

One very important thing to remember about reframing is that all human behaviors have a purpose in some context. If you smoke, you don't do it because you like to put carcinogens into your lungs. You do it because smoking makes you feel relaxed or more comfortable in certain social situations. You adopted this behavior to create some gain for yourself. So in some cases you may find it impossible to reframe the behavior without confronting the underlying need the behavior fulfills. This is a problem that sometimes comes up when people try electroshock therapy to cure their smoking. Perhaps they might be shocked into something just as bad, like feeling anxious all the time or overeating. I'm not saying this approach is bad; I'm simply saying it's useful for us to discover the unconscious intent so we can fill that need more elegantly.

All human behavior is adaptive in one way or another. Everything human beings do is designed to fill our six fundamental needs: certainty (comfort), uncertainty (variety), significance, connection (love), growth, and contribution. A complete discussion of these six human needs could fill an entire book, but for now, understand that we all are trying to fulfill these needs. It's no problem to make people hate smoking. The challenge is to create for them new behavioral choices that will fill their needs without negative side effects. If smoking made them feel comfortable and centered (that is, met their need for certainty), they need to come up with a more elegant behavior that will fulfill the same need, such as deep breathing or meditating.

Preserve the Benefits of the Old Behavior

It's important to note that you can reframe someone's representation, but if the person gets greater benefits from the old behavior than from the new choices, he or she will probably return to the old behavior. For example, if we work with a woman with an unexplainable numb foot, find out what she does in her physiology to create it, and help her learn to signal her body in a way that no longer creates numbness, her problem is now cleared up. But it may return when she goes home if she no longer gets the secondary benefits she had when her foot was numb, such as her husband's doing the dishes, paying attention to her, massaging her feet, and so on. For the first couple of weeks or months, he's thrilled that she no longer has the problem. However, after a while, since she no longer has the problem, he not only expects her to start doing the dishes, but he doesn't massage her feet, and he seems to pay less attention to her. Soon her problem flares back up mysteriously. She doesn't do this consciously. But to her unconscious mind, the old behavior works much better in giving her what she wants—and wham, her foot's numb again. To prevent this from recurring, she must find other behaviors that will give her the same or better quality of experience with her husband.

In one of Tony's trainings, a woman who had been blind for eight years seemed unusually adept and centered. I later discovered she was not blind at all. Yet she lived her life as if she were. Why? Well, she'd had an accident earlier in her life and developed poor eyesight. As she did, people around her gave her a tremendous amount of love and support, more than she had ever experienced before. In addition, she began to discover that even doing average everyday things brought her great recognition when people thought she was blind. They treated her as special, so she maintained this behavior, even convincing herself of her blindness at times. She had now found a more powerful way to get people to automatically respond to her in a thoughtful and loving way. Even strangers would treat her as special. The behavior would change only if she developed something bigger to move away from or something that gave her more benefits than her current behavior offered.

With this in mind, we can start to see how a child might join a gang and get into trouble. Perhaps the child is not getting the type of connection and attention at home that he or she needs. Perhaps the child gains a sense of significance or camaraderie from being part of a gang, even though the gang members are playing a dangerous life-and-death game that is all too real. If the child perceives the bonding of the gang as more important than the dangers and consequences of their actions, he or she will continue to play a losing game despite knowing better. This is why mentoring programs and activities that match youth up with people who will hold them to higher standards while simultaneously helping the child feel loved and significant have higher rates of success than prisons and other forms of correction.

There's a child in all of us, a person who believes in a glorious future.

—JASMINE GUY

So far we've been concentrating on ways in which we can reframe negative perceptions as positive ones. But we don't want you to think of reframing as a therapy, as a way of going from situations we consider bad to ones we consider good. Reframing is really nothing more or less than a metaphor for potential and possibility. There are very few things in your life that can't be reframed into something better. You would probably surprise yourself with how much you already do it.

One of the most important frames to consider is possibilities. We often fall into ruts. We might be getting comfortable results, but we could be getting *spectacular* results. So please do this exercise immediately. Make a list of five things you're doing right now that you're pretty pleased with. They could be relationships that are going well, successes at work, maybe something having to do with your children or your finances.

Now imagine them as even better. Spend a few minutes thinking about it. You'll probably surprise yourself by finding ways your life could be dramatically improved. Possibility reframing is something we can all do. All it takes is the mental flexibility to be alert for potential and the personal power to take action. Think of it in a broader sense as an ongoing process of exploring assumptions and finding useful contexts for what you do well.

Leaders and all other great communicators are masters of the art of reframing. They know how to motivate and empower people by taking anything that happens and making it a model for possibility. Virtually all the stories in this book about people who have overcome great obstacles are outstanding examples of how they reframed themselves and others to consider another alternative besides giving up. For that matter, if you look at people throughout history who have risen to the challenge and won, they all reframed the situation to their advantage. When Muhammad Ali was jailed for refusing the draft and stripped of his heavyweight title, he reframed the situation to mean this was an opportunity to find his soul in his religion and race. What's more, having his title taken from him provided him with the glorious opportunity to take it back. His miraculous comeback is part of this country's history.

Remember, there's a valuable lesson in everything that happens. We have only to look, and it will reveal itself. The best leaders are the ones who learn the lesson and put the most empowering frame on outside events. That works for politics, business, teaching, and your personal life as well.

We all know people who are reverse reframers. No matter how bright the silver lining, they can always find a dark cloud. No matter how far we as a race have come they are always ready, willing, and able to jump back into the past and drag up how bad things were and how horrible they will be in the future. No matter how successful a Black man or woman becomes, they still consider that person a sellout. No matter how far we've come as a culture and a race, they refuse to celebrate, because there's too much that's still not right. But for every disabling attitude, for every counterproductive behavior, there's an effective reframe, an inspiring role model or example of success. You don't like something? *Change it.* You're behaving in a way that doesn't support you? *Do something else.*

There's a way to not just produce effective behaviors, but make sure they're available when we need them. In the next chapter, we'll learn how to retrigger any useful behavior the moment we desire it, when we look at ways of . . .

CHAPTER NINETEEN

Anchoring Yourself to Success

When you expect good, it's available constantly and it makes itself a reality in your life.

—ALFRE WOODARD

THERE ARE SOME PEOPLE (I'm one; perhaps you are, too) who get chills and feel proud and inspired every time they hear the words "I have a dream." These words immediately flash me to a time when America was awakening to a bright new dawn of possibilities. A time when so many of our sisters and brothers rose to the call of life to be, do, and have more for ourselves and the ones we love. But why the chills, why the instant feelings when I hear those words? What is the source of their power? It's an odd reaction if you think about it analytically. After all, they're just words, sounds arranged in a certain order. There's nothing inherently magical about them. But of course that interpretation misses the whole point. Yes, they are just words. But at the same time, they have come to stand for all the virtues and characteristics of our nation and of our proud people. Whenever I hear those words, I also hear a powerful, resonant symbol of everything we stand for.

Those words, like countless other things in our environment, are an *anchor*, a sensory stimulus linked to a specific set of states. An anchor can be a word, a phrase, a touch, or an object. It can be something we see, hear, feel, taste, or smell. An anchor is anything that stimulates or causes us to go into a specific state of mind. Anchors have great power because they can instantly access powerful states. That's what happens when you hear "I have a dream" or see the American flag. You immediately experience the powerful emotions and sensations that represent how you feel about the nation as a whole, because these feelings have been linked to or associated with those specific anchors.

Our world is full of anchors, some of them profound, some of them trivial. If I start to say to you, "Winston tastes good like a . . ." chances are you'll automatically say, ". . . cigarette should." If I ask you, "How do you spell relief?" you will probably spell it R-O-L-A-I-D-S. You may think all cigarettes taste awful. You probably know that relief is spelled R-E-L-I-E-F. But advertising has been so effective that it's anchored an automatic response in you even though you don't even use the product. The same sort of response occurs all the time. You can see people instantly go into state—good or bad—depending on the feelings you have associated to them. For far too long the word *nigger* or the sight of a cross burning or a group of people in hooded white robes was an instant anchor for anger and frustration within the Black community. But what happens when you hear a powerful song like "We Shall Overcome"? You probably have an instantaneous change of state. Or how about if you smell pine trees and it reminds you of Christmas? Or smell cotton candy and think about the circus? Have you ever seen a stranger on the street who reminded you of someone you knew and were fond of long ago, then felt those feelings all over again? These are all the results of powerful anchors. You don't even have to consciously think about it; it just happens. Just as these experiences and memories and feelings are etched into your soul, so can you create any emotion or experience you choose to assist your upward spiral.

This section of the book ends with this chapter on anchoring for a very good reason: Anchoring is a way to give an experience permanence. We can change our internal representations or our physiology in a moment and create new results. Those changes require conscious thought. **However, with anchoring you can create a consistent triggering mechanism that will automatically cause you to create the state you desire in any situation without your having to think about it.** When you anchor something effectively enough, it will be there whenever you want it. You've learned any number of invaluable lessons and techniques so far in this book. Anchoring is the most effective technique we know for constructively channeling our powerful unconscious reactions so they're always at our disposal. Reread the quote that opens this chapter. We want the good things in life to be available constantly. Anchoring is a way to ensure that we always have access to our greatest resources, a way to make certain we always have what we need.

It's been said so many times that you get out of life exactly what you put into it. Well, here's at least one example of where that saying doesn't necessarily hold true. **By doing the exercises in this chapter, you will produce results far beyond the effort it takes to execute them.** These exercises were designed to produce immediate, lasting results. But I feel it's of the utmost importance to remind you to do all the exercises and to do them with as much energy, imagination, and enthusiasm as possible. So pull out all the stops, have fun, and give yourself the gift of state control and emotion on demand!

It's important to realize that we are anchoring all the time anyway. In fact, it's impossible not to. All anchoring is a created association of thoughts, ideas, feelings, or states with a specific stimulus. Remember Dr. Ivan Pavlov? He took hungry dogs and put meat where they could smell and see it but not get to it. This meat became a powerful stimulus to the dogs' feelings of hunger. Soon they were salivating heavily. While they were in this intense state of salivation, Pavlov consistently rang a bell with a specific tone. Pretty soon he no longer needed the meat—he could just ring the bell and the dogs would salivate as if the meat itself were in front of them. He had created a neurological link between the sound of the bell and the state of hunger or salivation. From then on, all he had to do was ring the bell, and the dogs would instantly go into a salivation state.

We, too, live in a stimulus-response world where much of human behavior consists of unconscious programmed responses. For example, many people under stress immediately reach for a cigarette, alcohol, or in some cases, a drug. They don't think about it. They're just like Pavlov's dogs. In fact, many of these people would like to change their behavior, feeling it is unconscious and uncontrollable. The key is to become conscious of the process so that if your anchors do not support you, you can eliminate them and replace them with new stimulus-response linkages that automatically put you into states you desire.

ANCHORS IN EVERYDAY LIFE

How do anchors get created? Whenever a person is in an intense state in which the mind and body are strongly involved together and a specific stimulus is consistently and simultaneously provided at the peak of the state, the stimulus and the state become neurologically linked. Afterward, whenever the stimulus is provided, the intense state automatically results. We sing the national anthem, create certain feelings in our body, and look at the flag. We say the pledge of allegiance and see the flag. Pretty soon, merely looking at the flag automatically triggers these feelings.

Many anchors are pleasant. You associate a particular Temptations song with a wonderful summer, and for the rest of your life, whenever you hear the song, you think of or relive that time. You finish off a perfect date by sharing an apple pie with chocolate ice cream, and from that point on it's your favorite dessert. You don't think about these things any more than Pavlov's dogs did, but every day you have anchoring experiences that condition you to respond in specific ways.

Yet not all anchors are positive associations. Some anchors are unpleasant or worse. After you get a speeding ticket, you get a momentary sinking feeling every time you pass the same section on the highway where you got pulled over. How do you feel when you see a red (or blue!) flashing light in your rearview mirror? Does it instantly and automatically change your state?

One of the things that determines the power of an anchor is the intensity of the original state. Sometimes people have such an intense unpleasant experience—like fighting with their spouse or boss—that from then on, whenever they see the person's face, they immediately feel anger inside. From that point on, their relationship or job loses all its joy. If you have such negative anchors, this chapter will teach you how to replace them with positive anchors. And once they're in place, you will not have to remind yourself to use them; it will happen automatically.

Most of us are anchored utterly haphazardly. We're bombarded with messages from television, radio, and everyday life. Some of these become anchors and others don't. A lot simply depends on chance. If you're in a powerful state—either good or bad—when you come in contact with a particular stimulus, chances are it will become anchored. Consistency of a stimulus is a powerful anchoring tool. If you hear something often enough (like advertising slogans), there's a good chance it will become anchored into your nervous system. The good news is that you can learn to control that anchoring process so you can install positive anchors and cast out negative ones.

Throughout history, successful leaders have known how to make use of the cultural anchors around them. When a politician is "wrapping himself in the flag," he's trying to link himself to all the positive emotions that have been linked to the flag. At its best, that process can create a healthy common bond of patriotism and rapport. Think of how you feel when you watch a Fourth of July parade. Is it any wonder that no self-respecting candidate for office will miss showing up at a July Fourth parade? At its worst, anchoring can provide frightening displays of collective ugliness. Hitler had a genius for anchoring. He linked specific states of mind and emotion to the swastika, goose-stepping troops, and mass rallies. He put people in intense states, and while he had them there, he consistently provided specific and unique stimuli until all he had to do later was offer those same stimuli—like raising his open hand in the gesture of *heil*—to call up all the emotion he had linked to them. He constantly used these tools to manipulate the emotions and thus the states and behaviors of a nation.

In our chapter on reframing, we noted that the same stimuli can have different meanings, depending on the frame put around them. For example, Hitler linked positive, strong, proud emotions to Nazi symbols for party members. For opponents, however, he linked them to states of fear. Did the swastika have the same meaning for a member of the Jewish community as it did for a storm trooper? Obviously not. Yet the Jewish community took this experience in history and created a powerful positive anchor that helped them build a nation and protect it under what would seem like impossible odds. The auditory anchor of "Never again" that many Jewish people use puts them in a state of total commitment to do whatever it takes to protect their sovereign rights. As I stated earlier, think of the letters KKK or men in hoods burning crosses. For many of us, now these same symbols no longer trigger fear, hate, and anger. For me they are a joke. They symbolize weak, fearful, confused human beings hiding behind their ignorance, pathetically trying to fill their need for significance. I recognize the heavy toll that hate and fear take on the human body, and I feel genuinely sorry for these misguided people who have chosen this particular hell to spend their precious lives in.

When General Colin Powell contemplated running for office in 1996, he linked himself to all the positive attributes of the American military to bolster support. He even chose the colors red, white, and blue for the cover of his best-selling autobiography. Anchoring isn't restricted to the most profound emotions and experiences. Comedians are masters of anchoring. Good comedians know how to use a specific tonality, phrase, or physiology to get laughs instantly. How? They do something to get you to laugh, and while you're in that specific intense state they provide a specific and unique stimulus, like a certain smile or facial expression or tone of voice. They do this consistently until the state of laughter is linked with that stimulus. Pretty soon they can just make the same facial expression, and you can't help laughing. Martin Lawrence, Eddie Murphy, and George Wallace are all masters at this. They've done it so many times before, we know what's coming and our minds trigger the same states.

Anchoring is a tool used by many professional athletes. They may not call it that or even be aware of what they're doing, yet they are using the principle. Athletes who are known as clutch players are triggered, or anchored, by do-or-die situations to go into their most resourceful and effective states, from which they produce their most outstanding results. Some athletes do certain things to trigger such a state. Tennis players use a certain rhythm for bouncing the ball or a certain breathing pattern to put themselves in their best state before they serve. I remember seeing the great Carl Lewis as he readied himself for each event in the 1984 Olympics. He'd snap his head to the side several times, shake his arms, and put that determined look on his face. You could literally see him putting himself in state. And that was the year he broke Jesse Owens' long-standing record. By the way, with all the publicity about Lewis going after the record, do you think the public anchored the same feelings we got from Jesse Owens when we watched Carl Lewis give it his all? You bet we did! Another example is when Tony used anchoring and reframing in working with Michael O'Brien, the gold medal winner of the 1500 freestyle in the 1984 Olympics. Tony reframed O'Brien's limiting beliefs and anchored his optimum states to the firing of the starter's gun. He did this by having him recall the stimulus of the music he had used earlier in a successful match against his opponent and to the black line on the bottom of the pool that he would focus on underwater as he swam. The results O'Brien produced in this peak state were the ones he desired most.

The Keys to Successful Anchoring

Let's review more specifically how you consciously create an anchor for yourself or others. Basically, there are two simple steps. **First you must put yourself, or the person you're anchoring, into the specific state you wish to anchor. Then you must consistently provide a specific, unique stimulus as the person experiences the peak of that state.** For example, when someone is laughing, she is in a specific congruent state—her whole body is involved at that moment. If you squeeze her ear with a specific and unique pressure and simultaneously make a certain sound several times, you can come back later, provide the stimulus (the squeeze and the sound), and the person will start laughing again. Remember how Pavlov would anchor the dogs? All he did was put each dog in state by showing it the food, and while it was in a state of salivation, he applied the stimulus (the bell).

One way to create a confidence anchor for someone is to ask him to remember a time when he felt the state he wishes to have available on cue, then have him "step back" into that experience so he is fully associated and can feel those feelings in his body. As he does this, you will begin to see changes in his physiology—facial expressions, posture, breathing. As you see these states nearing their peak, quickly provide a specific and unique stimulus several times.

You may enhance these anchors by helping the person get into a confident state more rapidly. For example, have him show you how he stands when he's feeling confident, and at the moment his posture changes, provide the stimulus. You then may ask him to show you how he breathes when he feels totally confident, and as he does, provide the same stimulus again. Then ask what he says to himself when he feels totally confident, and have him tell you in the tone of voice he uses when he's confident. As he does this, provide the exact same stimulus again (for example, pressure on his shoulder in the same spot each time).

Once you believe you have an anchor, you need to test it. First get the person into a new or neutral state. The easiest way to do this is to get him to change his physiology or think of something completely different. Then, to test your anchor, simply provide the appropriate stimulus and observe. Is his physiology the same as it was when he was in state? If so, your anchor is effective. If not, you may have missed one of the four keys to successful anchoring:

1. For an anchor to be effective, when you provide the stimulus you must have the person in a fully associated, congruent state, with his whole body fully involved. We call this an intense state. The more intense, the easier it is to anchor, and the longer the anchor will last. If you anchor someone while part of his attention is on one thing and another on something else, the stimulus will become linked to several different signals and thus will not be as powerful. Also, if a person is merely visualizing a time when he felt something and you anchor him in that state, then when you provide the stimulus in the future, it will be linked to seeing the picture rather than to having the whole body and mind associated.

2. You must provide the stimulus at the peak of the experience. If you anchor too soon or too late, you won't capture the full intensity. You can discover the peak of the experience by watching the person go into the state and notice what he does when it begins to fade. Or you can get his help by asking him to tell you as he's nearing the peak, then use that input to calibrate the key moment to provide your unique stimulus.

3. You should choose a unique stimulus. It's essential that the anchor give a clear and unmistakable signal to the brain. If someone goes into a specific intense state and you try to link it with, say, a look you give that person all the time, it will probably not be a very effective anchor because it's not unique and it will be difficult for the brain to get a specific signal from it. A handshake, likewise, may not be effective because we shake hands all the time, though it could work if you shook hands in some unique way (such as a distinct pressure, location, and so forth). The best anchors combine several representational systems—visual, auditory, kinesthetic, and so forth—at one time to form a unique stimulus that the brain can more easily associate with a specific meaning. So anchoring a person with a touch and a certain tone of voice will usually be more effective than anchoring with just a touch.

4. For an anchor to work, you must replicate it exactly. If you put a person in a state and touch his shoulder blade in a specific spot with a specific pressure, you cannot retrigger that anchor later by touching him in a different place or with a different pressure.

If your anchoring procedure follows these four rules, it will be effective. One of the things we do in our firewalk events is teach people how to produce anchors that mobilize their most resourceful, positive energies. We put them through a conditioning process where they make a fist every time they summon up their most powerful energies. By the end of the evening, they can make a fist and immediately feel a powerful surge of productive energy. I have an anchor on my right hand that when I pinch it, my scalp tingles, my whole physiology changes, and I get so determined and strong that nothing can stop me. I call it my "ballistic" state of mind. I created this anchor the same way you are learning to do. How powerful would it be for you to have an anchor that could instantly change you from unresourceful to ballistic?

Keys to Anchoring

Intensity of the State
Timing (Peak of Experience)
Uniqueness of Stimulus
Replication of Stimulus

Let's do a simple anchoring exercise now. Stand up and think of a time when you were totally confident, when you knew you could do whatever you wanted to do. Put your body in the same physiology it was in then. Stand the way you did when you were totally confident. At the peak of that feeling, make a fist and say, "Yes!" with strength and certainty. Breathe the way you did when you were totally confident. Again make the same fist and say, "Yes!" in the same tonality. Now speak in the tone of a person with total confidence and control. As you do this, create the same fist and say, "Yes!" in the same way. Come on, don't be shy—this is for you.

If you can't remember a time, think how you would be if you did have such an experience. Think of someone else who could do it and imagine how this person would feel. Put your body in the physiology it would be in if you did know how to feel totally confident and in control. Breathe the way you would if you felt total confidence. We want you to actually do this, like every other exercise in this book. Just reading about it won't help you. *Doing* it will work wonders!

Now as you stand there in a state of total, centered confidence, at the height of that experience, gently make a fist and say, "Yes!" in a powerful tone of voice. Be aware of the power at your disposal, of the remarkable physical and mental resources you have, and feel the full surge of that power. *Yell it out loud.* With power and certainty and conviction, say, "YES!" Say it like you mean it! Start over and do this again and again, five or six times, each time feeling stronger, creating an association in your neurology between this state and the act of making a fist and saying, "Yes!" Then change your state and your physiology. Now make your fist and say, "Yes!" in the same way you did when you anchored, and notice how you feel. Do that several times over the next few days. Get yourself into the most confident, powerful state you can, and at the peak of that state make a fist in a unique way.

Before too long, you'll find that by making that fist, you can bring forth that state at will, instantaneously. It may not happen after one or two times, but it won't take long for you to do this consistently. You can anchor yourself with only one or two repetitions *if the state is intense enough and your stimulus is unique enough.*

Remember, this is a science. This is how your body and mind

operate. You do it anyway, so you may as well use it to empower yourself now. Once you've anchored yourself in this way, you should use it the next time you're in a situation you find difficult. Make that fist and feel totally resourceful. Anchoring has such power because it aligns your neurology in an instant. Traditional positive thinking requires you to stop and think. Even getting yourself into a powerful physiology takes some time and conscious effort. Anchoring works *in an instant* to summon your most powerful resources.

How to Anchor

1. Clarify the specific outcome you want to use an anchor for and the specific state that will have the greatest effect in supporting the achievement of that outcome for yourself and/or others.
2. Identify the current state.
3. Elicit and shape the individual into the desired state through the use of your verbal and nonverbal communication patterns.
4. Use your sensory acuity to determine when the person is at the peak of the state, and at that exact moment, provide the stimulus (anchor).
5. Test the anchor by
   a. changing physiology to break state
   b. triggering the stimulus (anchor) and noting if the response is the desired state.

It's important for you to know that anchors can be made most powerful by being *stacked*—one piled on top of another—adding many of the same or very similar resourceful experiences together on a cumulative basis. For instance, the "ballistic" anchor I told you about is made up of hundreds of experiences of power and certainty and excitement from my past. Experiences like skydiving and scuba diving and firewalks, seminars and playing music in front of huge crowds. In each of these situations when I got myself most resourceful, at the peak of the experience I made a unique fist. Now, whenever I make the same fist, all those powerful feelings and physiologies are simultaneously triggered within my nervous system. It's a greater feeling than any drug could ever hope to create. I get the experience of swimming with sharks, bungee jumping, fighter pilot training, making love, floating down a Fiji river, swimming with dolphins—all at once. And the more often I get into that state and attach new, powerful, positive experiences to it, the more power and success is anchored to it. It's another example of the success cycle: **Success breeds success. Power and resourcefulness breed more power and resourcefulness.** And you know what? You don't even have to have had any of these experiences to get the emotions! Remember, as you think so you are. Use your imagination to get fully associated to how it would be if you were doing the things that excite you. Then build from there.

Here's my next challenge for you: Go out and anchor three different people in positive states. Have them remember a time when they were feeling exuberant. Make sure they are reexperiencing it fully, and anchor them several times in the same state. Then engage them in conversation and test the anchor while they are distracted. Do they return to the same state? If not, check the four key points and anchor again.

If your anchor fails to trigger the state you desire, you've missed one of the four points. Maybe you or the other person weren't in a specific and fully associated state (as the anchorer, you need to put yourself in the appropriate state as well, such as excitement or confidence). Maybe you applied the anchor at the wrong time, after the peak of the state had passed. Maybe the stimulus wasn't distinctive enough or you didn't replicate it perfectly when you tried to bring back the anchored experience. In all these cases, you simply need the sensory acuity to make sure the anchoring is being done correctly and, when anchoring again, make the appropriate changes in your approach until you produce an anchor that works. It's a great gift to give someone.

Ways to Calibrate (Identify) State Change

Note Changes in:

Breathing
location
pauses
rate
volume

Eye Movement

Lower Lip Size

Posture

Muscle Tension

Pupil Dilation

Skin Color/Reflection

Voice
tempo
timbre
tone
volume

Here's another task: Select three to five states or feelings you would like to have at your fingertips, then anchor them to a specific part of yourself so that you have easy access to them. Let's say that up till now you've tended to have a difficult time making decisions, but you'd like to change. You want to feel more decisive. To anchor the feeling of being able to make a decision quickly, effectively, and easily, you might select the knuckle of your pointer finger. Next, think of a time in your life when you felt totally decisive, step mentally into that situation, and fully associate to it so you feel the same way you did then. Begin to experience yourself making that great decision from your past. (If you can't think of a time, then associate fully to how you would be if you had made that great decision.) At the peak of the experience, while you feel most decisive, squeeze your knuckle and make a sound in your mind, such as the word *yes*. Now think of another such experience, and at the peak of that decision-making process create the same pressure and the same sound. Do this five or six times to stack a series of powerful anchors.

Now think of a decision you need to make. Take inventory of all the facts you need to know. Then reach down and fire off the anchor. You'll find you can make a decision quickly and easily now! You can use other fingers to anchor other feelings such as relaxation, if you need to. I anchored creativity feelings to a knuckle, enabling me to take myself in a matter of moments from feeling stuck to feeling creative. Take the time to select five states and install them, then have fun using them to direct your nervous system with pinpoint accuracy and speed. *Please do this now.*

FEAR INTO POWER: THE MAGIC OF ANCHORS

Anchoring can be remarkably successful in overcoming fears and changing behaviors. Let me give you an example of such an anchoring process Tony uses in his seminars. He'll ask a man or woman who has difficulty dealing with the opposite sex to come to the front of the room. On one occasion, it was a young man who somewhat timidly volunteered. When Tony asked him how he felt about talking to a strange woman or asking a strange woman out, we could see an immediate physical reaction. His posture slumped, his eyes went down, his voice got shaky. "I'm not really comfortable doing that," he said. But he didn't really need to say anything. His physiology had already told me what I needed to know.

Tony broke his state by asking him if he could remember a time when he felt very confident and proud and secure, a time when he knew he would succeed. The young man nodded, and Tony guided him into that state. He had him stand that way and breathe that way to feel as confident in every way as he did then.

Tony told him to think about what someone had said to him at that time when he felt confident and proud, and to remember the things he said to himself while he was in that state. At the peak of his experience, Tony touched him a specific way on the shoulder.

Next he took him through the exact same experience again several times. Each time Tony made sure the young man felt and heard the exact same things. At the peak of each experience, Tony did the same anchoring touch. Remember, successful anchoring depends on precise repetition, so he was careful to touch him in the same way and put him in exactly the same state every time.

By this point the reaction was pretty well anchored, so it was time to test it. Tony broke the young man's state and asked him again how he felt about women. Immediately he started to fall back into the depressed physiology. His shoulders went down; his breathing stopped. But when Tony touched his shoulder in the spot he had set as an anchor, the young man's body automatically began to shift back into that resourceful physiology. Through anchoring, it's amazing to watch how quickly someone's state can change from fright or despair to confidence and eagerness.

At this point in the process, a person can touch his shoulder (or whatever spot he's set as an anchor) and trigger his desired state whenever he wants to. Yet we can take things a step further. We can transfer this positive state to the very stimuli that used to create feelings of unresourcefulness, so that those same stimuli will now create feelings of resourcefulness! Here's how. Tony asked the young man to pick an attractive woman from the audience, someone he would normally never dream of approaching. He hesitated for a moment until Tony touched his shoulder. The minute he did, his body posture changed and he picked an attractive woman. I asked her to come to the front of the room. Then Tony told her this guy was going to try to get a date with her and that she was to reject him completely.

Tony touched his shoulder, and the young man went into his resourceful physiology—his eyes up, his breathing deep, his shoulders back. He walked toward the woman and said, "Hi, how's it going?"

She snapped, "Leave me alone." It didn't faze him. Before, even looking at a woman caused his whole physiology to go haywire. Now he just smiled. Tony continued to hold his shoulder, and the young man continued to pursue her. The more verbal abuse she dished out, the more he stayed in his power state. He continued to feel resourceful and confident even after Tony took his hand from his shoulder. He had created a new neurological link that now caused him to become *more* resourceful when he saw a beautiful woman or when he encountered rejection. In this case, the woman finally said, "Can't you leave me alone?" and he replied in a deep voice, "Don't you know power when you see it?" The whole audience exploded in laughter.

Now he was in a very powerful state by himself, and the stimulus that kept him there was a beautiful woman and/or her rejection—the same stimulus that had made him feel terrified before. In short, Tony had taken an anchor and transferred it. Because the young man was held in a powerful state while receiving rejection, his brain began to associate the woman's rejection with his calm, confident state. The more she rejected him, the more relaxed, confident, and calm he became. It's quite remarkable to see the transformation that occurs in a matter of moments. For several years I have assisted countless men and women in overcoming this and several other shortcomings using the same technique.

The logical response is, "Well, that's great in a seminar. Now what will happen in the real world?" What we do in the seminar is set up the same stimulus-response loop for everybody so they can take their new anchoring skills out into the real world and use them. In fact, we have the people we work with go out that evening and meet other people—and the results are amazing. Because the fear is gone, they begin to develop relationships with people they never would have approached in the past. It's really not that amazing if you think about it. After all, you had to learn how to respond to rejection as you grew up. There were plenty of models. Now you simply have a new set of neurological responses to choose from.

> *You can't just sit there and wait for people to give you that golden dream, you've got to get out there and make it happen for yourself.*
>
> —DIANA ROSS

It's crucial to be aware of anchoring, because it is always going on around us. With this awareness you can deal with it and change it. If you're not aware of it, you'll be mystified at the states that come and go seemingly without reason. I'll give you a common example. Let's say there's been a death in someone's family. She's in a state of deep grief. At the funeral, a number of people come over and touch her sympathetically on the upper part of her left arm, offering condolences. If enough people touch her in the same way, and she remains in a depressed state while they do, that kind of touch in that location can, and many times does, get anchored to her depressed state. Then, several months later, when someone touches her there with the same kind of pressure in a completely different context, it can set off the same feeling of grief, and she won't even know why she's feeling that way.

Have you ever had an experience like this, when all of a sudden you're depressed and you don't even know why? Chances are you have. Maybe you didn't even notice the song playing low in the background—a song you'd linked to someone you used to love a lot who is no longer in your life. Or maybe it was a certain look somebody gave you. Remember, anchors work without our conscious awareness.

Additional Anchoring Tools

Let me give you a few techniques for handling negative anchors. One is to "fire off" opposing anchors at the same time. Let's take that anchored feeling of grief triggered at the funeral. If it's anchored on the upper part of your left arm, one way to deal with it is to anchor an opposite feeling—your most powerful, resourceful feelings—in the same place on your right arm. If you trigger both anchors at the same time, you'll find something remarkable happens. The brain connects the two in your nervous system; then, anytime either anchor is touched, it has a choice of two responses. **The brain will almost always choose the more positive response.** Either it will put you in the positive state, or you'll go into a neutral state (in which both anchors have canceled each other out).

Anchoring is critical if you wish to develop a long-lasting, intimate relationship. There's a period in many relationships when a couple may have more negative than positive experiences associated to each other. If they are seeing each other consistently while in those states, the feelings get linked; sometimes just looking at each other makes them want to be apart. This especially happens if a couple begins to fight a lot, and if, during those angry states, each makes statements that are designed to hurt or anger the other. (Remember to use pattern interrupts!) These intense negative states then get linked to the other person's face. After a while, each of them wants to be with someone else, maybe someone new, someone who represents only associated positive experiences.

Virginia Satir, the world-famous marriage and family counselor, used anchoring in her work all the time. Her results were outstanding. In modeling her, NLP founders Richard Bandler and John Grinder noted the difference between her style and that of the traditional family therapist. When a couple comes in for therapy, many therapists believe the underlying problem is the suppressed emotion and anger the couple have for each other, and that it's helpful for them to say exactly how they feel about the other—all the things they're angry about, and so on. You can imagine what happens many times when they begin to do this!

To ensure this doesn't happen to you, you must be willing to work both at collapsing those negative anchors and creating new and exciting ones. When you catch yourself or your mate in an unresourceful state of mind, use pattern interrupts to put the person in a better state and anchor it. Create unique ways and special moments to enhance loving feelings, confident feelings, secure feelings—each time anchoring them with a touch, a smile, a hug. My girlfriend and I have such a powerful anchor with just a hug that it is hard for us to stay in any unresourceful state of mind around each other. All I have to do is think of her, and I smile and feel loving feelings.

By the way, isn't that how you fall in love with someone in the first place? Don't you associate all those great feelings to that person? Aren't you just anchoring yourself by thinking of the person while you are feeling great? When you are going to see the person, aren't you feeling excited and giddy? And while you're in that state of mind, aren't you anchoring those feelings to that person's face and presence?

Let me give you another powerful tool Tony taught me for dealing with negative anchors. First let's create a positive and powerful resource anchor. It's always best to start with the positive rather than the negative so that if the negative becomes difficult to deal with, you have a tool to help yourself get out of that state quickly and easily.

Now think of the most powerful positive experience you've ever had in your life. Place that experience and its feelings in your right hand. Imagine doing this, and feel what it's like to have it in your right hand. Then think of a time when you felt totally proud of something you did, and place that experience and feeling in your right hand as well. Next, think of a time when you felt powerful, positive, loving feelings, and put them in your right hand also, experiencing how they feel there. Now remember a time when you laughed hysterically, maybe a time when you had the giggles. Take that experience and put it in your right hand. Notice how it feels with all those loving, resourceful, positive, powerful feelings. Now observe what color these powerful feelings have come together to create in your right hand; just note what color first comes to mind. Notice what shape they have come together to form. If you were to give them sound, what would they all sound like? What is the texture of all these feelings together in your hand? If they were all to come together to say one powerful positive statement to you, what would it be? Enjoy all these feelings, then close your right hand and just let them remain there.

Now open your left hand, and in it place a negative, frustrating, depressing, or angry experience, something that is or has been bothering you. Maybe something you're afraid of, something that worries you. Place it in your left hand. There is no need to feel it inside. Make sure you disassociate from it. Just realize it's over there in your left hand. Now I want you to become aware of its submodalities. What color does this negative situation create in your left hand? If you don't see a color or have a feeling right away, act as if you did. What color would it be if it did have one? Run through the other submodalities. What shape is it? Does it feel light or heavy? What's the texture of it? What sound does it make? If it were to say one sentence to you, what would it say?

Now we're going to do what's called *collapsing anchors*. You can play with this in whatever way feels natural for you. One approach would be to take the color in your positive right hand, make believe it's a liquid, and pour it into your left hand at a very fast rate, making humorous noises and having fun as you do. Do it until the negative anchor in your left hand is the color of the positive experience in the right.

Then take the sound that your left hand was making and drop it in your right hand. Notice what your right hand does to it. Now take the feelings of your right hand and pour them into your left, noticing what they do to your left hand the minute they enter it. Bring your hands together in a clap, continuing to hold them there for a few moments until they feel balanced. Now the color in your right hand and left should be the same (the feelings should be similar).

When you're through, see how you feel about the experience in your left hand. Chances are you'll have stripped it of all its power to bother you. If you haven't, try the exercise again. Do it with different submodalities and a more active sense of play. After one or two times, almost anyone can utterly obliterate the power of something that used to be a strong negative anchor. You should now either feel good or at least have neutral feelings about the experience.

You can do this same process if you're upset with someone and want to change how you feel about him. You can imagine the face of someone you really like in your right hand and the face of someone you don't like very much in your left. Begin by looking at the person you don't like, then at the person you do like, the person you don't like, the person you do. Do this faster and faster, no longer labeling which you like or do not like. Bring your hands together, breathe, and wait a moment. Now think about the person you didn't like. You should now like him or at least feel okay about him. The beauty of this exercise is it can be done in a matter of moments, and you can change how you feel about almost anything! I did this three-minute process in a seminar recently with a whole group. One woman in the group put in her right hand someone she really liked, and in her left hand she put the face of her father, to whom she had not spoken in almost ten years. This way, she was able to neutralize her negative feelings about her father. She called him that night and spoke to him till 4:00 in the morning, and they have now redeveloped their relationship.

It's critical that we realize the impact of our actions in anchoring kids. For example, I have more than a little concern about the images that are associated to some of the violence and abuse on television and radio. In the case of certain gang-related videos and songs, there are many images of young men and women feeling proud and sometimes even celebrating crime or destructive behavior. It's possible that a child who experiences these things over and over again while in the state of mind produced by the music and the sexiness of the images may become anchored to the images as being attractive. The results could be quite destructive. Just as we are conditioned by the images we see in commercials and advertisements, these influences could and may already have dire consequences on our youth. Nothing would please me more than to start seeing a decline in that type of programming. It is argued that this is how it really is on the streets, and that may very well be so, but the fact remains that at least some of the reason is the constant glorification of criminal or destructive behavior. I do realize that the intention of the producers of these videos and commercials is not to decay the minds of our youth. I just would like to see programming that would counteract and balance the negative effects of the input that bombards us daily. Black on Black crime is at epidemic proportions in this country, and I wonder if children seeing Blacks killing each other in TV programs and movies in such detail and frequency, with no regard for the consequences, doesn't contribute to that epidemic.

Where Can You Use Anchors in Your Life?

Let's do one last exercise. Put yourself in that powerful, resourceful state and pick the color that's most resourceful for you. Do the same thing with a shape and a sound and a feeling you would associate with your most powerful, resourceful state. Then think of a phrase you would say if you were feeling happier, more centered, and stronger than you've ever felt before. Next, think of an unpleasant experience, a person who's a negative anchor, or something you're afraid of. In your mind, put the positive shape around the negative experience. Do it with the utter belief that you can capture the negative feeling within that positive shape. Then take your resourceful color and visualize blowing it all over the negative anchor, with such force that the anchor instantly dissolves. Hear the sound and feel the feeling that occurs when you're totally resourceful. Finally, say the thing you would say in your most powerful state. As the negative anchor melts away into a mist of your favorite color, say the phrase that accentuates your power. How do you feel about the negative situation now? Chances are you'll find it hard to imagine it bothered you so much before. Do this with three other experiences. Then go through the process with someone else.

If you've just been reading along, these will come across as odd, even silly exercises. But if you do them, you'll know the incredible power they have. This is the key ingredient of success: the ability to eliminate from your own environment triggers that tend to put you in negative or unresourceful states, while installing positive ones in yourself and others. One way to do this is to make a chart of the major anchors—positive and negative—in your life. Note whether they're primarily triggered by visual, auditory, or kinesthetic stimuli. Once you know what your anchors are, you should go about collapsing the negative ones and making best use of the positive ones.

Think of the good you can do as you learn how to anchor positive states effectively, not just in yourself but in others. Suppose you talked to your associates, got them in a motivated, upbeat frame of mind, and anchored it with a touch or expression or tone of voice you could produce in the future. After a while, by anchoring those positive mental states several times, you could elicit that kind of intense motivation at any time. Their work would be more rewarding, the company would be more profitable, and everyone would be much happier. Think of the power you would have in your own life if you could take the things that used to bother you and have them make you feel great or resourceful enough to change them. You have the power to do it!

Let me leave you with a final thought, not just on anchoring, but on all the techniques you've learned thus far. There's an incredible synergy, a processional sense, that comes from mastering any of these skills. Just as a rock thrown in a quiet pond sets off a pattern of ripples, success with any of these skills breeds more and more success. You should already have a strong and clear sense of how powerful these skills are. Our hope is that you will use them, not just today, but on an ongoing basis in your life. Just as the stacked anchors in my "ballistic" anchor get more powerful every time I use them, you will increase your own personal power with each skill you learn, master, and use.

There is a filter to human experience that affects how we feel about everything we do or do not do in our lives. These filters affect anchoring and everything else we've discussed in this book. Understanding them is the first element in mastering . . .

PART THREE

LEADERSHIP: THE CHALLENGE OF EXCELLENCE

CHAPTER TWENTY

Value Hierarchies: The Ultimate Judgment of Success

Races, like individuals, must stand or fall by their own merit; to fully succeed, they must practice their virtues of self-reliance, self-respect, industry, perseverance and economy.

—PAUL ROBESON

DO YOU KNOW WHAT'S MOST IMPORTANT TO YOU IN LIFE? Just this: The most important thing is to know the most important thing. I remember when Tony first told me that, we both laughed our heads off because it sounded so ridiculously simple. But as silly and simple as that saying may sound, it's so true about life in general. The most important thing is to know the most important thing in your life. So many of us are unfulfilled not because we aren't doing things that are worthwhile, but because we aren't doing the things that are most worthwhile to *us*. Most of us are playing out someone else's script rather than our own, working to create someone else's dream and not our own. One of the greatest shifts we've seen in people's lives is when they sit down and clarify exactly what is most important to them in their lives and what *needs* to be most important for them to achieve their ultimate desires.

The topic of values is something an entire book could be written about. It's covered extensively in another of Tony's best-sellers,

Awaken the Giant Within, and is the centerpiece of his intensive Date With Destiny seminar. But for now, we felt this book could not be balanced without making sure you took a moment to at least think about what's most important to *you.* This chapter is designed to give you an overview as to what values are and why understanding them is so essential as well as to help you take a look at your existing values and perhaps create some new ones. Please do not take this chapter lightly just because it's short. Take the time to explore these next few pages with wide-eyed curiosity and enthusiasm. We think you will get a wealth of insight as to what you really want and what makes you feel fulfilled. Just keep in mind this is not the end-all and be-all on this subject, and we hope you will explore it with us further at a later date.

VALUES: THE SOURCE OF SUCCESS OR FAILURE

So let's start with what values are in the first place. **Values are emotional states that, based on our life experience, we believe are most important for us to experience (move toward) or avoid (move away from).** The moving-toward values, or "pleasure" values, are emotions like love, happiness, success, security, adventure. These are known as *ends* values. It's important to make the distinction between *means* values, which are simply vehicles or instruments to achieve our ultimate outcomes, and *ends* values, which drive all of our behaviors as human beings. For example, some people may say that what they value most in life are their cars. Well, it's true they may value a car (i.e., it's important to them), but they value it as a *means,* a way to get what they're really after. The *end* a person who values a car might be seeking is a sense of convenience or a sense of freedom or, depending on the type of car, maybe a sense of power, fun, or prestige. Likewise, many people may think what they value most is money, but that's merely a means to an end. It's not the paper they want; it's what they think the money will give them. For some people, they believe that's security. For others, it's the ability to take control of their lives. And for some, it's the feeling of having lots of choices.

The secret in life is to know what you're really after: your ends values. The subject of values is critically important because our values guide all our decision making. **In fact, decision making is nothing but values clarification.** If you know what you value most, what you truly want most out of life, then you'll find you can make decisions much more effectively and rapidly.

HERE'S YOUR ASSIGNMENT

Most people would think that even attempting to define their own values is too big a task for a month, much less a single day. But if you've made it this far in the book, I know you are an extraordinary individual! Having said that, I would like to give you a six-step process that will require a significant amount of your time and energy, but for which the rewards are remarkable.

You might want to complete the first two of the six steps today and divide the rest of these tasks over the course of the next two days. I know how challenging this can be, but there are few things in the world more rewarding than being absolutely clear about what's important to you. So set yourself up to win on this assignment today by breaking it down into doable chunks. And be sure to have fun!

1. Ask yourself, *What's most important to me in my life?* Make sure you write down the feelings you're after, the states you value most, such as *love, passion,* or *happiness,* as opposed to means values like *money* or *business success.* If you think you want money or business success, ask yourself, *If I had that additional money, if I had that business success, what would it ultimately give me? How would it make me feel?* Those feelings are the true driving force in your life, your "moving-toward" values. See the following example of moving-toward values.

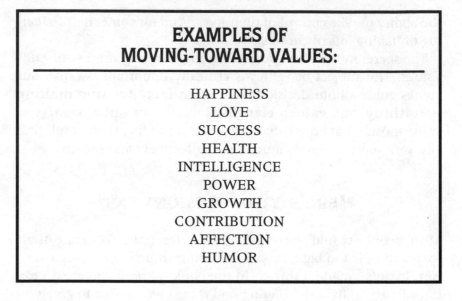

EXAMPLES OF MOVING-TOWARD VALUES:

HAPPINESS
LOVE
SUCCESS
HEALTH
INTELLIGENCE
POWER
GROWTH
CONTRIBUTION
AFFECTION
HUMOR

2. Rewrite your moving-toward values in the order of their importance. That is, which value is it absolutely most important for you to have—more than all the rest? That would be the number one value at the top of your value hierarchy. Then, which value is next most important? That would be number two, and so on. See the example below of a hierarchy of moving-toward values.

EXAMPLE OF A HIERARCHY OF MOVING-TOWARD VALUES:

1. HEALTH
2. SUCCESS
3. HAPPINESS
4. GROWTH
5. LOVE
6. CONTRIBUTION
7. HUMOR
8. INTELLIGENCE
9. POWER
10. AFFECTION

3. Make a list of all the negative feelings or emotions you'd do almost anything to avoid. For some people, this list might include *rejection* or *frustration* or *feeling overwhelmed* or *loneliness.* Discovering what you want to avoid will help you understand more about your drive. We are not driven just to get what we want. We're also driven to avoid those feelings we link the most pain to, our "moving-away-from" values. See the example below.

EXAMPLES OF MOVING-AWAY-FROM VALUES:

DEPRESSION
BOREDOM
FEELING OVERWHELMED
ANGER
WORRY
FRUSTRATION
RESENTMENT
SADNESS
JEALOUSY
SELF-PITY

4. Rewrite your moving-away-from values in the order of their importance, starting at the top of the list with the one you would do the most to avoid feeling. An example of a hierarchy of moving-away-from values follows.

EXAMPLE OF A HIERARCHY OF MOVING-AWAY-FROM VALUES:

1. ANGER
2. FRUSTRATION
3. BOREDOM
4. RESENTMENT

5. JEALOUSY
6. DEPRESSION
7. FEELING OVERWHELMED
8. SELF-PITY
9. SADNESS
10. WORRY

5. Now it's time to examine your *rules* for these values. That is, what has to happen for you to feel these emotions? For example, if success is one of your values, what has to happen for you to feel successful? (For some individuals to feel successful, they have to have a million dollars in the bank. For others to feel successful, all they have to do is wake up, look down, and see that they're aboveground—because they believe every day aboveground is a great day!) Similarly, for your moving-away-from values, what has to happen for you to feel them? (For some individuals, if they don't achieve a goal on time, they feel like a failure. For others, it's impossible to fail. Their rule for failure is, "I would fail only if I were to give up. As long as I keep trying, I'm successful.") It's important to understand the rules you have for feeling bad, because often we make it too hard to feel good and too easy to feel bad.

Have you discovered any rules that limit the quality of your life? If so, which rules are you willing to change now to improve your life forever? See the following examples of disempowering rules that ought to be changed.

EXAMPLES OF RULES THAT SHOULD BE CHANGED

"I have to do everything perfectly all the time in order to be successful."
"I feel intelligent only if I have an IQ of 180 or higher."
"In order for me to feel loved, my children must obey me 100 percent of the time without complaint."

"I must always breathe pure, unpolluted air to be healthy."
"To be a success, I must acquire several top-grossing businesses that pull in a minimum of $1 million each, with steadily increasing revenues every year thereafter, and set a new record for running the mile—all by age thirty."
"I will know I've succeeded when I win the state lottery."
"I know I'm successful when I never make any mistakes."

6. What new, more empowering rules can you start including in your life so that you are supported in moving toward the values you desire most and moving away from the values you want to avoid? Do these new rules make it easier for you to feel good and harder for you to feel bad? Following are examples of empowering rules you might want to adopt for a moving-toward value (health) and a moving-away-from value (boredom).

EXAMPLES OF RULES FOR MOVING-TOWARD AND MOVING-AWAY-FROM VALUES

"I feel healthy whenever I walk at least fifteen minutes a day."
"I feel healthy when I take care of myself by getting appropriate amounts of exercise, rest, structural support, and mental rejuvenation."
"Whenever I eat high-water-content foods, I feel healthy."
"I would feel boredom if and only if all the world's problems had been solved and there was nothing I could do to contribute to humanity."
"I would feel boredom if I cut off all contact with other people and set up residence in Antarctica."

In the next chapter, we are going to look at the five things every successful person has to confront and deal with to use all we've talked about in this book. I call them . . .

CHAPTER TWENTY-ONE

The Five Keys to Wealth and Happiness

The urge to explore, the push toward the unknown—this is inherent in the life of the child. It does not seem to be a response from without but rather the expression of some deep urge that wells up from within.

—HOWARD THURMAN

I RECENTLY RETURNED from what I can only describe as the most culturally rich experience of my life: AFRICA! I was invited to teach a series of reengineering and human design workshops to a group of entrepreneurs, bankers, and businesspeople in Lagos, the capital of Nigeria. My colleague and business partner, Steve Wright, and I spent eight days in this seaport city that was the hub of the African slave trade four hundred years ago.

While I was in Nigeria two very emotional things happened that I believe every Black American, if not every American, should experience. The first occurred the instant I stepped through the airport doors into the crowded streets of the city. As I looked all around me into the hundreds of Black faces—all of them so different, so unique, so beautiful—a warm wave of smooth energy washed through my body, while simultaneously a burden of pressure lifted from my soul. In that instant it suddenly hit me: For the first time in my life, my color was not an issue. *They were all like me.* Yes, I stood out because of my clothing and mannerisms, but I was just another human being, and so were they. I instantly felt self-pride and deep affection for my race, which I had never felt before in my life. This really blew my mind—I had no idea there was any remnant of racial pressure left in me to be replaced by this bliss. In my opinion, I of all people had evolved beyond that. A long time ago I had chosen to view my color as a definite asset of strength, power, and pride. But there it was, this feeling of unacknowledged pressure like a ton of raw iron ore scooped out of my being, dissipating into the warm African air. I was not a Black man, I was not an African American man, *I was simply a man.* There was so much power in that moment it brought tears to my eyes. To me, this was the way every human being on the face of the earth should feel. Yes, we are all special in our own way, but we also have the choice to feel free and without self-judgment. These wonderful souls all around me had already made that choice.

The second thing happened about fifteen minutes later. From the airport, we were driven through the city to the facility where the seminars were to be held. Along the way, we passed people living in poverty the likes of which I had never seen before. Conditions were so appallingly disgusting we could hardly stand it. Emaciated children crying real tears ran alongside our car, looking us in the eyes, chanting, "Daddy, Daddy! Please feed me, please feed me. Please feed me, I'm so hungry . . ." It literally broke my heart. All the money we could give them was not enough to fill the hole left in me from the sight of so many people in so much pain. We later found out that Nigeria really has only two classes of citizens: affluent and impoverished. But even though the poor were living substandard lives, they were still proud and strong of spirit. All of them, even the beggars, were actively doing something with their time—selling things on the streets, offering their labor for hire. As you looked into their eyes, you could feel and see the love in their souls. They laughed and smiled and were full of life. Throughout our time in Nigeria, we went out and talked to all kinds of people. Our consensus was that the impoverished multitudes live this way because they don't know any better. It's all they expect. They don't have the abundant opportunities we do to make changes in their lives. The government doesn't provide for the citizens of Nigeria the things we have easily grown accustomed to. They clearly do not have the choices we often take for granted. It made me feel so grateful for the life I have and the choices we all have every day of our lives.

I fully realize that things aren't nearly at the level they need to be in America, but they are a far, far cry from the standard of living we saw in Nigeria. It made me realize many of us don't utilize the personal and societal gifts we have at our fingertips each and every day. But you know what? Most people go through life looking for a helping hand, never realizing it's right there at the end of their own arm. We have to decide, and ask, and utilize what we have inside us. Ready or not, the future is coming, and our individual destinies are created by the actions we take in the present.

You now have the tools and resources to take absolute charge of your life. You have the ability to form the internal representations and produce the states that lead to success and power. But having the ability isn't always the same as using it. **Remember, knowledge is only potential power; most of us know what to do, but we don't always do what we know.** Action is power. There are certain experiences that time and again put people in unresourceful states. There are bends in the road, rapids in the river, that snag people time and time again. There are experiences that consistently prevent people from being all they can be. The road to success and fulfillment is often booby-trapped with dangerous curves and potholes that could threaten your forward motion. In this chapter, we want to give you a map showing you where the perils are and what you need to know to overcome them.

If you're going to use all the abilities you now have, if you're going to be all you can be, you're going to have to understand the five keys to wealth and happiness. Every person who is successful uses these keys sooner or later. If you can handle them consistently, your life will be an indomitable success.

Just as there are keys to success, there are also keys to failure, sadness, illness, and an uninspired life. Someone once said that if you don't want to be poor, don't do what poor people do. Obviously the same holds true for unhappy, miserable people as well. The best thing you can do for them is not to be one of them. As ridiculously simple as that sounds, everything you have learned so far supports this truth. We've learned we must ask for what we want out of life and ourselves. And if we are willing to do what is necessary to achieve what we want, then we will get what we desire. Ask for a quarter, and that's what you'll get. Ask for resounding joy and success, and you'll get that, too. **Everything we've studied convinces us that if you learn to manage your states and manage your behaviors, you can change anything.** You can learn what to ask of life and be sure to get it. I have met people who are poor and asked them about their lives and how they got there. I have asked wealthy people what brought them where they are in life. I've found that many of them have had the same types of experiences in their lives. The difference is what they did with what happened.

> *We create our own destiny by the way we do things. We have to take advantage of opportunities and be responsible for our choices.*
>
> —Benjamin Carson

Let me share with you five truths to use as road signs to success. There's nothing profound or difficult about them. But they're absolutely crucial. If you master them, there's no limit to what you can do. If you don't use them, you've already placed the limits on how high you can go. Affirmation and positive thinking are a start, but they're not the full answer. Affirmation without discipline is the beginning of delusion. Affirmation with discipline creates miracles.

Key No. 1: You must learn how to handle frustration. If there's one emotion I would say has gotten me the furthest, it's learning how to handle frustration. In the past I not only experienced this emotion frequently, but I would let it linger like a bad smell, stinking up my life and the lives of others around me. Frustrating situations happen to everyone. We don't have to become frustrated as a result. This is the first key to creating wealth and happiness. If you want to become all you can become, do all you can do, hear all you can hear, see all you can see, you've got to learn how to handle frustration. Frustration can kill dreams. It can change a positive attitude into a negative one, an empowering state into a crippling one. The worst thing a negative attitude does is to wipe out self-discipline. And when discipline goes, the results you desire go with it.

To ensure long-term success, you must learn how to discipline your frustration. Let me tell you something: The key to success is massive frustration. Look at almost any great success, and you'll find there's been massive frustration along the way. Anybody who tells you otherwise doesn't know anything about achieving. There are two kinds of people—those who've handled frustration and those who wish they had.

Let's consider a little company called Federal Express. A guy named Fred Smith built a multimillion-dollar business out of mounds of frustration. When he started the company (after financing it with every dime he had) he hoped to deliver approximately a hundred and fifty packages the first day. Instead, only sixteen packages were processed, five of which Fred Smith had sent to one of his employees. Things got worse from there. Periodically, employees cashed their payroll checks at convenience stores because the funds weren't available to cover the checks. Many times the company's airplanes were in the process of being repossessed; sometimes they had to bring in a certain amount in sales during a single day just to keep operating. Federal Express is now a billion-dollar company. The only reason it's still here is that Fred Smith was able to handle frustration upon frustration.

People get paid very well to handle frustration. If you're broke, it's probably because you're not handling very much of it. You say, "Well, I'm broke, and that's why I'm frustrated." You've got it backward. *If you handled more frustration, you would be rich.* A major difference between people who are financially secure and people who are not is how they handle frustration. I'm not callous enough to suggest that poverty doesn't have huge frustrations. I'm saying the way not to be poor is to take on more and more frustration until you succeed. I've heard it said, "People with money don't have any problems." If they take on enough frustration, they probably have *more* problems. Perhaps they just know how to deal with them better—and come up with new strategies, new alternatives.

Remember, being rich is not just about having money. A superb relationship, for example, also provides problems and challenges. If you don't want problems, you shouldn't have a relationship at all. There's great frustration on the road to any great success—in business, in relationships, in life. *The only people on this earth who have no problems are in the graveyard.* So if you find yourself with no problems, you might just get on your knees and ask God for some more. You definitely have an advantage in this area over most people because you know how to handle any emotion. And when you think about it, isn't that all frustration is—an emotion? You know exactly what to do with any emotion that does not serve you: Look in your toolbox and find something to handle it. You can take things that used to make you frustrated and program them so they make you excited. Tools like NLP are not just positive thinking. What we offer instead is a way to turn stress into opportunity. You already know how to take images that once depressed you and make them wither and disappear or change them to the images that bring you ecstasy. It's not hard to do.

Here's a two-step formula for handling stress. Step 1: Don't sweat the small stuff. Step 2: Remember, it's all small stuff. Use the Ultimate Success Formula, and take frustration as a signal to start looking for the opportunity to change your approach, and move that much closer to your goals.

Key No. 2: You must learn how to handle rejection. I'll even take it a step further: You must learn to get *excited* if it happens. This usually makes people's spines crawl and their toes knot up in their shoes. No one likes to be rejected. Rejection is the number one emotion most people will do nearly anything to avoid. Is there anything in the human language with more sting than the tiny word *no*?

If you're in sales, what's the difference between making $100,000 and making $25,000? The main difference is learning how to handle rejection so this particular fear no longer stops you from taking action. The best salespeople are those who are rejected the most. They're the ones who can take any no and use it as a prod to go on to the next yes.

Some time ago I borrowed a saying from a man who was a high-ranking figure in multilevel marketing. He said that he treats every no as one step closer to a yes. You see, he figured out that on average it took being told no fifty times before he got a yes, and one yes would cancel out all the no's. So he started getting excited every time he got a no because he knew that after fifty no's he would get his yes. According to him, the best part was never knowing when that yes would come; it could be the tenth or the fortieth or even the first time. So he was in the business of collecting no's. He would even thank the person for telling him no and helping him achieve his goal.

The biggest challenge for people in our culture is they can't handle the word *no.* Remember the question I asked earlier? *What would you do if you knew you could not fail?* Think about it. If you knew you couldn't fail, how would that change your behavior? Would that allow you to do exactly what you want? So what's keeping you from doing it? That tiny word *no.* To succeed, you must learn how to cope with rejection, to strip rejection of all its power.

Tony once worked with a high jumper who had been an Olympic athlete but had reached the point where he was no longer jumping at competition level. After Tony watched him jump, he immediately saw the problem. Whenever the athlete hit the bar instead of clearing it, he started going through all sorts of emotional gyrations. He turned each failure into a big event. He was storing the whole experience as failure; he was sending a message to his brain that reinforced the image of failure so it would be there the next time he jumped. Each time he jumped, his brain was more concerned with failing than with being in the resourceful state that brings success. Tony called him over and told him if he wanted any more private coaching, he must never do that again. Instead, if he hit the bar, he should tell himself, _Aha! Another distinction!_ not _*%$&*!%$*! Another failure._ He should put himself back into a resourceful state and go for it again. Within three jumps this man was performing better than he had in two years.

It doesn't take a lot to change. The difference between six feet four inches and seven feet is only 10 percent. It's not a big difference in height, but it's a big difference in performance. In the same way, small changes can make a big change in the quality of your life.

How many nos can you take? How many times have you wanted to go and talk to someone you found attractive, then decided not to do it because you didn't want to hear the word *no?* How many times have you decided not to try for a job or make a sales call or audition for a part because you didn't want to be rejected? Think about how crazy that is. Think how you're creating limits with your fear of that little two-letter word. The word itself has no power. It can't cut your skin or sap your strength. Its power comes from the way you represent it to yourself. Its power comes from the limits it makes you create. And what do limited thoughts create? Limited lives.

> *Treat failure as practice shots.*
>
> —DEBORAH MCGRIFF

When you learn to run your brain, you can learn to handle rejection. You can even anchor yourself so that hearing *no* turns you on. You can take any rejection and turn it into an opportunity. If you're in telephone sales, you can anchor yourself so that simply reaching for the phone puts you in ecstasy rather than raising the fear of rejection. Remember, success is buried on the other side of rejection.

Key No. 3: You must learn to handle financial pressure. Remember, we all grow with pressure—that's how muscles get stronger, diamonds become harder, and people get richer. *The only way not to have financial pressure is not to have any finances.* There are many kinds of financial pressure, and they've destroyed many people. They can create greed, envy, deceit, paranoia. They can rob you of your sensitivity or rob you of your friends. (Now remember, I said they *can*, not that they *will*.) Handling financial pressure means knowing how to get and knowing how to give, knowing how to earn and knowing how to save.

When I first started to make money, my friends started avoiding me and treating me like an ugly stepchild. They teased me and accused me of things I would never dream of doing. They said, "You're into money. What's your problem?" Even though money was what they all wanted the most, they made me out to be bad because I had it. I would tell them, "I'm not into money. I just have some." I even offered to show them how to do the same for themselves. They wouldn't see it that way. People somehow suddenly perceived me as a different person because I had a different financial status. So that's one kind of financial pressure.

I remember overhearing a conversation in a music studio about how many hard-core Black artists thought of M.C. Hammer as being a "sellout" because he got so popular. Here's a man who had done everything it takes to get on top, done all the things that others were not willing to do. And now, because he had reached a certain level of success, he was ridiculed for it. Even though the man contributes more than most people make in a year back into the communities, even though he has done so much to bring Black music into the mainstream, he was criticized. You have to wonder if this criticism has been an influence on the sometimes up-and-down nature of his financial success. This shows up in so many other ways in our culture. Many African Americans have ambivalence about succeeding for fear of being alienated from their peers. Well, just for the record, there are plenty of our peers at the top, and the numbers are growing.

Not having enough money is another kind of financial pressure. You probably feel that pressure every day. Most people do. But whether you have a lot of money or just a little, you still have to deal with financial pressure.

Tony has been an amazing model, not only of succeeding financially, but also of doing it by finding ways to add more value to other people's lives. He believes the only way a person becomes wealthy in this country is to find a way to do more for other people than anyone else is doing—and to do it at a level of quality no one else has dreamed of. He has also taught so many of us that you can never become truly wealthy or financially independent from your own income alone. **You must learn to become an investor, a skill few people master in our society.** We believe this is one of the main reasons that most people are having challenges in the area of their finances. You see, most people live their lives as consumers, not investors. So Tony and I encourage people, including young people, to become owners of companies either by entrepreneurship or by investing in the stocks of public companies. Anyone can become an investor, and the returns can be extraordinary if you are willing to invest through time.

One incredible example of the power of investing is Theodore Johnson, a Black man who was a postal worker from the early 1940s through the late 1950s. Theodore never earned more than $14,000 a year from his job. Yet he became wealthy beyond most of our wildest dreams. Every extra penny he had, he socked away in interest-earning investments. *He retired in 1954 and by the year*

1984, thirty years later, he was worth $30 million. Here's a man who made barely enough to take care of his family, even by 1940s and 1950s standards, yet he invested and became wealthy. Upon his death, Theodore Johnson left more than $7 million to various charity organizations.

One of the most exciting things we have been doing in recent years is learning and applying the strategies of investing. Tony has been teaching and sharing with people these strategies on how to produce amazing and virtually immediate financial results. When he first told me I could create not a 10 or 20 percent annual return on my investments but a 10, 20, or 30 percent *per month* return, I thought he was crazy. But I was more than willing to listen, because I knew he had modeled strategies of some of the most successful financial traders in the world. One of these was a man with whom Tony had spent almost two years, a well-known financial trader who made almost half a billion dollars in a single day. After having many challenges, he hired Tony and paid him several million dollars to help him turn his financial trading around. Tony, in turn, took this man's strategies and simplified them in order to create a system that he has used not only for himself, but also for my benefit and that of many others he's taught. As I'm writing these words now, I'm also celebrating a week's worth of investing in which I've produced 20 percent returns in this one week alone! **What changes our lives is profound knowledge—those skills, strategies, or tools that, once we understand them, can immediately and profoundly change the quality of our lives forever.***

The most important thing to realize is that we have to change our beliefs about what's possible or we will never find the strategies that enable us to achieve a greater result. The fact of the matter is, there are very specific ways for us all to invest and secure our financial futures, and it's much easier and faster than most of us ever dreamed. It only makes sense to model those who are succeeding at the highest level if we want to achieve the greatest financial freedom possible.

Remember, all our actions in life are guided by our philoso-

*Although this book is not specifically about finances, if you have an interest in finding out more about cash flow strategies or how to create the financial independence you desire, be sure to contact Robbins Research International, Inc. at (800) 898-8669.

phies, our guiding internal representations about how to act. They give us the models of how to behave. George S. Clason provided a great model for learning to handle financial pressure in *The Richest Man in Babylon*. Have you read it? If so, read it again. If not, run out and get it now. It's a book that can make you totally wealthy, happy, and excited. To me, the most important thing the book teaches is to take 10 percent of all you earn up front and give it away. That's right, give it away. Why? One reason is you should put back what you take out. Another is it creates value for you and for others. Most important, it says to the world and your own subconscious *there is more than enough*. And that's a very powerful belief to nurture. If there's more than enough, it means you can have what you want and others can, too. And when you hold that thought, you make it come true.

When do you start to give the 10 percent away? When you're rich and famous? No. You should do it when you're starting out, because what you give away becomes your "seed corn." You've got to invest it, not eat it, and the best way to invest it is to give it away so that it produces value for others. You won't have trouble finding ways. There is need all around us. One of the most valuable aspects of this practice is how it makes you feel about yourself. When you're the kind of person who tries to find and fill other people's needs, it makes you feel differently about who you are. And from those kinds of feelings or states, you live your life in an attitude of gratitude.

I have the good fortune of being able to give back in several ways. I often volunteer to work in schools and retirement homes and with youth groups. This is a special thing for me because these people are so full of love and learning that it shows in their faces and hearts. I also believe in letting the people who have helped you know how much you appreciate what they've done for you. I believe you can never do too much of that.

When I was eighteen years old, I was homeless, living in a cardboard box behind an old abandoned drive-in theater. On my nineteenth birthday, I was at the end of my rope and ready to give up. A very kind man gave me a copy of *Think and Grow Rich* and made me read it right then and there. He didn't have to do this, but he did, and it changed my life. When I went back to thank him for what he had done, he barked at me, "I didn't do it for your thanks; I don't want them. You can thank me by going out and doing the same for others." From that day forward I swore I would always find a way to give back. Not because I want something in return, but because I am so grateful for all that has been given me. Tony and I believe if we all take the time and give just a little to those who might need it, we can make some pretty amazing changes on this planet. You never know when a kind word or a donation or a book will change the course of someone's life.

After you give away 10 percent of your income, take another 10 percent to reduce your debts and a third 10 percent to build up capital to invest. You need to live on 70 percent of what you have. We live in a capitalistic society in which most human beings are not capitalists. As a result, they don't have the lifestyle they desire. Why live in a capitalistic society, surrounded by opportunity, and not take advantage of the very system our forefathers fought to create? Learn to take your money and use it as capital. If you are spending it, you'll never build up any capital and you'll never have the resources you need. It's been said that in California the average income is now $30,000 a year. The average outgo is $35,000. The difference is called financial pressure. You don't want to join that crowd.

The bottom line in money is like everything else: You can make it work for you, or you can let it work against you. You should be able to deal with money with purpose and elegance. Learn to earn, to save, and to give. If you can do that, you'll learn to handle financial pressure, and money will never again be a stimulus to put you in a negative state, causing you to be unhappy or treat others around you in a less than resourceful way.

When you master the first three keys, you will begin to experience your life as hugely successful. If you can handle frustration, rejection, and financial pressure, there's no limit to what you can do. Ever see Tina Turner perform? She is someone who has handled massive amounts of all three. After becoming a star, she lost her marriage, lost her money, and spent eight years in a show business purgatory of hotel lounges and cheap clubs. She couldn't get people to return her phone calls, much less offer her a recording contract. But she kept plugging, tuning out the no's, paying off debts, and putting her financial house in order. Eventually she came all the way back to the top of the entertainment world.

Okay, you can do anything—and that's where number four rears its ugly head:

Key No. 4: You must learn how to handle complacency. I'm sure you've seen celebrities or athletes or people in your life who reach a level of success and then stop. It's almost a cliché—fighters who lose their killer instinct, actors who lose their spark, writers who suddenly develop writer's block, models who let themselves go physically. Most of us look at them and say, "Boy, if I had what they have, I wouldn't take it for granted. I'd use it and be grateful for it every day." But these people have become too familiar and comfortable with what they have.

Life loves the liver of it. Life loves to be taken by the lapel and told: "I'm with you, kid. Let's go."

—MELVIN CHAPMAN

Comfort can be one of the most disastrous emotions anybody could have. What happens when someone gets too comfortable? That person stops growing, stops working, stops creating added value. You don't want to get too comfortable. If you feel really comfortable, chances are you've stopped growing. You're either climbing or you're sliding. Ray Kroc, the founder of McDonald's, was once asked if he had one piece of advice to guarantee a long life of success, what would it be? He said, "Simply remember this: When you're green, you grow; when you ripen, you rot." As long as you remain green, you grow. You can make any experience an opportunity for growth or an invitation to decay. You can see retirement as the beginning of a richer life, or you can see it as the end of your working life. You can see success as a springboard to greater things, or you can see it as a resting place. And if it's a resting place, chances are you won't keep it for long.

One kind of complacency comes from comparison. We should never compare our progress to others'. One of the biggest mistakes you can make is to feel you are doing well compared to your friends. Maybe it just means your friends aren't doing very well. Yes, look to others for possibility, but learn to judge yourself by your goals instead of by what your peers seem to be doing. Why? Because you can always find examples worse than you to justify what you're doing. It is too easy to get caught up in justifying your lack of action by comparing yourself to others: "At least I'm not as bad as ______________."

Didn't you do that as a kid? Didn't you say, "Johnny did this; why can't I?" Your mother probably said, "Well, I don't care what Johnny does," and she was right. You shouldn't care what Johnny or Mary or the Joneses do. Care about what you're capable of. Care about what you create and what you want to do. Work from a set of dynamic, evolving, enabling goals that will help you do what you want, not what someone else has done. There will always be someone who has more than you. There will always be someone who has less. None of that matters. You need to judge yourself by your goals and nothing else.

Here's another way to avoid complacency. Stay away from "coffeepot seminars." You know what I'm talking about: sessions where people's work habits, sex life, financial status, and everything else become fair game. You're putting attention on what other people are doing in their private lives instead of what you can be doing to enhance your own life. It's easy to get caught up in these "seminars," but just remember that people who do so are merely trying to distract themselves from the boredom created by their inability to produce the results they desire in their own lives.

There's a phrase that Rolling Thunder, the Native American wise man, used often: "Speak with good purpose only." What we put out comes back to us. So I challenge you to stay away from the garbage of life. *Don't major in minor things.* If you want to be complacent and mediocre, spend your time gossiping about who is sleeping with whom. If you want to make a difference, then challenge yourself, test yourself, make your life special.

The last key may be the most important of all because it virtually guarantees true happiness:

Key No. 5: Always give more than you expect to receive. There is an old saying, "Receiving is evidence that you are giving." If you want to make your life work, you have to start by focusing on how to give. Most people start by thinking about how to receive. Sometimes it seems our whole culture is based on what we can get—"what's in it for me." There was even a whole decade, the 1980s, named for this prevailing attitude: the "Me Decade." There's nothing wrong with receiving. But you've got to make sure you are giving so you can start the process in motion.

The problem is that often people want to receive first. Frequently people come to me because they are fighting with someone, sometimes even their spouse or mate. And even though the fight may be long over, they still have ill feelings and resentment for what was said and done. Often all they want is an apology, but they keep tight-lipped about the whole thing and stew in their own juices. They even admit they were just as much at fault as the other person, but they simply aren't going to make the first move. I always ask, "Are you forgiving?" Usually they bark back, "Of course—I'm a very forgiving person." Then I repeat the question very slowly and deliberately: "Are you FOR . . . GIVING?" They look at me puzzled for a few seconds, then they get it. Are you for *giving* first, breaking the ice and sometimes apologizing first? That is when you will receive what you want.

Don't let pride keep you from giving first. The key to any relationship is that you have to give *and then keep giving.* Don't stop and wait to receive. When you start keeping score, the game's over. You're standing there saying, "I gave, so now it's her turn," and she's already gone. You can take your score to the next spinning planet, because the scoreboard doesn't work that way here.

You've got to be willing to plant the seed, then patiently nurture its growth. What would happen if you stood over the soil and demanded, "Give me some fruit, give me some plants"? The soil would probably respond, "Excuse me, but you're a little confused. You must be new here. That's not the way things happen here." Then it would explain that you plant the seed. You take care of it. You water and fertilize it. You pull the weeds. You protect it and nurture it. Then, if you do it well, you will get your plant or fruit sometime later. You could yell at the soil forever, but it wouldn't change things. You have to keep giving and nurturing for the soil to bear fruit—and life's exactly the same way. When people ask me to help them reach a specific goal or outcome, I always ask them, "What are you willing to give in exchange for that prize?" Most people have to search their brains for the answer, because all they had been thinking about was receiving what they wanted, not what they could give.

The secret to living is giving.

—ANTHONY ROBBINS

Here's one last thing to know. You can make a lot of money. You can rule kingdoms or run huge businesses or control vast terrain. But if you're just doing it for yourself, you're not really a success. You don't really have power. You don't have real wealth.

Please remember this simple fact: Success is not something you achieve, conquer, climb, or complete. **Success is a process; it's a way of life.** Success is the journey, the path, the information, the superhighway to fulfillment. If you want to succeed, if you want to achieve all your outcomes, you have to view success as a habit of mind, a strategy for life. And that's when you start to come into your real power. That's what this chapter has been all about. You must know what you have, and you must know the obstacles along the way. You must have the ability to use your power in a responsible and loving way if you are to experience true wealth and happiness. And you must be willing to do—and not do—whatever it takes to make it happen for you. When you can learn to handle these five keys, you'll be able to use all the skills and powers taught in this book to do wondrous things.

Everything we do, including writing this book, has one goal: to move as many people as possible to create the lives they deserve. Without a doubt, the collective consciousness of a mass of people working toward bettering the human condition will result in an overall improvement of the world in which we live. If there is to be positive change in this culture, there must be change in ourselves first, then in our communities. We've already looked at the way change works on us as individuals. Now let's see how change works on the larger level of groups and communities and nations. We call it . . .

CHAPTER TWENTY-TWO

Trend Creation: The Power of Persuasion

There is hope for the future because God has a sense of humor.

—BILL COSBY

FOR MOST OF MY LIFE, I've felt that we are all alive in the best possible time on this planet. Think about it: Within this century, you and I have witnessed some of the greatest events of all time. We as a species have made more progress in the last ninety years than all of humanity has made in the history of the world. Aircraft, computers, space travel, medicine, you name it—we've defied all the odds, broken all the barriers. In some cases, we've even rewritten what we thought were unchangeable laws of nature. I often think that when God checks in on how we're doing as a species, he must be very proud. In my mind, the biggest leap forward has been in the area of communication. In seconds we can be talking to someone on the other side of the world, for literally pennies. The Internet, the telephone, even the ability to get an object from here to any spot on the globe in less than twenty-four hours has in effect shrunk the world down to a manageable size.

The idea of a global village has long since become a cliché, but it's still true. Never before in the history of the world have there been so many powerful mechanisms for massive, lasting group persuasion. That can mean more people buying Cokes, wearing Levi jeans, and listening to all types of music. It can also mean massive, positive shifts in attitudes around the world. It all depends on who's doing the persuading and why. In this chapter, we're going to look at the changes that occur on a mass scale, see how they happen, and consider what they mean. We'll pay particular attention to what it means to the Black community and how we can anticipate and utilize what lies ahead on the path we are all traveling. Then we're going to focus on how you can become a great persuader and what you can do with your abilities.

The Ever-Present Force of Persuasion

We think of our world today as being awash in stimuli, but that's not what really differentiates it from earlier times. A warrior walking through the jungles of Africa was constantly confronted with sights and sounds and smells that could mean the difference between life and death, between eating and starving. The biggest difference today is in the intent and reach of the stimuli. The African in the jungle had to interpret the meaning of the random stimuli. In contrast, our world is full of stimuli that are consciously directed to get us to do something specific. And as we've discussed earlier, the senders of these messages might not necessarily have our best interest in mind at all times. It might be a plea to buy a car or a mandate to vote for a candidate. It might be an appeal to save starving children or a pitch to consume more hamburgers and fries. It might be an attempt to make us feel good about having something or a message to make us feel bad we don't have something else. But the main thing that characterizes the modern world is the persistence of persuasion. We're constantly surrounded by people with the means, technology, and know-how to persuade us to do something, and that persuasion has global reach. The same image that's being force-fed to us can also be pounded into most of the rest of the world at the exact same instant. And with the advent of the many on-line services and the Internet, any one of us can likewise transmit our own personal visual and auditory form of persuasion to be viewed by the rest of the globe in a split second. The possibilities are endless.

Let's consider the habit of smoking cigarettes. People in earlier times could have pleaded ignorance. But today we know beyond a shadow of a doubt that cigarettes are harmful not only to our own health but to the health of those around us as well. They contribute to everything from cancer to heart disease to birth defects. What's more, it's now being shown that even secondhand smoke is killing people at an alarming rate. Along with all this overwhelming evidence, there's even a large amount of powerful public sentiment—expressed through local anti-smoking drives and referenda—making smokers feel they're doing something bad. People have every reason in the world not to smoke. Yet the tobacco industry continues to profit, and millions of people continue to smoke cigarettes, with more starting the habit all the time. Why is that?

Most smokers will probably tell you they enjoy the experience of smoking. But what got them started in the first place? They had to be taught how to use a cigarette as a trigger to create pleasure; it was not a natural response. What happened when they first smoked? They hated it. They coughed and gagged. Their nose ran, and their stomach twisted with nausea. Their body revolted and screamed, "What are you, CRAZY? This stuff is nasty; get it away from us. This crap will kill us!" In most cases, if the physical evidence of your own five senses tells you something is bad, you would expect to listen. So why in God's name don't all people do that with smoking? Why do they continue to smoke until the body gives in and finally becomes addicted?

They do it because they've been reframed as to what smoking means, and that new representation and state have been anchored securely into place. Someone with a great deal of knowledge about persuasion has spent millions and millions of dollars to convince the public that smoking is something desirable. Through skillful advertising, seductive images and sounds are used to put us in positive-feeling states; then those desired states are associated with or linked to a product called cigarettes. Through massive repetition, the idea of smoking is continually linked with various desirable states. There's no inherent value or social content to a piece of paper wrapped around tiny tobacco leaves. But we've been persuaded and seduced into thinking that smoking is sexy, suave, adult, macho, cool. Want to be like the *GQ* guy in the ads with all the sexy women clinging all over him? Smoke a cigarette. And not just any cigarette, the one he's smoking. Want to show you've come a long way, baby? Want to show you know your power and independence as a woman? Smoke a cigarette. You've come a long way all right—a long way closer to the possibility of lung cancer, just like one of the guys.

How crazy is this? What in the world does putting carcinogens into your lungs have to do with any desirable state? But advertisers consistently do on a mass scale exactly what we've talked about in this book. They send out images that put you in a receptive, elevated state, and at the peak of the experience, they anchor you with their message. Then they repeat it on television, in magazines, and on the radio so that the anchor is constantly reinforced and triggered.

Why do Jell-O and Coke pay Bill Cosby to sell their products? Why do politicians wrap themselves in the flag? Why is Miller brewed the American way? Why do we love baseball, hot dogs, apple pie, and Chevrolet? Why? Because these people and symbols are already powerful anchors in the culture, and the advertisers are simply transferring the feeling we have for these people or symbols to their products. They use them as ways to make us receptive to whatever it is they're selling.

You can break down any effective ad or political campaign and find it follows the precise framework we've set up in this book. First it uses visual and auditory stimuli to put you in the state the promoters desire. Then it anchors your state to a product they want you to buy or an action they wish you to take. This, of course, is done time and time again until your nervous system effectively links the state with the product or desired behavior. If it's a good ad, it will use images and sounds that engage and affect all three major representational systems: visual, auditory, and kinesthetic. TV is such a persuasive medium because it can make the best use of all three: It can give you pretty pictures, include a catchy song or jingle, and provide a message with emotional punch. Think of the most effective ads done for a soft drink like Coke or a beer like Miller or a fast-food restaurant like McDonald's. Think of the "Reach Out and Touch Someone" ads for the phone company. What they all have in common is a strong V-A-K mix that offers a hook for everyone.

Of course, there are some ads that are effective in producing the opposite image—they break the state in as stark a manner as possible. Think of anti-smoking ads. Have you ever seen the one showing a fetus smoking a cigarette in its mother's womb? Or

Brooke Shields looking dopey with cigarettes coming out of her ears? Those ads are most effective when they function as pattern interrupts, when they destroy the aura of glamour someone else has tried to create around an unhealthful product.

Remember, we still ultimately have control of our own associations, and we can change the trends that advertisers work so hard to promote. Here's an interesting statistic: It is estimated that some three thousand teenagers a day are beginning to smoke cigarettes for the first time. In spite of all the statistics showing that approximately a thousand of them will die of tobacco-related diseases, they are still lighting up at an alarming rate. But the good news for the Black community is that, despite this overall societal trend, young Black men and women have been much smarter in their choices. It's not necessarily because they are lucky or inherently smarter, it's just that they have been influenced to make that better choice. Part of this trend is due to a big movement in the Black community saying that cigarettes are sold by White companies taking advantage of the Black community and trying to kill us. Some Black leaders point out that we are easy targets and this is one way we are still enslaved by the White powers that be, that White advertisers are trying to make money off our death. And while that may be an extreme (think about it: cigarettes don't kill selectively; White people are dying off, too), the good news is this influence has caused a new awareness in the Black community and had a positive effect on us as a whole. This is definitely a prime example of trend creation that we should be proud of. By changing our associations we can change the trends of society en masse, not just follow them like puppets on a string.

Just as those who are masters of persuasion learned their skill, you can do the same as well. In a world full of persuaders, you can choose to be a persuader yourself. If not, you stay with the multitudes at the mercy of those who are the persuaders. In short, persuade or be persuaded. You can direct your life or be directed. When you come right down to it, this book has really been about persuasion. It's shown you how to develop the personal power that can put you in control so you can do the persuading, whether as a role model for your kids or as a positive force at work. The people in power are the persuaders. The people without power simply act on the images and commands that are directed their way.

Power today is the ability to communicate and the ability to persuade. If you're a persuader with no legs, you'll persuade someone to carry you. If you have no money, you'll persuade someone to lend you some. Persuasion may be the ultimate skill for creating changes in our lives. After all, if you're a persuader who's alone in the world and doesn't want to be, you'll find a friend or a lover. If you're a persuader with a good product to sell, you'll find someone who'll buy it. You can have an idea or a product that can change the world, but without the power to persuade, you have nothing. Communicating what you have to offer is what life is all about. It's the most important skill you can develop.

Putting Personal Power to Work

Let me give you an example of how powerful this technology is and how much you can do once you master the techniques. In 1986 when I attended my first NLP certification program, Tony devised a way to test us to see how well we had learned and integrated the skills we had been studying. The program took place in Palm Desert, California, about two hundred miles from Los Angeles. There were about four hundred of us in the class, and we had one more day before we graduated. At approximately 10:30 P.M. Tony announced he had a task for all of us to do. We were instructed to turn in our wallets, room keys, all of our money, and credit cards—everything but the clothes on our backs, an apple, and a quarter.

He told us he wanted to prove that to succeed in life we didn't need anything but our own personal power and persuasive abilities. We had the skills to find and fill people's needs, and we didn't need money, status, a vehicle, or anything else the culture teaches us we need to make our lives the way we want them. We were to leave the hotel premises within the next hour, find our way to either Los Angeles, New York, Hawaii, or San Diego, and return by 6:00 the following evening. If we were not off the premises by midnight they would call security and have us removed, and if we were arrested they would deny any knowledge of their affiliation with us. He told us to take excellent care of ourselves, to be safe, and to use our skills to help as many people as possible in the next 24 hours, arriving back healthfully in Palm Desert by the next evening. We were instructed to find a nice place to stay, eat well, and use our education and persuasion skills in any other ways that seemed effective and empowering, not only for ourselves but for the people we met along the way.

The first challenge was to find a way to get out of Palm Desert. This freaked me out, because the only other time I had ever hitchhiked I had been attacked by thugs hell-bent on beating the life out of me and leaving my carcass in the dirt. We all left in the middle of the night and set out on the adventure of our lives.

Picture four hundred people leaving Palm Desert at midnight, planning to hitchhike or find some other way out of town. I remember thinking, "This is crazy. How is everyone going to get picked up?" But within one-half hour there was no one on the streets. People did the most amazing things. Some of them got aboard private jets to Las Vegas to gamble. Many of us were able to get bank loans of from $100 to $500 simply on the force of our personal power and congruence. Remember, we had no identification whatsoever, and we were in a city we'd never been in before. One man made it all the way to Hawaii with no money and got to be onstage along with the conductor during a symphony at the local concert hall. One man got a job as a consultant for a large financial institution. Of the four hundred or so people who went on the adventure, about 80 percent were able to get a job, and virtually all of us ate well, slept well, and traveled without hitchhiking or putting ourselves in danger. One man went to an elementary school and conducted an assembly on personal power, first to the faculty, then to the student body. He was initially told it couldn't be done and that he had to submit a written proposal to the board of directors for approval and wait for a reply. But he developed so much instant rapport that he was allowed to come in and work there that very day.

I went to Los Angeles and made it into the number-one radio station in the city. I was interviewed live on the air by Rick Dees, the number-one disc jockey at the time. Afterward, I was limousined back to Palm Desert and given cash to ease my suffering.

While I was in Los Angeles, I had the honor of teaching some of the skills of personal power and helping many of the staff of the station with some of their emotional challenges. I made several new friends with whom, to this day, I keep in touch. But most important, I learned I didn't need all the things we are conditioned to believe we need to get what we want. **All we have to do is learn to give value first.**

That day, a number of resourceful individuals cleared up people's phobias and assisted with other emotional problems. The point of this exercise was to show us we needed nothing more than our own resourceful behaviors and skills to find our way around without all the usual support systems such as transportation, money, reputation, contacts, credit, and so on. What's more, the majority of us had one of the most powerful and enjoyable days of our lives. We all made great friends and helped hundreds of people. We made lifelong changes within ourselves as well.

In the second chapter, we talked about how people have different feelings about power. Some think it's somehow unseemly; it means having undue control over others. Let me tell you, in the modern world, persuasion isn't a choice. *It's an ever-present fact of life.* Someone is always doing the persuading. People are spending millions and millions of dollars to get their messages out with ultimate power and skill. So either you do the persuading, or someone else does. The difference in our children's behavior may be the difference between who is a greater persuader—you and I, or the drug pusher. If you want to have control of your life, if you want to be the most elegant, effective model for those you care about, you've got to learn how to be a persuader. If you abdicate responsibility, there are plenty of others ready to fill the void.

We must give our own story to the world.

—CARTER G. WOODSON

By now, you know what these communication skills can mean to you. Now we need to consider what these skills can mean to all of us together. We live in the most remarkable era in human history, a time when changes that once took decades can now happen in days, when voyages that once took months can now be made in hours. Many of those changes are good. We live longer, in better comfort, and with more choices and freedom than ever before.

Some of the changes, however, can also be terrifying. For the first time in history, we know we have the ability to destroy the entire planet, either through horrifying nuclear explosions (the Cold War is over, but membership in the "nuclear club" grows, and violence by international terrorists with access to nuclear, chemical, and biological weapons is a constant threat) or a long, slow death from polluting and poisoning the planet and ourselves. It's not something most of us want to talk about; it's something our minds move away from, not toward. But these situations are a fact of life. The good news is that while divine power (or human intelligence, or pure dumb chance, or whatever force or combinations of force you believe affect where we are today) has created these terrifying problems, it has also created the means to change them. Less than a decade ago there were thousands of nuclear warheads pointed at the U.S. from the former Soviet Union, and we had equally as many pointed at them. Today, a fraction of that exists, and this, too, is slated for dismantling. The Berlin Wall which stood for decades in stark defiance of human rights and democracy, has crumbled under the weight of the ever-growing human spirit. Without a doubt, broad changes are sweeping humanity. Underlying all of this, we believe in a source much larger than our present understanding. To say there is no source of intelligence we may call God is like saying Webster's dictionary is the result of an explosion in a print factory and everything just came together in perfect order.

The next time you are overwhelmed by the problems facing society, think about this: All human problems are behavioral problems! (I hope you're using your precision model right now and asking, "All?") Well, let me put it this way: If the source of the problem is not human behavior, there is usually a behavioral solution. For example, crime is not the problem—it's people's behavior that creates this thing we call crime.

Many times we take sets of actions and turn them into nouns as if they were objects, when actually they are processes. As long as we represent human problems as if they were things, we disempower ourselves by turning them into something big and beyond our control. Toxic waste in and of itself is not the problem. How we use our energy resources can be a problem if they're not handled effectively. The technology used to create chemical and biological weapons in and of itself is not the problem. The way human beings behave is what creates or prevents war. Famine in Africa is not in and of itself the problem. Human behavior is the problem. Destroying each other's land does not support the creation of a larger food supply. If food shipped in from other humans all over the world is rotting on the docks because humans can't cooperate, that's a behavioral problem.

If we can agree, as a useful generalization, that human behavior is the source of human problems or that new human behaviors can solve most other problems that arise, then we can become quite excited: We will understand that these behaviors are the results of the states human beings are in and represent their models of how to respond when they are in these states. We also know that the states from which behaviors spring are the result of people's internal representations. We know, for example, that people have linked the process of smoking to a particular state. They don't smoke every minute of every day, only when they're in a smoking state. People don't overeat every minute of every day, only when they are in a state they have linked to overeating. If you effectively change those associations or the linked response, you can effectively change people's behavior.

Remember, we are now living in an age where the technology needed to communicate messages to almost the entire world is already in place and being used, via radio, television, movies, the Internet, and print. The movies we see in New York and Los Angeles today are in Paris and London tomorrow, Beirut and Managua the day after that, and around the whole world a few days later. If those movies or books or television shows change people's internal representations and states for the better, they can change the world for the better, too. We've seen how effective the media can be for selling products and spreading cultural influences. We're just now learning how effective they can be in changing the world for the better. Think of the Live Aid concerts. If they weren't an awesome display of the positive power of communication technology, I don't know what is.

Therefore, the means to change massive numbers of people's

internal representations, and thus massive numbers of people's states, and thus massive numbers of people's behaviors, is available to us now. By effectively using our understanding of the triggers to human behavior and the present-day technology for communicating these new representations to the masses, we can change the future of our world.

The documentary film *Scared Straight* is a great example of how we can change people's internal representations and thereby change their behaviors by using the resources of the media. It documents a program in which kids who are producing destructive or delinquent behavior are brought to a prison where inmate volunteers proceed to change the kids' internal representations of what crime and imprisonment really mean. When these kids were interviewed in advance, most were real tough and said that going to prison wouldn't be a very big deal. Yet their internal representations and states were effectively changed when a mass murderer began to tell them what life in prison was really like, relating the details with an intensity that would change anyone's physiology! *Scared Straight* is must viewing. Follow-up on the program found it incredibly effective in changing the behaviors of these kids. Television was then able to carry that same experience to huge numbers of kids (and adults), simultaneously changing many people's thoughts and behaviors.

A similar program was introduced a few years ago to deal with the problem of teenage drinking and driving. Teenagers who had been arrested for the crime were taken into the hospitals and morgues of their cities and shown the consequences of driving while intoxicated. They were shown dismembered bodies and made to spend time with people whose lives had been shattered by someone else's irresponsible behavior. The program produced a 35 percent drop in drunk driving arrests among teenagers. The same is being done with gang-related arrests and would-be "gang bangers." By exposing the teenagers to the reality of what a bullet does to a human body and the horror the families go through as a result, it causes them to think first and take into consideration what they are really doing.

Sometimes trend creation can occur just by getting ourselves to think about and feel the consequences of our current actions. Too often we keep moving in a particular direction because we don't look at the consequences. I recently did a radio interview in Los Angeles on the topic of how to change the attitudes of crack cocaine dealers in the inner cities. One of the callers was a drug dealer who could see nothing wrong with what he was doing. He told us he wasn't about to take a job at McDonald's for minimum wage knowing he could make a thousand dollars a day on the streets selling dope. He said it was all about survival and feeding his three kids and that he would do anything to make sure they were taken care of. I asked him if it bothered him that people who use the drugs he sells are destroying their lives and that statistics have shown that 85 percent of the time a gang-related shooting happens in the inner city, it is either over drugs or has something to do with drugs. He told me it was not his problem and he didn't know any people who were hurt or killed in direct relation to his drugs. He also told me he believed that if he didn't sell the drugs to them, someone else would.

I then asked his permission to talk about his personal life and his family. He agreed, so I asked him if his kids used drugs. The man became very upset with me and told me that that would never happen. I asked what he would do if one of his kids were hurt as a result of drugs. He told me "I don't think about that." I asked him what he would really do if his child was hurt because of someone directly or indirectly selling someone drugs. The man was silent for a few seconds and then said he would use any means necessary to find out who was responsible. "What if the person who sold the drugs didn't know where his drugs would eventually end up and your child simply was in the wrong place at the wrong time?" I could feel the man's tension over the airwaves. He blurted out, "If anything ever happened to one of my babies, either me or my crew would find that %$#)%!* and kill him and everything he ever loved!"

"What if someone right now felt that same way about you and the ones you love? What if as a result of what you sold, someone else's child down the road was hurt, perhaps shot in a drive-by or overdosed on crack?" I asked. "That ain't going to happen," he insisted, his voice quivering.

"I know it won't," I said, "but what if it did?" The man didn't answer, but I guessed by his silence he was thinking about it.

Then I asked him, "Have you ever seen what a .44 magnum

does to a child's body? Have you ever seen what's left of their tiny heart when a bullet rips through their chest? Have you ever heard the cries of the mothers, fathers, and family members of a child who was a casualty of crack? Have you ever tasted the bitter sting of hopelessness in your mouth because there's nothing you can do for the pain of a child gone too far with drugs?" At the end of a long, pregnant pause the man who had been so cold and hard and abrasive said, "Man, that's a cold thing to make a brother think about. I never thought about it like that." He continued, "The truth of the matter is, I don't really know where the stuff goes after it leaves my hands. And if it could make it back to my babies then I'd be the one I'd be lookin' for to blame." He then told me he was going to look into other avenues of supporting his family and thanked me for being real with him. The host of the show gave him several numbers to call for assistance.

There is no guarantee this man stopped selling drugs, but I do know that now he will think first, and, hopefully, his honesty triggered some of the listeners to move in another direction. Whether he changes or not long-term, I honestly don't know for sure. But the point is, that's how people finally stop selling drugs—or doing anything destructive, for that matter: when they finally get associated to what it really means. All of us have the ability to do something about our lives and the way we affect others.

THE ANATOMY OF SOCIAL CHANGE

We can change massive numbers of human behaviors if we can make effective representations that appeal to people in all the primary representational systems and if we frame things in ways that appeal to all the major metaprograms. When we change the behaviors of the masses, we change the course of history.

For example, when asked to describe the 1950s, most Whites refer to that period as the happy days or the fun times. A time when there was no real war going on and America was innocent and growing up. Elvis was big, groceries were cheap, cars were cool, and people were optimistic about the future. Most everyone lived a fairly comfortable, secure life. Even people who were born later talk about how it must have been great to have lived in those times. They feel nostalgia based on TV representations of those times: *Father Knows Best, Leave It to Beaver, I Love Lucy. Happy Days* and the Fonz. Pretty positive, wasn't it?

On the other hand, when I ask Blacks the same question about the 1950s (myself included), we have quite a different opinion of those days. To have been Black in those days was to be denied all of the things the White population was enjoying. I remember the sign over an old dirty drinking fountain saying "Colored" while the sign over the nice clean fountain read "Whites Only." The segregation, the inequality, and all the injustice that plagued our country seemed to be pushed beneath the consciousness of the White population.

What finally happened to start bridging the gap between two such radical differences in perception of the same time? Slowly but surely, a different set of external stimuli was offered to huge numbers of individuals every night through a new technology called the evening news. It changed their internal representations on a daily basis. People saw real-life images that conflicted with the white-picket-fence mentality and began to represent the times as something quite different than previously. It was no longer all *Leave It to Beaver.* The horrid reality of racial injustice was now in our living room at dinnertime as we watched in vivid detail what was really going on. With increasing regularity in the 1960s, Whites received their first glimpses of the struggle and the fight to be recognized and respected by a nation of people who had been repressed far too long. Much of America chose to ignore the harsh reality, but the undeniable evidence was there in black and white. Whole segments of society began to focus on different aspects of the representations of the day, and what they chose to focus on changed their perception of life in the 1950s. As people's internal representations were changed, so was their behavior, all as a result of the media creating the vehicle for that change.

As society began to make these shifts on a mass scale, courageous individuals everywhere also made a tremendous impact by standing up for what was right. My own dear father told me of times when he was denied the same right as his White friends just because he was Black. My father was on the Air Force swim team in 1953. One night the whole team went on a trip to compete with another base. He and one other man were the only Blacks on the bus. When the bus stopped for food, my father and the other man were not allowed to eat in the same restaurant as the rest of the team and were sent to the Black side of town to find food. Another time while on the base, he and his friends went to the pool to swim. My father was an excellent diver, and when he went to the diving board, all the White people in the pool scrambled to get out. Soon after, the lifeguard came to my father and told him the base commander had ordered him to go to the Black side of the civilian town outside the base to swim. When my father refused, they closed down the pool rather than have a Black man swim in their White pool. He told me of several other incidents in the 1950s where being Black was a nightmare.

Through it all, my father was a trend creator in his own right. In the early 1960s he was president of the local NAACP chapter in Grand Forks, North Dakota. One night he and a friend went into a restaurant to eat and were denied service. He notified the police, and they did nothing. He then alerted the NAACP, and they sent a lawyer to represent him in court. When news of the lawsuit reached the Air Force base where we were stationed, many other Blacks on the base took up a collection to help fund the trial. In the end, we won the case. The restaurant was fined and made to hold themselves to a higher standard.

What my father did was fight injustice, not just for himself and his family, but for all involved. A lot of who I am and my own willingness to stand for justice came from his influences on me. What's equally as important is that, though my father endured some horrific challenges (as did a great deal of people in those days), he refused to stay angry about it. He became a role model for the philosophy of "Don't settle for it! Deal with it, take care of it, and get over it." Life is too precious to be angry and upset all the time.

WHO'S IN CHARGE HERE?

What would happen if you changed an entire world's internal representation of racism? What if the same power and technology that's used so seductively in films and TV to glorify violence and killing could be used effectively to bridge value differences and represent the unity of all peoples? Does the technology exist? We believe it does. Don't get me wrong—we're not suggesting this is easy, that all we have to do is make a few films or TV programs, show them to everyone, and the world will instantly change. What we are suggesting is that the mechanisms for change are as available as the tools for destruction. We're suggesting that we become more aware of what we see, hear, and experience on a consistent basis and that we pay attention to how we represent these experiences to ourselves individually and collectively. What we consistently represent on a mass scale tends to become internalized in mass numbers of people. These representations affect the future behaviors of a culture and a world. Thus, if we want to create a world that works, we might want to consistently review and plan what we can do to create representations that empower us on a unified global scale.

You can live your life one of two ways. You can be like Pavlov's dogs, responding to all the trends and messages sent your way. You can be romanced by war, lured by junk food, captivated by every trend that pours through the tubes. Someone once described advertising as "the science of arresting the human intelligence long enough to get money from it." Some of us live in a world of perpetually arrested intelligence.

The alternative is to try something more elegant. You can learn to use your brain so that you choose the behaviors and internal representations that will make you a better person and this a better world. You can become aware of when you're being programmed and manipulated. You can determine when your behaviors and the models beamed out at you reflect your real values and when they don't. Then you can act on the things that have real value as you tune out the ones that don't.

We live in a world where there seems to be a new trend every month. If you're a persuader, you become a trend creator rather than someone who just reacts to the multitude of messages. The direction in which things are going is as important as what is happening. Directions cause destinations. So it's important to discover the direction of the current, not just wait until you get to the edge of the falls and find out you're in a canoe with no paddles. The job of a persuader is to lead the way, map the terrain, and find the paths that lead to better outcomes.

Trends are created by individuals, individuals like you and me and those who have the imagination and tenacity to see a better world for themselves. In November of 1945, a young man with a heart of gold, a gleam in his eyes, and an overpowering vision set out to introduce a magazine for and about Blacks. John H. Johnson was a twenty-seven-year-old businessman in a time when Black businessmen had a difficult time making a living, let alone launching a magazine. When asked why he devoted his life's work to his vision, Johnson says, "We wanted Blacks to have a new sense of somebody-ness, a new sense of self-respect. We wanted to tell them who they were and what they can do. We believed then and we believe now that Blacks needed positive images to fulfill their potentials." Thank God for those beliefs! Over the years, *Ebony* magazine has been a constant source of inspiration for a race of people hungry for successful individuals to model. Johnson and his team of dedicated souls developed not just a magazine about Blacks, but an encyclopedia of references for all to glean pride and possibility from. Over its fifty-year reign as the number one Black publication in the world, *Ebony* magazine has brought to the forefront the issues, politics, accomplishments, and styles of a people who've gone far too long without respectful representation. He proved to the media that had systematically shut us out as a race from the mainstream of society that we were not only a force for good to be recognized, but a major economic force as well.

Let me offer you some possible models for effective trend creation. I have long felt that the impact that popular music can and does have on our society is a powerful force to be reckoned with. It's ridiculous for us to think the messages that are being beamed over radio airwaves and the images we see flashed in front of our retinas in brilliant, split-second Technicolor don't have an effect on our beliefs and perceptions. The controversy still drags on over whether or not the violence in today's music makes its listeners and viewers more prone to act out the behaviors they see and hear. I can't help but feel that trends set by certain types of music are eating away at the values and morals of our youth like a cancer. Several gangsta rap artists argue they are just telling how it really is in the streets and that the youth are not affected by what they see. I wonder what would happen if these same artists known for their violence and crime depiction would fashion their work to reflect the other side of reality as well, focusing on the good and the positive that happens each and every day. What if they wrote songs that reflected people's hopes and desires and the conquering of fears and shortcomings? Wouldn't those who are enamored of the artists be inspired to start acting out a different set of behaviors?

While I was in London last year, I had the pleasure of sharing a meal with a wonderful soul who I believe has made a huge trend change in the music world and the people who listen to her music. The artist is Des'ree, and she is the embodiment of the songs she writes and sings. Her signature song, "You Gotta Be," on her debut album, *I Ain't Movin'*, has become an international hit and has all the qualities any other hit song would. The beat is slammin', the melody is kickin', and the video is cutting-edge. The only difference is, Des'ree is singing about possibilities and what we can all find if we look inside and display the human spirit we all possess. I have never met a more alive singer in my life, and as this book is being written she is working on another album that promises to inspire us more. During our meal, she told me she thought "You Gotta Be" connected with so many people because the music and lyrics exude such powerful, positive energy. The song was inspired by her quest for a positive outlook on surviving the "slings and arrows of outrageous fortune" while paying homage to the most powerful life force of all—*love*. She told me that she got a lot of her inspiration from her mother as a child. When I listen to Des'ree's songs, I feel similarly inspired and energized.

There's a saying in the computer world: GIGO (garbage in, garbage out). It means that the quality you get out of a system depends entirely on what you put into it. If you put in bad, faulty, or incomplete information, you'll get the same kind of results. Many people in our culture today give little or no conscious thought to the quality of information and experience being input daily. According to the latest statistics, the average American watches television seven hours a day. *U.S. News & World Report* states that young adults between grades nine and twelve will see an average of 18,000 murders. They will watch 22,000 hours of television, more than twice the time spent in class during twelve years of schooling. It's critical we look at what we are feeding our minds if we expect them to grow and nurture our ability to fully experience and enjoy this thing we call life. Our "operating systems" are much like those of a computer. If we form internal representations that tell us blowing away people with guns is neat or that unhealthy junk food is what successful people eat, those representations will govern our behavior.

We have more power now than ever before to shape the inner perceptions that govern behavior. There's no guarantee we'll shape them for the better. But the potential is there, and we should start doing something about it. The most important issues we face as a nation and as a planet deal with the kinds of images and mass representations we produce.

Trend creation is what leadership is about, and it's the real message of this book. You now know how to run your brain to process information in the most empowering fashion. You know how to turn down the sound and turn off the brightness of the junk communication. **But if you really want to make a difference, you also need to know how to be a leader, how to take these persuasion skills and make the world a better place.** That means being a more positive, more skillful role model for your kids, for your employees, for your business associates, for your world. You can do this on the level of one-on-one persuasion, and you can do it on the level of mass persuasion. Instead of being influenced by images of muscle-bound strongmen gleefully shooting up other human beings, you might want to dedicate your life to communicating the empowering messages that can make the difference in getting this world the way you want it to be.

Remember, the world is governed by the persuaders. Everything you've learned in this book and everything you see around you tells you this is so. If you can externalize on a mass scale your internal representations about human behavior—what is elegant, what is effective, what is positive—you can change the future direction of your children, your community, your country, your world. We have the technology to change it right here. We suggest you make use of it.

That's ultimately what this book is about. Sure, it's about maximizing your personal power, learning how to be effective and successful in what you try to do. But there's no value to being a sovereign of a dying planet. Everything we've talked about—the importance of agreement frames, the nature of rapport, the modeling of excellence, the syntax of success, and all the rest—works best when it's used in a positive way that breeds success for others as well as for ourselves. My dear friend Sam Georges has a great saying when he talks about undeniable facts. He says, "Rocks are hard and water is wet; that's the way it is, and there ain't nothin' you can do about it." Well, the fact of the matter is, we all have to share this planet. None of us are going anywhere without the rest of us. I believe that as long as we have to inhabit the planet together, we might as well figure out how to live with each other in harmony.

Ultimate power is synergistic. It comes from people working together, not working apart. We now have the technology to change people's perceptions almost in an instant. It's time to use it in a positive way for the betterment of us all. Thomas Wolfe once wrote, "There is nothing in the world that will take the chip off one's shoulder like a feeling of success." That's the real challenge of excellence: using these skills on a broad level to empower ourselves and others in ways that are truly positive, in ways that generate massive, joyous, communal success. The time to start using them is now. It's time for . . .

CHAPTER TWENTY-THREE

Living Excellence: The Human Challenge

Determination and perseverance move the world; thinking that someone else will do it for you is a sure way to fail.

—Marva Collins

Well, congratulations! You've made it. Together we've come a long way. How much farther you'll go is now up to you. This book has given you tools and skills and ideas that can change your life and the lives of others around you. When you put this book down, you have two choices. You can feel you've learned a little something and go on as you used to. Or you can make a concerted effort to take control of your life and your brain. You can create the powerful beliefs and states that will produce miracles for you and the people you care about. But this will happen only if you make it happen.

Let's take a look at the things you've learned in the last twenty-two chapters. You now know that the most powerful tool on the planet is the biocomputer between your two ears called your brain. Properly run, your brain can enable you to achieve your dreams and desires. You've learned the Ultimate Success Formula: Know your outcome, take massive action, develop the sensory acuity to know what you're getting, and change your behavior until you get what you want. You've learned beyond a shadow of a doubt what you've known in your heart all along: Color, religion, gender, even socioeconomic standing have nothing to do with a person's true potential and ability to achieve. You've learned that we live in an age where fabulous success is available to all of us and that those who really achieve it are those who take action. Knowledge is important, but it's not enough. Plenty of people had the same information as a John H. Johnson or a Nelson Mandela, but it was only the ones who took action who created astounding success and changed the world.

You've learned about the importance of modeling. You can learn by experience, through laborious trial and error—or you can speed up the process immeasurably by learning how to model. If anybody can do something, you can follow the same system and compress decades into days with the modeling process. This is because every result produced by an individual was created by some specific set of actions in some specific syntax. You can dramatically reduce the time it takes to master something by modeling the internal (mental and emotional) actions and external (physical) actions of people who produce outstanding results. In a few hours, days, or months, depending on the type of task, you can learn what took them months or years to discover. And you have virtually thousands of Black role models to choose from.

You've learned that the quality of your life is the quality of your communication. Communication takes two forms. The first is your communication with yourself: The meaning of any event is the meaning you give it. You can send your brain powerful, positive, empowering signals that will make everything work for you, or you can send your brain signals about what you can't do. People of excellence can take any situation and make it work for them—Quincy Jones, Bonnie St. John Dean, Herdale Johnson—people who have taken severe adversity and even terrible tragedy and turned it into triumph. We can't go back in time. We can't change what actually happened. But we can control our representations to give us something positive for the future. The second form of communication is with others. The people who've changed our world have been master communicators. You can use everything in this book to discover what people want so you can become an effective, masterful, elegant communicator.

You've learned about the awesome power of belief. Positive beliefs can make you a master. Negative beliefs can make you a loser. And you've learned that you can change your beliefs to make them work for you. You've learned about the power of state and the power of physiology. You've learned the syntax and strategies that people use, and you've learned how to establish rapport with anyone you meet. You've learned powerful techniques for reframing and anchoring. You've learned how to communicate with precision and skill, how to avoid the fluff language that kills communication, and how to use the precision model to get others to communicate effectively with you. You've learned about value hierarchies and how they influence everything you do. You've learned about handling the five roadblocks in the way of success. And you've learned about the metaprograms and values that serve as the organizing principles for personal behavior.

We don't expect you to find yourself utterly transformed when you put down this book. Some things we've discussed will come easier to you than others. But life has a processional effect. Changes lead to more changes; growth leads to more growth. By starting to make changes, by growing in bits and pieces, you can slowly but steadily change your life. Like a rock thrown into a still pond, you create ripples that grow larger in the future. It's often the littlest thing, viewed over time, that makes the biggest difference.

Think of two arrows pointing in the same general direction. If you make a tiny change in the direction of one of them, if you push it three or four degrees in a different direction, the change will probably be imperceptible at first. But if you follow that path for yards and then for miles, the difference will become greater and greater—until there's no relation at all between the first path and the second.

That's what this book can do for you. It won't change you overnight (unless you go to work on yourself tonight!). But if you learn to run your brain in ways that empower you, if you understand and make use of things like syntax, submodalities, values, and metaprograms, the differences over six weeks and six months and six years will change your life. Some things in this book, like modeling, you already do in some form. Others are new. Just remember, everything in life is cumulative. If you use one of the principles in this book today, you've taken a step. You've set a cause in motion, and every cause creates an effect or result, and every result builds on the last one to take us in a specific direction. Every direction carries with it an ultimate destination.

Every time God's children have thrown away fear in pursuit of honesty—trying to communicate themselves, understood or not—miracles have happened.

—DUKE ELLINGTON

Here's a final question for you to consider. In five years someone new is going to show up in your life. This person will use a key to get into your home, walk around, and use all the things you have worked so hard to acquire. He or she will follow you around and look right back at you as you look into the mirror. This person will be *you*— the man or woman you've created as a result of the actions you took (or never took). The question is . . . Who is that person? What does this person believe, value, dislike, regret, feel proud of? Where does this person live? Who loves this person, and who does he or she love in return?

What direction are you currently going? If you follow your current direction, will that person you see in the mirror be different? In short, where will you be five years or ten years from now? Is that where you really want to go? Be honest with yourself. John Naisbitt, author of the popular *Megatrends* books, once said that the best way to predict the future is to get a clear idea of what's happening now. You need to do the same thing in your life. So when you finish this book, sit down and think about the direction you're going and whether it's where you really want to go. If it's not, I suggest you change. If this book has taught you anything, it's the possibility of creating positive change with almost lightning speed on both a personal and a global level. Ultimate power means the ability to change, to adapt, to grow, to evolve. **Unlimited power doesn't mean you always succeed or that you never fail. Unlimited power just means you learn from every human experience and make every experience work for you in some way.** It is unlimited power to change your perceptions, change your actions, and change the results you're creating. It's your unlimited power to care and to love that can make the biggest difference in the quality of your life.

Remember, we are alive in the greatest times in human history. There is no better time to be Black. We have more freedom, more choices, more opportunities than we have ever had since the beginning of time.

We'd like to suggest another way to change your life and ensure continued success: Find a team you want to play on. Remember, we've talked about power in terms of what people can do together. In every town and every community you can find groups of people and organizations aimed at bettering the quality of life, not the least of which are local Black empowerment and support groups like the NAACP and the Rainbow Coalition. I volunteer my time to youth-at-risk groups because I know how valuable a caring friend and mentor can be to a child or anyone who might need some direction in their lives. You never know what you will learn and how much of a difference you can make in someone else's life if you don't put yourself on a team that strives to be a force for good.

All it takes is a simple decision to be part of the trend for more unity and camaraderie amongst ourselves. When I think about the Million Man March and all those caring, concerned, forward-moving people gathered together for one noble cause—atonement—it brings tears of pride and positive expectancy to my eyes. I didn't see just a sea of Black men; I saw a sea of people. Women, children, White, Asian, you name it. People representing all walks of life were concerned about one thing: how to take this planet to a new level. No one can deny the love and the spirit of hope that permeated even the would-be negative aspects of the event. We all agree it is high time for atonement in this society, as shown by those thousands and thousands of people who were and are looking for the next step.

Well, my friend, you have some of the answers right here in your own two hands. The first step is spelled out in the chapters that have gone before this one. The next step—what you will do with all these new tools and understandings—is up to you. Perhaps you will share what you've learned with your team called family or friends or co-workers. In our opinion, the worst thing you can do is nothing at all. Unlimited power is the power of people working together, not pulling apart. That might mean your family, or it might mean good friends. It could be trusted business partners or people you work with and care about. But you work harder and better if you're working for others as well as for yourself. You give more, and you get more.

If you ask people about their richest experiences in life, they'll usually come up with something they did as part of a team. Sometimes it's literally that—a sports team they'll remember forever. Sometimes it's a business team that did something memorable. Sometimes the team is your family or you and your spouse. Being on a team makes you stretch, makes you grow. Other people can nurture and challenge you in ways you can't yourself. People will do things for others they won't do for themselves. And what they get in return makes it all worthwhile.

Just by being alive, you're already on a team of one kind or another. It can be your family, your relationship, your business, your city, your country, your world. You can sit on the bench and watch, or you can get up and play. Our advice to you is to be a player. Join the game; share your world. The more you give, the more you get; the more you use the skills in this book for yourself and for others, the more they'll bring back to you.

Above all, make sure you're on the team that challenges you. It's easy for things to get off track. It's easy to know what to do and still not do it; that just seems to be the way life is. All other things being equal, the tendency of objects at rest is to stay at rest and of moving objects to slow down. All of us have our off days; all of us have times when we don't use what we know. But if we surround ourselves with people who are successful, who are forward-moving, who are positive, who are focused on producing results, who support us, it will challenge us to be more and do more and share more. If you can surround yourself with people who will never let you settle for less than you can be, you have the greatest gift anyone could hope for. Association is a powerful tool. **Make sure the people you surround yourself with make you a better person by your association with them.**

Once you have a commitment to a team, the challenge of excellence is to become a leader. That can mean being the president of a Fortune 500 company, or it can mean being the best teacher you can be. It can mean being a better entrepreneur or a better contributor or a better parent. True leaders have a knowledge of the power of procession, a sense that great changes come from many small things. They realize that everything they say and do has an enormous power to inspire and embolden others.

I had the privilege of meeting General Norman Schwarzkopf at Tony's Mastery University program two years ago. "Stormin' Norman" said it best: "If you want to be a leader, remember these simple facts. A leader is someone who leads people, not things, but *people*. A leader is someone with a vision. And he or she uses that to inspire people to *willingly* do those things they wouldn't normally do on their own." The challenge of leadership is to have enough power and vision to be able to project in advance what outcome will result from your actions, large and small. The communication skills in this book offer critical ways to make those distinctions. Our culture needs more models of success, more symbols of excellence, and that's where you can make a difference, using the skills in this book.

My father was one such leader and mentor for me, even though I might not have understood it at the time. One of my earliest memories of how to create change in my life was seeing the power of a real decision. It was the day my father quit smoking cigarettes. I remember seeing him hold a pack of cigarettes in the air and say, "This is the last pack I'll ever smoke." With that, he crumpled the pack and threw it in the wastebasket. I never saw him smoke another cigarette. He taught me that decisions are real. Decisions change our lives.

Both my parents taught me the most important lesson of all, though: A true leader is a person who cares deeply, who doesn't allow the judgment of others to affect his or her judgment toward them. My parents taught us to get to know people rather than judge them—and certainly not to jump to conclusions based on the color of their skin, or we'd be making the same ridiculous mistake others have made with us. My mom's message was simple: "Always look for ways to be kind to people first." She was and is a trend creator in her own right. She has always believed that giving to others is the noblest gesture a person can make. Even though we didn't have money to spare, and things were pretty slim sometimes, my mother would bring underprivileged children into our home to share what we had and perhaps bring some light into their lives. Perhaps my favorite trait that I was able to model from my parents was their incredible ability to laugh and find humor in anything. My father was and still is a nut. His laugh, smile, and disposition are the same as those I call my own to this very day.

Without a doubt, my life has been graced by teachers and mentors who gave me and others lessons of immeasurable value. Not the least of these towering role models of possibility is my dear friend Tony. My goal in life is to give back some of what has been given to me, and that's what we hope this book has helped you to do.

What can you do for others, starting today? What if you made it a principle that every time you passed someone taking a collection for something, you always put some money in the collection plate? What if you made an automatic commitment always to buy from a Boy Scout, Girl Scout, or other youth involved with a group that builds positive values? What if you made it a point to seek out Black organizations and foundations and give some of your time and energy to helping their cause? What if you called the United Negro College Fund and offered to work or donate some time toward their efforts? There is an old saying, "Receiving is evidence that you are giving enough." What if you made it a point to call friends every now and then just to say, "I'm not calling for any special reason; I just wanted you to know I love you"? What if you made it a point to send little thank-you notes to people who have done things for you? What if you spent time and effort figuring out new and unique ways to get more joy out of life by adding value to other people's lives? That's what quality of life is all about. We all have the time; the question of the quality of life is answered by how we spend it. Do we fall into a pattern, or do we continuously work at making our life unique and special? These may seem like little things, but their effect on how you feel about who you are as a person is very powerful. They determine your internal representations of who you are and thus the quality of your states and life.

The chemist who can extract from his heart's elements compassion, respect, longing, patience, regret, surprise, and forgiveness and compound them into one can create that atom which is called love.

—Kahlil Gibran

Our final challenge to you is to share this information with others—for two reasons, really. First, we all teach what we most need to learn. By sharing an idea with others, we get to hear it repeatedly and remind ourselves of what we value and believe is important in life. Second, there is incredible, almost unexplainable richness and joy that comes from helping another person make a truly important and positive change in his or her life.

You know, one of the things I am definitely attracted to in people is a good heart. I think one of the strongest reasons Tony and I have been friends for so many years is because of who he is as a person. Not only has he been a great friend, he's been a great model of caring for all people.

Years ago Tony shared with me a story of an experience that really touched him. It was a great reflection of what he is all about and what I think we're all about together (I hope this includes you now, too!). Here is the story recalled in his own words:

"I had an experience last year at one of our children's programs that I will never forget. The camps are twelve-day programs during which we teach children a lot of what is discussed in this book and give them experiences that change their competency, their learning skills, and their confidence as fully alive human beings. During the summer of 1984, we ended the camp with a ceremony in which all the kids got gold medals like the ones in the Olympics. On the medals it said, 'You can do magic.' We didn't finish until about two in the morning, and it was a very joyous emotional event.

"I got back to my room feeling bone-tired, knowing I had to be up at 6:00 A.M. in order to catch a plane to my next event but also feeling the way you do when you know you've really made a day count. So I was ready to get to sleep around 3:00 A.M. when I heard a knock at my door. I thought, *Who in the world can that be?* I opened the door to find a young boy there. He said, 'Mr. Robbins, I need your help.' I started to ask him if he could call me in San Diego the following week, when I heard this sound behind him, and there was a little girl crying her eyes out. I asked what the matter was, and the boy told me she didn't want to go home. I said to bring her in, and I'd anchor her, and she'd feel better and go home. He said that wasn't the problem. He said she didn't want to go home because her brother, who lived with her, had been sexually abusing her for the last seven years.

"So I brought them both in, and using the tools we've talked about in this book, I changed her internal representation of those negative past experiences so that they no longer created any pain. Then I anchored her into her most resourceful and powerful states and linked them with her now altered internal representations so that the very thought or sight of her brother would immediately put her in a state of being in charge. After this session, she decided to call her brother. She got on the phone in a totally resourceful state and woke him up. 'Brother!' she said in a tone he'd probably never heard before in his life. 'I just want you to know that I'm coming home, and you best not even look at me in a way that makes me even think you're thinking of the things you used to do. Because if you do, you'll go to jail for the rest of your life and be totally embarrassed. You will absolutely pay the price. I love you as my brother, but I will never accept those behaviors again. If I even think you're moving toward them, it's over for you. Bear in mind that I am serious. And I love you. Good-bye.' He got the message.

"She hung up the phone, feeling totally strong and in charge for the first time in her life. She hugged her little boyfriend, and together they cried in relief. The night I worked with them, they both gave me the most incredible hugs I'd ever had. The young man said he didn't know how he could repay me. I told him that seeing the changes in her was the greatest thanks I could receive. He said, 'No, I've got to pay you in some way.' Then he said, 'I know something that means a lot to me.' He reached up and slowly took off his gold medal, and he put it on me. They kissed me and left, saying they would never forget me. I walked upstairs after they left and got into bed. My wife, Becky, who had been listening to the whole thing, was crying, and so was I. She said, 'You're incredible. That child's life will never be the same.' I said, 'Thanks, honey, but anybody with the skills could have helped her.' She said, 'Yeah, Tony, anybody could have. But you did.' "

Seize the time.

—BOBBY SEALE

You now know what to do, how to do it, and when and where to do it. The last step is—DO IT! That's the ultimate message of this book. **Be a doer. Take charge. Take action.** Take what you've learned here, and use it now. Don't just do it for yourself—do it for others as well. The gifts from such actions are greater than can be imagined. There are a lot of talkers in the world. There are a lot of people who know what's right and what's powerful, yet still aren't producing the results they desire. It's not enough to talk the talk. You've got to *walk the talk.* That's what unlimited power is all about—unlimited power to get yourself to do the necessary things to produce excellence. Julius (Dr. J) Erving of the Philadelphia 76ers has a view of life that I think sums up the philosophy of a "walker." It's worthy of modeling. He says, "I demand more from myself than anybody else could ever expect." That's why he's one of the best.

Let me give you one final story. There were two great orators of antiquity. One was Cicero, the other Demosthenes. When Cicero was done speaking, people always gave him a standing ovation and cheered, "What a great speech!" When Demosthenes was done, people said, "Let us march," and they did. That's the difference between presentation and persuasion. We hope to be classified in the latter category. If you just read this book and think, *Wow, that was a great book; it has lots of cool tools,* and don't use anything in it, we've wasted our time together. However, if you start right now and go back through this book and use it as an owner's manual for running your mind and body, as a guide to changing anything you want to change, then you have begun a life journey that will make even the greatest dreams of your past seem almost trivial. I know that's what happened to me when I began to apply these principles daily.

By reading this book you have joined an elite group of people. You've embarked on a journey that will change the quality of your life and the lives of those around you. We truly believe we all came from somewhere and we're all going somewhere when we leave here and that the color of your skin is not what matters most. What matters most is the depth of your soul. I've always looked at life as a story continually unfolding, an adventure that stretches through time. And the best part about the story of our lives is that we can write the pages that make up our adventure. You now have the tools to do so.

The future you hold in your dreams is your birthright. It is our sincere wish for you that the tools and strategies you have gathered from this book will help you make your own glorious future truly outstanding.

We challenge you to make your life a masterpiece, to live your life as if it's an incredible adventure. We challenge you to join the ranks of those people who live what they teach, who walk their talk. They are the models of excellence the rest of the world marvels about. Join this elite team of souls known as the few who do versus the many who merely wish—result-oriented people who produce their life exactly as they desire it.

May you dedicate yourself not only to strive for the goals you have set, but to meet them and set even more; not only to hold to the dreams you have had, but to dream greater dreams than before; not only to enjoy this land and its wealth, but to make it a better place to live; and not only to take what you can from this life, but to love and give generously.

It's time to grab hold of the steering mechanism that guides your life and aim it in the direction you most want to go. Put this bad boy called life in gear, slam the pedal to the floor, and quickly slide your foot off the clutch. Feel the sudden surge of human power, and hang on for dear life!

Yes, dear life . . . Dear, sweet, loving, happy, exciting, crazy, sexy, wonderful, wide awake, fast, slow, warm, grateful, dear life.

We thank you for this opportunity to share with you and walk with you along this portion of your journey. May your quest for greatness be filled with the fruits of joy and love. Until we meet again, Peace and God bless . . .

Index

About the Authors

JOSEPH MCCLENDON III is the founder and president of the Succeleration Research Group, a company that performs applied research for understanding human behavior and teaches people how to get the most out of themselves—to break through the barriers of fear, procrastination, and indecision.

As an instructor at the University of California, Los Angeles, he teaches two courses for the Department of Engineering and Management designed to give students the tools necessary to move further faster, with heightened awareness as to what makes them take action in the first place. He is well known, also, for his one-on-one personal achievement counseling, as well as seminars and workshops. He donates his time and expertise to helping the inner-city youth of Los Angeles and to programs committed to improving the quality of the community.

Aside from his notable career as a human-development resource, McClendon is a painter, sculptor, and accomplished composer/producer/recording artist. But this high degree of personal and professional success was not always his. On his nineteenth birthday, he nearly lost his two remaining possessions—his motorcycle and his life—when he was in an accident. That night, he huddled under a sopping-wet cardboard furniture carton, shivering as the rain poured down on his "home."

What changed his life dramatically, and later was the genesis of this book, was McClendon's attendance at an Anthony Robbins event in 1985. The two became friends, and since that day, McClendon has mastered a number of skills on the path that today leads him to collaborate with his friend on *Unlimited Power: A Black Choice*. He made his financial breakthrough in the real estate market, studied psychology for two years, capitalized on his talents as a studio vocalist and bassist to gain a recording contract in 1990 with Sony, and became one of only eight master trainers—and eventually head trainer—with the Anthony Robbins Companies based in San Diego, California.

Joseph McClendon III lives in Encinitas, California.

ANTHONY ROBBINS is the nation's expert in the psychology of peak performance and personal, professional, and organizational "turnaround." The diversity of his work is reflected in the variety of people he has helped, including the 1992 America's Cup Winner, *America³*; 1993 Stanley Cup finalists, the Los Angeles Kings; 1994 U.S. Open champion, André Agassi; and the 1995 San Antonio Spurs; as well as organizations such as Hallmark, Southwestern Bell, and the U.S. Army. In addition to having had the privilege of advising the President of the United States, Robbins has also served as an adviser to members of two royal families, and is the primary consultant for the regeneration of Sheffield, the fourth largest city in England.

An entrepreneur, Robbins has founded nine companies in industries as varied as medical practice management to a resort in the Fijian Islands. In addition, his nonprofit Anthony Robbins Foundation's volunteers feed more than 125,000 people in sixty-five cities in North America every Thanksgiving; he personally sponsors a college education fund for thirty students in Houston, Texas; and he provides scholarships to all of his live events, and offers his books, tapes, and multimedia seminars to any government-recognized social organization, such as prisons, homeless shelters, and public school systems. His work has been covered worldwide, including articles in *Time, Newsweek, Life,* and *Success* magazines; and segments on *CBS Evening News* with Dan Rather, *NBC News,* and *PrimeTime Live.*

Robbins is a best-selling author with four titles published in fourteen languages worldwide: *Unlimited Power, Awaken the Giant Within, Giant Steps,* and *Notes from a Friend.* He has produced the best-selling personal development series of all time, *Personal Power,* with 24 million educational audiotapes sold in less than five years. More than a million people have attended his live events. Using the knowledge that he has gained over the last seventeen years of his life interacting with people from virtually every socioeconomic category, Robbins has also developed a series of books, tapes, seminars, multimedia packages, and coaching systems that are utilized by people around the world.

In 1995, Robbins was selected as one of the Ten Outstanding Young Americans by the U.S. Junior Chamber of Commerce, and he is the recipient of two Timmie Awards given by the Touchdown Club of Washington, D.C.: the 1994 Outstanding Humanitarian and the Justice Brian White Award. Further, Toastmasters International recognized him as one of the world's top five speakers in 1993, and in 1995 awarded him the Golden Gavel Award, their most prestigious honor.

Anthony Robbins lives in La Jolla, California, with his wife, Becky. He is the father of four children.

About the Anthony Robbins Companies

We are an inspired force of leaders: Men and women who are driven to constantly improve the quality of life for all those who desire it.

We empower individuals and organizations by discovering and creating resources that can transform people's lives. We simplify these resources so that their profound impact is delivered to a mass number of people in a manner that inspires action and entertains in the process.

We are the recognized leader in human-development training, an organization whose dynamic contributions are constantly creating positive transformations of individuals and organizations worldwide.

THE **ANTHONY ROBBINS COMPANIES** (ARC) offer cutting-edge technologies for the management of human emotion and behavior and empower individuals not only to recognize but also to *utilize* their unlimited choices.

We believe there is only one way to succeed in the long term, and that is through commitment to the discipline of **CANI!™**, Constant and Never-ending Improvement. No corporation or individual is satisfied with achieving a certain level of success. True fulfillment occurs only through a sense that we are constantly growing and contributing. Profound growth is the direct result of continual improvement. By sharing the finest technologies for personal and corporate change, ARC's mission is to assist all those who are committed to taking their lives and companies to the next level through personal and professional mastery.

The Anthony Robbins Companies fulfill this promise of sustained growth by constantly pursuing **profound knowledge**—simple strategies, ideas, systems, and plans that are universally applicable and, the minute we understand them, we can use them to increase the quality of our individual and corporate lives. We seek out excellence in all forums, modeling the strategies of its creation and sharing the steps that are required to produce lasting impact for change.

We believe that all change occurs through individuals, and ARC is committed to improving the world by teaching its citizens to improve themselves, for it is through the forging of each link that the mightiest chain is built.

Although we may never exactly duplicate the achievements of the world's greatest individuals, we can duplicate their excellence in our own lives. Each of us can use more effective tools to shape our personal, social, political, and corporate environments—and to enjoy our lives more in the process!

Listed below is a sampling of some of the Anthony Robbins Companies that can provide useful resources for you or your organization. For a complete list of available services, please call 1-800-445-8183.

Robbins Research International, Inc.

This research and marketing arm of Anthony Robbins' personal development businesses conducts personal development, sales and corporate seminars that cover a wide range of topics, from mental conditioning and personal achievement systems to communication mastery.

Anthony Robbins & Associates

The Anthony Robbins & Associates Franchise and Distributor Network brings video-based seminars to local communities and businesses worldwide. Owning an Anthony Robbins & Associates franchise offers you the opportunity to be a source of positive impact and growth for the members of your community. Anthony Robbins & Associates provides its franchisees the training, visibility, and ongoing support to create a business that truly makes a difference in people's lives.

Robbins Success Systems

Robbins Success Systems (RSS) provides Fortune 1000 corporations with state-of-the-art management systems, communication, and teamwork trainings. Presented in conjunction with RRI's network of Personal Development Consultants, RSS teams combine thorough pretraining diagnostics, customized facilitation and training, and post-program evaluation and follow-up. Through customized training programs and unequaled follow-up, RSS is a catalyst for constant and never-ending improvement in the quality of life within corporations worldwide.

Fortune Management

Fortune Management is a full-service, practice-management company that provides health care professionals with vital strategies and support for increasing the quality and profitability of their practices. Fortune Management is committed to making a difference in the quality of health care and in the quality of life of its practitioners.

Namale Plantation Resort

The ultimate hideaway and Fijian retreat of Anthony Robbins, Namale is a private paradise nestled in the heart of the South Pacific. Activities range from a relaxing stroll on a coral reef to tennis, water skiing, and volleyball with the locals, to spectacular snorkeling and scuba diving. The innocence and purity of the Fijian people, in addition to their "bula" attitude of happiness and playfulness, make this an ideal destination to restore and nurture the balance we need in our lives. For reservations, or a brochure, call 619/535-6381.

The Anthony Robbins Foundation

THE ANTHONY ROBBINS FOUNDATION is a nonprofit organization, a coalition of caring professionals who have committed to consistently reach and assist people who are often forgotten by society.

Specifically, we are aggressively working to make a difference in the quality of life for children, people who are homeless, the prison population, the deaf community, and the elderly.

The Anthony Robbins Foundation is dedicated to providing the finest resources for inspiration, education, training, and development for these important members of our society.

A VISION REALIZED

The Foundation is a lifelong dream come true for Mr. Robbins. He has been a committed philanthropist since the age of eighteen and has worked extensively with the Salvation Army in the South Bronx and Brooklyn as well as with the homeless in the San Diego area. Currently, we are offering a complimentary copy of his national best-selling "Personal Power" audio library, as well as copies of his national best-selling books *Unlimited Power, Awaken the Giant Within,* and *Notes From a Friend* to every homeless shelter, high school, and prison in the country. At this writing, eighty-seven schools and fifty-four correctional institutions, plus a broad range of other social service organizations, have received these materials from the Foundation.

Your Commitment

The Foundation's charter is expressed through the theme of Commit-2. It means that as a member of the Foundation you will commit to two projects, one from each of the following categories:

1. Monthly Commitment—As a member of the Foundation, you will be asked to make a one-year commitment to visit an assigned prisoner, elderly person, homeless individual, or child on a monthly basis. Your visits will be designed so that as you listen to your partner and share your experiences with them, you will ultimately, through your skill, caring, and commitment, help them to increase the quality of their life.
2. Annual Commitment—As a member of the Foundation, you will also be asked to commit to help support, organize, or sponsor at least one of the following programs once per year within your community.

Opportunity to Give

"The Basket Brigade"—This program takes place during Thanksgiving and involves making up food baskets (including a copy of Robbins's powerful little book *Notes From a Friend,* which was written expressly for this audience) and delivering them to the homeless, as well as to the elderly and poor families who are not able to make it to a shelter or a soup kitchen. Efforts in the last several years have nourished the bodies and souls of hundreds of thousands of people around the world.

The Challenge

Life is a gift, and all of us who have the capacity must remember that we have the responsibility to give something back. Your contributions, both financial and physical, can truly make a difference. Please join us now and commit to helping those less fortunate enjoy a greater quality of life.

People interested in more information about the Foundation may write to the Anthony Robbins Foundation, 9191 Towne Centre Drive, Suite 600, San Diego, California, 92122, or call 619/535-6295.